W9-ABI-449

Incest and the English Novel

PUBLISHING FOR THE WORLD
125 Years

THE JOHNS HOPKINS UNIVERSITY PRESS

Incest and the English Novel, 1684–1814

Ellen Pollak

The Johns Hopkins University Press
Baltimore and London

© 2003 The Johns Hopkins University Press
All rights reserved. Published 2003
Printed in the United States of America on acid-free paper
9 8 7 6 5 4 3 2 1

The Johns Hopkins University Press
2715 North Charles Street
Baltimore, Maryland 21218-4363
www.press.jhu.edu

Frontispiece: From Frances Burney's *Evelina,* vol. 2 (1794), engraved by J. Collyer after a drawing by E. F. Burney. Courtesy William Ready Division of Archives, McMaster University Library, Hamilton, Ontario, Canada.

Library of Congress Cataloging-in-Publication Data
Pollak, Ellen.
  Incest and the English novel, 1684–1814 / Ellen Pollak.
  p. cm.
Includes bibliographical references (p.) and index.
  ISBN 0-8018-7204-9 (alk. paper)
  1. English fiction—18th century—History and criticism.
2. Incest in literature. I. Title.
PR858.I63 P65 2003
823.009′353—dc21
2002009448

A catalog record for this book is available from the British Library.

*This one is for
Tessa,
Nigel,
and my Dad*

Contents

Acknowledgments

Many individuals and institutions have sustained me during the writing of this book. The Andrew W. Mellon Faculty Fellowship Program in the Humanities at Harvard University and the Harvard Center for Literary and Cultural Studies supported my early research, and the Office of the Vice President for Research and Graduate Studies at Michigan State University provided two generous grants to assist my writing during the project's later stages. I am also grateful to the MSU English Department for a semester's research leave and for the extraordinary support and friendship of Victor Paananen and Patrick O'Donnell, who served as Chairpersons during the period when the manuscript was in process. Special thanks go also to Howard Anderson, Clint Goodson, Joyce Ladenson, and Bob Uphaus, whose graciousness and encouragement when I came to Michigan State helped to make it a welcoming and inspiriting academic home.

I have enjoyed the rare wisdom and generosity of numerous friends and colleagues as I worked. Deborah Epstein Nord, Carol McGuirk, and Nigel Paneth continue to be my most steadfast critics and supporters, giving amply of their precious time, advice, and goodwill even amid the welter of life's growing demands. Scott Juengel and Susan Greenfield have unstintingly shared their enthusiasm, critical acuity, and work, providing the sort of intellectual exchange and scholarly community that buoys the spirit and inspires one to write. Many others have offered valuable encouragement and assistance along the way. Doug Buchholz, Jill Campbell, Doug Canfield, Julia Epstein, Bob Markley, Ellen McCallum, Scott Michaelsen, David B. Morris, Judith Lowder Newton, Ruth Perry, Judith Roof, Ellen Cronan Rose, Michael Seidel, Jyotsna Singh, and Tony Willson all read portions of the manuscript and made important suggestions for improvement. Marcia Aldrich, Jenifer Banks, Peter Berg, Bruce Boehrer, Irene Fizer, Richard Isomaki, Minaz Jooma, Roland Racevskis, Betty Rizzo, and Agnes Widder contributed meaningfully in a variety of other ways. Kathleen McGarvey and Maureen Lauder provided invaluable research assistance with exceptional intelligence and efficiency. Lois Crum supplied wisdom and an eagle eye. Cheryl Nixon generously shared her unpublished work on guardianship with me. The Harvard University Houghton Library, the Yale University Lewis Walpole Library, and the William Ready Division of Archives at the McMaster University Library provided crucial resources and assistance. Special appreciation goes as well to Guy Holborn of the Lincoln's Inn Library, A. S. Adams, librarian of the Society of the Middle Temple, and Nicole Rivette, Assistant Registrar of Collections at the Toledo Museum of Art.

My family has lived with this book for many years. My daughters, Rachel and Tessa, have grown up with it. For their perspicacity and high spirits, and for the love and respect they give so freely, I am grateful. My deepest debts are to my husband, Nigel, who helps me juggle and who immeasurably enriches the round of rest and work; my brother, Roger Pollak, who (in addition to performing numerous other helpful acts) first taught me to find the eighteenth century online; my father, John Pollak, who models vitality and determination, as well as patience, good humor, fortitude, and a respect for history; and my late mother, Tania, from whom I learned to think beyond.

An earlier version of chapter 3 appeared in *Rereading Aphra Behn: History, Theory, and Criticism,* edited by Heidi Hutner (Charlottesville: University Press of Virginia, 1993), and is reprinted here by permission of the Rectors and Visitors of the University of Virginia. Shorter versions of chapters 4 and 5 also appeared in article form, in *The Eighteenth Century: Theory and Interpretation,* volumes 39.3 and 30.1, respectively. They are reprinted by permission of Texas Tech University Press. The frontispiece, from Frances Burney, *Evelina,* vol. 2 (London: W. Lowndes, 1794), was obtained from the William Ready Division of Archives, McMaster University Library, Hamilton, Ontario.

Incest and the English Novel

CHAPTER ONE

Introduction

Modernity, Incest, and Eighteenth-Century Narrative

> We must not forget that the discovery of the Oedipus complex was con-
> temporaneous with the juridical organization of loss of parental authority.
>
> MICHEL FOUCAULT, *The History of Sexuality*

A striking number of English prose fiction narratives written between 1684 and
1814 predicate their plots on the tabooed possibility of incest. Aphra Behn's
popular *Love-Letters between a Nobleman and his Sister* (1684–87), arguably the
first extended epistolary fiction in English, is based on an incestuous affair
between Ford, Lord Grey of Werke, and his sister-in-law, Lady Henrietta Berkeley. Multiple stories of incest, one between siblings and several between guardians and wards, punctuate Delarivier Manley's popular anti-Whig scandal novel
The New Atalantis (1709). The eponymous heroine of Daniel Defoe's *Moll Flanders* (1722) inadvertently marries her own brother, and variations on the theme
of incest are played throughout her text. The hero of Henry Fielding's *Tom Jones*
(1749) has sexual relations with a woman he later mistakenly believes to be his
mother. The loving siblings Camilla and Valentine in Sarah Fielding's *David
Simple* (1744) are falsely accused of incest and cruelly banished from their father's house. Frances Burney's *Evelina* (1778) weaves an elaborate incest plot
around the figure of Mr. Macartney and displays a general fascination with the
problem of incestuous desire between fathers and daughters. Even Jane Austen
demonstrates a preoccupation with the question of incest, most notably in

Mansfield Park (1814), a novel that resolves its linked obsession with brother-sister relations and intrafamilial exchange through the marriage of the heroine to her cousin. These are just some of the better-known examples, if we restrict ourselves to the genre of the novel.[1]

This book examines such narrative representations of actual, averted, or imagined incest in the context of changes in class and kinship organization that occurred in England in the late seventeenth and eighteenth centuries. It seeks to illuminate the ways in which early modern incest narratives are shaped by and in turn participate in the production of Restoration and eighteenth-century discourses of gender and of class. To that end, it explores the relationships among those class and gender discourses and debates surrounding marriage prohibitions that took place during the period in the domains of religion, moral philosophy, and the law. Further, through analyses of prose fiction by women as well as men, it investigates the continuities and differences in the ways that male and female writers of the period use representations of incest to configure the relationship between power and sexual difference.

Broadly speaking, *Incest and the English Novel* approaches eighteenth-century incest narratives as part of the history of modern cultural formations. As such, it challenges two dominant existing accounts of literary incest in the long eighteenth century. The first of these accounts privileges Romantic models of culture and human desire and minimizes the importance of incest in eighteenth-century texts; the second privileges anthropological and psychoanalytic models of society and the human subject and assesses the importance of eighteenth-century incest plots in terms of the extent to which they exemplify (and thus corroborate) the axioms on which those models rest. In the first instance, scholars observe the presence of incest as a plot device in the prose fiction of the period, but they dismiss it as a mere surface effect—one readily exploited for comic or sensational purposes but not especially worthy of sustained analysis. (Significantly, no book-length treatment of the topic yet exists.)[2] Such critical neglect is largely a consequence of the Romantic teleology that has dominated discussions of literary incest since Peter Thorslev's pronouncement that while incest appears in eighteenth-century fiction, it does so "only incidentally, never as a major theme," and does not assume the status of a literary symbol until the advent of Romanticism and its Gothic forerunners.[3] Even relatively new studies that look at incest specifically in Restoration or eighteenth-century writing reproduce this narrative, as is readily illustrated by Richard McCabe's recent assertion that "[a]lthough [after Dryden] incest remains a comic possibility in the novels of Fielding, it was not until the Gothic and Romantic periods that it again emerged as a major focus for the examination of human nature."[4]

To the extent that the Romantic bias of such accounts locates literary meaning not in the surface effects of narrative (the external mechanics of mere plot) but rather in narrative's mimetic relation to truth (in this case, the "human nature" that is presumed to precede narrative and to constitute its object of "examination"), they share a certain circular logic with more recent attempts to read eighteenth-century incest narratives through the theoretical lens of the modern human sciences. Thus, for example, in his essay "Incest in the Early Novel and Related Genres," T. G. A. Nelson appeals to the words of Claude Lévi-Strauss as authorizing evidence for the conclusion that the fear of incest manifested (according to Nelson) in eighteenth-century narratives is "at some level related to a wish, not on the existential level of a desire for mating with actual relations, but on the level of memory and nostalgia for a primal state in which no revulsion from incestuous acts or longings was felt."[5] Nelson makes claims for the importance of incest in eighteenth-century narrative; but because, like Thorslev and McCabe, he reads the eighteenth century from the privileged epistemological vantage point of a later and presumptively more insightful moment, he is less concerned with the cultural work being performed by such representations than with the cultural and psychic truths they do or do not reaffirm.[6] My reservations about both of these trends pertain to what they have in common, whether they privilege Romantic or psychoanalytic and anthropological models of culture and human desire: namely, their treatment of Restoration and eighteenth-century representations of incest as part of the prehistory of more enlightened modes of understanding rather than as part of the history of modern epistemological and discursive forms.[7]

Incest and the English Novel seeks to reverse this critical move. Instead of reading eighteenth-century narratives of incest either as foils for a more enlightened Romanticism or as proving grounds for the "truths" discovered by twentieth-century anthropology and psychoanalysis, it seeks to illuminate the ways in which modernity's dominant theoretical formulations about incest and incestuous desire are themselves rooted in the Enlightenment and, particularly, in the emergent genre of the novel.[8] It thus allies itself with postmodern efforts to historicize and demystify Enlightenment cultural formations that helped to shape the discourses of the human sciences in the nineteenth century and continue to dominate many Western theoretical formulations at the turn of the twenty-first century. In fact, I argue, it is precisely in the surface effects of narrative (specifically, in the structural position of incest in eighteenth-century plots) that we can discern the incipient formation and naturalization of narrative constructions of modern gendered subjectivity and of that very representation of a surface and depth relation that has led critics since the Romantic era to read the incidental appearance of incest in early English fiction as inconsequential rather than symptomatic of broader cultural and ideological practices.

While the "sciences of man"—as theorists have come to call the disciplines of sociology, linguistics, statistics, economics, psychology, and ethnology/ anthropology—did not come into their own until well into the nineteenth century, many of the psychological, sociological, and cultural "realities" they undertook to explain and codify (and in the production of which they in turn participated) were already in the process of formation during the preceding century.[9] Where modern constructions of incestuous desire are concerned, this fact is evidenced not simply in the writings of eighteenth-century jurists, moral philosophers, and theologians but also in the proliferation of prose fiction narratives about incest that pervade that body of early modern writing we now refer to as the novel. The following pages examine the extent to which such textual representations of actual, averted, or imagined incest might fruitfully be said to contribute to the production and consolidation of the power/ knowledge discourse that grounds modern theories about incest.[10] Although my readings sometimes draw on the theoretical work of Freud, Lacan, and Lévi-Strauss, they do not position themselves within the ontological assumptions of anthropological or psychoanalytic discourse. On the contrary, they proceed on the premise that whatever unique power the formulations of modern anthropology and psychoanalysis might have to illuminate the dynamics of eighteenth-century prose fiction emanates neither from the timeless or universal applicability of modern theory nor from the immanent truth value of eighteenth-century fiction, but rather from the fact that modern theory reproduces so many of the early novel's structuring presuppositions about human nature and society.

My argument entails several distinct but related propositions: first, that fictional representations of incest in the eighteenth century are part of the history of the formation of a discursive construct in which incest is transgressive and liberatory;[11] second, that this construction of incest has its roots in discourses of political and religious liberation that emerged during the Reformation and evolved over the course of the seventeenth century, when they became additionally implicated in emergent theories of natural law; third, that because these liberatory discourses presuppose naturalized notions of gender asymmetry, women occupy a fundamentally contradictory position within them, particularly in relation to incest's transgressive force; fourth, that while early English novels contribute to the elaboration of discursive strategies for obscuring the contradictions surrounding women's relation to incestuous transgression, they also function as sites where such contradictions can be revealed; and finally that, like dominant modern theories about incest's function in the human psyche and human culture, early English prose fiction implicitly gives the narrative of incest and its prohibition centrality as a discursive matrix within which "truths" about culture, gender, and desire are produced.[12]

To establish the broad theoretical frame for this argument and for the analyses that accompany it, I turn now briefly (and in a necessarily general way) to examine the overdetermined character of incest in some of the key works of modern and postmodern theory in the domains of anthropology, psychoanalysis, and philosophy, with an eye particularly toward illuminating the productive intersections of gender, incest, and narrative within those theories. From there I move to an equally general discussion of the history of such formations in the early modern period. Sustained readings of the historical record and of individual novels are reserved for ensuing chapters.

Gender, Incest, and Narrative in Twentieth-Century Theory

> It could perhaps be said that the whole of philosophical conceptualization, systematically relating itself to the nature/culture opposition, is designed to leave in the domain of the unthinkable the very thing that makes this conceptualization possible: the origin of the prohibition of incest.
>
> JACQUES DERRIDA, "Structure, Sign, and Play in the Discourse of the Human Sciences"

> If the crime of Oedipus is the destruction of differences, the combined work of myth and narrative is the production of Oedipus. The business of the mythical subject is the construction of differences. . . . The work of narrative . . . is a mapping of differences, and specifically, first and foremost, of sexual difference into each text; and hence . . . into the universe of meaning.   TERESA DE LAURETIS, *Alice Doesn't: Feminism, Semiotics, Cinema*

While contemporary theory has sought to distinguish itself by an antifoundationalist refusal to privilege any stable point of origin, the centrality of the narrative of incest and its prohibition within both modern and postmodern theory seems incontestable. Though advanced as only a necessary fiction, this narrative nevertheless functions in philosophical, anthropological, and psychoanalytic paradigms as the discursive matrix for the production not just of culture, gender, and desire but of narrative itself. A brief summary of some of the major twentieth-century versions of this narrative should suffice to illustrate my point.

That incest is intimately tied to gender in modernity's dominant theoretical formulations about human society and the human subject will hardly take a reader familiar with contemporary cultural analysis by surprise. Acknowledgment of the critical conjuncture of these two categories in the discourses of the human sciences has been a staple of poststructuralist thought since the 1970s. Its most pointed articulation may be Gayle Rubin's feminist critique of the master narratives of structural anthropology and psychoanalysis in her influential essay "The Traffic in Women: Notes on the 'Political Economy' of Sex." Using the overlapping work of Claude Lévi-Strauss and Sigmund Freud as the basis of her analysis, Rubin exposes the key role played by the incest prohibition in the social construction of gender. Although she recognizes that both Freud and Lévi-Strauss presuppose the existence of a natural gender hierarchy, Rubin argues nevertheless that their theories both also implicitly construe gender difference as an effect of the social and intrapsychic workings of kinship structures produced and sustained by the incest taboo.[13]

For Lévi-Strauss, prohibition against incest is the linchpin of a particular organization of sexuality in which men are constituted as the agents and women as the objects of exchange. Similarly, in Freudian theory the Oedipus complex is the critical moment in individual psychosexual development from which the human subject (ideally) emerges as a gendered being. Because Lévi-Strauss identifies the institution of the incest taboo as the origin of culture, and Freud in his later work links resolution of the Oedipus complex (in which the child must resolve conflicts triggered by its desire for the parent of the opposite sex) to the production of the superego and the human subject's entry into the processes of cultural reproduction, both tacitly inscribe gender asymmetry as a cultural necessity. They represent the incest taboo, that is, not simply as a culture-instituting but also as a gender-instituting prohibition.[14] Rubin's project is to historicize such universalizing gestures by appropriating these two "sophisticated ideologies of sexism"[15] as "implicit theor[ies] of sex oppression" (171)—a somewhat idiosyncratic undertaking that she accomplishes by filtering her reading of Freud and Lévi-Strauss through the lens of the psychoanalytic work of Jacques Lacan (159).

Lacan returns to Freud through both structural linguistics and Lévi-Strauss's suggestion of "the implication of the structures of Language with that part of the social laws which regulate marriage ties and kinship."[16] His project is to rewrite the theory of the Oedipus complex as a mechanism for the production of gender, desire, and narrative by situating the oedipal drama not at the level of human drives or instincts, as Freud did, but rather exclusively at the level of language (though Lacan acknowledges that the effects of this drama are very real). The human subject, for Lacan, is constituted as a subject only through language, which Lacan conceives not as an instrument created or mastered by the subject but as a self-contained and nonreferential system of differences, including gender and kinship statuses, that names and positions the subject in a sociolinguistic order structured around paternal prohibition. Sexual identity, indeed subjectivity itself, is a function of those differences already inscribed in language prior to the subject's emergence as such. It is in this system of differences that Lacan locates the structure of the unconscious: "For where on earth would one situate the determinations of the unconscious if it is not in those nominal cadres in which marriage ties and kinship are always grounded . . . , in those laws of the Word where lineages found their right. . . ?"[17]

The figure of incest occupies a complex but critical position within this structure. Following Saussure, Lacan argues that the relation between signifier and signified is an arbitrary one. The paternal Law, he thus insists, is the law not necessarily of the biological father (whose paternity, in any event, is always open to doubt) but of a "neutralized" paternal signifier (the Phallus), which represents the Law of the Name-of-the-Father. By the same token, the primordial absence or "structural defect in being" upon which the Lacanian subject is founded—that ontological condition of lack that triggers the substitutive movement of desire in discourse—is not necessarily the irrecoverable maternal body.[18] Incest, nevertheless, remains the privileged figure for that conceptual knot or "lack of a fixed point" at the center of the Lacanian Symbolic order, where according to the standard Lacanian narrative (in which the subject is assumed to be male), a pre-oedipal state of Imaginary fusion with the m/Other is disrupted under the sign of the father's Name and Law (a pun in French, *Nom/Non*). To use Lacan's own words: the "interdiction of incest," that "primordial Law . . . which in regulating marriage ties superimposes the kingdom of culture on that of nature abandoned to the law of copulation," constitutes the "subjective pivot" of the Symbolic order.[19]

Like Lacan, Jacques Derrida situates the figure of incest on the border between signification and meaning and gives it a privileged place in the production of systems of cultural and gender difference. Expressly alluded to in an epigraph from Jean-Jacques Rousseau,[20] incest provides the subtext of Derrida's deconstructive reading of Western phonocentrism in part 2 of *Of Grammatology*, which investigates Lévi-Strauss's genealogical debt to Rousseau's Enlightenment philosophy. Here the prohibition against incest—which Derrida expressly identifies as the unstable center of structuralist thought—becomes the very condition of the possibility of meaning. In Derrida's "sexual fable of the production of meaning,"[21] incest figures as the ever-elusive condition of pure presence, whose endless deferral (differance) through prohibition is the locus of that originary lack on which the entire order of supplementarity (for Derrida, the sine qua non of meaning production and thus of writing) depends.

Although the incest prohibition is "neither named nor expounded" in Rousseau's accounts of the origins of civil society, Derrida's reading of those accounts uncovers incest as the absent presence at the heart of both *The Essay on the Origin of Languages* and *The Social Contract.*[22] It is in this sense, Derrida suggests, that Lévi-Strauss considers Rousseau to have been "the *founder*, not only the prophet, of modern anthropology."[23] The place occupied by incest in Rousseau's symbolic economy is, for Derrida, nothing less than "the point of orientation for the entire system of signification, the point where the fundamental signified is promised as the terminal-point of all references and conceals itself as that which would destroy at one blow the entire system of signs." It is a nonexistent point, "always elusive or, what comes to the same thing, always already inscribed in what it ought to escape or ought to have escaped, according to our indestructible and mortal desire."[24] This "fictive and unstable" point, Derrida maintains, is reflected in the primitive festival that Rousseau imagines at the watering hole prior to the birth of society. "The festival *itself* would be incest *itself*," writes Derrida, "if some such thing—*itself*—could *take place*; if, by taking place, incest were not to confirm the prohibition: before the prohibition, it is not incest; forbidden, it cannot become incest except through the recognition of the prohibition. We are always short of or beyond the limit of the festival, of the origin of society" (267). Remembering Lévi-Strauss on the "equivocal character" of the incest prohibition ("the prohibition of incest is where nature transcends itself"), Derrida reads the "*birth of society*" in Rousseau as that "ungraspable limit" when "culture is . . . broached within its point of origin."[25]

In the deconstructive account of Western philosophy, in other words, incest, far from standing outside the order of culture and prohibition, actually props that order up from within; it is itself constituted by prohibition. Incest occupies the place outside of culture that makes the very thinking of culture possible; like its prohibition, it stands on a border that simultaneously enables and threatens the distinction between nature and culture. As such, it represents at once the absence of those systems of difference that constitute culture and a fiction conceived to make it possible to think those differences.

If the work of Freud, Lévi-Strauss, Lacan, Derrida, and Rubin suggests, from varying epistemological vantage points, that the narrative of incest and its prohibition is constitutive of the categories of culture, gender, and desire, feminist narrative theorists argue explicitly that it is also constitutive of the category of narrative itself. "The Oedipus story . . . is . . . paradigmatic of all narratives," writes Teresa de Lauretis.[26] "It is the 'ur' narrative of narrative as well as the 'ur' narrative of subjectivity," Judith Roof avers, "standing in for the lost origin of both, functioning as the point of origin for stories of origins."[27] Tracing the reification and reinscription of this persistent cultural formation in the work of such narrative theorists as Roland Barthes and Peter Brooks, de Lauretis and Roof both expose the classic oedipal story as a primary site for the production and reproduction of heteronormative narrativity. As de Lauretis writes in her gloss on René Girard's identification of Oedipus as the "slayer of distinctions," quoted as an epigraph to this section, "if the crime of Oedipus [i.e., incest, regicide, and parricide] is the destruction of differences, the combined work of myth and narrative is the production of Oedipus. The business of the mythical subject is the construction of differences. . . . The work of narrative . . . is a mapping of differences, and specifically, first and foremost, of sexual difference into each text; and hence . . . into the universe of meaning."[28]

Judith Butler's effort to subject discursive constructions of the incest taboo to a Foucauldian analysis helps further to illuminate the mutually constitutive relations among incest, prohibition, and narrative within this structuralist frame. The figure of incest deployed in both psychoanalytic and anthropological narrative to signify a time before the law, she demonstrates, is always already a product of that law, whose generativity cannot be separated from its repressive function.[29] Incest may appear to precede prohibition in the temporal ordering of narrative, but in fact the two categories are conceptually synchronic. In the psychoanalytic narrative of development, incest is thinkable only from a postoedipal vantage point (to appropriate Derrida's words from another context, "before the prohibition, it is not incest"), just as any anthropological narrative of origins that speculates retrospectively on a time before the law can do so only postjuridically (as Butler puts it, "speculative origin is always speculated about from a retrospective position" [78]). It is thus as true to say that the founding prohibition of incest produces incestuous heterosexuality as it is to say that the founding presupposition of incestuous heterosexuality sustains the law that prohibits it.

As Butler also demonstrates, furthermore, the constitutive force of the law manifests itself not simply in the production of what is expressly prohibited (in this case, incestuous heterosexuality), but also in the unarticulated assumptions that underwrite that law (here, in the implicit discursive construction of bisexuality and homosexuality). The mobilizing of a distinction between what is "before" and "during" culture, that is, not only institutes a distinction between what is "inside" and "outside" of normative sexuality but also functions preemptively to foreclose other cultural possibilities from the start (77–78). As Rubin observes, "the incest taboo presupposes a prior, less articulate taboo on homosexuality. A prohibition against *some* heterosexual unions assumes a taboo against *non*-heterosexual unions."[30] The temporal logic of narrative obscures the conceptual simultaneity of incest and its prohibition as mutually sustaining categories within a closed and self-supporting system of differences at the same time that it produces the illusion of the naturalness and inevitability of that system's founding terms. What the incest taboo most decisively regulates, in other words, is not so much incest itself as the multiplicity of forms that, in the absence of that prohibition, it might be possible for sexuality to take.[31]

What is at stake in the working and reworking of oedipal narrative, to which both elite and popular culture seem to return in an endless cycle of dissolution and reinscription, then, is nothing less than the cultural production, reproduction, and naturalization of its own founding presuppositions, among which modern notions of gendered subjectivity and incestuous heterosexuality rank preeminent. One way to disrupt or block that reproduction, Roof suggests, may be to rethink our very notions of story. Another, I suggest, may be to write the history of incest narratives. This book seeks to contribute to that project by examining the relationship between gender and incest in British prose fiction produced during the period of the institution of the novel and of modern notions of gender and sexuality. As we shall see, this was also a time when changes in social and economic structure as well as in prevailing epistemologies and systems of representation worked together to transform the relationship between kinship and politics and, with it, the discursive role of incest in the cultural imaginary.

What can we learn by looking at incest narratives produced at the moment when the sexual and social order of modern class-society first emerged? If Terry Eagleton is right that "the symbolic order of which Lacan writes is in reality the patriarchal sexual and social order of modern class-society,"[32] what sort of genealogical link might we posit between early modern incest narratives on the one hand and modern and postmodern theoretical configurations of the relationship between gender and incest on the other? *Incest and the English Novel* approaches early modern prose fiction plots structured around the violation or potential violation of incestuous prohibition not simply as fruitful sites for exploring eighteenth-century ideologies of gender and of class; it also reads such stories as part of an ongoing narrative tradition—a stage, as it were, in a more or less continuous, if varied and often contested, project of cultural representation that begins in the Enlightenment and culminates in the theoretical discourses of the human sciences, of which psychoanalysis and structural anthropology are among the most salient twentieth-century manifestations.[33] This book thus aligns itself theoretically with postmodern efforts seeking not to reproduce but to historicize, demystify, and ultimately think beyond the heteropatriarchal formations of modern culture by opening conceptual space in which to redefine the grounds of prohibition and reimagine the structures of desire.

Incest and the Emergence of the Modern Family

> Capitalism . . . liberates the flows of desire, but under the social conditions
> that define its limit and the possibility of its own dissolution, so that it is
> constantly opposing with all its exasperated strength the movement that
> drives it toward this limit.
>
> GILLES DELEUZE AND FÉLIX GUATTARI, *Anti-Oedipus*

The period of British cultural history when the novel emerged witnessed two historical developments whose confluence is key to understanding the cultural work performed by eighteenth-century incest narratives: the advent of a burgeoning print culture and a massive reordering of class and kinship structures. Family historians have long emphasized the extent to which the importance of kinship ties in late seventeenth- and early eighteenth-century England receded as early modern culture increasingly privileged social relations based on class and individual desire. The institution of kinship had traditionally been the dominant mechanism for regulating economic, political, sexual, and religious life, but it underwent a significant reduction and narrowing of influence over the course of the seventeenth and eighteenth centuries with the emergence of the modern British state and the nation's gradual shift from a domestic to a market economy.[34] The movement of productive activity outside the home and Lockean liberalism's challenge to Robert Filmer's identification of paternal with political authority resulted in a gradual segregation of the domains of political, economic, and domestic life—spheres that had formerly been united within an exclusively agrarian, household economy organized by kinship obligation. As we shall see in chapter 2, one manifestation of the decline in kinship's regulatory force was the gradual transfer of legal jurisdiction over cases of incest from church to state (from the ecclesiastical to the civil courts) and a reduction in the scope of marriage prohibitions. Kinship ties, of course, continued to regulate relations between individuals within the now increasingly nuclear family unit. Nevertheless, as Nicholson observes, John Locke's distinction between "Conjugal" and "Political" power—manifest among other places in his assertion that "the Power of a *Magistrate* over a Subject, may be distinguished from that of a *Father* over his Children, . . . [or] a *Husband* over his Wife"—was a critical discursive move that took kinship out of the realm of politics and grounded the form of the modern family in nature.[35] Gender asymmetry was no longer understood as one aspect of a hierarchical principle of social obligation structuring society as a whole, as in the feudal codes of honor and obligation; it was now conceived, rather, as a natural relation based in biology and in the imperatives of social reproduction—a conception inscribed as a given in the discourse of early modern liberalism.

Thus, while kinship relations continued to organize the newly emergent private sphere of the family, the assumptions of Lockean contract theory provided a necessary cultural support for those relations by grounding them in the state of nature. In a sense we might say, building on the work of Jürgen Habermas and Michel Foucault, that the public circulation of an ideology of natural gender asymmetry through the medium of print came to supplement and to some extent to supplant kinship as one of the Enlightenment's new mechanisms of social regulation.[36] The dissemination of such an ideology was by no means confined to the genre of political theory, but as numerous scholars have observed, it emerged in a variety of discursive forms, including conduct literature and educational theory. Since the private sphere was defined at its inception as essentially independent of the state, these new methods of social discipline took the form not of explicit state controls but of textual bodies of knowledge about the nature of society and humanity.[37]

Because the era of the "decline of kinship" was also the period when the "affective" nuclear family established itself as the place where gender is created and where power is psychosocially organized, naturalized, and reproduced, the cultural contradictions inherent in the historical shift from patriarchal to "egalitarian" models of familial order emerged most powerfully within the family. Lockean individualism promoted social relations based on the principles of equality, autonomy, competition, and exchange, but it defined the family as "hierarchical, and based on social relations of obligation and concern."[38] There was thus a social and ideological contradiction surrounding the relationship between class and kinship in early capitalist society, and women stood at its crux. Juliet Mitchell has analyzed this contradiction and women's relation to it tellingly. In economically advanced societies, she argues, economic forms of exchange other than kinship exchange dominate, and class structures rather than kinship structures prevail. While capitalism renders kinship structures archaic, however, it also preserves them in a residual way in the ideology of the biological family, which posits the nuclear family with its oedipal structure as a natural rather than a culturally created phenomenon. In other words, the ideology of the biological family comes into its own against the background of the remoteness of a kinship system but masks the persistence—in altered forms—of precisely those archaic patterns of kinship organization. "[M]en enter into the class-dominated structures of history," writes Mitchell, "while women (as women, whatever their actual work in production) remain defined by the kinship patterns of organization . . . harnessed into the family."[39] It is an interesting twist of Anglo-European intellectual history that in the human sciences the systematic study of kinship as a mechanism for regulating social life should produce as its proper object of scrutiny not the modern family at all but rather the ethnologically primitivized cultural Other and that this development should occur during the very period when the modern European family, on the pretext of displacing kinship as a political force, assumes increasing importance in the structuring of affective life, eventually becoming the privileged object of modern psychological theory. The "Othering" of kinship in this context has the force of a disavowal of the political nature of gender in the modern family, camouflaging even as it exposes kinship's displacement as merely the flip side of its psychic, familial, and national domestication.

The contradictions outlined in Mitchell's characterization of the modern family emerge in a variety of forms in the work of other cultural theorists. Habermas, for example, alludes to "[t]he ambivalence of the family as an agent of society yet simultaneously as the anticipated emancipation from society . . . : on the one hand, [family members] were held together by patriarchal authority; on the other, they were bound to one another by human closeness." Juliet Flower MacCannell characterizes the Enlightenment's turn toward modernity as embodying a similar familial paradox: just at the moment when the overthrow of patriarchy promises a "new form of human community," patriarchy reasserts itself in a "distinctive variation" that she calls the Regime of the Brother.[40] Of all contemporary accounts, however, Michel Foucault's characterization of the family as "the interchange of sexuality and alliance" is unique in expressly theorizing the link between the privileged place of incest in modernity and the modern family's distinctive double character as a matrix of both desire and the law.[41] Foucault's narrative of the history of sexuality and of the modern European family thus provides a critical point of departure for my effort here to explore the cultural continuities between eighteenth- and twentieth-century constructions of incestuous desire.

In Foucault's account, sexuality—itself a modern European invention—is inherently incestuous. Before the eighteenth century, Foucault observes, relations of sex were regulated by "the deployment of alliance," a phrase he uses to denote traditional, feudal systems of marriage, kinship, and inheritance. From the eighteenth century onward, however, a new apparatus of social discipline emerged in the West that was superimposed on the deployment of alliance, without entirely supplanting it: this Foucault calls "the deployment of sexuality." "The family, in its contemporary form," he writes,

> must not be understood as a social, economic, and political structure of alliance that excludes or at least restrains sexuality, . . . preserving only its useful functions. On the contrary, its role is to anchor sexuality and provide it with a permanent support. It ensures the production of a sexuality that is not homogeneous with the privileges of alliance, while making it possible for the systems of alliance to be imbued with a new tactic of power which they would otherwise be impervious to. The family . . . conveys the law and the juridical dimension in the deployment of sexuality; and it conveys the economy of pleasure and the intensity of sensations in the regime of alliance.[42]

Anchored within the conjugal family unit, which became "its privileged point of development" (108), sexuality was thus from its inception dependent on the family and on the primacy of familial affections. At the same time, Foucault points out, the family became reciprocally dependent for its survival on the production of incestuous desire:

It may be that in societies where the mechanisms of alliance predominate, prohibition of incest is a functionally indispensable rule. But in a society such as ours,
where the family is the most active site of sexuality, and where it is doubtless the
exigencies of the latter which maintain and prolong its existence, incest . . . occupies a central place: it is constantly being solicited and refused; it is an object of
obsession and attraction, a dreadful secret and an indispensable pivot. It is manifested as a thing that is strictly forbidden in the family insofar as the latter functions as a deployment of alliance; but it is also a thing that is continuously demanded in order for the family to be a hotbed of constant sexual incitement. (109)

In the Foucauldian formulation, in other words, the emergence of sexuality
as a discursive construct in the modern era coincides with the cultural instantiation of incest as both the model and the limit of desire. Through the
paradoxical interpenetration of the imperatives of desire and the law, incest is
both demanded and forbidden. Within a single cultural economy, it is constituted as both the ultimate cultural transgression and the ultimate solution to
the problem of repression—as a veritable requirement, within the liberatory
ethics of individualist ideology, for gaining access to an authentic human core.

On the one hand, this structuring cultural paradox provides a built-in safe-
guard on desire, constituting it—along the lines suggested in my epigraph from
Deleuze and Guattari—as a drive toward precisely the thing that defines its limit.
As Foucault notes, even psychoanalysis, though it seemed to position itself
outside the imperatives of familial and communal obligation (from which it
aspired to emancipate an essential subjectivity), would become a reassuring
accomplice to the law by rediscovering "the law of alliance, the involved workings of marriage and kinship, and incest at the heart of . . . sexuality, as the
principle of its formation and the key to its intelligibility. The guarantee that
one would find the parents-children relationship at the root of everyone's sexuality made it possible . . . to keep the deployment of sexuality coupled to the
system of alliance" (113), or—as Deleuze and Guattari put it—to keep "European
humanity harnessed to the yoke of daddy-mommy."[43] Normative sexuality is
inherently incestuous because all legitimate love objects are always already
substitutes for the objects of incestuous longing. The processes of displacement
and substitution that ensure the reproduction of gender, family, and exchange
are themselves grounded in the assumption of the naturalness of incestuous
desire; incest thus functions simultaneously within this discursive matrix as a
trope of escape from the imperatives of gender, family, and exchange and as an
occasion for reinscribing the historical value of those very imperatives.

But if the tensions inherent in these conceptions of the modern family make for an incestuous sexuality whose transgressive force is neutralized because it is ultimately configured as an extension of the law, it is also precisely in its paradoxical nature that this configuration takes on its most disturbing implications (a circumstance perhaps not too surprising, given the paternal aegis of that Law). Freud, Lévi-Strauss, Derrida, and Lacan all privilege incestuous desire as the natural ground of cultural reproduction, but their theories all also systematically deny a conceptual place to the possibility of incestuous practices. They represent incest, rather, as a productive impossibility—as endlessly deferred, a fiction, a nonexistent point, an unconscious wish, an ungraspable limit. The material dangers of what we might call this modern "hystericization" of incest as mere cultural fantasy with no basis in social fact (a practice tacitly reproduced by critics like Nelson) are incisively suggested by Judith Butler in a gloss on Lévi-Strauss, where she critiques his "rather astonishing statement . . . [that] acts of incest 'have never been committed!' "[44] Resisting Lévi-Strauss's pronouncement that the "ancient and lasting dream" of incest dramatized in Freud's *Totem and Taboo* is a dream whose magic and "power to mould men's thoughts unbeknown to them, arises precisely from the fact that the acts it evokes have never been committed, because culture has opposed them at all times and in all places," Butler insists that we understand such theoretical constructions of reality—from a Foucauldian perspective—as themselves mechanisms or *technologies* of power.[45] The question, she contends, is not how prohibition is generated as a consequence of incestuous desire but rather "how . . . such phantasms [i.e., dreams of incest] become generated and, indeed, instituted as a consequence of their prohibition? Further, how does the social conviction, here symptomatically articulated through Lévi-Strauss, that the prohibition *is* efficacious disavow and, hence, clear a social space in which incestuous practices are free to reproduce themselves without proscription?"[46] Incestuous practices, one would have to reply, are free to reproduce themselves because the model of desire that underwrites belief in the efficacy of incestuous prohibition is hegemonically male. Never mind that in Western cultural practice the scene of incest usually involves paternal abuse of daughters;[47] the primal scene of incest posited in Western theory occurs between mother and son according to an oedipal logic of substitution and exchange. By relinquishing his desire for his mother and acceding to his father's phallic authority over her—and, for the time being, over him—the son acquires phallic authority over his own future family (or, in the Lacanian narrative, by relinquishing his desire for the m/other's desire, the child gains access to the Symbolic order organized around the phallic signifier).

Butler's queries recognize (in a way that Foucault's limited and often problematic analysis of gender relations does not) what feminist scholars like Florence Rush and Judith Herman have long observed, that what is at stake in modern theory's representations of incest and its prohibition is not so much protection against the acting out of incestuous pleasures as it is the maintenance of a whole structure of social relations and the asymmetrical power dynamics of their attendant sexual arrangements (some of which arrangements tacitly encourage incestuous acts).[48] What is produced by the incest taboo as it is understood within modern discursive configurations, that is, is not just the conceptual fiction of an "original" incestuous desire but also an entire nexus of social relations and cultural practices, which the prior postulation of a strong endogamous heterosexual impulse appears not merely to justify but to require. If we are interested in changing those cultural stakes by dislodging and dismantling such powerful and inherently dangerous representations, we would do well first to understand their material and discursive histories.

Incest Narratives in the Long Eighteenth Century

> The relation of narrative and desire must be sought within the specificity of textual practice, where it is materially inscribed.
>
> TERESA DE LAURETIS, *Alice Doesn't: Feminism, Semiotics, Cinema*

I have argued that the historical realignment of the categories of class, kinship, and representation that took place in England in the late seventeenth and eighteenth centuries marked a transformative moment in the cultural construction of incest that rendered narratives about incest a peculiarly dense transfer point between two overlapping but distinct forms of cultural power. The chapters that follow undertake to show how, through their varied and complex representations of the interlocking cultural economies of kinship, class, and textuality, incest narratives of the long eighteenth century work both to articulate and to obscure the ideological contradictions occasioned by the shift from patriarchal to "egalitarian" models of familial order. Each narrative that I study mobilizes several interlocking exchange systems—the economic, the sexual, and the semiotic. My readings focus on how the relationships among those systems of exchange are organized. Typically in these texts, the challenge of class to kinship opens the dual threat of incest and unruly representation. My analyses explore the varied ways in which this double threat is related to broader social concerns about unlicensed sexual and cultural reproduction—concerns precipitated by the explosion of print and by changes in gender ideology and in prevailing modes of representing power. In particular, I am interested in understanding how the threat of incest posed by middle-class challenges to aristocratic or landed ideology gets articulated in early novels around the contested cultural sites of textuality and the female reproductive body.

In order to establish the discursive context for my readings of individual texts, I begin, in chapter 2, by examining the regulatory discourses that circulated around incest from the Reformation through the end of the eighteenth century, with an eye toward teasing out the process whereby, over the course of the seventeenth and eighteenth centuries, the category of incest increasingly became discursively naturalized. The first section of the chapter focuses on the history of debates and uncertainties surrounding definitions of incest (a history that dates back at least to the beginning of the Protestant Reformation) and on the ambiguous legal status of incestuous marriage that resulted from long-standing conflicts between civil and ecclesiastical courts. It then proceeds to examine the convergence and interimplication of early modern regulatory discourses about incest with other dominant cultural discourses of the era. British discussions of incest had been embedded in larger questions of political and religious liberation at least since the time of Henry VIII's break with Rome. Over the course of the seventeenth and eighteenth centuries, I undertake to show, those discussions were further implicated in emergent discourses of natural law and eventually became part of a discourse of natural liberty that posited the existence of a prejuridical human subject with innate propensities for incestuous freedoms—a construct that remains central to twentieth-century theoretical formulations about incestuous desire.

In the final section of chapter 2, I make the case that seventeenth- and eighteenth-century discussions about incest were always already discussions about gender. Here I take issue with several existing studies of eighteenth-century juridical uncertainties surrounding incest in arguing that the assumption of natural gender asymmetry implicit in early modern discourses of political and religious liberation accounts more consistently than historical and class differences for the vexed and contradictory nature of incest regulations as they developed in the early modern West. In his account of the marriage prohibitions controversy in *The Rise of the Egalitarian Family,* for example, Randolph Trumbach focuses on the different class stakes implicit in defenses of cousin marriage on the one hand and wife's sister marriage on the other. By shifting the primary focus of analysis away from class politics and onto the gender politics that cut across those class distinctions, my inquiry urges an alternative perspective on what is fundamentally at stake in the marriage prohibitions controversy. Discussion of those stakes reemerges and is developed at further length in relation to developing racial ideology in my concluding chapter, on *Mansfield Park*.

In much the same spirit in which Foucault attributes a regulatory function to the discourses of the human sciences (which, he suggests, replace the law with the viewpoint of the objective), I argue here that during the long eighteenth century, when legal impediments to marriage were being questioned and incest was increasingly being naturalized within emergent theories of natural law, stories about incestuous relations contributed to the cultural work of regulating desire through the mechanism of its discursive production in the newly expanded medium of print. To suggest that the human sciences have reproduced "truths" about incest and its prohibition that early novels worked to found and naturalize, however, is by no means to suggest that eighteenth-century fictions about incest are simple rehearsals of oedipal plots or that they elaborate such "truths" in monolithic or univocal ways. On the contrary, because they are situated at a historically formative moment, these narratives often expose the contested nature of such representations more visibly than do their twentieth-century critical reconstructions. Just as often as they serve as occasions for the naturalization and consolidation of new discursive formations, they function as sites of resistance to such unifying processes. At a time when class transformations and new epistemologies were undercutting traditional justifications for the operations of power within the family and in English culture generally, stories about incest sometimes worked to defend against the erosion of patriarchal power; but they also sometimes served to critique the reinscription of patriarchal structures within emergent individualist ideologies that promised to open possibilities for cultural change that they in fact foreclosed.

Thus, as I argue in chapter 3, Aphra Behn's *Love-Letters between a Nobleman and his Sister* destabilizes incest as a gesture of liberatory rebellion against prohibitive patriarchal law by exposing it as the site of individualism's complicity with the very ancestral royalism that it endeavors to displace. Intuiting that incest's transgressive force is inextricably related to the law that produces it as an object of repression, Behn advances a model of transgression inflected by gender and thus not stably determined by the binary of reciprocity and incest that informs emerging Whig ideology and that structures the plots of Fielding and Defoe. Her heroine, Silvia, acquires transgressive agency not, as some have argued, through incest but rather by exploiting the performative possibilities open to her by virtue of her symbolic status as a woman within masculine economies of power and desire. Through her powers of performance, Silvia moves beyond the limits of an oedipal drama in which women are mere conduits for relations between men into an imaginative space generated by a parodic repetition of its terms.

My reading of Delarivier Manley's *New Atalantis* in chapter 4 similarly examines how the crisis of political and familial authority staged by the drama of incest opened new possibilities for female agency in the domain of representation. Tracing the complex link between Manley's stories of guardian-ward incest and the changing role of guardianship after the Restoration, I tie Manley's guardian-ward incest narratives simultaneously to an intricate network of legal, economic, and political developments and to Manley's own personal struggle—as a woman, a Tory writer, and an incestuously abused ward—to negotiate the complicated project of self-representation. The figure of the incestuously abused female ward, I argue here, became a highly charged cultural signifier for both the promises and the dangers attendant on Charles II's legal empowerment of private-property-owning fathers through the institution of testamentary guardianship. Manley critiques the precariousness of paternal privilege within this increasingly republican dispensation even as she takes advantage of the instabilities it generates to authorize her own Tory project of self-representation as a female ward and a victim of incestuous abuse. In the second part of the chapter, I read Manley's representation of the incestuous twins Polydore and Urania both as symptoms of and as familial scapegoats for the Whig corruptions figured throughout *The New Atalantis* by the condition of defective guardianship.

Because as women Behn and Manley exploited representational opportunities opened up by the very epistemological and political changes that as Tories they resisted, their writing has a peculiarly double edge. On the one hand, they use incest narratives to expose women's purely intermediary role in dramas of masculine desire and privilege, highlighting the passive and merely secondary function of the female reproductive body in male economies of exchange; on the other hand, by their very entry into the market for representation through the circulation of such narratives, they suggest the possibility of alternative models of desire and agency. For each, this move is both subversive and regressive: Behn appropriates theatrical strategies of performance and display from a classical discourse of sovereignty to recast the drama of male desire with another emphasis; Manley appropriates the classical figure of the Crown as a minor ward under sovereign guardianship to forge her own version of a modern narrative of succession. Whether there is, in fact, a stable place to stand outside the drama of masculine succession or whether that place is always already recuperated by the limits of cultural intelligibility is a question, of course, that ever haunts their texts, and it is one that Manley herself ventures to broach without resolving in her utopian vision of the exclusively female, cooperative community of the New Cabal.[49] It is clear, nevertheless, that both Behn and Manley sought to challenge, even as they exploited, the discursive regimes available to them. If early modern incest narratives function as imaginative sites—or theaters—for the enactment of dramas of male succession and desire, the work of Behn and Manley examines women's dual status in the unfolding and the production of those dramas, their function both as theaters across which the contest for masculine privilege gets played out and as performative agents (at the level of plot as well as narration) in the resignification of incest as a symbolic and discursive entity.

Behn and Manley use incest narratives, then, as sites of resistance to both traditional and emergent forms of patriarchy, deftly exploiting the discursive openings created by modernity's challenges to patriarchal law to expose the contradictions within those challenges. By contrast, as I argue in chapters 5 and 6, Defoe and Fielding deploy narratives about incest as occasions for consolidating and naturalizing the contradictory logic of emergent Enlightenment ideologies. Incest functions in *Moll Flanders* and *Tom Jones* not, as it does in *Love-Letters* and *The New Atalantis,* as a complex discursive site where two oppositional forms of patriarchy intersect; it functions rather as a representation of patriarchy's "Other"—an act of transgression against paternal order that must be recuperated and assimilated through a logic of substitution and exchange. *Tom Jones*—the most canonical and probably the most familiar of eighteenth-century incest narratives for its famous scene in which both protagonist and reader are led to believe, momentarily, that the hero has unwittingly had sex with his own mother—is also the novel most often invoked as evidence in arguments for eighteenth-century incest's essential literary insignificance. This may be not because the incest in Fielding's novel *is* in fact insignificant or merely incidental but because, as I argue, incest functions more seamlessly in *Tom Jones* as a site for negotiating the cultural contradictions occasioned by Enlightenment realignments of class, kinship, and representation than in any earlier narrative of the age.

Given Behn and Manley's position of double alienation from republican discourse (as women and as conservatives), it stands to reason that they should be less invested in mobilizing the recuperative function of the narrative of incest and its prohibition than in exposing the problematic nature of the emancipatory claims made for incest within emergent discourses of Whig liberalism. It does not necessarily follow, however, that all incest narratives by Whig men trace so "classic" a trajectory as *Tom Jones* does or produce so transparent a version of what Christine van Boheemen has called the " 'plot' of patriarchy."[50] Consider, for example, Defoe's *Moll Flanders*. Like *Tom Jones,* Defoe's more loosely organized narrative tells the story of an orphan's exile and return, in which the protagonist—though marked by illegitimacy, misfortune, and a life outside the law—ends up repentant and in possession of a substantial fortune. Nonetheless, the fact that Defoe's eponymous novel features a woman whose incest, though inadvertent, is not averted but realized has marked it for some readers as an ideal counterexample to Fielding's narrative of neatly recuperated lawlessness. Granted, the incest in *Moll Flanders* is between half-siblings rather than parent and child (a possibly somewhat mitigating circumstance); but since Moll's husband-brother functions as a conduit for reunion with her lost mother, there is also a sense in which Moll's incest (in a gesture of displacement necessitated by the heterosexual economy in which she moves) becomes an indirect signifier for a return to maternal presence (and thus signals, even as it disavows, the possibility of a lesbian economy). In other words, because Defoe's outlaw protagonist is a woman who moves in what Juliet Mitchell has called "a society without a father"[51] (in contrast to Fielding's hero, around whom father figures seem to multiply), some critics view her story as an exception to normative narrative patterns, in which female protagonists ultimately either assimilate to patriarchal structures or suffer tragic fates as a consequence of their failure to conform.[52] As I undertake to show in my analysis of the structural place of incest in the novel, however, Defoe's text, no less than Fielding's, inscribes the heterosexual exchange of women as a cultural necessity. The imperative of sexual exchange emerges in *Moll Flanders* as both logically and psychologically prior to the capitalist drive that Moll otherwise seems so fundamentally to embody, structuring the novel's class drama and harnessing it within a naturalized version of traditional gender hierarchy. Although one might argue that Defoe's novel represents a more incipient (and therefore, perhaps, less seamless) attempt than Fielding's to reinscribe kinship's limiting conditions within a narrative of class ascent, incest ultimately operates in *Moll Flanders,* as it does in *Tom Jones,* as a structural and ideological fulcrum around which narrative possibilities for transgression are delimited and contained—a narrative pivot toward and away from which the protagonist must move in order for the story to resolve itself and for Defoe to manage the narratological problems inherent in representing a female individualism within the limits of Whig ideology.

My readings of *Moll Flanders* and *Tom Jones* reveal, I hope, some of the broader implications of my approach to the history of the early English novel as a history of gender-inflected incest narratives. In particular, I hope to show how reading some of the more canonical, male-authored versions of the genre against their lesser-known counterparts by women works to destabilize conventional binaries that have structured traditional discussions of the genre by exposing the ideological continuities that subtend the differences between, for example, formally closed and open texts, or between representations of male and female protagonists, and between averted and actual or intergenerational and intragenerational incest.

The unstable distinction between parent-child and sibling incest and the dynamic of narrative displacement whereby Moll Flanders's marriage to her half-brother mediates her return to maternal presence are matters that I take up in a more sustained fashion in chapter 6, where I discuss a range of incest narratives published after 1740 that address questions of maternity, textuality, and origins. My point of departure for this discussion is analysis of a little-known, anonymous pamphlet entitled *Eleanora; or A Tragical but True Case of Incest in Great-Britain* (1751), whose striking treatment of the problems of origins, maternal desire, textuality, and intertextuality provides a useful paradigm for thinking about the structural and symbolic continuities among narrative representations of different varieties of heterosexual incest (i.e., parent-child and sibling). Critics have sometimes been inclined to read representations of intergenerational and intragenerational incest as embodiments of distinct power differentials (sibling incest being, it is assumed, a more egalitarian relation than parent-child incest). My readings in this chapter, however, suggest strong intertexual links between such representations as functions of a totalizing symbolic order. *Eleanora* helps to illuminate these links not simply because it includes versions of mother-son, father-daughter, *and* sibling incest but also because it demonstrates how inextricable is the relation between incest and textuality in the modern episteme, where problems of linguistic indeterminacy become the subject matter of fictive narrative and incest becomes a figure for the impossibility of discursive immanence. Indeed, because it exemplifies the intertextual logic whereby incest in mid- to late-eighteenth-century fiction comes to signal the absence of origin that haunts all textuality, *Eleanora* might be said to represent an early case of that modern instantiation of incest as the "ungraspable limit" or lack of a fixed point that twentieth-century theory has so consistently identified as the unstable ground of meaning,[53] a ground so fundamental that, like kinship, it seems "to condition the sphere of politics without entering into it."[54] An obscure Enlightenment narrative of maternal desire and deceit, *Eleanora* stands as a kind of ur-text through which I have found it both possible and fruitful to read a variety of other midcentury narratives concerned with the dangerous possibilities of deceitful maternity.

Containing a startling scene in which its hero literally ingests an incest narrative, *Eleanora* also signals the reterritorialization of incest that occurs when kinship is discursively detached from the realm of politics and resituated in the domain of private life—that is, when incest narratives become psychic rather than overtly "political" dramas. Interestingly, of all the texts that I analyze in this study, the one that is most invested in elaborating such a drama of interiority, *Mansfield Park,* is also the one that most squarely addresses the national and racial politics of kinship—in particular, the ways in which kinship uses gender asymmetry to establish external or communal as well as internal or familial boundaries. These are matters that come up earlier, though much less insistently, in my discussions of *Moll Flanders's* casual invocation of a global colonial context in chapter 5 and of *Evelina's* thematic preoccupation with problems of "belonging" in relation to strangers and foreigners in chapter 6. My concluding discussion of *Mansfield Park* takes up the question of kinship's politics in a more sustained fashion, however, in a reading that explores the interimplication of tropes of incest and slavery in the novel in connection with evolving concepts of British liberty as they pertain, on the one hand, to eighteenth-century defenses of close kindred marriage and, on the other hand, to the political freedoms of enslaved Africans transported from the colonies to English shores.

If Behn and Manley use incest narratives as sites of resistance to both traditional and emergent forms of patriarchy, Jane Austen deploys narrative tropes of incest to lay bare the internal instabilities of an already consolidated modern patriarchy founded on an ideal of authenticity. Tropes of incest and representation intersect in *Mansfield Park*, where the heroine's insistence that she "cannot act" becomes the very ground for her successful performance of the role of dutiful daughterhood and thus, ultimately, for full incorporation into her foster family through marriage to her cousin and surrogate-brother, Edmund Bertram. Like Henry Fielding's *Tom Jones*, Austen's novel is a story of adoption in which the protagonist's internal qualities of dutifulness and sincerity earn her symbolic filial status in her uncle's family. An extreme introvert, Fanny may be the psychological antithesis of Fielding's gregarious hero, but she is like Tom in being a f(am)ilial interloper who comes to displace more "natural" children in that family's affective and material economy. Through her, I argue, Austen exposes the instabilities at the heart of early modern notions of domesticity that privilege affect over birth in the constitution of "true" family and that, in this case, render the acting rather than the actual daughter the more genuine article.

In some ways, the vertiginous ironies created by Austen's collapsing and complication of the difference between affect (as feeling) and affect (as performance), and between inside and outside (manifest not simply at the level of the individual but also at the level of the group, in such oppositional categories as family and not-family or home and not-home), recall Aphra Behn's much earlier problematizing of such categories in *Love-Letters* in order to expose the mutually constitutive nature of sexuality and politics. But *Mansfield Park* goes yet further in disclosing the discursive mechanisms whereby emergent notions of the sentimental family that idealize the asymmetrical relation between brother and sister as an emancipatory incestuous space and a psychological model for normative heterosexuality also provide the sustaining ground for naturalized notions of racial purity.

If, as I argue in chapter 2, studies like Trumbach's *Rise of the Egalitarian Family* or Jack Goody's *Development of the Family and Marriage in Europe* take the mediating role of women in cultural economies as a given, it is my aim in this study to make that position of mediation my primary object of analysis—a ground worth interrogating rather than a question to be begged—in attempting to understand the preoccupation with incest that manifested itself in the cultural debates and literary representations of the long eighteenth century. While I trace these questions through readings of early English novels published between 1684 and 1814, I am less interested in offering a totalizing account of the development of the early English novel than I am in identifying and exploring the distinct role that incest came to play within an emerging modern episteme. My readings demonstrate that incest functions as a site both for the production and for the critique of gendered subjectivity within this emergent cultural formation. I am interested in plotting the arcs of change that transpired in the movement from patriarchal to "egalitarian" models of familial order, but I am also interested in identifying the cultural continuities by which the paradigms of modernity installed old power dynamics and social hierarchies at new cultural sites—most notably, in the domains of gendered sexuality and psychic interiority. Because the novels of many early women writers work so powerfully to resist and critique these emerging paradigms, they provide a productive point of departure for interrogating the cultural necessity of incest economies. I thus return to those novels here as a potentially fruitful place to begin rethinking the structures of desire and exchange that have for so long defined the terms of our psychic and our global "realities."

CHAPTER TWO

Incest and Its Contingencies

Debates in Britain from the Reformation
through the Eighteenth Century

> To know whether his idea of *adultery* or *incest* be right, will a man seek it
> anywhere amongst things existing? Or is it true because any one has been
> witness to such an action? No: but it suffices here, that men have put to-
> gether such a collection into one complex idea, that makes the archetype
> and specific idea; whether ever any such action were committed *in rerum
> naturâ* or no.   JOHN LOCKE, *An Essay Concerning Human Understanding*

> Because the father, the mother, and the child, though they be three per-
> sons, yet are they but (*una caro*) one flesh; and consequently no degree of
> kindred—or any method of acquiring one *in nature*—There you push the ar-
> gument again too far, cried Didius—for there is no prohibition *in nature*,
> though there is in the Levitical law—but that a man may beget a child upon
> his grandmother—in which case, supposing the issue a daughter, she would
> stand in relation both of—But who ever thought, cried Kysarcius, of laying
> with his grandmother?—The young gentleman, replied Yorick, whom Sel-
> den speaks of—who not only thought of it, but justified his intention to his
> father by the argument drawn from the law of retaliation—"You laid, Sir,
> with my mother," said the lad—"why may not I lie with yours?"—
>
>   LAURENCE STERNE, *Tristram Shandy*

This chapter examines regulatory discourses about incest in early modern England as manifestations of gender ideology. It chronicles the history of juridical uncertainties and instabilities surrounding incest from the Reformation
through the eighteenth century, exploring the intersections of early modern
discourses about incest with both contemporary discourses of political and
religious liberation and emergent discourses of natural law. In an effort to discover what kinds of cultural work the confluence of these mutually constitutive
discourses might perform, I examine a variety of opposing arguments by biblical commentators, jurists, and philosophers regarding the limits of natural law

in determining questions of incest. In all these arguments, the Bible figures prominently as an authoritative text. How were scriptural narratives about incest—most notably the originary story of Adam and Eve, which was repeatedly read by early modern commentators as a story of authorized incest—deployed hermeneutically both to naturalize a particular nexus of assumptions about gender and to order the relationship between the categories of gender and kinship? How, over the course of more than two centuries, did the changing discursive role of incest figure in the process whereby early modern theories of natural law transformed a Reformation discourse of religious liberation into a constitutional discourse of natural rights? And, finally, to what extent can the assumption of natural gender asymmetry implicit in these discourses of political and religious liberation account for the persistently vexed and contradictory nature of incest regulations as they developed in the early modern West?

Juridical Uncertainties and the Prohibited Degrees of Marriage

When in 1660, on the occasion of the Stuart Restoration, Jeremy Taylor published his monumental work of English casuistry, *Ductor Dubitantium or, The Rule of Conscience,* he observed a certain lack of clarity among his contemporaries regarding the degrees of kinship that legitimately could be considered impediments to marriage. Because of his assessment that "the questions of degrees and the matters and cases of incest are not so perfectly stated as the greatness of the matter and necessities of the world require," he set himself as one of his tasks to illuminate the extent and limits of the law in matters pertaining to marriages between kin.[1]

Taylor wrote his treatise with the express design of providing Anglican clergymen, who formerly had been forced to rely on Roman Catholic manuals or on the writings of foreign theologians, with an authoritative English system of conduct. But while the *Ductor* may have been the most comprehensive, it was by no means the first work of casuistry in English to address uncertainties surrounding restrictions on marriages within families.[2] Controversy over such prohibitions had been going on since at least the time of Henry VIII, when, as Taylor himself notes, the question of the status of the Levitical prohibitions in binding Christian conduct "was strangely tossed up and down" in connection with Henry's efforts to divorce his first wife, Catherine of Aragon, the widow of his deceased brother Arthur.[3] The Catholic Church had traditionally forbidden both marriage and sexual intercourse within a broad range of kindred relation-ships. In the early sixteenth century, these impediments extended to the fourth degree of kinship, or to third cousins, and they included relationships through marriage (affinity) as well as blood (consanguinity).[4] It had been necessary, therefore, for Henry and Catherine to obtain a papal dispensation of the imped-iment of affinity in the first degree (in the collateral line) before their marriage—contracted by an international treaty between Spain and England—could be solemnized.[5] Pope Julius II issued a papal bull to this effect in 1503, and the couple were publicly married in 1509 (when Henry was fifteen). When, twenty years later, the marriage had failed to produce a surviving male heir, however, Henry (who by then had already entered into an adulterous liaison with Anne Boleyn) found it personally, diplomatically, and dynastically expedient to de-velop scruples regarding the lawfulness of his marriage on theological grounds. Remembering Leviticus 20:21 ("if a man shall take his brother's wife, it is an unclean thing: he hath uncovered his brother's nakedness; they shall be child-less"), he construed his own failure to produce an heir as divine punishment for his transgression of the Levitical injunction against a man's having sexual rela-tions with his brother's wife (18:16). In the hope of obtaining a formal annul-ment of his marriage, Henry therefore brought a case against Julius's bull, argu-ing that the pope had no authority to dispense with a divinely ordained law.[6]

Against the arguments of Henry and those he marshaled in his defense, Catherine's supporters invoked the text of Deuteronomy 25:5–6. Here Scripture expressly enjoined a man to marry his brother's widow in cases where the brother had died without issue: "If brethren dwell together, and one of them die, and have no child, the wife of the dead shall not marry without unto a stranger: her husband's brother shall go in unto her, and take her to him to wife, and perform the duty of an husband's brother unto her. And it shall be, that the firstborn which she beareth shall succeed in the name of his brother which is dead, that his name be not put out of Israel." Such marriages obliging a man to produce heirs for his dead brother for the sole purpose of carrying on the family line were called levirate marriages (from the Latin word *levir,* meaning brother-in-law). According to Henry's opponents, they were a special case and the single legal exception to the Levitical precepts.[7]

The apparent scriptural contradiction between Leviticus and Deuteronomy had been previously and extensively commented upon by religious scholars;[8] and the rules of consanguinity and affinity had been invoked in earlier cen-turies as justification for dissolving the marriages of European nobility.[9] Never before, however, had the nuances of scriptural interpretation generated public debate on quite so grand a scale. As Scarisbrick's account makes clear, the Henrician divorce produced an intellectual controversy of international significance:

> A galaxy of Greek and Hebrew scholars, Christian and Jew, of theologians and canonists, of religious houses and universities, first in England and then on the Continent, were . . . called upon to provide evidence for the king. Soon English agents were abroad, in France and Italy especially, quizzing and cajoling, ransacking libraries, interrogating university faculties, drawing up lists of signatories in this or that friary, urging canonists and Scripture scholars to take up the pen. By the end they had assembled a weighty corpus of *libelli*, tracts, opinions and *obiter dicta* from scores of scholars and institutions. Meanwhile, of course, the other side had been no less energetic. Men great and small rallied to defend Queen Catherine, meeting tract with tract, opinion with opinion. By 1529–30 the king's divorce had occasioned an international debate as violent and swift-moving, though on a much smaller scale, as the contemporary conflict between Catholic and Protestant polemicists. It was the sort of competition in scriptural exegesis which the printing press and the recent renewal of Greek and Hebrew studies made easy and, to some, highly congenial.[10]

Perhaps in part because the Holy Roman Empire was at that time under the control of Queen Catherine's nephew, Charles V, Henry ultimately failed to persuade the church to grant an annulment. Thus began the protracted process whereby—with the help of Thomas Cromwell, Lord Privy Seal, and Archbishop Thomas Cranmer—Henry would in due course deny papal supremacy and establish himself as head of the Church of England. In 1533, Cranmer declared Henry's marriage to Catherine null and void, and shortly thereafter Henry secretly married the already pregnant Anne Boleyn.

For all the exegesis it generated, the Henrician divorce did not once and for all resolve the knotty points of canon law regarding marriage; on the contrary, it exacerbated what Jack Goody has called "the general level of uncertainty" surrounding those rules.[11] Henry's determination to make the rules bend to dynastic and personal interests made them seem arbitrary. As Jeremy Taylor put it more than a hundred years after the fact, while the questions surrounding Henry's divorce had "very much imployed and divided the pens of learned men," the occasion as a whole ultimately "gave too great testimony . . . with how great a force a king that is rich and powerful can make his own determinations."[12] It hardly simplified matters, moreover, that Anne's sister Mary had been Henry's former mistress. Since at the time affinity was established through extramarital as well as marital intercourse, some argued that Anne stood in precisely the same relationship to Henry of first degree collateral affinity as Catherine had—although Henry's insistence on a strictly literal interpretation of Leviticus (which expressly mentioned the brother's wife but not the mistress's sister) prevented him from seeing his relationship with Mary as an impediment to marrying Anne.[13] Nor, given the fact that consanguinity and affinity were then considered equally powerful impediments to marriage, did it seem to all observers entirely unproblematic that Henry should issue a statute legalizing marriage between first cousins by blood or in-law in 1540, the same year he married Anne's first cousin, Catherine Howard.[14]

By the end of his reign, Henry VIII had issued four statutes regarding prohibited marriages, not all of which seemed entirely consistent with one another. The first two (issued in 1533 and 1536) designated which kin were off-limits as sexual or conjugal partners, including in their restrictions all the relatives mentioned in Leviticus 18 and 20, with the addition of the wife's sister, who is not mentioned there. The second two Henrician statutes (of 1536 and 1540) declared that all marriages not expressly forbidden by divine law or not outside the Levitical degrees were legal. Did these second two statutes, then, contradict the earlier rulings prohibiting marriage with the deceased wife's sister? This question would be debated for centuries.[15] Confusion over the prohibited degrees of marriage was multiplied, moreover, by the fate of Henry's statutes under the reigns of his two daughters, Mary and Elizabeth. Repealed in 1553 and 1554 under Mary (whose legitimacy as the daughter of Catherine of Aragon depended on such a measure), they were partially reenacted in 1558 under Elizabeth (whose legitimacy as the daughter of Anne Boleyn depended on their restitution). Finally in 1560 Matthew Parker, archbishop of Canterbury under Elizabeth I, drew up a *Table of Kindred and Affinity* to be publicly displayed in every parish church for the guidance of both clergy and laity. Within a few years, Parker also proposed a series of articles for the Church of England, which, after several revisions, were published in the new English translation of the Bible of 1571, subsequently further revised, and at last officially adopted into the church canons in 1603, eventually to be included as well in *The Book of Common Prayer*. While Parker's table was originally designed to help codify and clarify the rules first formulated by Cranmer in 1553, however, its stipulations differed significantly from the Henrician statutes in their particular interpretation of Scripture, prohibiting a number of relatives not "literally" mentioned in Leviticus but thought to be implied there by virtue of their equivalence in degree of relatedness to those expressly mentioned.[16] Parker's effort to fix prevailing law and to eliminate ambiguity thus served in its own way to introduce further areas of uncertainty and inconsistency.

Taylor's remarks in 1660 about the need for a more perfect statement of "the questions of degrees and the matters and cases of incest" make it clear that the ambiguities first generated by debates and legislation surrounding the Henrician divorce and compounded by changes wrought under Mary and Elizabeth were by no means resolved by the Restoration. The fate of the ecclesiastical courts during the intervening years of Civil War and parliamentary rule only further complicated an already complex situation. The Canons of 1604 had defined incest as a spiritual offense punishable exclusively under the jurisdiction of the ecclesiastical courts, along with other sexual misdemeanors not punishable as crimes under the common law (e.g., bigamy, procurement, and adultery). The normal punishment for incest was public penance or excommunication and included the bastardization (and consequent disinheritance) of the children of couples married within the prohibited degrees. In the late 1630s, however, the rising tide of Puritan opposition to the church courts for their alleged laxity, corruption, and inefficiency led gradually to a decline in the effectiveness and authority of the ecclesiastical court system and finally, in 1640, to its collapse. Falling outside the cognizance of any existing court, incest now became legally unpunishable.

The revolutionary decade of the 1640s witnessed a variety of challenges to traditional authority, not the least of which involved the rules of sexual conduct. Indeed, according to John Gillis, there occurred during this period "what can justifiably be called the first modern sexual revolution."[17] To many, the general threat of sexual license posed by such radical sects as the Ranters now seemed especially intense. The particular threat of sanctioned sexual relations between close kindred was inflamed, for instance, by the 1646 publication of an anonymous pamphlet entitled *Little Non-Such,* which argued that the Bible did not in fact forbid incestuous marriages. The Levitical prohibitions against "the uncovering of nakednesse," *Little Non-Such* maintained, pertained to fornication only and not to kindred marriage.[18] In fact, its author argued, ecclesiastical efforts to restrict such marriages were themselves violations of Christian law, which authorized natural liberty of conscience:

> that marriage is most just, which is made without any ambitious or covetous end; and if this liking and mutuall correspondency happen betwixt the neerest of kindred, then it is also the most naturall, the most lawfull, and according to the

primitive purity and practice: nor is there now any *Popish Canons* to restraine it. . . .
And indeed we would not argue any thing here against higher powers that are in
true orthodox authority; but onely desire that no Law or prohibition should bind
the conscience in matters that the *Gospell of Christ* hath left free unto Christian
people. (13)

The vehement attack of so staunch a defender of the established church as
Thomas Edwards, who in the third part of his *Gangraena* of 1647 animadverted
against the author of *Little Non-Such,* whom he identified as an Independent (of
whose sect Edwards claimed to know the names of three members within the
same county who had married incestuously), only served to generate renewed
defense of the freedom to question received interpretations of scriptural authority, prompting in that same year the publication of another pamphlet—*The
Counter Buffe*—which debunked Edwards's censures and further vindicated incestuous marriages.[19]

In such a climate of open challenge to traditional standards of sexual behavior, leaving conduct like adultery and incest (in Clarendon's words) "as
unpunishable as any other acts of good fellowship" seemed a less than prudent
course of action to Puritans and Royalists alike.[20] In 1650, therefore, as part of a
general movement for moral reform, the commonwealth enacted alternative
measures for the regulation of sexual conduct in the form of an ordinance for
"suppressing the detestable sins of Incest, Adultery and Fornication."[21] Under
this act incest, formerly an exclusively spiritual sin, was reclassified as a secular
crime, becoming a felony punishable by death. The new measure, however,
would be short-lived. When in 1660 the monarchy and the ecclesiastical courts
were restored, the Puritan act of 1650 was allowed to lapse, and ecclesiastical
jurisdiction over incest was revived. From that point on, violation of the prohibited degrees of marriage continued to be treated as a purely spiritual offense
until 1908, when incest (confined by then to blood relations) became the last
strictly "moral" offense in England to become a statutory crime.[22]

Despite revival of its official cognizance over incestuous conduct, nevertheless, by 1660 the church judicial system had lost much of its practical authority and effectiveness. As Christopher Hill notes, excommunication had ceased
by then being an effective censure among the laity, and Puritan emphasis on
the role of individual conscience in the punishment of sin was supplanting
more traditional beliefs in externally imposed sanctions for immorality.[23] There
seems to have been a marked discrepancy, moreover, between church canons
on the one hand and popular opinion regarding the punishment of incest on

the other. Jack Goody alludes to the prevalence in post-Reformation England of what he calls a "dual economy of kinship, one at the level of rules, one at the level of practice, one open, one hidden," noting that throughout the sixteenth and seventeenth centuries, prosecutions for incest were infrequent and actual sentences fairly light.[24] To Polly Morris, who has looked more recently at the plebian practice of incestuous marriage in Somerset between 1730 and 1835, the relatively high proportion of affinal marriages within the prohibited degrees that were solemnized and the children of which were baptized by local clergy "suggests that, alongside the canonical definition of incest, there existed a popular definition that was far less restrictive and distinguished very clearly between affinity and consanguinity."[25] Whether Morris's findings should be construed as evidence of lay ignorance of official rules or of complicity on the part of local clergymen in a popular rejection of the canonical definition of incest remains an open question.[26] It seems clear, nevertheless, that where the prosecution of such moral offenses as incest was concerned, by 1700, as Ingram notes, "the spiritual jurisdiction was only a shadow of what it had been a few generations earlier."[27]

A number of legal precedents that expressly limited ecclesiastical jurisdiction in cases involving marriages between kin further contributed to the ambiguous status of incestuous marriages under the law. The case of *Hill v. Good,* reported by Lord Chief Justice John Vaughan in 1677, for example, addressed the question in the Court of Common Pleas as to whether the temporal courts had the power to prohibit a case involving marriage to a deceased wife's sister from being heard and presumably dissolved by the ecclesiastical courts.[28] The case of *Harrison v. Burwell* had already established a precedent in which the temporal courts had prohibited prosecution by the spiritual courts of a case involving marriage to a great-uncle's widow on the grounds that the marriage was *not* within the Levitical degrees (206–50). Such intervention on the part of the common law courts was replicated in 1692 in the case of *Harris v. Hicks,* in which an ecclesiastical court was prohibited from annulling a man's marriage to his deceased wife's sister and bastardizing the children of the marriage, although the court was allowed to proceed to punish the incest.[29] In the case of Thomas Good, the temporal courts initially granted a prohibition on the grounds that the precept forbidding a man to take his wife's sister "to vex her . . . in her life time" (Lev. 18:18) referred only to "having two Sisters for wives at the same time"; but ultimately a consultation was granted that returned the case to the ecclesiastical courts.[30] As John Fry observed some years later, nevertheless, this ambiguous ruling did not deter others from making future appeals to the civil courts on similar grounds: "Since the Determination of this Case, *viz.* of *Hill* and *Good,* many Marriages have been contracted within the Degrees prohibited by the [Parker's] Table, and some of the Persons that contracted them have been prosecuted for such their Marriages in Ecclesiastical Courts, and have applied to the Courts of Law for Prohibitions, as may be seen in the Books of Reports."[31] Nor did the fact that such appeals were often unsuccessful dissuade Fry from the position that prohibitions of this sort were within the "rightful Power of his Majesty's Temporal Courts" (139). In his view, the last clause of Henrician Statute 32, H. VIII c 38—providing that "no Reservation or Prohibition, God's Law except, shall trouble or impeach any Marriage without the *Levitical* Degrees" (102) and that "no Person . . . be admitted in any of the Spiritual Courts . . . to any Process, Plea, or Allegation, contrary to this aforesaid Act" (104)—had effectually taken all cognizance over marriage to the deceased wife's sister (a relation that some argued was not explicitly mentioned in Leviticus) away from the ecclesiastical courts. By 1750, this was by no means a maverick opinion. Virtually the same argument had been handed down by a council of judges under Charles II, reasserted in Thomas Salmon's *Critical Essay Concerning Marriage* of 1724, generally reaffirmed in James Johnstoun's *Juridical Dissertation Concerning the Scripture Doctrine of Marriage Contracts, and the Marriages of Cousin-Germans* of 1734, and rehearsed at length in *The Gentleman's Magazine* of 1746; it would be reiterated in the 1770s in John Alleyne's *Legal Degrees of Marriage Stated and Considered, in a Series of Letters to a Friend.*[32] Clearly, as Boehrer justly observes for an earlier period, Henry VIII's establishment of the king "as the supreme head of both the secular and sacred legal regiments" had effected a mingling of jurisdictional categories from which the church courts would never fully recover.[33]

Anticlericalism, Natural Law, and the Discourses of Religious and Political Liberation

Seventeenth- and eighteenth-century attacks on the spiritual courts and canon law tapped into a long-standing tradition of anticlerical discourse that originated in the writings of Martin Luther and reemerged in the statutes of the Henrician monarchy. In the 1520s, Luther criticized the mercenary practices of the Catholic Church with its "artificial, money-seeking impediments," through which laws he elsewhere averred, "the Romanists of our day have . . . become merchants [selling] . . . [v]ulvas and genitals."[34] In a similar vein, Henry issued a statute suggesting that the Catholic church courts had invented prohibitions purely "for their Lucre . . . , the Dispensations whereof they . . . reserved to themselves. . . . And all because they would get Money by it."[35] Although Protestantism was to return believers to a truly natural, authentic Christianity, by the eighteenth century this association of rule-making with corruption extended as well to the Anglican spiritual courts, which, in jurist James Johnstoun's view, adhered to a poorly reformed version of the Roman canon law. It seemed something of a contradiction to Johnstoun, writing in 1734, that "a Protestant Nation, which professes to abjure the Church of *Rome,* and therefore the Canon Law; and to make the Bible the Law of Faith and Manners: On [which] Ground *Luther* publickly burnt the Canon Law," should call Anglican ecclesiastical courts "Christian" courts when they founded themselves on none other than that very same canon law. This, he declared, was but "reforming Backwards."[36] Indeed, by the 1750s, the discursive association of marriage prohibitions and corrupt church practices was so firmly entrenched that John Fry would casually link the forces of paganism with the impulse to prohibit close kindred marriages. "The greatest and most famous Prohibitors of such Marriages," he asserted (alluding here mainly to marriages between cousins and between brothers and sisters-in-law), were that *"Great Cut-throat* of the Age in which he lived," *"Alexander* the Great"; the "great Impostor, *Mohammed,"* whose "two predominant Passions were Ambition and Lust"; and, as Bishop Jeremy Taylor had earlier implied, "those barbarous People (the *Goths*)."[37]

But discussions of the prohibited degrees of marriage after 1660 engaged other discursive contexts besides the anticlerical. Perhaps chief among these was the early modern discourse of natural law.[38] The Henrician canonists of the sixteenth century had grounded their attack on Rome on the view that Henry's marriage to Catherine was not just a sin against God but also "a wicked sinne ageynst nature." Since divine and natural law traditionally were presumed to exist in a relation of perfect commensurability—"the law of nature and reasone, [being] moved by the lawe and the worde of God," no pope, they argued, had the authority to dispense with natural law.[39] The Catholics, on the other hand, had taken the position that only marriages in the direct ascending and descending lines of consanguinity and affinity (i.e., between parents and children or children-in-law) were violations of natural law; marriages in the collateral line (such as Henry's marriage to Catherine) were prohibited not by natural law as it existed in the Garden of Eden, but only by positive divine law instituted after the sons and daughters of Adam and Eve had sufficiently increased and multiplied as to preclude the original necessity of incestuous coupling. Violations of such "secondary" natural laws, they argued, were therefore subject to papal adjudication.[40]

Given the profound and long-term impact on British history of Henry's break with Rome, it may seem somewhat paradoxical that of these two positions on incest and natural law, the Catholic argument is the one that comes to dominate Restoration and eighteenth-century discourse about incest. The intervening century saw the emergence and evolution of an increasingly secularized natural law philosophy that implicitly challenged the metaphysical assumptions of the Middle Ages and the Renaissance, particularly those positing a stable correspondence between divine and natural law. The work of such seventeenth-century thinkers as the Dutch humanist-lawyer Hugo Grotius and the German jurist and historian Samuel Pufendorf were translated widely throughout Europe and had a profound impact both in England and on the Continent. Both Grotius and Pufendorf emphasized the difficulties inherent in justifying the prohibited degrees of marriage on natural grounds.[41] Wrote Grotius, "if one tries to assign definite natural causes why . . . marriages [of those united by blood or affinity] are unlawful—just as they are forbidden by laws or customs—he will learn from experience how difficult, if not impossible, the task is."[42] And Pufendorf observed that while in all civilized nations people allied by blood or affinity within the prohibited degrees are under a moral restraint not to marry, "yet to assign a solid Reason for it . . . seems . . . a Point of no ordinary Difficulty." Addressing early theories of natural aversion to incest, he elaborated on some of the specific problems inherent in the argument from nature:

> Some Enquirers are content to fly to the Abhorrence of Human Affections in this Case. "All Persons, say they, who are not corrupted by Ill Education or Wicked Habits, do find in their very Senses, a Repugnancy and Aversion to such Impurities; which is a plain Argument that those Things are prohibited by the Law of Nature." But indeed this Repugnancy of Affections is not equally to be discover'd amongst all People, nor always, even amongst those who pretend to the Art of Culture and Refinement: And when Authors urge it for a Reason, it would not be altogether absurd to answer them, that the Abhorrence may perhaps arise not so much from any in-bred Principle, as from long Use and Custom, which often counterfeit Nature.[43]

While both Grotius and Pufendorf were generally inclined to regard the incestuous conjunction of parent and child as unnatural because it overturns the proper of order of familial authority,[44] they also both agreed that prohibitions against consanguineous marriages in the first degree in the collateral line "do not come from the pure law of nature."[45] These views, their anti-Henrician echoes notwithstanding, were to have a major influence on even so profound an Erastian as Jeremy Taylor, who followed Grotius in asserting that "Nothing else is against the prime laws of nature, but a conjunction in the right ascending and descending line. . . . The marriages of brothers and sisters is incestuous, and the worst degree of it, and so forbidden by the laws of all civil nations; but . . . it cannot be accounted against the prime law of nature."[46] Neither, according to Taylor, could marriage between uncle and niece be forbidden on the ground of natural law, although it was prohibited in Leviticus by positive command. Unions between first cousins, Taylor argued further, are prohibited neither by natural law nor by Levitical decree.[47]

Taylor's views would become a touchstone for writers throughout the Restoration and eighteenth century. Samuel Dugard's *Marriages of Cousin Germans* (1673) was declared on the title page of an anonymous early edition to have been "mostly taken . . . from Dr. Jer. Taylor's book called Ductor Dubitantium, &c.";[48] and many others—among them the Anglican Bishop Simon Patrick in *A Commentary Upon the Historical Books of the Old Testament* (1695-1710), Thomas Salmon in *A Critical Essay Concerning Marriage* (1724), and John Fry in *The Case of Marriages between near Kindred* (1756)—quoted Taylor's treatise extensively.[49]

Despite its pervasive and long-standing influence, however, *Ductor Dubitantium* would by no means put the winds of controversy surrounding kindred marriages to rest. That the juridical status of the prohibition on the marriage of first cousins remained a contested issue in 1673—as it had been in 1660, when Taylor described it as "a great question amongst all men"—is evidenced by the very existence of Dugard's effort to defend such marriages from "the Censures of the Many."[50] Indeed, as Randolph Trumbach has observed, Chief Justice Vaughan's declaration of the legality of cousin marriage in 1669, because it challenged canon law, merely created the conditions for increased conflict between the secular and spiritual courts.[51] Marriage to a deceased wife's sister, moreover, continued to be a widely debated topic. While many, like John Quick, still considered such marriages to be "pernicious Snares," others, like Fry and John Alleyne, pleaded for them on behalf of those "sober, sedate and prudent persons, who have happily formed the matrimonial union, and yet are fearful, lest the sable rod of *remaining superstition*, should one day, inflict a scourging too severe for a feeling creature."[52] The question of the legitimacy of marriage to the deceased brother's widow continued to be debated at midcen-

tury on the pages of *The Gentleman's Magazine,* where a correspondent in August of 1746 referred to it as a "Gordian knot" of scriptural exegesis and lamented that efforts to resolve the difficulty seemed only to render it more
"intricate and perplex'd." So persistent were the ongoing disagreements and
conflicts of authority over such matters that as late as the 1770s, Alleyne urged
the propriety of applying to Parliament "to have the legal degrees of marriage
considered, and precisely ascertained, by legislative authority." "The difficulty
of fixing, with precision, the limits of natural law," he observed, "calls for the
interposition of legislature in every country," but especially in England, where
"the doubts of many, the difference of opinion which certainly prevails among
Civilians, and the intricacy of *legal* disquisition . . . make this, in a peculiar
degree, a fit subject for parliamentary inquiry."[53]

Every text that attempted to resolve the crisis of definition first introduced by
debates over the Henrician divorce, it seems, served in the end only to expose its
own unstable ground. But while the climate of controversy and confusion over
the status of the Levitical prohibitions that characterized the Reformation and
Renaissance persisted up to and through the Restoration, the period after 1660
did see some significant shifts in emphasis. If sixteenth-century writers tended
with Henry and his canonists to invoke the law of nature to justify a wide
variety of matrimonial prohibitions, and seventeenth-century writers challenged those arguments almost exclusively in negative terms—asserting typically that many affinal and consanguineous unions were *not contrary* to natural
law—writers after 1700 became increasingly likely to invoke the authority of
nature *positively* to vindicate varieties of close kindred marriages. At the same
time, those opposed to such marriages were increasingly *unlikely* to use nature
as the measure of legitimacy. Thus, for example, while Fry proposed to demonstrate that marriages "contracted . . . with the Sister of a deceased Wife, may
be . . . justified by the Authority of the Law of Nature, and the Laws of our
National Constitution," a writer like Quick, who invoked Henry VIII's divorce
from his brother's relict as evidence "by parity of reason" against the legality of
such marriages, felt compelled to go out of his way *not* to mount his case on
natural grounds.[54] Anticipating the objection that the prohibition against affinal marriage "cannot be a moral natural Law . . . [or] Mankind must have
perished in their Root," Quick invokes an argument that a century earlier would
have been marshaled by the papacy in support of precisely the antithetical
position. "'Tis none of my Assertion," insists Quick, "that this is a Moral Natu-

ral; but a Moral Positive Law: So that this Objection doth not here in the least affect me."[55]

Restoration and eighteenth-century thinkers generally adhere to the claim, made rather tentatively by Pufendorf, that it *"would not be altogether absurd* to answer" proponents of the argument from nature with the suggestion that "Abhorrence [of incest] *may perhaps* arise . . . from long Use and Custom"; but they assert it with much more confidence (emphasis added). In his ruling in the case of *Harrison v. Burwell,* for instance, Vaughan considers the sense in which "any *Marriages* and *Copulations* of Man with Woman, may be said to be Natural, and in what not," asserting baldly that "nothing is unnatural but that which cannot be, and consequently nothing that is, is *unnatural,* and so no *Copulation* of any man with any woman, nor an effect of that *Copulation* by *Generation,* can be said *unnatural."*[56] Certain copulations may be said to be unnatural "by Custome," Vaughan explains, "When Laws Divine or Humane, do supervene upon *mans original nature* with great penalty for transgressing them" and thus *"implant a horrour and averseness* to break them" (emphasis added). But in this case, the faculty whereby *"Copulation* with the Mother, Sister, and the like, do become odious and reluctant to Nature . . . which in the original state of nature . . . had been as indifferent as with other women" is only a kind of "secondary Nature" (224–25). Bernard Mandeville strikes a similar note in the 1723 expanded version of *The Fable of the Bees,* which includes his "Search into the Nature of Society," when he summarily dismisses the notion that the horror of incest has a basis in nature. Incestuous practices, such as those "In the *East* [where] formerly Sisters Married Brothers, and it was meritorious for a Man to Marry his Mother, . . . are abominable," Mandeville concedes; but, he insists, "it is certain that, whatever Horrour we conceive at the thoughts of them, there is nothing in Nature repugnant against them, but what is built upon Mode and Custom."[57] Mandeville's general views concerning the essential artificiality of human virtue remained highly controversial throughout the eighteenth century, but only a few writers directly challenged his remarks on incest. The most notable was Francis Hutcheson, who, in *An Inquiry into the Original of our Ideas of Beauty and Virtue* (1725), argued expressly against Mandeville's principles and in defense of the late earl of Shaftsbury's belief that human beings have an innate moral sense. Incest, however, presented something of a problematic target for benevolist doctrines predicated on the virtues of natural human sociability. (If such sociability were inherently virtuous, then why would it require regulation? And if it were natural, then why would it be necessary, as many argued that it was, to institute out-marriage in order to promote wider and more peaceful social ties?) Hutcheson reworked the grounds for his belief in the natural repugnancy of incest at least three times during the course of his career, but he always seemed to concede at least as much to his opponents as he was ever able to controvert effectively. In his earliest effort in the *Inquiry*, for instance, he attacks Mandeville's contention that incestuous practices in other cultures undermine all justifications for their prohibition, but he manages to mount only a shaky and somewhat circular counterargument. The very existence of a horror against incest in European culture, an abhorrence that asserts itself in the face of the palpable absence of demonstrable "natural" evidence of the detrimental effects of incestuous unions where they do occur, he asserts, constitutes proof that human sentiments will spontaneously dispose men to virtuous actions. And later, in his posthumously published *System of Moral Philosophy* (1755), his argument founders on the same apparent inconsistency in scriptural imperatives that Vaughan earlier invoked when observing that "the World could not have been peopled, but by Adams Sons going to their Sisters, being Brothers and Sisters by the same Father and Mother, or by a more incestuous coupling than that."[58] Hutcheson grants this point quite liberally: "that there is not a necessary invariable turpitude or moral impurity in all these marriages ordinarily called incestuous, antecedently to the prohibition of them, must be owned as [sic] such as consider that God laid the immediate children of Adam under a necessity of inter-marrying, and for some political reasons ordered such marriage on certain contingencies as were ordinarily prohibited."[59] He persists in arguing that legislators are justified in prohibiting incest because they thereby ensure that the "bonds of affection" do not remain "too much confined" (172) within families but are diffused throughout society and because the restriction apparently has no "grievous" consequences (173); but his concessions put him clearly on the defensive.

Like Mandeville, Henry St. John Bolingbroke concludes that the abhorrence of incest is "artificial, and . . . has been inspired [not by nature but] by human laws, by prejudice, and by habit."[60] Observing that natural and ecclesiastical laws are not always mutually supportive, but that "positive laws, ecclesiastical and civil," will often "forbid those things arbitrarily, and by mere will, which the laws of nature permit," he concedes no natural or logical justification for the incest prohibition, echoing Pufendorf but without the diffidence: "They scarce deserve an answer, who would prove these marriages prohibited by the law of nature, on the supposition that there is a repugnancy in nature to any such copulations; as if consanguinity, like fire, produced an agreeable sensation at certain distances, and pain and abhorrence at a nearer approach . . ." (4:226–27). Bolingbroke observes both a logical contradiction in the presumed necessity of proscribing actions for which all human beings are supposed already to have a natural aversion and, like Vaughan and others, a scriptural contradiction between the Levitical prohibitions against incest and God's injunction to the first humans to increase and multiply: "as if a multitude of nations, civilised and uncivilised, could have been determined to act unnecessarily against so strong an instinct of nature, as this repugnancy or abhorrence is assumed to be; and . . . as if the first men, who could not increase and multiply without committing incest, had been commanded to do it by the author of nature, against the law of that nature he had just before given them" (4:227).

Like Vaughan's passing reference to a coupling in Eden "more incestuous" than that between Adam's sons and daughters, however, Bolingbroke's gloss on Genesis opens a more radical possibility than most other commentators of the time were willing to entertain: the possibility that incest between parent and child may be an originary act. To Bolingbroke, "prohibition cannot be deduced, in *any* [degree] . . . , from instinct, or animal nature" (4:228; emphasis added). Following Taylor and many others in his conviction that "no color of an argument can be drawn . . . from the constitution of nature" (4:229) against sibling marriages, he nevertheless controverts prevailing views when he speculates that parent-child unions may also have some "natural permission," though of "the lowest sort" (4:228). Vaughan's ambiguous insinuation about couplings "more incestuous" than those between siblings opens itself to several readings, including the possibility of copulations between Adam's children and their parents; but Bolingbroke makes explicit his conclusion that Eve was a direct descendent of her husband:

> Eve was in some sort the daughter of Adam. She was literally bone of his bone, and flesh of his flesh, by birth, if I may call it so, whereas other husbands and wives are so in an allegorical manner only. But to pass this over, the children of the first couple were certainly brothers and sisters, and by these conjunctions, declared afterwards incestuous, the human species was first propagated. (4:229)

Though both Vaughan and Bolingbroke seem eager to "pass over" the possibility of originary parent-child incest with dispatch, it is worth pondering the implications of Bolingbroke's construction of the original, heterosexual relationship between Adam and Eve as the prototype of all incestuous relationships—with its corollary insight that conjugal relations in society are, in fact, substitutive replications (or "allegories") of a primal father-daughter incest. Such a construction not only encodes the foundational instability of incest as that which is at once desired and proscribed but also exposes the way in which early modern biblical hermeneutics constituted the categories of gender and kinship as simultaneous and mutually dependent. For just as there is in this narrative of origins neither family nor sexual difference without femaleness (both, after all, come into being with the creation of Eve), so in Eden there is no femaleness not determined by kinship structures. In this formulation, in other words, femaleness is always already a "relative" term (the first woman is simultaneously the first daughter and the first wife) and heterosexual relations are always already hierarchical and primally incestuous.

While the increasing dissociation of natural law theory from traditional theology that occurred over the course of the seventeenth century affected virtually all eighteenth-century discussions of incest, not all writers who favored the dictates of natural law felt equally compelled to repudiate Leviticus. If some—like Bolingbroke—preferred the principles of natural over revealed religion, others—like Fry—simply recuperated Scripture by bringing it into line with (their understanding of) natural law. Criticizing Bolingbroke for attempting "to vilify the Sacred Writings, as being inconsistent with the Law of Nature," Fry offers a gloss on Leviticus that is reminiscent of some of the most radical interpretations of the 1640s in an effort to prove "the Inconsistency . . . not real."[61] Basing his position on the observation that throughout the Bible marriage is signified by the figure of a covering (as in "spreading a skirt over" a woman), he reasons that the Levitical phrase "thou shalt not uncover the nakedness" of a person refers not to marriage, as theologians traditionally had assumed, but rather to adultery and fornication. Thus, he argues, lawful commerce between close kin is not forbidden by Mosaic law; the defiling object of prohibition instead is sexual commerce occurring outside the covenant of marriage. This interpretation was not—as the almost identical gloss elaborated in *Little Non-Such* had been in 1646—a maverick view conceived, summarily attacked, eventually silenced, and soon forgotten;[62] on the contrary, it was taken up by others later in the century, most notably by lawyer Alleyne, who cites the attestations of Hebrew scholars that Fry's reading of Leviticus is "the most correct and accurate comment on that chapter to be any where found."[63] Fry's and Alleyne's treatises both generated considerable popular interest and exerted widespread influence, appearing in multiple editions, the latter enlarged by a variety of supporting letters from lawyers and clergymen in 1775.[64]

Alleyne's treatise offers a compelling instance of how, through its concurrent engagement of the discourses of Reformation anticlericalism and seventeenth-century natural law, eighteenth-century writing about incest eventually reconstitutes its subject as part of a discourse of natural liberty. To Alleyne, a successful "attempt to reduce matrimonial prohibitions to the standard of rational law and sound policy" (that is, to parents and children, siblings, and siblings' children, but not beyond) would be prologue to "a vast accumulation of happiness."[65] On behalf of the "numbers, whose natural liberty is now unwisely restrained" by the "illiberal absurdities of papal relicts" (5), he seeks to render the laws of England worthy of "a nation whose constitution nearly has reached perfection,—wherein political freedom, has been secured by the most illustrious decisions; . . . the rights of nature . . . asserted and vindicated . . . ; domestic liberty . . . acknowledged, and the very air pronounced too pure for slavery to exist in it" (vi).

We begin to glimpse here a conception of the relationship between human subjects and the law that has not emerged so clearly heretofore, one informed more by benevolism, sentimentalism, and Enlightenment rationalism than by traditional humanist or Augustinian assumptions.[66] The Reformation, as its name implied, sought to throw off the yoke of Rome in order to reestablish the authority of a scriptural text conceived as the pure and simultaneous embodiment of both divine and natural law—hence Henry's appeal to a strict interpretation of Leviticus, whose law would restore him, and by extension the entire Tudor dynasty, to the precincts of grace. By contrast, in Alleyne's liberatory deployment of a discourse of natural rights, we encounter a conception of the law as repressive rather than reformative—as the imposition of a slavish system of Anglican ecclesiastical restraint on fundamental human happiness. Actual laws regarding incest have not varied much over the course of more than two centuries;[67] but the discursive role of incest has begun to change. No longer the logical antithesis of a monolithically conceived domain of Law, where the categories of the natural, the civil, and the divine come together in a relation of perfect commensurability, incest has now become aligned with the domain of an increasingly independent Nature, where human subjects precede the institution of (positive) divine or civil law. Granted, Alleyne's reinterpretation of Leviticus as the law of adultery and not the law of marriage enables him to avoid abandoning revelation altogether by arguing only that its strictures have been improperly applied to marriages between kin; but his appeal to "the free operation of natural justice" (14) as the support of a "general system of happiness" whose principles carry "internal conviction" (7) and therefore need no external justification (though they may not in fact contravene the law of God) makes his emphasis on the primacy of nature fairly clear. The truths of nature for Alleyne are intrinsic and self-evident, while those of Scripture require exegesis in order to be made to jibe with nature's law. What precisely those self-evident, natural truths were and how, specifically, Alleyne conceived the prejuridical human subject he invokes are questions that bear directly on his views on incest and that require more sustained analysis.

Untying the Gordian Knot: The Gender Politics of Incest and Its Prohibition

The historical and ideological distance between the two versions of liberatory rhetoric deployed by Henry VIII in the sixteenth century and John Alleyne in the eighteenth is perhaps nowhere more apparent than in the simple fact that Alleyne undertakes to defend the legality of a close kin marriage that Henry had specifically outlawed: marriage between a man and his deceased wife's sister. This was also a relation of first-degree collateral affinity and thus equivalent by parity of reason to the kindred relation between Henry and his first wife, Catherine, the repudiation of which had led directly to the decisive political moment of the Reformation, Henry's denial of papal supremacy. This irony, however, does not keep Alleyne from locating his own spiritual and intellectual roots in the Reformation, which he celebrates as the "noblest struggle, gilded with the happiest success, in the history of Christianity!"—one produced "[b]y surmounting prejudices—reasoning by sound logic, and concluding with free-thinking—and giving full rein and fair play to human understanding."[68] However one might question the ultimate coherence of such claims with Alleyne's simultaneous assertion that his argument is indisputable because "it brings conviction to [his] mind" (12), his sense of the cultural indebtedness of his own Enlightenment rationality to the liberatory principles of the Reformation is evident.

That some of the same liberatory arguments deployed by Henry to retain the force of legal impediments on kindred marriage should here be used in defense of their reduction suggests that there was something more at stake in the ongoing debates over the legal degrees of marriage than the legitimacy or illegitimacy of particular prohibitions. Indeed, it suggests that particular restraints themselves may even have had a certain irrelevance. Whether one points to internal contradictions in the principles according to which Henry VIII justified marrying and divorcing his various wives or to discrepancies within the scriptural text itself, the history of marriage prohibitions is one of practical ironies and inconsistencies. Boehrer suggests that there was a certain "political utility" in maintaining the climate of controversy surrounding these prohibitions in the Renaissance, as such controversy perpetuated the conditions under which individuals or interest groups could "[convert] the incest taboo into political capital."[69] A similar argument had been advanced in the eighteenth century by Bolingbroke, who attributed the fact that "restraints on marriage [have] been very inconsistently laid" to their arbitrary and essentially "political" nature. If, as Bolingbroke reasoned, the law of nature is to "[i]ncrease and multiply," an injunction easily fulfilled whether we "marry among our kindred, or . . . marry strangers," then the regulation of the "manner" in which the propagation of the species is executed must be "the law of man," and "[a]s occasions are various, circumstances different, and will above all uncertain," that law will vary with political expediency.[70]

What, then, *were* the politics underlying the regulation of kindred marriage, and did they operate according to any coherent rules? According to Jack Goody's 1983 study *The Development of the Family and Marriage in Europe,* the political stakes in Western culture have been largely economic. The vastly extended range of prohibitions on kindred marriage that were instituted by the Catholic Church in the eleventh century and somewhat reduced in the thirteenth, Goody contends, increased church revenues not only by forcing individuals to seek dispensations, a practice Luther and Henry both lamented, but also by controlling the "strategies of heirship" whereby lay property was routinely transferred to the church.[71] Because extensive prohibitions made it difficult for individuals to marry, consolidate holdings, and produce legitimate heirs, they increased the likelihood that property owners would leave their lands and money to the church. In other words, as Goody's argument makes eminently clear, the regulation of marriage and its politics in the history of the West has had everything to do with property and its transmission. The Reformation was no exception to this rule. As Goody observes, "[t]he search of Henry VIII for other wives was not a demonstration of the lusty sexuality of an English hero; it was a quest for an heir, a male heir, to perpetuate the newly confirmed royal line. On the political level, the conflict between the ecclesiastical and noble views of marriage represents an aspect of the struggle between 'Church' and 'State,' between the interests of the two most powerful bodies in the land; in Henry VIII's case, marriages were political attempts to achieve continuity by using procedures forbidden in Church doctrine" (185).

There remains, however, a largely repressed or unelaborated subtext in this narrative of struggle between those two powerful male "bodies" represented here by church and state, as there does in virtually all debates regarding the prohibited degrees of marriage in the Restoration and eighteenth century. For missing from Goody's economic explanation is any express account of the place of that indispensable, if not politically powerful, female body through which the drama of inheritance—in this case, noble inheritance—was played out, indeed which provided the very condition of its possibility. At stake in ongoing debates over matrimonial impediments, that is, were not just the family and marriage as they were pressed into the service of one or another social institution, but the place of the female reproductive body within that larger institutional frame. As reproducers, women alone made possible the orderly transmission of property and patronym from father to son. As objects of exchange in an exogamous kinship system, they were the conduits through which heirs were produced and fraternal bonds between men were established and extended; through the regulated circulation of women, men literally became brothers-in-law.[72] Hence men's urgency to consolidate control over women's bodies. Unregulated sexual activity on the part of women, especially if they were married, had the potential to disrupt successions—to "confuse the issue," so to speak, by creating uncertainty about paternity; and uncertain paternity meant not only uncertainty regarding the genetic identity of one's immediate heirs but also, consequently, the future danger of unwitting incest among one's descendents. A male heir unaware of his true paternity might inadvertently marry his own sister, creating the potential for long-range economic consequences. For as we have seen in the case of Henry and his daughters, a man who married a woman from among those prohibited to him by prevailing matrimonial laws ran the risk of rendering his children ineligible to inherit his property or to carry on his estate.[73]

If Goody explains sixteenth-century debates over the regulation of kindred marriage as a manifestation of institutional struggle, Randolph Trumbach identifies such debates in Restoration and eighteenth-century Britain as expressions of class conflict. Since "cousin marriage (in which a daughter married the son of her father's brother) prevented the loss of a family's name or land," Trumbach observes in *The Rise of the Egalitarian Family,* its legitimation represented an effort on the part of the aristocracy to consolidate its assets in the face of the determination of the more socially mobile middle classes to perpetuate class alliances by encouraging marriages to close affines (for example, to the deceased wife's sister).[74] The difference between favoring marriages with close consanguineal relations and close affines, he explains, "was the difference between seeing marriage as an act of incorporation that *maintained* a family's standing . . . and seeing it as an alliance that could *improve* a family's social standing" (18–19).

Although Trumbach's emphasis on the "egalitarianism" of emergent kindred systems in the eighteenth century seems to me overstated, his argument, to the extent that it implicitly recognizes the politico-economic utility of marriage, does acknowledge that gender plays a role in the distribution of property. His primary focus, nonetheless, like that of Boehrer and Goody, is on period-specific plays for power between groups of men—not on the gender politics on which such plays depended. One of the broad socio-ideological continuities that cut across the vagaries of class and historical change, these politics generally have been treated more as a tacit *given* than as a sustained object of cultural or historical analysis. Historians of the family have been intent to point out that the struggle for power over the regulation of marriage was in fact a struggle for power over the regulation of access to property, but they have been less quick to emphasize the extent to which the struggle for power over access to property was in fact a struggle for power over access to women.[75] At the most manifest level, Trumbach's discussion foregrounds class and kinship (while downplaying gender) as analytic categories; in effect, however, what his analysis demonstrates is that a man's ability to maintain or improve his social standing by incorporating or accumulating property depended largely on which women he had legal access to—on whether, to be precise, he was permitted to take his cousin or his sister-in-law to wife.

It is easy for gender politics to become obscured in modern historical accounts of the prohibited degrees of marriage because, historically, the discourse of liberation that in varied manifestations surrounded discussion of those prohibitions from the Reformation through the eighteenth century and beyond is itself *inexplicit* about the social arrangements and structures of subordination that it presupposed. In this sense, it is very like the social contract theory that grew out of seventeenth-century philosophies of natural law, whose implicit "sexual contract" Carole Pateman has so persuasively identified. When John

Alleyne asserted that the "fundamental truth" of natural law was contained in the proposition "Let man so conduct himself, as to secure his own happiness, without invading the present, or future happiness of another," how, precisely, and for whom, did he envision the ideal of human happiness?[76] Are women included in his designation either of "man" or of "another"? Who in his conception of "political freedom," "domestic liberty," and "the rights of nature" was and was not implicitly recognized as a political subject entitled to the pursuit of happiness? Whose subjection and whose domination was he thinking of when he pronounced the British air "too pure for slavery"? Neither that of women, nor—the 1772 Mansfield Judgment notwithstanding—that of West African slaves in the Caribbean. That would be understood.[77]

As we work to expose the false universals within hegemonic discourses by examining the complex and interlocking hierarchies of class, gender, national, ethnic, and racial difference that such discourses presuppose, we ought not to lose sight of the broad ideological structures that sometimes establish cultural commonality among otherwise historically, socially, or ideologically disparate groups or individuals. As representatives of two very different views on in-law marriage at two distinctly different historical moments, Henry VIII and John Alleyne present an interesting instance of such cultural affinity. For if differences in their positions can be accounted for in Trumbach's terms largely as a function of class ideology, those historical and class differences are also bridged by the shared implication of both men, as white European men, in a common set of cultural assumptions. Those assumptions recognize no explicit contradiction between the cause of "liberty" and the circulation either of nonwhite populations in the British colonial system of slavery or of women as legal tender in male homosocial sexual economies.

As Judith Herman and Florence Rush both demonstrated persuasively in the early 1980s, the incest taboo historically has been neither about the protection of women from sexual predation by family members nor about their liberation as desiring subjects.[78] It has been, rather, about the protection of male property (in a cultural context in which women were included in that category) from being infringed on by the "happiness" of other men. Writing of the injunctions of Leviticus 18:6–18, which begins "None of you shall approach to any that is near of kin to *him*" (emphasis added), Herman notes that

> [t]he biblical law is addressed to men. It is assumed without question that men initiate and women submit to sexual relations. The wording of the law makes it clear that incest violations are not offenses against the women taken for sexual use

but against the men in whom the rights of ownership, use, and exchange are vested. What is prohibited is the sexual use of those women who, in one manner or another, already belong to other relatives. Every man is thus expressly forbidden to take the daughter of his kinsmen, but only by implication is he forbidden to take his own daughters.[79]

Herman finds the omission of any express prohibition of father-daughter incest in Leviticus striking, considering that "almost every other conceivable breach of the incest taboo is explicitly named and condemned" (60); she nevertheless recognizes that such an omission is not inconsistent with the male proprietary ethos that underwrites the law. "Though the incest taboo forbids [the father] to make sexual use of his daughter in marriage, no particular man's rights are offended, should the father choose to disregard this rule. . . . The man who has the power to give a woman away also has the power to take her for himself. That power can be contested only by other men, not by the women who are given or taken. No kinsman, and certainly no man outside the family, is in a position to challenge a father's power over his daughters" (60–62).

In the West, this proprietary sexual ethos historically underpins both incest and its prohibition and, I would submit, provides the common logic behind such apparently contradictory scriptural injunctions as those of Leviticus on the one hand and of Genesis and Deuteronomy on the other. Indeed, it is only when we acknowledge how embedded issues of succession and property are in the dynamics of sexual exchange that the myriad of contradictions and inconsistencies we have observed in the rules controlling kindred marriage begins to dissipate, only when we understand the basic grammar of sexual exchange that the history of marriage prohibitions begins to disambiguate. If the incest taboo exists not for its own sake, as an arbitrary and absolute injunction, but contingently, for its instrumentality in preserving the continuity of the male estate, then it will be warranted only in those circumstances in which that purpose might be served. In some circumstances—such as in Eden, where without incest Adam would have no heirs, or in the case of a brother who dies without issue—close kindred marriage may be more conducive than its prohibition to preserving the male line.[80] Thus, Henry VIII's marriage to Catherine of Aragon was called for by the levirate obligation; and thus it lost its raison d'être when it did not produce an heir.[81]

The contradictory logic of this ethos was understood by eighteenth-century commentators on kindred marriage. As those who argued for the legality of cousin marriage or other varieties of close kindred marriage often pointed out, close marriages were not only often not prohibited in the Bible; they were sometimes, as in the case of the levirate, expressly commanded. One of the most frequently invoked scriptural examples of enjoined incest was the story of the daughters of Zelophehad (Num. 27:4). In Bolingbroke's account of this story, the principle that requires that women be used to mediate succession is made quite explicit. Observing that "if it be agreeable to the law of nature and of right reason, in many cases, to extend the bonds of society by a prohibition of marriages between persons too near akin, it is in many cases at least as agreeable to this law, to preserve possessions and wealth in the families to which they belong, and not suffer them to be carried by any female caprice into others,"[82] Bolingbroke explains what happens when, at their request and also at God's command, Moses "cause[s] the inheritance of their father to pass unto" (Num. 27:7) Zelophehad's daughters after their father's death:

> when the chief fathers of the families of the sons of Joseph came before Moses and the elders of Israel, to complain of this law, the precaution we speak of here was immediately added, and the law amended. Moses declared in the name of God, that "every daughter who possessed an inheritance" by virtue of the former law [that "If a man die, and have no son, then ye shall cause his inheritance to pass unto his daughter" (Num. 27:8)], should be obliged to marry one of the family of the tribe of her father, and no other: and the reason is annexed, "that the children of Israel may enjoy every *man* the inheritance of his fathers." In obedience to this law, the daughters of Zelophehad "were married unto their father's brother's sons." (4:230; emphasis added)

Simon Patrick earlier pointed to the commonality of principle informing this law and the Deuteronomic law of the levirate marriage when he observed that although Zelophehad's daughters had come before Moses quite literally in the name of their father (asking "Why should the name of our father be done away from among his family, because he hath no son?" [Num. 27:4]), that name "could not be thereby preserved, but by the Son of one of these Daughters taking upon him, not the Name of his Father that begat him, but of his Mother's Grand-father, *viz. Hepher;* which was ordered afterwards by a general Law, XXV *Deut.* 6." For as Patrick also observed in another connection, within a patrilineal and patronymic context "[t]*he Family, or Kindred of the Mother* . . . hath not the effect of a Kindred in Successions to Inheritances."[83]

As in the matter of the levirate marriage, the circumstance of Zelophehad's daughters was, in Jeremy Taylor's words, "a special case"; "what was in all cases lawful," wrote Taylor, "was made in this case necessary. For if the woman was an heiress she was to pleasure her own family rather than strangers."[84] It is an exception, moreover, that proves the rule. For though Taylor may be in the process of arguing the legality of cousin marriage, his assertion that a woman is obliged to "pleasure" her family only in this special circumstance tacitly concedes that out-marriage (the pleasuring of strangers) is the norm. Through his use of "pleasure" as a verb whose object is either the family or strangers (both objects implicitly encoded here as male) and of language associating the pleasure of that object with a woman's performance of economic obligation, Taylor suggests that a daughter's filial indebtedness can be dispensed by sexual means. He reveals, furthermore, that an identical logic of sexual ownership underwrites both the law that prohibits incest and its apparent antithesis: the law that requires it. Like Bolingbroke's use of the term *female caprice* to refer to the economically disruptive effects of wayward female desire, Taylor's language confirms Herman's observation that, despite the critical role played by female sexuality here, female pleasure is not a factor centrally at stake in either the endorsement or the prohibition of incestuous marriage.

Another remarkable example of incest in Scripture involved both parent-child and extramarital sex; but, despite the almost universal condemnation of incestuous marriage in the direct line and of fornication of any sort as unnatural abominations, this incest found sanction in the eighteenth century on the grounds that it was motivated by a desire to preserve the paternal bloodline. This was the story of Lot's two daughters, who, believing that there was "not a man in the earth," plied their father with wine and lay with him that they might preserve his seed (Gen. 19:30-38). Bolingbroke cites the story as a remarkable instance of the care that was taken among the families of the early patriarchs to preserve the genealogy and perpetuate the race whence the Messiah was to proceed. Here is his paraphrase of part of Bishop Patrick's commentary on Genesis:

> If the daughters of Lot committed incest with their father, we are not to ascribe it to unnatural lust, but to their innocence, their simplicity, and a laudable concern for the preservation of their father's family; for they believed all mankind destroyed, according to Irenaeus; or, at least, they might believe that none were left who might go in unto them, "juxta morem universae terrae." Our learned Bishop assumes, much more ingeniously and with greater regard to virgin modesty, that these young women had the same eager desire, which then possessed the hearts of

good people, to fulfill the promise of the Messiah. It was that which put them on this otherwise monstrous crime. It was that which sanctified it, in the intention, though not in the event; for the two accursed races of the Moabites and Ammonites were the fruits of this incest.[85]

Besides confirming that he sees incest not as intrinsically but only as contingently evil, this emphasis on the preservation of patriarchy in general (and through it of the divine seed in particular) may explain why at the end of his commentary on Leviticus Patrick demurs with the following caveat regarding strict adherence to a purely moral law. The operations of conscience, he counsels, must be judiciously balanced against economic considerations: "in contracting Marriage we are not only to have regard to our own Conscience . . . but to Succession also, and to Inheritances. And therefore . . . that is to be done, both which good Men judge to be honest, and is allowed by lawful Governours."[86] This idea of moral consensus by a community of "good men" is one to which we will have occasion in chapter 7 to return.

The incestuous union of Tamar and her father-in-law, Judah, is treated by Patrick as a similar kind of case (Gen. 38). When Judah's son Onan refuses the levirate obligation to "raise up seed" to his deceased brother, Er, by marrying the latter's widow, Tamar, instead spilling his seed upon the ground (Gen. 38:8–9), Judah promises Tamar his youngest son, Shelah. But Judah fails to fulfill this promise even after Shelah is grown; so Tamar dresses as a harlot and thereby tricks Judah into conceiving a child by her. Although, according to Patrick, Tamar has clearly committed the crime of incest, her apparent motivation by a higher purpose—the preservation of the name of her late husband's family—mitigates the moral seriousness of her offense. Of Judah and Tamar, Patrick writes, "Tho he did not know her, yet she knew him: Which aggravated her Crime, and made it *Incest* in her, tho only *Fornication* in him. Unto which, one would think, she was tempted, by her vehement desire to have a Child, by one of this Family; unto which the Promise of the *Messiah* belonged. For tho she seems to have been one of the Seed of *Canaan*, (as I said before, *ver*. 6) yet embracing the Religion of *Jacob*, she renounced the Impiety of the *Canaanites*: And so is mentioned in the Genealogy of our Saviour, as well as *Rehab* and *Ruth*" (Gen. 38:18). Thus, in his gloss on Judah's statement upon learning of Tamar's deception—"She hath been more righteous than I"—Patrick explains, "These words do not signify that she had in this matter committed a less Sin than he, (for she had committed a greater) but that in another matter, which was the occasion of this, he had broken his word with her, when she had, till now, kept her Faith with him; and lived a Widow honestly in expectation of his Son. Besides, she committed this Fact out of desire to have a Child; he to satisfy his Lust" (Gen. 38:26).[87]

Yet another instance in Jewish history of sanctioned incest in the direct line is found in the story of the birth of Hyrcanus, son of Joseph, originally told by Josephus in his *Antiquities* and recounted in Humphrey Prideaux's *Old and New Testament Connected in the History of the Jews* of 1718.[88] This story involves a man's prostitution of his own daughter to her uncle for the greater good of preventing the uncle from committing the sin of taking a foreign wife. In it, Joseph (in the time of Ptolemy) travels to Alexandria, as he is wont to do in his official capacity as collector of the king's revenue in Coelo Syria and Palestine. He is accompanied by his brother, Solymius, who brings along one of his daughters, intending to marry her there to a Jew of suitable quality. At court, Joseph falls in love with a young dancer, whom he asks his brother to procure for him in secret, it being a sin and shame for a Jew to take an alien woman.[89] To avoid that sin, Solymius brings Joseph not the dancer but his own daughter. Joseph, being drunk, does not perceive that the woman with him is his niece, sleeps with her on several different occasions without discovering the deception, and finally falls desperately in love. Still believing the woman to be his dancer, he bemoans the fact that Jewish law prohibits his marrying her, whereupon Solymius reveals the truth: "That he had chosen rather to do this wrong to his own child, than suffer him to do so shameful and sinful a thing, as to join himself to a strange woman, which their holy law forbad."[90] Thanking his brother for this kindness, Joseph marries his niece, by whom he has a son, Hyrcanus, a future Jewish leader of outstanding virtue and sagacity. In the end, by exercising his paternal right to either give his daughter away or keep her in the family, Solymius does successfully execute his plan to marry her to a Jew of suitable quality.

Josephus's account, which ends with the birth of Hyrcanus, makes no comment on the moral status of this union. Prideaux, however, appends a statement justifying the marriages of uncles and nieces under Hebrew law, in which he makes clear his own, eighteenth-century assumptions about the essential and mutually constitutive character of systems of kinship and systems of gender difference:

> according to the *Jewish* law an uncle might marry his niece, tho' an aunt could not her nephew, for which the *Jewish* writers give this reason; that the aunt being in respect of the nephew in the same degree with the father or mother in the line of

descent, hath naturally a superiority above him; and therefore for him to make her his wife, and thereby bring her down to be in a degree below him (as all wives are in respect of their husbands) would be to disturb and invert the order of Nature. But that there is no such thing done where the uncle marries the niece: For in this case both keep the same degree and order, which they were in before, without any mutation in it.[91]

Generational firstness confers authority; but within the same generation, the rule of male supremacy prevails. We see here clearly, moreover, the subtle articulation of kinship and miscegenation laws (a topic to be further addressed in ensuing chapters). If one contingency affecting the status of in-marriage is the desire for extended kin groups, another is the fear of diluting national, ethnic, or racial purity by failing to preserve the integrity of geographic and cultural boundaries.[92]

Discussion of the moral and legal contingencies surrounding determinations of incest in the eighteenth century is not confined to the pages of juridical tracts and biblical commentaries but emerges as well in the popular press. Perhaps the most notable instance of periodical writing on this subject is a sustained exchange of letters appearing in *The Gentleman's Magazine* between 1746 and 1750. Prompted by two brief inquiries made in June and July of 1746, one from a Mr. Budge about the legality of marrying one's brother's widow and another from J.L. regarding the legality of marriages between first cousins,[93] there ensues a protracted exchange of conflicting epistolary opinions on close kindred marriages that seems intent on parodying the welter of contrary arguments circulating in the reigning authoritative texts.

J.P., the first to respond to Budge's query, points out that the prohibition does not apply to the brother's *widow,* but only to the brother's *wife* during her husband's lifetime; in fact, he reminds Budge, Deuteronomy expressly enjoins marriage to the sister-in-law when the husband dies childless.[94] This point is reiterated in a subsequent missive by Obed. Reperet, with the dutiful qualification that the levirate injunction was never absolute and that childlessness is the *only* condition under which such a marriage would be lawful (July 1746, 363). These letters prompt a contrary response from a Widower, who argues on the grounds both of "natural liberty," and of parity of reason with the case of the deceased wife's sister, that marrying the brother's widow *is* legal regardless of the brother's parental status (Aug. 1746, 410).[95] A month later, nevertheless, obedient Obed. reasserts the simplicity of the prohibition, this time at much greater length and with the marshaling of many finer points of exegesis (Sept. 1746, 461).

If anything is clearly established for the reader by this exchange, it is above all else the profoundly vexed and indeterminate character of the question. Where the Widower (whose own marital status may give him a vested interest in the cause of in-law marriages) invokes the statutes of Henry VIII to authorize marriage to the brother's widow (Oct. 1746, 544–45), Reperet, ever intent on repairing prohibitions complicated over time by hermeneutic uncertainty, had invoked the very same statutes to establish its illegality. At this point, an anonymous correspondent from Seighford, Staffordshire, intervenes in the debate, insisting in a letter written in August but published in October that these two "ingenious gentleman . . . according to the custom of the time, have talk'd a good deal, and said nothing." He, in contrast, will "untie [the] Gordian knot" by reconciling apparent scriptural inconsistencies. Both Reperet and the Widower, he asserts, have missed the point. The levirate obligation is obsolete on the grounds that it is no longer possible to "raise up a brother's name in *Israel;*" after all, he reasons, "*Israel* is no more!" All marriages to the brother's wife or widow, he thus pronounces, are incestuous (545).

In December, a Batchelor joins the discussion (Dec. 1746, 658–60). After giving the nod to the unanswered question of J.L. regarding marriages between first cousins (which the Batchelor declares unproblematically legal), he turns to Mr. Budge. Noting that Budge's question is dealt with at length in the opinions of the Jewish rabbis as set down in Bishop Burnet's *History of the Reformation,* where the dispute between Reperet and the Widower is also "very fully handled," he tosses several learned textual references to his male readers, as a tub to a leviathan, to divert their attention while he addresses the ladies privately. Arguments in favor of matches between first-degree collateral in-laws, the Batchelor warns his female readers, "are generally brought by such as lie in wait for some of you" (659). Women should be wary of yielding to men's false rationalizations of such unions, for illegal matches have potentially dire consequences. Here the example of Queen Catherine is invoked; this union having been justified as an exception to Leviticus, Henry had a ready pretext for repudiating his wife when it suited his purposes to do so. It is prudent, therefore, for women not to gamble on unions surrounded by so much doubt; predatory men are ever ready to take advantage of hermeneutic uncertainties, to deploy the project of scriptural interpretation to their own ends. Ironically, of course, the Batchelor's letter archly exemplifies precisely the male vices it condemns. Discouraging collateral in-law marriages by discrediting his competition with the ladies may serve a bachelor's interests by keeping more marriageable women (some perhaps with dowagers' estates) in circulation.

There now ensues a hiatus of almost three years before *The Gentleman's Magazine* resumes discussion of marriage prohibitions. Then, in July of 1749, A. Fontan begins *An Enquiry into the Foundation, Extent, etc. of the Prohibitions forbidding to marry within certain Degrees.* Truly a fountain of learned excess, Fontan rehearses, ad nauseam, all the familiar arguments on both sides of the issue, invoking every authority on the subject, from Pope Gregory VII to Cardinal Cajetan to Grotius to Hammond to Taylor to Patrick and beyond, and citing legal precedents both old and recent to make the case—with Obed. Reperet—for the illegality of marriage to the brother's wife (July 1749, 297–301). In December of the same year, the editors of the magazine confess to having hoped, after several lengthy installments over several months, "to conclude the *Enquiry* with the year" (Dec. 1749, 598), but Fontan's remarks spill over into January of 1750, where at last they terminate inconclusively. Fontan's extraordinary proliferation of authorities and texts ultimately thrusts his arguments into an equivocal light. Arguing that the Deuteronomic exception to the Levitical prohibition against marrying the brother's wife is exclusive to the customs and inheritance system of the ancient Jews and therefore is *not* applicable to other nations, for whom the prohibitions of Leviticus are morally and eternally obligatory, he nevertheless caps his argument with Bishop Patrick's statement epitomizing the moral contingencies of the law: viz. "that, In contracting marriage, we are not only to have regard to our own conscience . . . but to succession also, and inheritances: and therefore . . . 'That is to be done both which good men judge to be honest, and is allowed by lawful governors'" (Jan. 1750, 10). Fontan admits that even though he has "taken the liberty freely to produce the opinions of several learned men," some matters nevertheless remain so "dark, and hard to be understood" that they can only be submitted to the discretion of his readers (12). Ironically, nevertheless, this acknowledgement does not discourage him from advising those contracting doubtful unions "first to consult with men learned in the laws, to understand what is lawful, what is honest, and expedient, before the finishing of their contracts" (10). In Fontan's *Enquiry,* the proliferation of authoritative texts points to nothing more clearly than the ultimate absence of stable textual authority.

One is not surprised, therefore, to find in the same issue that the *Enquiry* has inspired a letter to Mr. Urban from a Timothy Trytruth asserting, with a certain arbitrary force, the mistaken premises of all the foregoing authorities and the legality of marrying a brother's wife (12–14). This—with the exception of a brief, if convoluted, query in February from Ophelia as to *"Whether a woman married to a man's wife's nephew, and afterwards single, and the aunt-in-law's husband so likewise, can be counted kindred of blood?"* (Feb. 1750, 69) and a response in October from Trytruth answering "No"—is the last we hear on the matter of close kindred marriages in *The Gentleman's Magazine* (Oct. 1750, 449).

Analysis of English regulatory discourses and commentaries regarding incest from the Reformation through the eighteenth century thus discloses several striking phenomena. First, paradoxically, it reveals that such regulatory discourses are critically bound up with—even mutually dependent upon—emergent discourses of political liberation. Indeed, whether they argue for or against particular prohibitions, discourses about incest during this period emerge essentially *as* discourses of liberation—from either ecclesiastical authority, religious superstition, political oppression, or some combination of these forces.

Second, like other liberatory discourses of the period, incest discourse presupposes a certain set of hierarchical social arrangements, including implicitly a structure of gender subordination authorizing male sex right as a natural law. This law of male sexual privilege had the potential to justify both incest and its prohibition and thus simultaneously to authorize apparently contradictory narratives. In this sense, the shifting and contradictory nature of incest regulations in early modern England might be said to point to, even as it works to mask, the operation of a prior axiom: that women are the natural sexual property of men. Manifestly, early modern debates over the regulation of kindred marriage dwell at length on the question of whether incest or its prohibition has a basis in nature when, in fact, what is at stake in these controversies is the naturalization not of incest at all but of the gender categories that underwrite the natural rights of men. The naturalization of gender difference as such was the stabilizing ideological ground on which incest was either sanctioned or proscribed. As long as the story of women's natural subordination to men remained repressed within early modern liberatory discourses, the juridical ground of incest and its prohibition would *appear* to be inherently unstable. But while the rules regarding incest may have been shifting and contradictory, the underlying cultural logic of masculine privilege that sustained those contradictions was not. Paradoxical though it may seem, the interpretive disagreements of rival male authorities evince, even as they obscure, the coherence and simplicity of that logic.

CHAPTER THREE

Beyond Incest

Gender and the Politics of Transgression in Aphra Behn's
Love-Letters between a Nobleman and his Sister

> If subversion is possible, it will be a subversion from within the terms of the
> law, through the possibilities that emerge when the law turns against itself
> and spawns unexpected permutations of itself. The culturally constructed
> body will then be liberated, neither to its "natural" past, nor to its original
> pleasures, but to an open future of cultural possibilities.
>
> JUDITH BUTLER, *Gender Trouble*

> The *appearance of substance* is precisely that, a constructed identity, a per-
> formative accomplishment which the mundane social audience, including
> the actors themselves, come to believe and to perform in the mode of be-
> lief. . . . The possibilities of gender transformation are to be found precisely
> in the arbitrary relation between such acts, in the possibility of a failure to
> repeat, a de-formity, or a parodic repetition that exposes the phantasmatic
> effect of abiding identity as a politically tenuous construction.
>
> JUDITH BUTLER, *Gender Trouble*

> So well he dissembled, that he scarce knew himself that he did so.
>
> APHRA BEHN, *Love-Letters between a Nobleman and his Sister*

Expressly incestuous and deeply embedded in the politics of regicide and political rebellion, Aphra Behn's *Love-Letters between a Nobleman and his Sister* is also a
text insistently preoccupied with questions of gender, identity, and representation. Published in three parts between 1684 and 1687, Behn's novel is based
loosely on an affair between Ford, Lord Grey of Werke, and his wife's sister, Lady
Henrietta Berkeley, a scandal that broke in London in 1682, when Lady Berkeley's father published an advertisement in the *London Gazette* announcing the
disappearance of his daughter. Lady Berkeley had in fact run off with Grey, the
well-known antimonarchist figure whom Dryden alluded to as "cold Caleb" in
Absalom and Achitophel (1681) and who serves Behn here as a model for her

character Philander. Prosecuted by Lord Berkeley for abducting and seducing his daughter, Grey was eventually found guilty of "debauchery" but never sentenced.[1] Shortly thereafter, he was also implicated in the Rye House Plot to murder Charles II and was later active in Monmouth's rebellion against Charles's brother James. In Behn's fiction Grey figures as a political follower and friend of Cesario, the French prince of Condé, whose failed attempt to overthrow his king is modeled on the parallel exploits of Charles's bastard son. Lady Berkeley is Silvia, the dutiful Royalist daughter whom Philander seduces and corrupts. Like the crown for Cesario, she is for Philander a sign of male prerogative and desire, her body the theater across which several dramas of masculine rivalry are played out.

It is not surprising that a text situated so expressly within the political context of the Duke of Monmouth's rebellion against the royal authority of both his father and his uncle should be structured around the repetition of a series of analogously configured masculine rivalries. Through her elaborate foregrounding of the figure of a woman, however, Behn adds a dimension to this drama of political and familial succession that is manifestly absent from such comparable Royalist efforts as *Absalom and Achitophel*. To what extent Behn's choice to develop the love interest here was motivated by her recognition that the role of romance historian was more acceptable for a woman than the role of political poet, we cannot know for sure;[2] but when Lady Berkeley's father published his advertisement announcing her disappearance and offering two hundred pounds for her return, Behn clearly perceived an opportunity to explore the narrative possibilities (as well as the discursive instabilities) inherent in comparing stolen daughters with stolen crowns.

Behn incorporates the scandalous historical fact of the Berkeley-Grey affair into the political, thematic, and figural dimensions of her fiction by situating Philander's justifications for his adulterous and incestuous desire for Silvia squarely within the context of Restoration debates over the relationship and relative authority of nature and conventional morality. As Susan Staves has amply demonstrated, the increasing dissociation of natural law theory from theology during the second half of the seventeenth century effectively established the conditions both for changes in the institutional treatment of moral crimes and for the emergence of a new brand of heroism in the imaginative literature of the age. Herculean and libertine stage heroes captured the popular imagination through their bold allegiance to a nature defined not in accordance with, but in opposition to, religion, law, custom, and conventional mo-

rality. Such heroes appealed to nature to justify a range of behaviors traditionally regarded as crimes against nature as well as God. The deployment of
incest as a figure for rebellion against traditional forms of authority became a
favorite device on the Restoration stage (along with adultery, sodomy, and
parricide) for articulating cultural anxieties and for giving dramatic play to the
multiple tensions inherent in contemporary efforts to rethink the connections
between the laws of nature, religion, and social morality.[3]

Behn's libertine hero, Philander, fits the profile of this new literary type in his
elaboration of natural justifications for his socially criminal desire for Silvia.
From as early as his very first letter, he invokes the liberatory ethos of a return to
original pleasures. The legal institutions of kinship and of marriage, he insists,
are mere practical creations inspired by material interests, while his own incestuous and adulterous passion has a primacy that transcends the prudent
imperatives of tradition. Philander uses the fact that his relation to Silvia is
affinal (a legal relation created through his marriage to her sister) as opposed to
consanguineal (a blood relation) to further question the natural basis for the
rules that prohibit his having sex with her: "What Kin my charming *Silvia* are
you to me? No tyes of blood forbid my Passion; and what's a Ceremony impos'd
on man by custome? . . . what Alliance can that create? why shou'd a trick
devis'd by the wary old, only to make provision for posterity, tye me to an
eternal slavery."[4] In point of legal fact, as Sybil Wolfram's work has shown,
because the English concept of marriage in the seventeenth century was based
on the legal and religious doctrine of the unity of husband and wife, "intercourse between affinal relations was . . . on a footing with and as much incest as
intercourse between close blood relations."[5] But Philander represents an emergent strain of thought that radically questioned the received assumption that
incest controverted natural law.

Scripture, as we have seen, was a site of theoretical controversy among
seventeenth-century moral philosophers, especially at those points where God
appeared arbitrarily to command behavior elsewhere prohibited by his law. Of
numerous instances of apparent biblical inconsistency regarding the legitimacy
of incestuous practices, the most pervasively cited involved differences between the injunctions of Leviticus, which forbade incest, and those of Genesis,
which bade Adam and Eve (whom most commentators regarded as siblings) to
increase and multiply. Philander's arguments do not emerge ex nihilo, therefore, when he invokes Genesis to justify his incestuous desires. In a manner
typically modern and predictably Whig, he disdains the beaten track of con-

ventional morality to assert the prerogatives of an originary state: "let us . . . scorn the dull *beaten road,* but let us love like the first race of men, nearest allied to God, promiscuously they lov'd, and possess'st, Father and Daughter, Brother and Sister met, and reap'd the joys of Love without controul, and counted it Religious coupling, and 'twas encourag'd too by Heav'n it self" (*L-L,* 12). As Ruth Perry has observed, Philander speaks for the authenticity of nature over the artifice of social codes. Posing as the ultimate pastoral lover, he emulates the freedom of creatures in the natural world. There is "no troublesome Honour, amongst the pretty inhabitants of the Woods and Streams, fondly to give Laws to Nature," he insists, "but uncontroul'd they play and sing, and Love; no Parents checking their dear delights, no slavish Matrimonial tyes to restrain their Nobler flame." Only "Man . . . is bound up to rules fetter'd by the nice decencies of Honour."[6]

Given Behn's Royalist politics, Philander's defense of incest may seem at first blush a simple alignment of Whiggism with transgression, the act of regicide— as René Girard has noted in another context—constituting an equivalent in the political realm of parricide or incest within the family.[7] Those who violate loyalties to their king, Behn seems to want to say, are also apt to violate the other bonds on which the social order and its civilizing systems of difference depend.[8] Behn's creation of a heroine of Royalist birth who draws the better part of her appeal from her success in outdoing Philander at the game of transgressiveness, however, destabilizes this easy, politicized opposition between authority and rebellion and suggests a more complex and heterogeneous notion of transgression than a simply negative political coding would allow.[9] As more than one critic has noted, Behn's treatment of gender often seems to complicate and refract, if not indeed to contradict, her party politics, creating in her work the sense of multiple and incommensurate ideological agenda.[10] *Love-Letters* exemplifies this tendency through its own rhetorical excess, inviting itself to be read with a certain burlesquing tongue-in-cheekiness, as if it wants to make us ask—and it does make us ask—why (if this is first and foremost a political scandal novel) Behn would choose to defend the royal cause through so protracted a portrait of untamed female insubordination.

Is it true, as Janet Todd and Maureen Duffy both suggest, that Behn wants to promote the values of sincerity and authenticity as they are embodied in the figure of Philander's friend and rival, Octavio, by showing us that Philander's appeal to nature is nothing more than base hypocrisy?[11] Perhaps, at the most manifest level. But why then does her narrative *feel* so much like a celebration of the pleasures and powers of role-playing and artifice whereby the indomitable Silvia sacrifices Octavio to her revenge against Philander? If, as Perry suggests, Behn's characters are designed to show us "where disrespect for law and order can lead," why does Behn's relation to her heroine's depravity seem so very fraught with irony?[12] The narrator tells us that Silvia is imperious, proud, vain, opinionated, obstinate, censorious, amorously inclined, and indiscreet (*L-L*, 257–58); and yet Behn appears to revel in the emotional resilience that the heroine's duplicity affords. Jane Austen rarely assumes a more heteroglot relation to her heroines than Behn does when, reflecting on the ease with which Silvia is able to transfer her affection from one lover to the next, she writes: "Nature is not inclin'd to hurt it self; and there are but very few who find it necessary to die of the Disease of Love. Of this sort was our *Silvia*, tho' to give her her due, never any Person who did not indeed die, ever languished under the Torments of Love, as did that charming and afflicted Maid" (261). The "nature" appealed to here is elusively construed, gesturing ironically toward an unstable opposition between female nature and artifice in a world where a "natural" female impulse toward self-preservation requires the performance, nearly unto death, of the artifice of languishing femininity.[13]

Feminist critics have taken differing positions regarding the significance of the incest in Behn's text. To Janet Todd, on the one hand, it is merely a sensationalist device meant to keep Behn's book in print, not an important theme developed at any length.[14] For Judith Kegan Gardiner, on the other hand, Silvia's willing participation in an incestuous adultery with her brother-in-law is the paradigmatic instance of her transgressiveness as a heroine and the conceptual point of departure for a complex reconfiguration of literary history.[15] Reading *Love-Letters* as a story of brother-sister incest that does not follow a familiar and traditionally valorized oedipal logic but instead avoids "both father-son and mother-daughter paradigms for a transgressive sexuality in which the woman is not exclusively a victim but a willing and desiring agent" (207), Gardiner makes the case that a revaluation of the importance of Behn's text in the history of the novel genre opens the way to imagining an alternative paradigm of literary history, one that displaces an oedipal by what she calls "an incestuous model of the novel's origins" (218).[16]

But *is* Behn's heroine stably figured as a willing agent of incestuous desire? Does the text of *Love-Letters* in fact support Gardiner's assessment that incest functions for Silvia, as it does for Philander, as the expression of a liberatory eros? Behn may indeed refuse an oedipal model of female desire; but does she therefore necessarily embrace an incestuous ideal of feminine transgression? I shall argue that, on the contrary, far from replacing an oedipal with an incestuous ideal, Behn's narrative effectively displaces the conceptual grounds of a heterosexual matrix of assumptions that encodes incestuous desire as a form of freedom from patriarchal law.

There is a great deal more at stake here than a subtle difference of reading. Where we locate the transgressiveness of Behn's heroine has critical implications not just for the place Behn will occupy in contemporary conceptions of aesthetics and of literary history but also for a feminist analysis of narrative representations of incestuous desire, especially for efforts to theorize the role of incest in modern discursive inscriptions of female desire.[17] In making the case for Silvia's incestuous agency without taking into account how she is located *specifically as a female subject* in relation both to incest and to the law that produces it as an object of repression—without regard, that is, to the patriarchal power structure within which incest derives its meaning and transgressive force to begin with—Gardiner allows a dangerous slippage to occur in her argument. Assuming that incest always inevitably constitutes transgression (indeed, reading incest as the ultimate transgression), she relies on a characteristically modern discursive coding of incestuous desire as natural—an emergent cultural inscription in seventeenth-century England, as we have seen, but one that I would argue Behn's narrative actively refuses to underwrite.

In fact, I would suggest that, far from elaborating a simple equivalence or correspondence between incest and transgression, Behn uses both categories to register the shifting positionality of gendered subjectivities, producing a variable model of the transgressiveness of incest and the incestuousness of transgression for her male and female characters. Rather than inscribing incest as a stable and univocal marker of transgression, she destabilizes incest as a trope of liberation by exposing the ways it is differently constituted for her hero and her heroine. In the process, she radically problematizes the question of desire's origins, representing what Gardiner reads as original desire in Silvia not as an intrinsic essence but as an effect of power.[18] Silvia's transgressiveness as a heroine is situated not in her incestuous agency but elsewhere; it emerges rather in a conceptual and performative space made available to her only by the eventual recognition that Philander's exaltation of incest as a liberation from prohibitive patriarchal law actually functions as an instrument of power. Incest operates in Behn's text, in other words, not as a simple figure for transgression but as a complex discursive site where the oppositional ideologies of patriarchy and individualism intersect, at once confronting each other and, in the process, exposing their joint complicity in (and their shared dependence on) the appropriation and co-optation of female desire.

This is hardly to revert to Todd's assessment of the essential insignificance of the incest in Behn's text. On the contrary, it is to read Silvia's incest as a necessary part of Behn's complex critique of Whig libertarian politics. At the level of plot, after all, it is the incest that moves Silvia outside her father's house, and thus it is the incest that establishes the conditions within which Behn is able to show that that outside is always already inside—always on the verge of re-inscribing the very law it would subvert. To be successfully transgressive on Behn's terms, Silvia will have to move *beyond* the illusory liberation of natural-ized incestuous desire—*outside* the outside of an oedipal dyad in which women are mere theaters for the playing out of male desire. The serial nature of *Love-Letters* allows Behn to effect these consecutive displacements compellingly by creating an opportunity for her to write her heroine out of and beyond the limits of the typical romantic plot.[19]

Philander's "Phallic Handshake" and the Limits of the Libertine Critique of Patriarchy

I approach my subject through a reading of several key episodes that help to establish the context within which the incest in Behn's narrative acquires meaning. My aim is to illuminate the extent to which the incestuous relation between Philander and Silvia is conditioned by the dynamics of a system of homosocial exchange in which the daughter's desire functions not as a locus of agency but as a site of confrontation between paternal and fraternal interests. Because familial conflict is coded politically in Behn's novel, this reading also necessarily involves discussion of the way Silvia's body functions in a double symbolic register as a political as well as a familial battleground.

This is not to say that Silvia entirely lacks transgressive agency. It is rather to suggest that we must first understand the structuring homosocial frame within which her incest is enacted ultimately to appreciate the process whereby she manages to move beyond the possibilities for transgression delimited by that frame into a space subversively generated by a parodic repetition of its terms. For however paradoxically, it is only after Silvia comes to recognize her status as a sign within a drama of masculine rivalry, to understand that as a woman she is always already a representation within a homosocial matrix of desire, that she opens herself to the possibility of taking performative control of her enactment of desire and gendered subjectivity.

I take as my point of entry Philander's account of an episode that occurs relatively early in part 1, immediately after his first nocturnal tryst with Silvia. As a dutiful Royalist daughter, Silvia early expresses considerable anguish over Philander's attempts to prevail upon her "honour"; she finally concedes, nevertheless, to a private interview, which she justifies as a trial of her virtue and resolution. And as Philander's letter recounting the details of their first night alone together reveals, Silvia does remain "a maid" despite the opportunity for physical conquest on his part.

The cause of Philander's forbearance, as he explains, is neither his regard for Silvia's honor (on the contrary, he says, her resistance inflames him all the more) nor her physical attractions (these, he insists, are overwhelming) but a fit of sexual impotence brought on by a state of overstimulation. Having "overcome all difficulties, all the fatigues and toyles of Love's long Sieges, Vanquisht the mighty Fantôm of the fair, the Giant Honour, and routed all the numerous Host of Womens little Reasonings, past all the bounds of peevish Modesty: Nay even all the loose and silken Counterscarps that fenc'd the sacred Fort," instead of receiving "the yielding treasure," Philander had fallen "fainting before the surrendering Gates," a circumstance he goes on to associate with the weakness of old age. In a rhetorical maneuver that underscores his physical prowess even as it acknowledges a lapse in his "[(]till then) never failing power," he attributes his attack of impotence to the envy of the gods; one "malicious at [his] Glory," he suggests, has left him full of "mad desires" but "all unactive, as Age or Death it self, as cold and feeble, as unfit for joy, as if [his] Youthful fire had long been past, or *Silvia* had never been blest with Charms." Indeed, the excess of passion has so paralyzed Philander that he curses his youth and implores the gods to give him "Old Age, for that has some excuse, but Youth has none" (*L-L,* 56–57).

The dialectic of youthful vigor and old age within which Philander here encodes what amounts to an averted incestuous consummation is, as we have to some extent already seen, precisely the dialectic within which he has attempted to justify his incestuous and adulterous desire from the start. From as early as his very first letter to Silvia, he has idealized his affection for her by casting the older generation as guardians of a threatened domain of power, invested only in the jealous retention of control over the future. The institutions of kinship and of marriage are mere "trick[s] devis'd by the wary old" (11), who, like the gods, arbitrarily wield the reins of political power even as they fear and envy Philander's authentic passion and youthful virility.

Philander reproduces this dialectic at a more literal level in his reference later in the same letter to a parallel sexual plot involving another male predator and another "reluctant maid." For even as Philander, "the Young the Brisk and Gay" (57), is engineering an interview with Silvia, Silvia's father, that "brisk old Gentleman" (61), has been counting on a garden assignation with Melinda, her refreshingly worldly serving maid. Few readers will forget the hilarious "accident" by which plot and comic subplot here intersect, enabling Behn to play irreverently with the ironies, multiple meanings, and shifting power relations produced when the "maid" Silvia, "mistress" of Melinda, plays "mistress" to Philander while her "maid," Melinda, plays "mistress" to Silvia's father. Much as Defoe would later point to the ironies inherent in the homonymous relation contained within the honorific "Madam," Behn here uses the shifting and multiplying of subject positions to baldly expose the illusory forms of power invested in all varieties of mistresses and maids.[20]

According to Philander, no consummation takes place between master and "mistress" here any more than between Philander and Silvia. Alarmed by a noise that makes the young lovers fear discovery, Philander steals into the garden disguised in Melinda's nightgown and headdress, only to be mistaken for Melinda by the eager old gentleman. Here is his account of events as they unfold:

> *Monsieur* the Count, . . . taking me for *Melinda* . . . , caught hold of my Gown as I would have pass'd him, and Cry'd, Now *Melinda* I see you are a Maid of Honour,— Come retire with me into the Grove where I have a present of a heart and something else to make you. . . . (*L-L,* 60)

It is now Philander's turn to play the role of reluctant maid:

> With that I pull'd back and whisper'd—Heavens, would you make a Mistress of me?—Says he—A Mistress what wouldst thou be a Cherubin? Then I reply'd as before—I am no Whore, Sir,—No crys he, but I can quickly make thee one, I have my Tools about me, Sweet-heart, therefore let's lose no time but fall to work: . . . with that he clapt fifty Guinnies in a Purse into one hand, and something else that shall be nameless into the other, presents that had both been worth *Melinda's* acceptance. (61)

Combining many of the key motifs and topoi of *Love-Letters* (among them masquerade, gender reversal, class and generational encounter, and homosocial exchange of a most literal variety)—and all within an epistolary frame— Philander's garden adventure offers a veritable object lesson in the problematics of reading Behn. It is possible to take Philander's narrative at face value, to accept the hero at his word, as Gardiner does when she reads Philander's disguise as providing a sort of comic externalization of his demeaning impotence. Philander, as she sees him here, is a whining buffoon—"a ludicrously declassed and feminized figure" whose exposure through Behn's publication of his private correspondence realizes his own worst fear, as he expresses it in his letter, of being publicly ridiculed ("Where shall I hide my head, when this lewd Story's told?" [*L-L*, 57]). In Philander's account of his comic adventure with Count Beralti, Gardiner suggests, Behn not only casts doubt on the virility of the notoriously promiscuous Lord Grey but also "undercuts the admiration accorded to Don Juans" generally. His withdrawal from the garden, which leaves his father-in-law in a state of sexual frustration, is, she argues, a burlesque of "his own frustrated romantic seduction of Sylvia."[21]

But Gardiner's reading does little justice to the hermeneutic instabilities generated by the epistolary nature of Behn's text, instabilities that produce the possibility that Philander may be feigning impotence. The only ground we have for validating what really happened on that disappointing night is, after all, Philander's word—his own dubious representation of events. And in light of the strategies of seduction he has deployed up to this point, it is certainly plausible to read his attack of impotence not as a fact but as a performance (what might more fittingly be called a magnificent antiperformance in this case). Indeed, one could argue that, far from constituting a form of humiliation, this episode actually helps Philander to consolidate his power over Silvia.[22]

Philander's "retreat" from consummation at this moment of peak excitement and opportunity is thoroughly in keeping with the strategies of deferral by which he has gained entry into Silvia's bedchamber in the first place. From the outset, he has moved with a certain deft belatedness. As early as her third letter, Silvia pines for word from Philander: "Not yet?—not yet?" she laments, "oh ye dull tedious Hours when will you glide away? and bring that happy moment on, in which I shall at least hear from my *Philander*; . . . Perhaps *Philander*'s making a tryal of Vertue by this silence" (*L-L*, 21–22). In her next, still waiting ("Another Night oh Heav'ns and yet no Letter come!" [23]), she even entertains the thought that Philander may in fact be toying with her: "is't a trick, a cold fit only assum'd to try how much I Love you?" (24). Predictably, Philander has an excuse, though in presenting it he also betrays a certain disingenuousness: "When I had seal'd the inclos'd, *Brilljard* told me you were this Morning come from *Belfont*, and with infinite impatience have expected seeing you here; which defer'd my sending this to the old place; and I am so vain (oh Adorable *Silvia!*) as to believe my fancy'd silence has given you disquiets, but sure my *Silvia* cou'd not charge me with neglect" (19).

It may be revenge for Silvia's ambivalence about surrendering herself to him, indeed for the tenacity with which she clings to the imperatives of honor, that drives Philander to these delays. For although Silvia often longs for him, she is just as often grateful for his neglect: "let me alone, let me be ruin'd with Honour if I must be ruin'd.—For oh! 'twere much happyer I were no more than that I shou'd be more than *Philander*'s Sister; or he than *Silvia*'s Brother: Oh let me ever call you by that cold name" (22). Philander, however, will not be satisfied with gaining anything less than absolute control over the representation of Silvia's desire. Early on she describes herself as the very embodiment of disorder and indeterminacy: "cou'd you but imagine how I am tormentingly divided, how unresolv'd between violent Love and cruel Honour: You would say 'twere impossible to fix me any where; or be the same thing for a moment together" (24–25). Onto this doubt and indecision, Philander fixes his own desire, reading Silvia as he wishes—like Adam, dreaming her doubt into desire for his advances and then naming it as love (15–16). "I know you Love," writes Philander to Silvia (31); he "soon taught her to understand 'twas Love," asserts the narrator in the novel's "Argument" (10); "thou art the first that ever did inform me that there was such a sort of wish about me," writes Silvia to Philander (66)—such phrases sound a refrain throughout part 1. And Silvia does at last defer to the authority of Philander's reading of her, both in finally accepting his diagnosis of her alienation from desire and in conceding to his accusations of her fickleness and inconstancy along the way.

In the context of this series of deferrals, Philander's impotence simply constitutes a culminating moment in the production of desire in Silvia. Although in prior letters she has vacillated wildly between attraction to her brother-in-law and a perfectly catechismal defense of patriarchal honor, in the two letters that she writes in quick succession immediately following Philander's "lapse" in potency, she describes herself as experiencing a degree of desire she has previously not known. "I have Wishes, new unwonted Wishes," she writes, "at every thought of thee, I find a strange disorder in my blood, that pants and burns in every Vein, and makes me blush, and sigh, and grows impatient, asham'd and angry" (67). She now further concedes that her previous "coldness" must have been dissembled, as she was "not Mistress of" it (67). (This concession by Silvia is of interest for our reading of Philander, as it admits the possibility that coldness may be feigned.) "[T]here lyes a Woman's Art," she continues, "there all her boasted Vertue, it is but well dissembling, and no more.—But mine alas is gone, for ever fled" (67–68). In the process of increasingly surrendering to Philander's "cause," Silvia now begins in several instances to echo his very words and arguments, mirroring his early references to "fond custom" and "phantom honour" as well as the opportunistic and somewhat desperate arguments he used to justify his commitment to the political interests of the treacherous Cesario. Just as he there described himself as being "in past a retreat" (46) and declared that "though the glorious falling weight should crush me, 'tis great to attempt" (47), so Silvia now casts herself in the role of heroic martyr to her love: "I am plung'd in past hope of a retreat, and since my fate has pointed me out for ruine, I cannot fall more gloriously. Take then, *Philander*, to your dear Arms a Maid that can no longer resist, who is disarm'd of all defensive power: She yields, she yields, and does confess it too" (69). Silvia's response to Philander's impotence, in short, is to renounce every doctrine she has hitherto been taught by the "Grave and Wise" (67). He induces her to give up a "coldness" she is "not Mistress of" by, in effect, being master of his own. One more instance of deferral (occasioned this time by Cesario's calling him away) will secure his romantic victory; to prove his passion, Philander will offer to disregard the summons, but Silvia—now thoroughly identified with his interests—insists that he respond, promising that Philander's obedience to the commands of Cesario (whom earlier she regarded as a rival) will be rewarded in her arms (72–73).

If, as Silvia is here driven to presuppose, affecting coldness is "a woman's art"—a prerogative or sign of femininity—then feigning impotence is for Philander, in more than one sense, "putting on" the maid. It is a way of putting Silvia on both in the sense of controlling her through deception and in the sense of performing a woman's part (affecting coldness), a strategy made literal in Philander's garden performance as Melinda.[23] Appropriating to himself a dissembled coldness that he identifies as a female strategy, Philander does not invite Silvia to become a better mistress of her own standoffishness but instead maneuvers her into accepting the coercive fiction of her own natural desire for him. Her longing for him is thus understood not as the effect of a performance on his part but as an essence intrinsic to her, a "natural propensity" (*L-L*, 65) poorly masked in her case by a shabby cloak of artificial virtue. As she does at several other points throughout her text, Behn here problematizes the question of desire's origins in depicting Silvia's grasping after a causal narrative: "I am the

Aggressor," she declares eventually, "the fault's in me, and thou art innocent" (65).[24] Thus does Philander take control rhetorically of their courtship by inducing Silvia to own an "unaccountable" passion (*L-L*, 66) over which she has neither prior knowledge nor control.

It remains, however, to determine the role of Philander's garden performance as a reluctant maid in his project of displacing all traces of reluctance in Silvia. I have argued that what to Gardiner is whining and buffoonery on Philander's part can also, if we refuse to assume the hero's authenticity, be understood as a form of strategic self-dramatization whereby Philander acquires power by performing impotence. Philander's account of his "pleasant adventure" in the garden similarly serves his ends with Silvia by enlisting her collusion as a reader in a comic undermining of paternal authority. By reducing the Count to a rather embarrassing travesty of the predatory excesses of youth, it offers a repetition and amplification of Philander's successful manipulation of the signs of impotence and femininity to establish the conditions for sexual victory.[25] It is not just that Philander has prior knowledge from Melinda of Beralti's sexual indiscretions while Beralti himself remains ignorant of Philander's dalliance with his daughter. There is also the fact that the old man is prepared to pay for Melinda's "services," a detail that, while it bespeaks Beralti's economic prowess, also makes him compare unfavorably with Philander. The fifty guineas intended for Melinda may stand as a mark of Beralti's class as well as gender supremacy, but they are also a sign of his "maid's" affective indifference to him—an indifference that, as we have seen, stands in stark contrast to the passion Philander arouses in Silvia (despite, if not indeed because of, his temporary lapse in potency). In fact, the comic circumstance of Melinda's physical absence at the moment when the fifty guineas is bestowed makes an utter mockery of the Count's physical power over her. The scene in which the father both literally and figuratively attempts to impose the phallus is also the scene in which the paternal phallus is inadvertently exposed, not simply to the laughter of the son-in-law but, through him, to the daughter's laughter too.

But Beralti's garden vigil for the daughter's maid takes place at the very moment when Philander is preparing the stage for the theft of the daughter's maidenhead. The identity of role between Philander and the Count as predatory males is thus complicated by their status as rivals. They are not simply mirrors of one another—males in quest of separate objects of desire—but also competitors for control of Silvia. (Couldn't Beralti's dalliance with the "maid" in fact be read as a phantasmatic rendering of the eroticized relation between father and daughter that underpins the entire sexual drama of part 1?)[26] To the extent that they situate Silvia's alienation from her father within the context of a drama of masculine rivalry in which she figures not as an agent but a sign, the familial dynamics here are critical. Philander's inclination to flout paternal authority and to infringe upon the father's right of rule is an aspect of his political character as a follower of the regicidal Cesario. But the link does not end there. Like Cesario, Philander functions in the capacity of a son, a role he has acquired by his marriage to Silvia's sister, Mertilla, and that involves not just the acquisition of certain privileges but also the institution of specific prohibitions. The rules of kinship that give Philander freedom of access to Beralti's daughters also presuppose the assumption of countervailing filial responsibilities. Silvia alludes to both these prerogatives and their limits when she contemplates the consequences of her father's discovery of their affair: "my Father being rash, and extremely jealous, and the more so of me, by how much more he is fond of me, and nothing would inrage him like the discovery of an interview like this; though you have Liberty to range the house of *Bellfont* as a Son, and are indeed at home there, but . . . when he shall find his Son and Virgin Daughter, the Brother and the Sister so retir'd, so entertain'd. —What but death can insue; or what's worse, eternal . . . confusion on my honour?" (49). In seducing Silvia (by, in effect, usurping the father's prerogative to dispose of her virginity), Philander violates the authority vested in him as a brother—an authority that, as the following passage testifies, Silvia recognizes as lawful. Describing herself as impaled by a sense of familial obligation in the face of his advances, as "a Maid that cannot fly," she entertains a moment of regret: "[W]hy did you take advantage of those Freedoms I gave you as a Brother, I smil'd on you, and sometimes kist you too;—But for my Sisters sake, I play'd with you, suffer'd your Hands and Lips to wander were I dare not now; all which I thought a Sister might allow a Brother, and knew not all the while the Treachery of Love: Oh none, but under that intimate title of Brother, cou'd have had the opportunity to have ruin'd me, . . . by degrees so subtil, and an authority so lawful, you won me out of all" (22).[27]

Within the discursive economy of Behn's text, in short, Silvia's honor—represented both by her virgin body and by her desire to fulfill her f(am)ilial obligations—becomes Philander's political battleground. As "Daughter to the great *Beralti,* and Sister to *Mertilla,* a yet unspotted Maid, fit to produce a race of Glorious Hero's," Silvia recognizes that all her actions reflect on the honor of "the noble House of the *Beralti*" and that Philander seeks "to build the trophies of [his] Conquests on the ruine of both *Mertilla*'s fame and [her own]" (*L-L*, 25–26). From a political perspective, it is not sufficient that he ruin Mertilla only, as Silvia yet remains to "redeem the bleeding [Royalist] Honour of [her] Family" (30). As Mertilla puts it in her one admonitory missive to her sister, Silvia is "the darling child, the joy of all, the last hope left, the refuge" of "the most unhappy [family] of all the race of old nobility" (75). Philander's corruption of Beralti's dutiful younger daughter through the illicit appropriation of sexual rights over her in this sense constitutes a Whig usurpation of the Royalist right of rule.

One sees here, better perhaps than at any other point in her text, the logic of Behn's interweaving of sexual and political narratives; for what Behn's complex structuring of her tale makes evident is the profound interimplication—indeed the mutually constitutive nature—of sexuality and politics. The relationship between plots here is more than merely analogical, more than the simple matter of a metaphor in which sexual conquest serves as a figure at the level of private life for a more public, political form of victory. It is rather a relationship of discursive interdependence in which the categories of the private and the public, materiality and meaning, desire and the law reveal their inherently contingent and unstable identities. Gardiner accepts the efficacy of a stable distinction between private and public life when she rests her reading on the difference between Philander's positive political power and his lack of familial authority over Silvia. But this is precisely the distinction Behn destabilizes when she exposes the intensely political nature of individual desire. Philander's binary opposition between private and public life is, she suggests, an illusion created to sustain the liberatory fiction that legitimates the operations of masculine privilege.

Philander represents his incestuous love for Silvia as an expression of unconstrained desire that marks a liberation from a materialist economy of sexual exchange. Against the institution of marriage—"a trick devis'd by the wary, old only to make provision for posterity" (11)—he urges the authenticity of "Pleasures vast and unconfin'd" (28). And eventually, in the invective against marriage to which she devotes her penultimate letter in part 1, Silvia too comes to embrace such a libertine philosophy, asserting that only adulterous love can occasion genuine heterosexual reciprocity ("that's a heavenly match," she writes, "when two Souls toucht with equal passion meet . . . , when no base interest makes the hasty bargain, . . . and . . . both understand to take and pay" [111–12]). Ultimately, however, by showing how the very act of erotic transgression

that Philander proffers as an individualist solution to the problem of hierarchical repression ultimately reinscribes Silvia's specular status in reciprocal
relations between men, Behn exposes the limits of the libertine critique of
patriarchy.

The asymmetrical and nonreciprocal character of Silvia and Philander's relationship will become increasingly clear, both to Silvia and to the reader, as the
events of parts 2 and 3 of the narrative—especially those involving the relationship between Philander and Octavio—unfold. But even within the limits of the
love plot of part 1, that inadvertent "phallic handshake" between father and
son-in-law in the garden—a savage burlesque of the gentleman's agreement by
which the gift of the daughter is legitimately exchanged—reveals (even as it
figures the bypassing of legitimate succession) the homosocial ground of *both*
patriarchal law *and* its transgression. Fifty guineas and that "nameless" entity,
the father's penis, may be "presents . . . both . . . worth *Melinda*'s acceptance,"
but only Silvia—phallic representative of the father's name and law—is worth
Philander's. Just as Silvia's ensuing marriage to Philander's "property," Brilljard,
will expose the underlying ironies of the libertine's dependence on the legal
artifice of marriage to secure control over the body of his lover, so Behn here
shows that an incestuous challenge to the law of patriarchal prerogative does
not necessarily constitute a challenge to the law of masculine privilege.

Role-Playing, Cuckoldry, and Cross-Dressing: Silvia's Semiotic Education

It is crucial to recognize the extent to which Philander's performative strategy of playing the maid in part 1 of Behn's narrative is embedded in the male
homosocial dynamics that organize her plot more generally. Abounding in the
representation of erotic triangles, *Love-Letters* may be read as a veritable proving
ground for analysis of what Eve Kosofsky Sedgwick identifies as the homosocial
bases and gender asymmetries of triangular heterosexual desire. Of special rele-
vance here is Sedgwick's analysis of the dynamics of cuckoldry and their relationship to the "masculinizing potential of subordination to a man" as it is
elaborated in psychoanalytic accounts of male psychosexual development.[28]
Sedgwick quotes Richard Klein's gloss on Freud's account of "the little boy's
progress towards heterosexuality" in order to call attention to the way in which
modern constructions of heterosexual masculinity presuppose the existence
(and repression) of a prior homosexual stage of feminized subordination to

another male. The male child, writes Klein, "must pass . . . through the stage of the 'positive' Oedipus, a homoerotic identification with his father, a position of feminized subordination to the father, as a condition of finding a model for his own heterosexual role."[29]

A dynamic of homoerotic identification similar to the one Freud posits and Klein describes is central to the male relationships represented in Behn's text. It is evident not just in Philander's struggles with his father-in-law, where playing the maid becomes simultaneously the means by which the hero usurps paternal authority and the occasion (however burlesque) for a homoerotic encounter with the father, but also in the prolific instances of cuckoldry recounted elsewhere in the narrative. For Silvia is not just the space across which Philander aspires to homosocial sameness with "the father"; she is, interestingly, also the conduit whereby he asserts masculine identity with Cesario.

A brief review of the prehistory of the incestuous lovers' affair clearly reveals the extent to which Silvia functions for Philander simultaneously as a locus of deflected homoerotic love and as a means of resolving his own desire to be like Cesario. The founding circumstance of Silvia and Philander's love is a prior sexual rivalry between Philander and Cesario over the heart and body of Silvia's older sister, Mertilla. After promising to marry the prince, Mertilla is drawn instead into a marriage with Philander, only to return at last to an adulterous affair with Cesario. Here again, as in the matter of the affair between Philander and Silvia, Behn makes the origins of desire problematic, introducing ambiguity in her "Argument" as to whether the impulse toward conjugal infidelity originates in Philander or Mertilla. Philander nevertheless produces his own causal narrative in an early letter to Silvia, where he makes the case that Mertilla was the first to violate her vows. Especially striking here is his response to that alleged betrayal:

> *Mertilla*, I say, first broke her Marriage Vows to me; I blame her not, nor is it reasonable I shou'd; she saw the young *Cesario*, and Lov'd him. *Cesario*, whom the envying World in spight of prejudice must own, has unresistible charms, that Godlike form, that sweetness in his face, that softness in his Eyes and delicate Mouth; and every Beauty besides that Women doat on and Men envy: That lovely composition of Man and Angel! with the addition of his eternal Youth and Illustrious Birth, was form'd by Heav'n and Nature for universal Conquest! and who can love the charming Hero at a cheaper rate than being undone: And she that wou'd not venture Fame, Honour, and a Marriage Vow for the Glory of the young *Cesario*'s heart, merits not the noble Victim. (*L-L*, 16–17)

Instead of faulting Mertilla for her disloyalty, Philander identifies with her desire for Cesario. Granted, his letter is part of an elaborate textual strategy of seduction—one that requires that he provide Silvia with irrefutable justifications for his own adulterous love. But the hyperbolic portrait he paints of Cesario, surpassed in erotic extravagance only by the protracted and probably parodic inventory of Mertilla's physical attributes in the novel's "Argument," exceeds the demands of Philander's rhetorical project and prepares us for his ensuing account of the joyful submission and "shameful freedome" he experiences when Cesario cuckolds him:

> but when I knew her false, when I was once confirm'd,—When by my own Soul I found the dissembl'd Passion of her's, when she cou'd no longer hide the blushes or the paleness that seiz'd at the approaches of my disorder'd Rival, when I saw Love dancing in her eyes and her false heart beat with nimble motions, and soft trembling seize every Limb, at the approach or touch of the Royal Lover, then I thought my self no longer oblig'd to conceal my flame for *Silvia;* nay, e're I broke silence, e're I discover'd the hidden Treasure of my heart, I made her falshood plainer yet: Even the time and place of the dear assignations I discover'd; certainty! happy certainty! broke the dull heavy chain, and I with joy submitted to my shameful freedome, and caress'd my generous Rival, nay and by Heav'n I lov'd him for't, pleas'd at the resemblance of our Souls, for we were secret Lovers both, but more pleas'd that he loved *Mertilla,* for that made way to my passion for the adorable *Silvia!* (17)

At the climax of this passage, it is difficult to disentangle Philander's pleasure from Mertilla's. But Philander's text ultimately takes a turn whereby its writer comes to occupy more than a single position in the complex network of triangular desire. At one and the same time, he manages to identify with Mertilla's pleasurable submission to Cesario and, through the mediating figure of Silvia, with Cesario's position of conquest over him. For Philander, that is, Silvia is not just a double for Mertilla (not just another version of prohibited womanhood) but a locus of deflected homosocial love—a substitute, in effect, for Cesario. As in Philander's night of impotence or his garden encounter with Beralti, where playing the maid serves as a strategy for appropriating paternal prerogatives, so here identification with the position of Mertilla becomes a conduit for his assertion of masculine privilege.[30] By providing the possibility for Philander to occupy multiple subject positions simultaneously, Silvia creates the conditions whereby he is able to convert his sense of admiration and envy for his rival into a version of identification with him.

" 'To cuckold,' " writes Sedgwick, "is by definition a sexual act, performed on a man, by another man. . . . The bond of cuckoldry . . . [is] *necessarily* hierarchical in structure, with an 'active' participant who is clearly in the ascendancy over the 'passive' one." In the homosocial scheme that underwrites this bond, moreover, "men's bonds with women are meant to be in a subordinate, complementary, and instrumental relation to bonds with other men."[31] The world of *Love-Letters* both exemplifies this ethos and, through the heroine's ability to identify it, provides a critique of its structuring principles.

As Philander notes early on, being cuckolded is hardly an abuse over which it is worth risking one's life, let alone one's friendship with a male rival. "Let the dull hot-brain'd jealous fool upbraid me with cold Patience," he writes in defense of his response to Cesario's cuckoldry, "Let the fond Coxcomb whose Honour depends on the frail Marriage Vow, reproach me, or tell me that my Reputation depends on the feeble constancy of a Wife, perswade me 'tis Honour to fight for an unretrievable and unvalor'd Prize, and that because my Rival has taken leave to Cuckold me, I shall give him leave to kill me too" (*L-L,* 18). Silvia displays a similar cynicism when she demands in a moment of resistance of Philander, "What Husband is not a Cuckold? Nay and a friend to him that made him so?" (26). Philander, of course, claims transcendent passion for Silvia as grounds for his casual dismissal of Mertilla, insisting that "only she that has my Soul, can . . . ingage my Sword" (18). But his actions in the ensuing narrative will belie these early protestations and expose the deep contradictions inherent in Philander's libertine debunking of the interested codes of patriarchal honor. Silvia will perceive these contradictions with clarity by the middle of part 2, where, pregnant and betrayed by Philander after having joined him in his flight to Holland to escape political prosecution (as in real life Henrietta Berkeley had in a similar circumstance followed Grey), she angrily begins a course of increasing cunning and self-sufficiency. Entertaining the advances of another suitor while allowing Philander to continue to believe in her fidelity to him and in her ignorance of his infidelity to her, she will ultimately outstrip Philander at the game of inconstancy. The Dutch nobleman Octavio, illegitimate son of the House of Orange (192) as well as Philander's confidant and friend, fittingly becomes her instrument of revenge.

The ensuing rivalry between Philander and Octavio reproduces the competing demands of love and honor that dominate Philander's seduction of Silvia, only to recast them in an ironic light. To all appearances, Octavio is the very embodiment of honor and authenticity; but Behn makes a mockery of his honorable punctilios in her portrait of his bumbling efforts to "protect" Silvia from the secret of Philander's infidelity. Unable to restrain his love for the abandoned Silvia, Octavio dutifully confesses all in letters to Philander, only to discover that the latter has taken up with Octavio's own virtuous married sister, Calista, and is altogether willing to surrender Silvia's body to the encroaching erotic advances of a friend. While Octavio nourishes resentment over the honor of Calista (of whose familial identity Philander yet remains ignorant), he nevertheless resolves that his friendship for Philander will surpass all other ties, including both his duty to his sister and his passion for Silvia. Finding solace in being able to act honorably toward (i.e., with permission from) his rival in satisfying his desire for his new object, Octavio thus agrees to what amounts to a double transaction with Philander: namely, the prostitution of his sister to gain a lover ("rifle *Calista* of every Vertue Heaven and Nature gave her," he declares, "so I may but revenge it on thy *Silvia!*" [178]) and the exchange, in effect, of his sister for Philander's. Behn underscores the similarity in difference between incest and exchange here by building a clearly incestuous charge into Octavio's voyeuristic consumption of letters in which Philander elaborately details his erotic encounters with Calista. Through her repeated doubling of the categories of sister and lover, she lodges a deft critique of aristocratic codes of masculine honor that deploy sisters, as well as lovers, as enabling grounds for the enactment of male prerogative.

Cognizant of the extent to which Octavio and Philander's gentleman's agreement reduces her to a mere object of circulation among men, Silvia at length confronts Octavio with the double moral standard underlying his devotion to male honor:

> Oh, you are very nice, *Octavio* . . . in your Punctilio to *Philander,* but I perceive you are not so tender in those you ought to have for *Silvia*? I find Honour in you men, is only what you please to make it, for at the same time you think it ungenerous to betray *Philander,* you believe it no breach of Honour to betray the eternal repose of *Silvia.* You have promis'd *Philander* your friendship, you have avow'd yourself my Lover, my Slave, my Friend, my every thing, and yet not one of these has any tye to oblige you to my interest. . . . And here you think it no dishonour to break your word or promise; by which I find your false Notions, of Vertue and Honour, with which you serve your selves, when int'rest, design, or self Love makes you think it necessary. (194–95)

Finally, it is neither Silvia's inconstancy with Octavio nor the latter's erotic rivalry that inspires Philander to raise his sword against his friend; it is rather the perception that, in betraying the "Secrets of Friendship" to Silvia (356),

Octavio has allowed a heterosexual tie to supersede their homosocial bond. This transgression alone is able to move Philander, as it were, out of the boudoir and onto the battlefield (356–57).

On the day before he is to take Holy Orders in part 3 of the narrative, Octavio—now broken by Silvia's treachery—is visited by Philander, who comes to beg Octavio's pardon for offenses he has committed against him and to persuade him to abandon his determination to retire from the world. Not only has Philander debauched Octavio's sister, who has by now retired pregnant to a convent; he has also ravished from him Silvia, the very mistress he had not long before abandoned to his friend. As a pledge of his friendship at this critical moment in the text, Philander now assures Octavio that he would never have violated Calista, had he known of her relationship to him. He would, moreover, as he wryly notes, gladly "quit [Silvia] to him, were she Ten times dearer to him than she was" (376), if doing so would deter Octavio from his desperate intent. While these protestations of friendship from Philander fail to dissuade Octavio from his resolve, they do nevertheless elicit this reciprocal profession of his love:

> "Sir, I must confess you have found out the only way to disarm me of my resentment against you, if I were not oblig'd, by those Vows I am going to take, to pardon and be at peace with all the World. However these Vows cannot hinder me from conserving intirely that Friendship in my Heart, which your good qualities and beauties at first sight ingag'd there, and from esteeming you more than perhaps I ought to do: the Man whom I must yet own my Rival, and the undoer of my Sisters Honour. But Oh—no more of that, a Friend's above a Sister, or a Mistress." At this he hung down his Eyes and sigh'd——. (376–77)

Uttered on the eve of the hero's initiation into the fraternal order of St. Bernard, this simple maxim—"a Friend's above a Sister, or a Mistress"—is perhaps the baldest statement we have of the sexual hierarchies that underpin Behn's plot. Granting the pardon Philander begs, Octavio seals it by taking "a ring of great value from his Finger" (377), which he presents to Philander as a pledge of his love, in much the same spirit that Philander had earlier pledged his Silvia. Like the ring, Silvia is the gift that cements and the token that signifies relations between men.

Silvia's specular status in relations between men is neatly literalized by her frequent appearances in the text in male attire. It is, in fact, during the first of these episodes of cross-dressing that Octavio initially falls in love with her. Drag enhances Silvia's attractions as an object of male desire (she "never appear'd so charming and desirable" as when dressed as a man [123]), if for no other reason than that it enables her male admirers both to identify with the sexual conquests of the young cavalier whom she impersonates and to experience a certain rivalry with him. These at least are the peculiar pleasures of Octavio's experience: "*Octavio* every day saw the abundance of pleasure the little revenges of Love on those Womens hearts who had made before little conquests over him, and strove by all the gay presents he made young *Fillmond* (for so they call'd *Silvia,*) to make him appear unresistable to the Ladies, and while *Silvia* gave them new wounds, *Octavio* fail'd not to receive 'em too among the crow'd, till at last he became a confirm'd slave to the lovely unknown; and that which was yet more strange she captivated the Men no less than the Women" (127).

In the long run, however, cross-dressing has another—a productive as opposed to a merely specular—potential that Silvia in time learns to exploit with increasing skill and that goes beyond according her that freedom of physical movement and those other "little Priviledges . . . deny'd to Women" (126).[32] Over the course of her career, Behn's Ovidian letter writer undergoes a dazzling metamorphosis from corrupted innocence to triumphant depravity—a transformation that culminates in part 3 of the narrative in an exhilarating escapade in which she elevates the game of sexual conquest from a means of revenge into an art. Having become a consummate fiction maker and role player (as well as a wealthy courtesan who capitalizes on the weaknesses of unsuspecting men), she here undertakes as a "Frolick to divert herself" (*L-L,* 385–86) conquest of the heart of Don Alonzo, a young Spanish-born gentleman distinguished most significantly for being the only man ever to have succeeded in outdoing Philander at the game of inconstancy. When Alonzo boasts of having "reduced . . . to . . . a Lover" an unconquerable Dutch countess whose heart even Philander could not command, Silvia resolves to go him one better by determining to fix his own wandering heart on her (392). She succeeds in her determination by enacting a masquerade in which she plays both male and female parts: a handsome cavalier named Bellumere and his lovely sister, Mme *de____* .

By means of a ring that Alonzo gives to Bellumere as a pledge of male friendship and that Mme de ____ later vaunts upon her tour, Silvia deftly turns Bellumere into a suspected rival of Don Alonzo for her favors. She thus plays an interesting variation on the homosocial code whereby mistresses typically stand in as obligatory heterosexual displacements of prohibited objects of homoerotic male desire. By creating a male version of herself through which to lure her victim into a homoerotic attachment, she paradoxically ensures her own status as a primary object of desire instead of merely an intermediate term in a phallocentric sexual and symbolic economy. In this instance, she also cleverly turns Alonzo's imagined rival into a brother, to whose authority over the disposal of her favors she presents herself as determined to defer. Silvia imposes her own authority, that is, by means of the pretense of deferring to Bellumere's, thus creating a drama in which she at once reproduces and subverts the hierarchy of authority that informed her early relation with Philander. Both producing and controlling Alonzo's desire for her, she now manages her own circulation as a sign of femininity.

This episode makes stunningly clear the extent to which Silvia has appropriated Philander's performative strategies of symbolic deferral by the novel's end. As we have seen, the relation between sign and referent in Philander's garden escapade with Beralti following his alleged attack of impotence in part 1 is neither as stable nor as transparent as Gardiner suggests when she reads it as a simple externalization of the hero's demeaning impotence. Nor does it involve a simple masking of the "truth" of Philander's inherent dominance. It is, rather, a productive relation in which Philander consolidates his power by using theater to produce material effects. This, we might say, is his type of sorcery, the basis of that power to charm by which he creates effects in some instances as tangible as those wrought by philters upon the body of Brilljard or by alchemy on the heart and eyes of Cesario. For Behn, his performances are occasions for displacing the natural ground of the opposition between inner and outer experience, psyches and surfaces, artifice and authenticity. Philander treads an extraordinarily fluid line between role-playing and reality, dissembling so well at times that, as Behn's narrator notes late in the text, "he scarce knew himself that he did so" (344).

By the time Silvia encounters Don Alonzo, she has learned how to exploit the productive nature of performance so as to move beyond her status as a specular representation of male desire, a mere player in a drama controlled by men, both to create and to variously represent herself. She has not, however, always recognized the productive potential of her own radical deracination as a sign (a performer) of femininity. Although she has from the start intuited the insufficiency of the written word to express her soul completely, she is fairly confident initially of its ability to simulate, if not entirely to substitute for, presence. "While I Write," she declares in an early letter to Philander, "methinks I'm talking to thee, I tell thee thus my Soul, while thou methinks art all the while smiling and listening by; this is much easier than silent thought, and my Soul is never weary of this converse, and thus I wou'd speak a Thousand things, but that still, methinks words do not enough express my Soul" (37). Still a fairly naive reader, Silvia believes this insufficiency can be made up for by the supplement of presence, by merely adding voice to text: "to understand that right there requires looks; there is a Rhetorick in looks, in Sighs and silent touches that surpasses all! there is an Accent in the sound of words too, that gives a sense and soft meaning to little things, which of themselves are of trivial value, and insignificant; and by the cadence of the utterance may express a tenderness which their own meaning does not bear; by this I wou'd insinuate that the story of the heart cannot be so well told by this way as by presence and conversation" (37–38). A more savvy reader of Philander might by now have recognized the dangers of ventriloquism, which he betrays in his third letter when he describes the emptiness of his public performances: "I move about this unregarded world, appear every day in the great Senate House at Clubs, Caballs and private consultations . . . I say I appear indeed, and give my Voice in publick business, but oh my Heart more kindly is imployed" (20). But Silvia, though she sometimes doubts his word, still finds Philander's letters more reassuring than ominous. Clinging to an idealized notion of presence, she buys into the rhetorical opposition between private and public life on which Philander erects the fiction of his own sincerity.

While the Silvia of part 1 may still believe naively in the possibility of her own and others' authenticity ("I have no Arts Heav'n knows, no guile or double meaning in my soul, 'tis all plain native simplicity" [24]), her maid and "too fatal Councellor" (29) Melinda nevertheless detects her mistress's performative potential early on. In the letter she writes to Philander just before his fateful night of impotence, Melinda alludes to the late occurrence of "many ominous things" (52). Among these she cites an incident that has aroused suspicions in Silvia's mother regarding her daughter's romantic activities. Melinda presumably wants to alert Philander on the eve of his assignation with Silvia to the perils of heightened parental vigilance, but her letter also provides him with a warning glimpse of Silvia's budding semiotic education. It shows the heroine's incipient ability to exploit not just the dangerous excesses of script but also the dangerous supplementarity of presence and voice itself. While Silvia early laments the intransigence of her "guilty pen" (32), bemoaning the insidious tendency of writing to betray her best intentions, she here shows an almost instinctive urge to master the treachery of the letter and to exploit its openness as a form of self-defense. Discovered by her mother in the act of writing to Philander, physical evidence in hand, Silvia brilliantly avoids being implicated in her own guilt through an ingenious act of textual deferral. In the exigency of the moment, she concocts the fiction that she is writing as a surrogate for Melinda to Melinda's lover, using pseudonyms to protect *that* guilty "maid," and she adds demonstrative proof of her claim by, in effect, performing her own text aloud with an altered—an essentially ironic—emphasis. As Melinda reports, she "turned it . . . prettily into Burlesque Love *by her manner of reading it*" (53, emphasis added).

This cunning transformation of material fact into plausible fiction by creating a multiplicity of referents through the act of reading forms a stark contrast with the later example of Samuel Richardson's Clarissa Harlowe, who is characteristically victimized by the uncontrollable openness of her own letter texts. When Clarissa finally does learn to exploit the ambiguities of script, moreover, she can do so only by closing them around the referent of the father. Writing to Lovelace that she is "setting out with all diligence for [her] father's house," in her famous trick of lying truthfully, Clarissa points to a superabundance of father figures, not to an open field of interpretive possibility.[33] And indeed one can not help feeling that the imperatives of honesty and sincerity that control Clarissa's writing play a rather sinister role in determining the range of choices she is able to imagine for taking retributive action against Lovelace's treachery.[34] It is not until the topos of the daughter's guilty pen recurs in Frances Burney's *Evelina* or Jane Austen's *Lady Susan* that we again encounter an exploitation of the formal openness of the letter as subtle and subversive as the one Behn offers in this single episode from her text.

This scene, in which Silvia reads her own love letter as if she were only playacting the lover, resonates in several crucial ways throughout Behn's text. In one sense, it serves as a paradigm in small of Behn's novel as a whole—a figure, as it were, for the distancing effect of parody that Behn herself achieves at the level of narration through her characteristic cultivation of rhetorical excess. As the first instance in the narrative when Silvia instinctively plays the role of "maid," moreover, it foreshadows the freedom she will ultimately realize by abandoning the presupposition that she possesses a natural bedrock of desire and a core of stable self-identity. By introducing the possibility that Silvia's "authentic" letter text may be itself only a script—that the very text she generates as the sincere expression of her soul may be symptomatic of a role she plays but over which she does not have performative control—it exposes the radically contingent nature of her desire and the performative as opposed to natural basis of her subjectivity.

If Silvia's original letter text is merely an imitation of originality, and if presence and voice are not reliable markers of substance but dangerous forms of supplementarity, then the very possibility of an origin—of an authentic ground from which one's actions and one's utterances proceed—becomes problematic. In the space opened by these unsettling possibilities, Silvia is freed from the promise of an incestuous fulfillment of original desire into an open field of signifying possibility. Behn gestures toward this openness in the penultimate paragraph of her text, where she sends her heroine daily in search of new conquests "where e'er she shows the Charmer" (439). The physical body—that most corporeal of figures—finally emerges as the most unstable of all sites of meaning. The ultimate "charmer," it obliterates the very ground of truth and falsehood required for the enactment of personal authenticity. In Behn's world of apparently infinite displacements, there is finally no essence or original that is not constituted in the dialogics of performance or the contestations of power politics. Even so allegedly authenticating a gesture as incest is finally exposed as substituting for the law it would subvert.

Coda

Libertine rhetoric exalts the female as an iconic substitute for the father-king, promoting the flattering fiction that woman is the source of both desire and prohibition. "Glorious Woman! was born for command and Dominion," declares Philander, ". . . though custom has usurpt us the name of Rule over all." In fact, he insists, Silvia's sovereignty is the motive force for all his political ambitions. He seeks political empire only to be able to trade it for romantic slavery:

> [L]et me toyl to gain, but let *Silvia* Triumph and Reign, I ask no more . . . than the led slave at her Chariot Wheels, to gaze on my Charming Conqueress, and wear with joy her Fetters! oh how proud I shou'd be to see the dear Victor of my Soul so elevated, so adorn'd with Crowns and Sceptres at her feet, which I had won; to see her smiling on the adoring Crown, distributing her Glories to young waiting Princes. . . . Heavens! methinks I see the lovely Virgin in this state, her Chariot slowly driving through the multitude that press to gaze upon her, she drest like *Venus* richly gay and loose, her Hair and Robe blown by the flying Winds. (44–45)

By novel's close, Philander's vision of Silvia's triumph as spectacle (however disingenuously it has been offered) is realized, as the heroine, "drest in perfect Glory," is pursued by gazing crowds through the streets of Brussels (417), a rival of even Cesario's elegant mistress, Hermione. But unlike Hermione, who invests all her own ambition in Cesario's success only to meet her demise in his defeat, Silvia does not depend for her glory on Philander's toil and enterprise; she achieves it on her own.[35] She makes the punctilious Octavio an instrument of her revenge against Philander, and to that passion she eventually sacrifices him. By the end of the narrative, moreover, she has resourcefully managed to turn even Philander's servant Brilljard (originally deployed to maintain Philander's authority over her) to the promotion of her material interests. Now using Brilljard as a prop in her own self-serving schemes, she manipulates him (by once again exploiting a homosocial bond) into extorting an inheritance from the retired Octavio on the spurious promise of her own penitence and retirement. Then, "impatient to be seen on the *Toure,* and in all publick Places," she promptly furnishes herself with "new Coach and Equipage, and . . . lavish . . . Clothes and Jewels" (414–15).

The irony of Behn's political defense of Royalism is that it ends with the triumph not only of the king but also of the woman who most quintessentially embodies unrecuperated female defiance of male supremacy. Cesario's rebellion fails and Philander opportunistically embraces monarchy, while in a savagely ironic twist on this double defeat of the Whig cause, Silvia makes good the libertine promise of female sovereignty. At one level Behn seems to want to point to divinely appointed kingship as the ultimate locus of truth and authority—the original object of worship of which all other objects of desire are failed imitations and empty substitutes. But the figure at center stage in *Love-Letters between a Nobleman and his Sister,* the one that absorbs the reader's gaze, is not the king at all but the spectacularly protean body of Silvia. That this body is also figured without much comment for the better part of Behn's narrative not as the virgin body Philander invokes but as an eroticized maternal presence, a curiously denaturalized point of physical origin in the shape of a pregnant eros, is perhaps not so very insignificant a detail after all, so thoroughly disruptive as it is of any binary relation between displacement and origin.[36] Much as Silvia signifies the physical power to generate nameless and presumably endless substitutions, so Behn proliferates meanings beyond the binary frame that constitutes incest as a counter to patriarchal law, or legitimate kingship as an ultimate site of meaning and of power.

CHAPTER FOUR

Guarding the Succession of the (E)state

Incest and the Dangers of Representation in Delarivier Manley's *The New Atalantis*

> INTELLIGENCE: 'Tis impossible a Prince can come to the knowledge of things but by Representation; and they are always represented according to the Sense of the Representator; . . . yet, how is it possible to prevent it?
>
> DELARIVIER MANLEY, *The New Atalantis*

Guardians and Wards

Several stories of incest or quasi-incest punctuate *The New Atalantis*, the popular Tory scandal chronicle of 1709 in which Delarivier Manley satirizes the duke of Marlborough and a variety of other prominent Whigs. The most sensational, and therefore perhaps the most memorable, of these incestuous intrigues is a tale of fatal attachment between siblings, the orphaned twins Polydore and Urania, which occupies the early pages of volume 2 and to which I turn in the final pages of this chapter. Wards of their maternal aunt, a baroness who sequesters them, Polydore and Urania yield under the influence of their confinement and a faulty education to a mutual passion culminating first in pregnancy and eventually in their tragic death. Consanguinity, however, is by no means the only ground of incest in Manley's text. In fact, no incestuous relation occurs more prominently or more frequently in *The New Atalantis* than that between male guardians and their female wards. The most notable accounts of such relations include the narratives of Charlot and the Duke and of Hernando and Louisa in volume 1, and Delia's sustained relation of her bigamous seduction by Don Marcus in volume 2. In the last of these tales, generally considered an autobiographical rendering of Delarivier's own unfortunate marriage to John Manley, consanguinity continues to play a role, since the guardian to whom Delia is bigamously united is (as was Manley's guardian) her first cousin. But blood relatedness is not primarily what gives this story its illicit, incestuous charge. Since the time of Henry VIII, the marriage of first cousins had not been prohibited by either civil or canon law. The incestuousness of the marriage between Delia and Don Marcus derives not from the fact of their second-degree consanguinity but from the status of their union as *a representation* of another kind of bond—namely, marriage between a father and his daughter.

Even so forward-looking a thinker as John Fry, writing at midcentury in defense of men's marriages to their deceased wives' sisters, thought marriages between guardians and wards as unnatural as those between parents and children. Arguing on a principle of analogy similar to that of parity of reason, Fry advances this as a view so universally acknowledged that it requires no defense:

> . . . as Marriage in the right ascending and descending Line, is . . . prohibited by the Law of Nature; so, *proportionably* all such as stand in the Place, or are the Representatives of such; as all Fathers and Mothers-in-law, and all that are appointed Guardians, with those that are left under their Care (at least as long as they are so under their Care, and till their Trust is legally discharged) are to be looked on as *effectually* barred from marrying one another. This hath been set forth by the Learned in different Lights, and is so plain, and I think so intirely agreed on all Hands, that I shall insist no longer on it.[1]

Similarly, Justice William Blackstone describes the relation of guardian and ward as bearing "a very near resemblance" to that between parent and child, from which it is "plainly derived . . . : the guardian being . . . a temporary parent."[2]

When Manley published *The New Atalantis* in 1709, this definition of guardians as parental representatives—with its concomitant assumption of the incestuousness of sexual relations between guardians and wards—was actually of fairly recent date. Late-seventeenth-century changes in guardianship law—including, most importantly, Charles II's institution of the practice of testamentary guardianship[3]—rearticulated the legal relationships among property inheritance, authority, and representation in a way that significantly affected the nature of the relationship between fathers and guardians on the one hand

and between guardians and wards on the other. Marking a shift in economic power from king to private-property-owning father, these changes provide an indispensable context for understanding the logic of Manley's treatment of guardian-ward incest in her text—particularly as it pertains to the larger problem of succession. *The New Atalantis* marks a complex moment in British literary and political history. Offering a Tory history of the Exclusion Crisis from the vantage point of Queen Anne's reign under the Whigs, it emerged at a time when monarchical power was becoming at once increasingly decentralized and increasingly dependent on the representative function of early ministerial governments. This was also the era of the emergence of what Jürgen Habermas has called the bourgeois public sphere, a time when political authority was undergoing a process of redistribution from the body of the king to a public body more broadly and more plurally conceived, and when the very concept of representation was expanding to include new political as well as aesthetic meanings.[4] Representation becomes a key point of connection between Manley's treatment of incest in *The New Atalantis* and her Tory critique of Whig individualism. Indeed, *The New Atalantis* draws extended metaphoric links between the familial dangers posed by the new, representative status of guardians and the national dangers inherent in modern representative governments—dangers that manifest themselves repeatedly in *The New Atalantis* in narratives of thwarted succession. At the same time, Manley herself undertakes to exploit those dangerous powers of representation through an intricate articulation of stories of public and private guardianship in which her own history as an incestuously abused ward plays a pivotal role.

This chapter begins by examining seventeenth-century legal changes surrounding guardianship as a basis for understanding the role that representation came to play in establishing the incestuous potential of guardian-ward relations after 1660. It then proceeds to read the episodes of guardian-ward incest in *The New Atalantis* as succession stories implicated in the text's larger concern with the problem of national succession. Its aim, ultimately, is to illuminate the complex strategies whereby Delarivier Manley simultaneously exposes and takes advantage of the de-centered representational possibilities inherent in emergent print culture to authorize her own politically charged project of self-representation as a female ward and a victim of incestuous abuse. At the end of the chapter, I turn to Manley's narrative of Polydore and Urania. This plot, I argue, reconfigures the guardian-ward incest plots that unfold elsewhere in the text, feminizing the figure of the corrupt guardian and displacing incest from a guardian-ward to a sibling dyad. It is, as I go on to demonstrate in subsequent chapters, a plot configuration that recurs in a variety of forms in prose fiction published after 1740 that mobilizes incest as a trope in probing the powers and the dangers of representation.

Guardianship and the Law

Prior to 1660, wardships were a prerogative of the Crown.[5] As feudal landlord, the king had historically leased the greatest part of his landed wealth to his subjects in return for military service, such tenure in chivalry historically having been, in Blackstone's words, "[t]he first, most universal, and . . . most honourable species of tenure" in the realm. Should a tenant by knight-service die leaving an underage heir incapable of performing such service, his land ultimately reverted to the king along with rights to the wardship of his heir. Such wardship included both supervision of the child's education into a good citizen and worthy tenant and the right to dispose of the child in marriage. Nonmilitary tenures, which accounted for a much smaller proportion of lands, were called tenures in socage and consisted of those lands held by any services or duties other than knight-service, such as by homage, fealty, rent, or husbandry. Feudal lords held no wardship over the minor heir orphaned by the death of a tenant by socage. Since, as Blackstone explains, "in this tenure no military or other personal service [is] required, there is no occasion for the lord to take the profits, in order to provide a proper substitute for his infant tenant: but his nearest relation (to whom the inheritance cannot descend) shall be his guardian in socage, and have the custody of his land and body till he arrives at the age of fourteen."[6]

Having lost its original function as a guarantee of national security, knight-service was by the sixteenth century only nominally a military tenure.[7] The Tudors nevertheless retained the practice of royal wardship as a strictly revenue-generating institution. When Henry VIII assumed the throne, the gift, lease, and sale by the Crown of the wardship of orphans and lunatics had long been an important royal prerogative and a substantial source of national income; however, Henry's formal establishment in 1540 of the Court of Wards and Liveries, a centralized administrative mechanism for overseeing the disposal of wardships and marriages, dramatically increased the number of prerogative wardships as well as the royal profits accruing from the sale of orphans.[8] The power and profits of the Court of Wards grew rapidly during Elizabeth's reign, its income accounting for nearly one-half of the total revenues of the Crown under Charles I.[9]

Within this essentially feudal system of property inheritance, kinship played a remarkably insignificant role. Because the Crown typically sold wardships to the highest bidders, mothers and other relatives of orphans, though they sometimes tried, were often unable to compete financially for the wardship of their own kin. Guardians and wards within this system were thus, typically, not related to each other, a circumstance of which guardians commonly took economic advantage either by marrying their wards to one of their own children or by marrying them themselves. Where the tie between guardian and ward was economic but not familial, such marriages were, by definition, nonincestuous.[10]

This circumstance changed radically when in 1660 Charles II legally abolished the Court of Wards, converting all military into socage tenures and granting fathers free testamentary disposal of the custody of their minor children. By the time of the Restoration, long-standing resistance to the Court of Wards among the propertied classes had already significantly eroded its influence. There had been an aborted attempt to abolish it under James I, and a parliamentary ordinance for its dissolution was enacted in 1645–46, an action reaffirmed under Cromwell in 1656. The Crown, however, had never ratified such measures, so that, had the political climate allowed, Charles might have revived the court when the monarchy was restored. Instead, he effected what amounted to a concession of the royal prerogative to livery and wardship, providing in Statute 12 Car.II.c.24 "that all sorts of tenures, held of the king or others, be turned into free and common socage."[11] In Blackstone's view, this abolition of the most oppressive of the feudal tenures "was a greater acquisition to the civil property of this kingdom than even *magna carta* itself" (2:5.77).

But, as Cheryl Nixon has recently shown, 12 Car.II.c.24 made a provision of perhaps even greater significance when it vested fathers with the statutory power to designate testamentary guardians for their children. In theory, the shift from a system of land tenure by knight-service to a system of universal socage tenure meant that, instead of automatically becoming a ward of the Crown, an underage orphan automatically became a ward of the closest relative who did not stand to inherit his or her estate. According to the traditional common law definition of socage tenure, such wardship legally ended when the ward arrived at the age of fourteen, at which time he was deemed capable of choosing his own guardian until the age of twenty-one. The father played no role in the designation of the guardian. In order to minimize the likelihood that youthful heirs might perpetrate their own economic ruin by the improvident choice of guardians (or in the case of young women, husbands), however, Charles stipulated in his statute that a father could appoint a guardian for any unmarried child under the age of twenty-one at the time of his death.[12] This stipulation complicated the common law practice of automatically locating the guardian within the family, replacing it with a statutory law that "enshrine[d] personal choice" by authorizing "the individual's ability to determine what kin or non-kin he consider[ed] most suitable for his child's surrogate parent."[13] Both the older, "feudal, politically-driven system of institutionalized guardianship" and the more modern, privatized "family-driven" system of testamentary guardianship, Nixon acknowledges, were essentially economically motivated (3). With 12 Car.II.c.24, however, the locus of economic power over wards and their property had shifted from the king or the royally assigned guardian to the father. "For the first time, the property-owning father is given legal control over the fate of his children after his death. The father, foreseeing a time when he will no longer have power over his family, can perpetuate some of his present power by using the last will to create the testamentary guardian who will *stand in his place*. The last will becomes a private, self-created means of preserving paternal agency" (4, emphasis added). In this system, that is, the guardian functions *in loco parentis* as the father's surrogate or representative.

In contrast to the feudal system of court-appointed guardianship, which "recognized that the guardian secured a ward in order to gain access to the child's estate and income,"[14] moreover, statutory guardianship was erected on a principle of trust. In both systems, the guardian's official responsibility was custodial: to manage the orderly descent of property by protecting the ward's estate until such time as the ward either married or passed out of minority. Income from the estate was to be used for the care, education, or other benefit of the ward, not for the personal aggrandizement of the guardian. As H. E. Bell observes, however, although in the earlier system the Court of Wards was quick to intervene legally on a ward's behalf for any infringement on his or her property, its motivation for safeguarding a ward's interests was typically more "profit-making" than "protective."[15] Under the Court of Wards, a guardian purchased a wardship with "the tacit understanding that he could abuse [his] economic powers with little fear of reprisal."[16] By contrast, the testamentary guardian who took advantage of the privileged access bestowed on him by a father to a ward's body and estate violated both a personal and a legal trust. With 12 Car.II.c.24, the father acquired unprecedented control over the identity of his child's future guardian; at the same time, however, he became more dependent than ever before on that individual's good faith as "the trustee of the family's economic future."[17] What had formerly been a primarily fiscal arrangement between a king and the tenant who acquired one of his wardships had now become a privatized relation of trust between men wherein, at one and the same time, fathers were unwontedly privileged and at risk.

Guardianship in The New Atalantis

Manley's treatment of guardian-ward incest in *The New Atalantis* deftly dramatizes the instabilities of paternal privilege in this relation. Each of the three key episodes of guardian-ward incest in the text depicts the social and economic ruin of a young woman by a male guardian who puts his own libidinal needs above the interests of either his ward or the father under whose authority he serves. Two of these episodes foreground the issue of betrayed paternal trust. All are stories of failed succession in which orphaned heiresses function as the bearers of family promise, conduits through whom family honor and property are to descend. In the stories of Charlot and Delia, ruin of the ward is tantamount to the dishonor and disempowerment of the father. In this sense, the female ward in these stories becomes a figure for the dependency of deceased fathers on testamentary guardians. One might even say that incestuous heterosexual relations between guardians and wards double in these accounts as sites of homosocial struggle in which guardians violate paternal trust by usurping the posthumous rights of fathers over daughters.

The orphaned Charlot [Stuarta Werburge Howard], a noble heiress with a dowry amounting to forty thousand crowns (such that "there was almost nothing but what she might pretend to"), is left by her father in the custody of his friend, a widowed duke.[18] Though he is modeled on the person of William Bentinck, an exceptionally trusted friend and favorite of the childless William III, Charlot's guardian—in keeping with his Whig allegiances—does not honor every trust. Overcome by physical desire for his ward, by a passionate urgency that assumes the force of ruthless need, he is moved to "possess" her despite his role as "Trustee of her Family" (1:75/1:347) and despite "who she [is], the Daughter of his Friend! . . . who had at his Death left the charge of her Education to him!" (1:58/1:330). Charlot loves the Duke "as a Benefactor, a Father" (1:60/1:332), and he takes full advantage of that confidence. Though the Duke initially uses his supervisory power over Charlot's education to raise her as a pattern of female virtue, even designing her as a match for his own son, he in time becomes so tormented by his own desire for her that his sexual desperation eventually overpowers his sense of duty or self-interest. He now uses his unregulated access to his ward's mind and body to corrupt her, seducing her with Ovid's story of the incestuous love of Myrrha for her father, Cinyras. Bestowing unwonted favors that seem to distinguish her from his own children, among whom she has grown up, the Duke flatters young Charlot's sense of self-importance, even holding out the promise of eventually making her his wife. Finally, unable to "contend with a Fire that consumed him, he must be gratified, or die" (1:70/1:342); and so, when Charlot's defenses are down, he brutally rapes her:

> he nail'd her down to the Bed with Kisses; his love and resolution gave him a double vigour, he wou'd not stay a moment to capitulate with her; whilst yet her surprise made her doubtful of his designs, he took advantage of her confusion to accomplish 'em; neither her prayers, tears, nor struglings, cou'd prevent him, but in her Arms he made himself a full amends for all those pains he had suffer [sic] for her.
>
> Thus was *Charlot* undone! thus ruin'd by him that ought to have been her Protector! (1:72/1:344)

Although the Duke does not succeed easily in appeasing the injured Charlot, she does eventually yield to his flattery and professions of urgent love, "espous[ing] his Crime, by sealing his Forgiveness" (1:72/1:344). In the end, perhaps predictably, the Duke—having gratified his lust—abandons his ward for another woman—her own friend and confidante [Martha Jane Bentinck, née Temple, countess of Portland]; and Charlot—with nothing any longer to pretend to—is left in a "Scene of Horror, Sorrow, and Repentance," amid the ruins of her "shipwrack[ed] . . . Honour," a "true Landmark: to warn all . . . Virgins" who believe "the Vows and pretended Passion of Mankind" (1:83/1:355).

Like the Duke, Hernando Volpone [William, first Earl Cowper] takes advantage of the privileged access that guardianship gives him to his ward, Louisa [Elizabeth Culling]. Married by his father to a woman whom he hates [Judith Booth], Hernando resolves to seduce Louisa both to gratify his lust and to injure his wife, who, having "a great kindness for" her husband's ward, has devoted herself to the young woman's moral education (1:214/1:486). Hernando is as amorous as Charlot's Duke but more unscrupulous in his pursuit of selfish pleasures. Although Louisa has no large fortune, her beauty and innocence represent a personal challenge for him: an opportunity to "blow up her Chastity"—which seems invincible—and, in the process, to undermine his wife's careful tutelage (1:225/1:497). Like the Duke, Hernando is inflamed by the "little Freedoms . . . permitted . . . him" as a guardian and takes "all occasions for those pretty Liberties" (1:216/1:488). Like the Duke, moreover, he distinguishes his ward with his attentions: "*Mademoiselle Louisa* found nothing so obliging as her Guardian, what ever she requested was granted; what ever she but seem'd to wish, she enjoy'd. . . . [H]er Bed-side was not refus'd him when he us'd to view her there in a Morning, he would fix his sparkling wishing Eyes, cross his Arms, and sigh . . . ; he would alway [*sic*] affect to sit near her, to take the Place she had quitted; to touch what she had but touch'd" (1:215-16/1:487–88). Just as Charlot responds gratefully to the Duke's flattery, Louisa thinks "her self oblig'd by these Distinctions; they even [create] a sort of Gratitude" (1:216/1:488). But Hernando makes no move until incited by jealousy. When an advantageous prospect in the form of a suitor—a relation of his lady, handsome, young, and amorous—threatens "to take [Louisa] from his very Table" (1:217/1:489), Hernando shows where his priorities lie: not with his ward's best interests but with his own selfish desires. Faced with the loss of Louisa's dependency on him, Hernando manipulates his rival, Wilmot, into defending the lawfulness of polygamy in Louisa's presence, thus ruining Wilmot's credit with Louisa, only to turn around and himself artfully seduce her into a bigamous mock-marriage. When Lady Volpone discovers the affair, she is incensed and upbraids Louisa, accusing her not just of adultery but of incest (the seduction not simply of a male guardian but of the husband of one who "had been as a Mother to her") and parricide ("since 'twas impossible [Lady Volpone] could survive the loss of [her husband's] Affection" [1:236–37/1:508–9]). In the end, Hernando gives Louisa two illegitimate children and venereal disease, from which she dies just at the moment when she becomes "a considerable Heiress" by her brother's death (1:244/1:516). As there are no legal heirs, Louisa's premature death marks another aborted economic future.

The tales of Louisa and Charlot, however, are mere rehearsals for the story Delia tells much later on. Indeed, by virtue of its autobiographical firstness, Delia's narrative might even be considered a kind of prototype of theirs. Incorporating key aspects of both earlier stories, it is of all the tales Manley presents of incestuous commerce between guardians and wards the most broadly "representative" in that it most clearly situates the guardian-ward incest plot within a larger political, historical, and moral frame.[19] Like both Charlot and Louisa, Delia yields to the advances of her guardian out of a sense of gratitude and abject dependency. Because Don Marcus has cared for her during a life-threatening illness, Delia feels a sense of obligation to yield to his amorous importunities (2:184/1:716); with her father and her brother both dead, he alone is "the nearest remaining Relation of a Man" to guide and protect her (2:188/1:720). Like Louisa, Delia is bigamously married in a private ceremony that, she later learns, is fraudulent.

Don Marcus's relationship with Delia's father [Roger Manley] casts the cousin at once as father figure and sibling to Delia, thus multiplying the story's incestuous possibilities. On the one hand, Don Marcus's relation to his uncle is fraternal; as Delia declares, Don Marcus "was about two or three and twenty Years older than I was, and as I have often heard him say himself, a *Man,* and with my Father in the next Chamber, when I was born" (2:185/1:717). On the other hand, he is a surrogate son to the chevalier. Don Marcus thus occupies the position of older brother to Delia, except that legally (as her father's collateral rather than direct descendent) he is subordinate to her in the line of inheritance. His corruption of his ward and subsequent squandering of her fortune, which now "was in his Hands" (2:188/1:720), is thus a clear disruption of the order of familial succession. According to Delia's account, Don Marcus recognizes the full enormity of his crime:

> my Fathers Form perpetually haunt[ed] his troubled Dreams, reproaching him as a Traitor to that Trust, which in the Pangs of Death, he had repos'd in him; and as a double Villain, casting an impure, an indelible Stain upon the Honour of a Family, which was so nearly his own: Representing to his tortour'd Imagination, all the Expence ond [sic] Care he had of his Education; more like a Father, than an Uncle, for which he had so ungratefully rewarded him, in the ruin of a Daughter, who, but for him, might have flourish'd Fair, an Ornament to his House, at least not a Reproach to it. (2:187/1:719)

Don Marcus violates filial as well as homosocial obligation. As the figure of Intelligence later points out, he commits an inextricable complication of offenses (as a guardian, a man, a friend, a son, a nephew, and a type of ward himself) "in corrupting a young Creature under his Care, so near a Relation, the Daughter of a Father to whom he had a thousand Obligations, to whom he ow'd his Education, who honour'd him with so many Marks of his Indearments, and receiv'd by him into the nearest Trust." His marriage to Delia obstructs "her Advancement in the World," but more seriously it corrupts her innocence, thus undermining her father's efforts to preserve, through her, the true principles of Tory morality (2:193–94/1:725–26).

In this respect, Don Marcus represents the perfect antithesis of the chevalier, who embodies a fading cultural ideal of royal service. A military man, Delia's father is represented as the vestige of a feudal past based on respect for familial as well as political authority, but giving the latter clear priority. His ancestral estate, having been "lavish'd in the Royal Service" during the late civil wars, was inadequately restored with the monarchy as a consequence of precisely the sorts of Whig political pressures that led to such Restoration compromises as Charles's decision to dismantle the Court of Wards (2:182/1:714). Nevertheless, despite his "suffering Loyalty," the chevalier has attempted through his nephew to compensate the "Error in Education" that caused his own brother, Don Marcus's father, to join "the Factious Party" and become "an unpitied Example of Rebellion" (2:182/1:714). Don Marcus's corruption of Delia marks the chevalier's ultimate failure to stem the erosion of Tory values. The treacherous and opportunistic nephew not only squanders her estate, leaving her with an illegitimate child and an indelibly tainted reputation, but, in so doing, he thoroughly undermines his uncle's moral legacy. Delia's story thus sets the plot of guardian-ward incest within the broader political frame of party conflict. Offering a Tory view of the dangers of emergent individualism and the inherent precariousness of the private-property-owning father, it provides a context for understanding *The New Atalantis*'s earlier episodes of sexual encounter between female wards and their paternal representatives. The very empowerment of the father within an individualist economy produces the seeds of its own corruption in the predatory figure of the testamentary guardian.

Guardianship of the Monarchy

At the level of the family, then, guardian-ward incest figures the economic empowerment of fathers as dangerously subject to the unruly sexuality of male guardians who disrupt lines of succession and disable rather than facilitate the descent of property. But Manley does not limit her use of the guardian-ward incest trope to the realm of domestic life; she uses it to engage the problem of succession at the level of the monarchy as well. Through a complex crossing of the private tragedies of Charlot, Louisa, and Delia on the one hand and the public history of the descent of British sovereign power on the other, she puts in play a constellation of metaphoric relations linking fathers, wards, and guardians to monarchs and ministers. The Exclusion Crisis offered a national narrative of disrupted succession for which the more personal dramas of ruined wards seem to serve as allegories. Manley plays on the traditional, patriarchalist metaphor of the king as father of the nation in which the family is divine in origin and the authority of the father is absolute. But she also develops a corollary association between modern guardians and ministers, establishing a complex, extended analogy between the power testamentary guardians have in a privatized system of land ownership to imperil the authority of the fathers they represent and the powerful but dangerous influence courtiers and favorites have over monarchs in early modern ministerial governments.

This analogy first emerges in a short sequence bridging Charlot's story and that of Madame de St. Amant. Lady Intelligence escorts her listeners into the palace where the body of King Henriquez [William III] lies in state, but to the party's great astonishment, the king's body is unattended: "all was a Desart; the numerous Croud of Guards and Attendance, nay even his menial Servants were vanish'd." Such circumstances, Intelligence explains, are "the way of the World": "Alas! this is nothing new, were you to peruse History, you wou'd find few faithful to the Dead. I have read of Kings that have dy'd in peace, amidst a great and flourishing People, yet have not found any to bestow the decent Rites of Washing or Covering to the Royal Carkass, till the Embalmers, who are paid for what they do, come two or three Days after, to find if 'tis time for them to fall to work" (1:84–85/1:356–57). Like dead fathers, dead kings leave their estates in jeopardy. They cannot count on the loyalty of former favorites. Courtiers who celebrated the king when he was alive now "run to make their Court to the new Successor" [in this case Anne]. Nor do they hesitate to keep the wealth of their former master from going where it belongs. "This very Morning," Intelligence recounts, "the youngest and most beloved of all the Favourites [Arnold Joost van Keppel, earl of Albermarle], as soon as ever he saw that his Master cou'd not live, accepted of the Key he gave him to his strong Box, to secure for himself, in Bills and Gold, Seventy eight thousand Crowns, which was all the personal Wealth the Monarch was possess'd of: His extreme Sorrow for losing so good a Prince did not prevent him from doing all that was necessary to hinder that Money from falling into the Successor's Hands, to whom of right it belong'd" (1:84–85/1:356–57). It is difficult not to read this account of Albermarle's pursuit of personal gain over the interests of the king's successor, coming as it does in the immediate wake of Charlot's story, as a variant of the Duke's violation of his responsibilities as the guardian of his friend's estate. Like Charlot, the king's successor is simultaneously courted and cheated of her rightful inheritance.

It is not only fathers, however, who have a metaphorical relation to sovereignty in *The New Atalantis*'s tropological scheme. Through the topos of inconstancy, Manley also activates the traditional courtly convention whereby heterosexual love is figured as a relation of dominance in which women (as objects of desire and admiration) hold sovereign power over men. What are the implications of this figure? Delia and Henriquez are both victims of the inconstancy of men over whom they formerly held sway. The infidelity of the Duke to Charlot once the loss of her virginity ends her empire over him becomes, like his infidelity to her deceased father, a figure for the infidelity of courtiers to dead kings. The romance trope, however, cuts both ways. Manley plays on the courtly exaltation of women even as she exposes its illusory ground. Under a Whig regime, patriarchs, royal or domestic, are like seduced and abandoned women, flattered and betrayed by those whose charge it is to represent and serve them.

This topos of inconstancy, with its tropological identification of women and monarchs, reemerges in the story of Utopia and goes far to explain Manley's gendered allegory of the Protestant succession, where in a phantasmatic reversal, succession descends exclusively through the women, who (like British Protestants) alone are "capable of the Crown" (2:118/1:650). Where Charlot earlier stands a "true Landmark" to virgins who believe the flattering lies of men (1:83/1:355), the Princess Ormia [James II] here emerges a "fatal Sea-Mark" to warn monarchs of the dangers of succumbing to the flattery of favorites (2:142/1:674). Ormia herself is guilty of inconstancy in endeavoring to change the succession to masculine [i.e., Catholic] (2:119/1:651); and she is the victim of inconstancy when, after flattering her "wretched Thirst of Arbitrary Power" (2:142/1:674), her followers (of whom the most notable is the Marquis de Caria [the duke of Marlborough]) desert her. Ormia's error has been allowing the *"Pride* and *Avarice* of *Favourites"* to blind her to the fact that a monarch is "made for his People, and not his People for him" (2:158–59/1:690–91). Ormia, that is, ceases to represent her people adequately when, instead of giving all her subjects an "equal Title to the *Benefit* of [her] *Attributes,"* she allows a few favorites to "[appropriate] the Royal *Ear"* (2:159/1:691). In much the same fashion, the monarchy under Olympia [Anne] is "reduced to an *Oligarchy.* A Council of *six"*; sovereign authority is undermined by the usurping power of a few who leave Olympia only the appearance of rule, having raised "a Government among themselves within the Sovereignty" (2:151–52/1:683–84). In such a government, sovereign authority is no longer concentrated in the body of a single monarch but is dispersed among a cadre of ministers who purport to "represent" the nation's interests but who in fact pursue their own. Such ministers violate their public trust as guardians of the succession when they "[repre-

sent] things through their *false, mischievous,* or *flattering* Glass" (2:159/1:691).
To Manley, Whig parliamentary politics—by dispersing—compromises the
power of the Crown, much as testamentary guardianship—while appearing to
extend paternal authority—ultimately compromises patriarchal power. In Manley's narrative economy, ministers and favorites are, like testamentary guardians, signs of a de-centered and destabilized authority—figures for the dangerous supplementarity of representation itself.

Manley's metaphoric yoking of legal guardians and royal ministers is a complex but telling gesture for a Tory writer whose father's death (portending a
tragic familial aftermath) occurred in the same year that the Glorious Revolution disrupted the Stuart succession and deposed the last of England's feudal
kings. At the very moment when Manley herself is delivered into the hands of
an unscrupulous guardian, England becomes the charge of the Whigs. Indeed,
so profound is the force of this conceit for Manley that she is ultimately moved
to imagine Anne's story as a rehabilitated version of her own. In her allegorical
rendering of Anne's reign under the Whigs (published months before the Tories
rose to power), a pregnant Olympia dies in childbed, leaving as heir to the crown
an infant daughter, the ward of her husband [George of Denmark] and Don
Geronimo de Haro [Robert Harley], both of whom she appoints regents while
"intrusting the Care of her [daughter's] Education wholly to the Conduct of . . .
Hilaria [Abigail Masham]" (2:153/1:685). Thus is the Crown—figured here as an
orphaned, female minor—"delivered" from the corrupt influence of the Whigs,
as it had come to be embodied in the Princess Olympia, each of whose favorites
subsequently meets his or her own tragic fate.[20] Manley deploys a feminized
version of the traditional trope of the "King's Two Bodies" in her allegory to offer
a wishful rendering of England's political future.[21] Through her phantasmatic
account of the death of Anne, who in fact had no surviving heirs, she effects a
figurative separation of the weak, corruptible person of the human monarch
from the idealized and incorruptible royal body—the body politic. In the death
of Anne, one might say, Manley kills off the "body natural" of the monarch in
order to save or restore the soul of the monarchy, figured here as the infant ward
of proper and trustworthy guardians. Unlike her immediate predecessor, William, Anne is figured as a generative force in advancing the succession.

Guardianship, Representation, and the Woman Writer

I have argued that, thematically, Manley locates the root of Whig corruption
in an excessive reliance on the privileged power of the sign in a system of repre-

sentation unregulated by any stable or centralized moral or political authority. Such representational unruliness manifests itself politically in *The New Atalantis* in the excessive power of courtiers over kings or of testamentary guardians over fathers; but it also works at the discursive level in the rampant circulation of stories about real people and events in a world where signs, having gained primacy over their referents, instead of simply imitating the truth have become dangerously productive of it.

And yet nothing partakes more fully of such semiotic instability than the narrative strategies Manley herself deploys to represent this crisis of substitutions. Like guardians and royal ministers, who figure the destabilization of authority because of their representative status as stand-ins for fathers and for kings respectively, Manley's stories of guardian-ward incest are themselves nothing less than stand-ins for or textual variants of one another. Even the one story that Manley posits as the type and original of all the others, the apparently grounding narrative of her own victimization, bears a precarious relationship to truth. In it, Manley's fictional counterpart, Delia, confronts a textual version of herself over whose circulation she has had little or no control by offering another, an ostensibly truer, version of events. But a certain slippage occurs in the relation between representation and referent when Delia identifies herself as "wanting of Fourteen, without any *Deceit* or *Guess* of it in others" (2:184/1:716) at the time of her bigamous marriage to Don Marcus, since Delarivier was in fact at least fifteen at the time of her father's death and at least seventeen when she married John Manley.[22] Why is minority conferred on Delia here? Is the discrepancy in age between Delia and Delarivier simply an aspect of Manley's project of self-vindication—her way of absolving Delia (and by extension herself) from responsibility for her own actions and thereby ensuring that the reader knows where in this story of "extreme *Youth* and *Innocence*" (2:181/1:713) to locate moral culpability?[23] This would be a plausible explanation if it were not for the fact that Delarivier technically required no such vindication; Roger Manley's testamentary designation of a guardian for his daughter would automatically have denied her the legal right to choose either her own guardian or her husband until the age of twenty-one, in effect extending her minority well beyond the usual age of legal discretion. Delia's minority is thus gratuitous with respect to any attempt Manley might be making to forestall an accusation of poor judgment on her part. Could its function simply be to dramatize the always already unstable relation of writing to truth?

Manley and Delia both seem mindful of the inherent precariousness of the project of self-representation, Delia in her appeal to the persuasive force of the Grand Druid's eloquence to authorize her tale, and Manley in her decision to frame her narrative at every point by voices not her own. The moral but sometimes overly judgmental figures of Astrea and Virtue and the voluble but informative and entertaining figures of Intelligence and Mrs. Nightwork are all versions of Manley herself, though limited in their referentiality by a certain representational excess. Manley seems to understand that stories always circulate in a contested discursive space—indeed, that knowledge is always also a form of power. As Intelligence avers, there is no more defense against the corruption of knowledge than against the corruption of favorites and ministers: "alas!" she declares, ". . . 'Tis impossible a Prince can come to the knowledge of things but by Representation; and they are always represented according to the Sense of the Representator; either Avarice, Revenge, or Favour, are their Motive, and yet, how is it possible to prevent it?" (1:204/1:476). The most representative aspect of Delia's story finally may be its metadiscursive figuration of its own status as an allegory of representation.[24] But even as Delia's minority signals the inherently interested character of representation, it demonstrates Manley's determination to use the circumstances of her own life as a representative trope to foreground the broadly political implications of her personal experience. The value of her own story, she suggests, extends beyond the local details of her individual case to a more general critique of modern patriarchy under the Whigs. As the case of a generic ward, Delia's story evinces that the destabilization of patriarchal power within a decentralized sovereignty rendered the female ward a peculiarly vulnerable site of cultural conflict.

For Manley, in other words, though the project of self-representation may be precarious, it is not impossible. The very crisis of authority that at once privileged and threatened the private-property-owning father also opened a discursive space for the woman writer. Manley inserts herself into that space both as a public actor (endeavoring to restore the soul of the monarchy by championing the Tory cause) and as a private citizen (an orphaned female ward incestuously ruined by corrupt representation in the form of a predatory father surrogate). In this dual capacity, if not by virtue of it, she challenges Whig notions of the perfect separability of public and private life in a critique that distinguishes her particular intervention into the public sphere as a political writer. In her crossing of domestic dramas, including her own, with the public history of the accession of Queen Anne, she produces both a new kind of political writing and a new kind of fiction—that hybrid, the British scandal chronicle—erected on the understanding that activities that go on in private spaces *do* have public consequences, and vice versa. The corruption that pervades the world of *The New Atalantis* proceeds both from the infiltration of royal spaces by private individuals with private interests (those who, like the Marquis and Marchioness de Caria [John and Sarah Churchill], gain privileged physical and psychological access to the monarch) and from the impact of public actions (the privatization of guardianship, for example) on domestic life. The two spheres—the public and the private—are not simply analogs of one another, Manley suggests; they are mutually constitutive and profoundly interimplicated.

Like the Utopian fiction of Olympia/Anne's infant heir, Delia's minority activates the tropological convention of the "King's Two Bodies." As Kantorowicz explains, within the corporational concept of the monarchy represented by this trope, the Crown was conceived as a perpetual minor. As such, it enjoyed all the privileges of an underage person within the conventions of early English law, which declared a ward's property inalienable and the ward invulnerable to any disinherison consequent upon a guardian's neglect. The association of the king as idealized "body politic" with the figure of the minor heir was a way of establishing "the exceptional position of the king and his rights, that is, the perpetuity which he shared with the Crown."[25] The king as "body natural," on the other hand, was, like his representatives (e.g., councillors, magnates, or members of Parliament), understood to be a guardian of the Crown (379–82). Given this intertextual frame of reference, it is tempting to speculate about the meaning Manley's trope of the monarchy as a female minor might have had for her in light of her personal history. Was there some wishful, wistful urge on her part to associate herself as a female ward with the sovereign privilege of inalienable rights—a privilege that, in 1709, fallen women (abused wards though they might be) did not enjoy? Manley well knew that the courtly trope of woman as sovereign did not guarantee women the same inalienable rights that were being extended to propertied men within the emergent philosophies of Whig individualism—a recognition that might explain her fictional representation of herself, in the figure of a thirteen-year-old Delia, as perpetually underage.

By dramatizing a crisis in cultural authority at a pivotal moment in British political history, the plot of guardian-ward incest in *The New Atalantis* articulates at once the anxieties and the promise of social change. Manley's tales of incestuous, heterosexual passion between guardians and wards are narratives of male homosocial transgression in which heroines function not as desiring agents but as theaters of male desire across whose bodies and estates masculine dramas of thwarted succession get played out. But they also introduce the possibility of a new kind of filial agency when they become the discursive vehicles though which Manley herself champions the legacy her father once hoped her cousin-guardian, John, would carry on. Through them, Manley becomes—in lieu of her cousin—a stalwart representative of her Tory father and a faithful guardian of the Crown, determined to restore the soul of the monarchy if she can. Insofar as she figures that ideal of sovereignty as a minor female ward, the very figure she uses in Delia to represent herself, she becomes—deftly and dangerously—her own "Representator" and guardian as well.

Corrupt Female Guardians and Manley's Incestuous Twins

Having examined the relationships among guardian-ward incest, familial succession, and the dangers of representation in *The New Atalantis,* let us turn now to the story of tragic incest between the twins Polydore and Urania. Here Manley doubly reconfigures the guardian-ward incest plot as it emerges in the narrative prototype of Delia and Don Marcus, but she continues to explore many of the same concerns. The figure of the greedy and dishonest cousin-guardian represented by Don Marcus in Delia's tale is here feminized and split into two separate but related figures—the materialistic Baroness and her scandal-mongering daughter, Harriat, and the act of incest is displaced from a guardian-ward to a sibling dyad. Although the dangers of unruly representation do not emerge directly in the incestuous bond that this story features, they remain a dominant focus of the important framing tale of the twins' cousin and detractor, Harriat.

The parable of Olympia's orphaned daughter entrusted to the protection and care of virtuous guardians constitutes an idealized intertext here as it does in the stories of Charlot, Louisa, and Delia. Polydore and Urania are wards of their maternal aunt, a baroness, their widowed mother having died—like Olympia—"in Childbed" (2:19/1:551). But like those other corrupt guardians— the Duke, Hernando, and Don Marcus—the Baroness shirks her fundamental responsibility for the suitable marriage and education of her wards when she turns to her personal advantage the power that guardianship gives her over the sexual circulation of her niece. The guardian's motive for abuse in this instance is not desire for the ward's virginity or inheritance, the latter in Urania's case being very small; it is, rather, elimination of Urania as competition for her own daughters in the market for husbands.

Despite the orphans' humble origins, the Baroness at first makes "no distinction" between the twins and her own children (2:20/1:552). When Urania reaches the critical age of fourteen, however, her physical beauty threatens to overshadow that of her guardian's daughters. Since Urania has reached the age at which she may legally consent or disagree to marriage, the only way for the Baroness to maintain control over her ward's attachments is to refuse to allow her to appear in public: "tho' she did not cease to love her, she ceas'd to carry her abroad as usual, or to suffer her Appearance in her own Family when Visiters were there; because she so far eclips'd her Daughter's, that with all the advantage of Fortune, 'twas impossible they should have any Lovers where *Urania* appear'd" (2:20/1:552). Thus sequestered and forced into dangerous proximity to her brother, the only man she ever sees, and being of a passionate nature, Urania eventually develops a "fatal Tenderness for the too lovely *Polydore*" (2:22/1:554); and Polydore, for his part, responds in kind. Too young to come into possession of the modest fortune left them by their mother, the sibling lovers resolve to retire penniless from the world together to enjoy their "guilty Love" (2:27/1:559).

The Baroness's effacing of her ward's beauty to enhance her daughters' economic prospects does not on the face of it violate paternal trust, Urania's father—a man of no fortune—being long since deceased. Like the stories of Charlot, Louisa, and Delia, nevertheless, this is a narrative of familial succession disrupted by a guardian's venal quest for social and financial self-aggrandizement. From a Tory point of view, the Baroness displays all the distinguishing features of a Whig lust for power. She insists on economic over nonmaterial considerations (such as, in this instance, Urania's great beauty) in the determination of her children's marriages, ensuring—contrary to Virtue's dictates—that their unions are the result of "*Interest*" rather than "Inclination" (2:2/1:534).[26] Abandoning family loyalty in favor of sororal competition, she ultimately prevents her sister's children from producing legitimate heirs.

If the Baroness exemplifies a corrupt modern privileging of the imperatives of class over kinship (a motif we later see developed in the machinations of Sarah Fielding's Livia, the neglect of Frances Burney's Madame Duval, and the hypocritical "benevolence" of Jane Austen's more prosperous Ward sisters— particularly of that corrupt female "guardian" Mrs. Norris), her daughter Harriat emblematizes a corrupt modern investment in the dangerous powers of representation. In contrast to Urania, who embodies unguarded sincerity and enmity toward "the Art of Dissimulation" (2:19/1:551), Harriat values reputation not only more than truth but even more than life itself (2:8/1:540). It is Harriat's voice, groaning in labor and crying for assistance under a moonlit sky, that first draws her to the attention of Virtue and Astrea as the first "Adventure" of volume 2 begins (2:7/1:539). We recall these groans and cries when, several pages later, we hear of Urania, in "Mother-Pains" at the birth of her "*Offspring* of *Incestuous Joy*," fatally drinking her tears, suppressing her cries, forbearing to call or groan, or groaning only "inwardly" (2:34–35/1:566–67). Harriat's more audible suffering is a fitting, if cruel, emblem of the power of publicity that she wields over her silenced cousin, whose withheld cries and reincorporated tears, like her reluctantly delivered stillborn child, stand as figures both for her faith in the power and innocence of a pure interiority and for the tragic consequences such faith incurs.

While the Baroness assumes control over Urania's circulation within the heteropatriarchal economy of marriage by keeping her niece in "reserve from the other Sex" (2:22/1:554), Harriat takes charge of her cousin's circulation as a sign within the ethico-discursive domain of public opinion by appropriating Urania's faulty innocence as a badge of her own virtue and superiority. In a sense, Urania becomes the ideal scapegoat for Harriat and her mother, who displace onto their poor relation the entire burden of moral responsibility for familial and societal corruptions. Driven out of public circulation by her family's avarice and thus into "guilty Commerce" (2:27/1:559) with her brother, only to have the shocking circumstance thereby created later brutally publicized by her cousin as the scourge of vice, Urania becomes the primary jettisoned object in relation to whom Harriat (who thinks "it render[s] her *Virtue* more conspicuous to find a Defect in any other's" [2:34/1:566]) constructs her own public image and the vehicle whereby she sustains the fiction of her family's moral rectitude. The same motive of protecting the family name drives the Baroness in forbidding Harriat to speak of the affair and in sending the pregnant Urania away.

After all, as Polydore points out to Harriat, in "exposing *them,* she expos[es] but a part of her *self*" (2:29/1:561). Polydore is referring literally to the bloodline that he and Urania share with their cousins, but his words resonate at a figurative level too. Whereas to the puritanical Harriat the incest of Polydore and Urania stands as the very essence of unregulated desire, to Manley, Harriat embodies the fundamental prurience of Whig morality. As the "Admiration" mixed with her *"Aversion"* for her cousins' crime insinuates (2:26/1:558), the incest of Polydore and Urania is a veritable mirror image of Harriat's own unregulated lust for power and pleasure—a lust she later pays for when, like Urania, she becomes the victim of a *"lawless Passion"* (2:33/1:565) and a "guilty *Pregnancy"* (2:26/1:558).

As Manley conceives her, in other words, Urania is the abject and unassimilable "trace" whose exclusion enables the modern family to secure and consolidate its own ontological boundaries—an early version of that "thing lacking within" that Jane Austen's Fanny Price at once stands for and redeems in the ailing Bertram family. By first confining Urania within its contracted affective space, the Baroness's family produces within itself the very desire that it then sustains its self-identity by condemning. As such, it comes to exemplify for Manley the internal dynamics of a Whig hypocrisy produced by the competing claims of honor and self-interest. Manley's project in *The New Atalantis* is to expose the moral and ideological contradictions whereby incest becomes the product as well as the vanishing point of Whig morality.

Indeed, in the world of *The New Atalantis,* incest is a vice at once profoundly stigmatized and utterly typical. As Polydore himself points out to the implacable Harriat in defense of his incestuous passion for his sister, domestic crimes are commonplace among the Whig aristocracy, incest being "no new thing even in the Age they [live] in" (2:27/1:559). Like polygamy, incest had long been held a prerogative of kings determined to preserve their royal lines.[27] What troubled Manley was that in a privatized system of property ownership where power and its transmission depended both on class mobility and on the acquisition of landed wealth, such traditionally royal prerogatives were becoming the personal privilege of ordinary men. Within Whig circles, she observed, the practices of incest and double marriage continued to be officially proscribed even as their prevalence was quite casually assumed.[28]

Whig notions of the separability of public and private life, Manley suggests, made possible (and plausible) what would otherwise be regarded as wildly contradictory—for example, that Hernando Volpone, Louisa's guardian and the destroyer of her honor, should be of the "precise Party [that] held it a violent Scandal for a marry'd Man to corrupt a young Woman, especially under his *Ward"* (1:215/1:487). According to Manley, it was necessary only to exploit the distinction between public and private truth in order for men to mitigate such crimes: "care was to be taken that [Hernando's corruption of Louisa] should not be known, and then it would be as it were undone" (1:215/1:487). The same tension between public power and private morality characterizes the several cases of Whig incest that Polydore invokes in his effort to elicit merciful treatment from his cousin; for example, the case of a count [identified in keys as Henry Sidney, the earl of Romney] who "had had two Children by his *Sister; of the latter of which she dy'd in *Child-bed*—Yet was it no *Article* against his *growing Greatness;* nor did any one make the Objection to his *Character,* when they found him at *Court,* in Power, caress'd and favour'd; Master of the King's Ear, and often (by the Duties of his Place) in the Royal *Bed-chamber!*" (2:28/1:560).

Manley targets Whig doctrines of natural goodness here as well. Polydore invokes such doctrines at length in his defense of his criminal passions. Like Behn's Philander, he questions the authority of "Human Laws and Customs" over "that happy Instinct, that forbids not the *Brothers* and *Sisters* of the *feather'd kind,* to indulge their Appetites to each other: They pair; they breed; and know no Kindred; no Law, but Love" (2:22/1:554). Indeed, like Shakespeare's Edmund, he invokes nature as a deity (2:23/1:555). But Polydore's flawed notions are as much the products of a faulty education (of an overinvestment in "outward Behaviour" at the expense of that "much more *noble Part,* the uncultivated Mind" [2:24/1:556]) as they are the tokens of corrupted innocence. Harriat's incestuous cousins are mere symptoms of the corruption of a society in which avaricious guardians fail to properly educate their wards; by the same token, Whig doctrines of natural goodness are no more than convenient fictions created to license vicious desires and to lead untutored innocence astray.

Only a proper humanist education can guard natural virtue from being victimized by natural corruption. Like Swift, Manley is fond of reminding her readers that traditional Tory values are those of neither the cynic nor the idealist; they are, rather, the creed of the humanist. In her allegory of Polydore and Urania, she places the Baroness's Hobbesian machinations and Harriat's puritanical and self-righteous overinvestment in honor in a direct line of kinship with the Lockean idealizations of nature that characterize Polydore's rejection of "Human Laws and Customs." When Polydore idealistically invokes the sexual freedom of "the *feather'd kind*" or, like the cynical Edmund, erects nature as a deity, he demonstrates an individualism as morally bankrupt as his cousin's and his aunt's. A proper education acknowledging the inherent frailties of human nature and thereby guarding against them might have protected Urania from the importunities of her brother by alerting her to the dangers of overreliance on individual judgment. But such Tory wisdom comes to her too late and then, significantly, from a relation who can afford to be charitable toward others' flaws only because, in contrast to the Baroness and Harriat, she attributes her own virtue not to any superior personal powers but to the "Gods" (2:32/1:564).[29]

Manley's emphasis on a humanist education bears a critical relation both to her historical moment and to the larger aims of her narrative. The importance of a proper education is, in fact, established in the very opening pages of *The New Atalantis,* where Astrea explains to her mother, Virtue, the motive for her mission upon earth: she will honor the memory of her votary, that unfortunate innocent, Elizabeth, queen of Bohemia, by assuming the role of guardian and guide to that suffering monarch's young descendant, the future George II. Though "born indeed with generous Inclinations," this young prince is, she fears, "in danger of suffering under the greatest of Misfortunes, the want of a Royal Education" (1:8/1:280). Armed with full knowledge of the corruption of earthly courts and cabinets, Astrea will see to it that her prince receives all the civilizing refinements that education can bring to human nature. For as she observes in reflecting on Urania's crime, "*Nature* in it self was never yet so *Bright,* but that it wanted the Refinement of *Education:* The Ore is but in the Lump till *Education* has separated it from all those *dark* and *sordid* Mixtures, or intervenings of *Earth. Earth!* that *Native* Source from which it took its earliest Form, its first Original" (2:37/1:569). It is only under the influence of a proper education that Urania's "guilty Passion" finally gives way to those more refined instincts (a veritable second nature) of "serene *Horror*" (2:33/1:565) appropriate to her crime.

As in her stories of guardian-ward incest, Manley relies here on a productive crossing of public and private narratives. Like innocent female wards, young princes require a proper education to protect them from seduction by corrupt courtiers or from becoming (like George Augustus's grandmother) martyrs to the crimes of their oppressors. Such measures were especially imperative at a time when political authority was becoming increasingly decentralized and dispersed among royal advisers and ministers, and when the power of representation seemed to be taking precedence over the influence of truth. Just as Manley undertakes, in writing *The New Atalantis,* to champion her father's Tory legacy and become guardian to the interests of the Crown, so through the education of George Augustus, Astrea sets out to protect the legacies both of that prince's grandmother and of her own mother, Virtue, whose influence on earth she will endeavor to preserve, if not restore.

The idea elaborated in the narrative of Polydore and Urania that human instincts can be educated—that is, that human nature in its original, instinctual form may be refined through education into a type of second nature—reaches as far back as classical times and reemerges repeatedly in the Renaissance and the seventeenth century. Sir John Vaughan, for example, invokes it in his 1677 reports, where—citing Selden and, through him, such ancient authorities as Simplicius, Lucan, and St. Paul—he alludes to the "horrour," "averseness," and "loathing" that custom can "implant" in men. "This kind of secondary Nature," he insists, can "supervene upon mans original nature" and incite an abhorrence of certain foods or certain kinds of sexual partners that is not the effect of "*primitive* Nature."[30] But the concept of an education of taste or desire that institutes a distinction between mere sensual pleasure and a pure pleasure cleansed of such "*sordid* Mixtures" (2:37/1:569) as result from incest, polygamy, or the mere self-interest characteristic of a market mentality—a "pleasure purified of pleasure" that becomes "a symbol of moral excellence and a measure for the capacity for sublimation which defines the truly human man"—also points forward to the late eighteenth and early nineteenth centuries.[31] In my final two chapters, I track this idea as it evolves around the problem of incest through a series of narratives published between 1744 and 1814 in which several plot configurations introduced in *The New Atalantis* reemerge, among them stories about female wards and male guardians, corrupt female guardians and incestuous siblings, and the dangerous powers of representation. With *Mansfield Park*, as we shall see, a number of these disparate storylines coalesce in a narrative in which the figure of the female ward (the dependent outsider inside the family) becomes a signifier for the increasingly ambiguous status of the daughter, as both the family's moral center and its dangerous supplement, in a cultural context where affect was displacing birth as the basis for domestic relations and sibling incest was increasingly being inscribed as the ground of normative sexuality. First, however, I turn to *Moll Flanders*—another story about sibling incest in which the narrative of individual desire is delimited by the institution of a split or internal division within the heroine herself.

CHAPTER FIVE

Moll Flanders, Incest, and the Structure of Exchange

Any gift or debt alienates the individual into the circuit of exchanges, compromises one's integrity and autonomy. But assertion of one's uncontaminated selfhood is no practical way out of the circuit.

JANE GALLOP, *The Daughter's Seduction*

The need to think the limit of culture as a problem of the enunciation of cultural difference is disavowed.

HOMI K. BHABHA, *The Location of Culture*

In many ways, Defoe's Moll Flanders moves impressively and resiliently outside the constraints of familial, and especially maternal, obligation.[1] Her story, however, reminds us that there are dangers attendant upon being or believing oneself outside the family. Like the story of Sophocles' Oedipus, another memorable literary figure whom circumstance early removes from the place and knowledge of familial origins, it demonstrates that families are biologically determining and that incest is a possibility always present in not knowing where one belongs. For Moll, who discovers midway through her quest for economic independence that she has unwittingly become the wife of her own brother, the coincidental return of family follows a dual and paradoxical narrative logic: it at once emblematizes an endogamous dissolution of family structure and testifies to kinship's persistent force.

Both *Oedipus the King* and *Moll Flanders* presuppose the existence of certain social necessities or rules governing the distribution of intrafamilial power. As René Girard observes, Oedipus violates a system of family distinctions that limit the son's access to his father's wife.[2] What the rules of familial differentiation are in Moll's case—and how far Defoe's text goes in endorsing them as a cultural, or even a natural, necessity—is, to a large extent, the subject of this chapter. Suffice it to say here that for Moll the problem of incest is inextricably intertwined with the problem of sexual difference, as it is figured by Defoe, both inside and outside the family.

There is, to be sure, a salient code of sexual differentiation at work in Sophocles' play as well, since—as Girard notes—Jocasta, "the father's wife and son's mother," is casually assumed to be "an object solemnly consecrated as belonging to the father and formally forbidden the son" (74). But a son may incestuously challenge paternal authority without bringing into question (or even into consciousness) the fact that that authority involves the social domination of a woman. In Defoe's text, in which the mythical subject of incest—and thus the transgressor against those systems of difference that organize social relations—is a woman, such relative indifference to the category of gender is difficult, if not impossible, to sustain. Here, a system of social relations that posits the female as a passive form of masculine property at least *appears* to be exposed or put in doubt.

Moll's marriage to her brother violates not one but two interlocking codes of difference: it violates the rules that prohibit sexual union between the offspring of a common parent; and, by virtue of the fact that it is transacted at the point in Moll's career when she attempts to take the reins of sexual power into her own hands, it also violates those rules that constitute her socially as a woman. Moll, nonetheless, seems to thrive as a result of this dual transgression. Though initially she is horrified by the discovery of her familial circumstance, by the end of her narrative she has managed to turn her disaster into a source of economic gain. The psychic costs of her brush with incest, furthermore, prove minimal. As several critics have noted, while for Roxana the reemergence of family means the utter dissolution of the self, for Moll it means the dissolution of family. Moll's brother-husband gradually succumbs to both physical and mental disintegration, but Moll both physically and mentally distances herself from demoralizing family ties. Recouping the financial losses that she sustains on an unlucky voyage back to Europe, she will at last return to America to capitalize on her maternal inheritance. That she also thereby acquires the filial offices of a loyal and forgiving son with a good head for business and plantation management simply amplifies the material benefits she is able to reap as a result of her incestuous history.[3]

But if, as Michael Seidel aptly observes, Moll Flanders " 'capitalizes' the incest taboo," her repugnance at the discovery of her consanguineous relation to her husband leaves certain lingering questions unresolved.[4] The specific terms of Seidel's remark require pause: what Moll turns to profit is not the crime of incest itself but its prohibition. Why? As intent as Moll is on material gain in every other circumstance in her life, why is it that Defoe chooses to portray her as so irresistibly moved to repudiate her incestuous liaison?[5] She might much more profitably capitalize on the incest by staying put. Although Moll proves magisterially duplicitous in many another circumstance and has already manipulated her third husband into marriage under fraudulent pretenses, Defoe denies her recourse to bold deception in this case.

It is clear that Moll considers remaining married to Humphrey technically criminal once she has knowledge of their consanguinity: "O had the Story never been told me," she writes, "all had been well; it had been no Crime to have lain with my Husband, since as to his being my Relation, I had known nothing of it."[6] But it is equally clear that, for Defoe, Moll's remaining in her marriage under false appearances is a perfectly imaginable possibility. Although Moll acknowledges that she has been living in "open avowed Incest and Whoredom," she declares that she "was not much touched with the Crime of it" (89). In fact, at first she seems to place her own self-interest as fully as ever in front of any other consideration. She continues "under the appearance of an honest Wife" for more than three years, during which time, she tells us, she was capable of giving "the most sedate Consideration" (89) to the losses she might incur upon sharing her knowledge with another living soul. It is, moreover, only when the risks of secrecy begin to outweigh its benefits—when Moll's "riveted Aversion" (98) to Humphrey so strains relations with him that he threatens to commit her to a madhouse—that Moll decides to reveal her true identity to her mother. Moll, it appears, has come by her knack for lying honestly. Her mother advises continued secrecy on precisely the grounds that have moved the daughter to take her into confidence: Humphrey might respond irrationally and, among other possibilities, take advantage of the law to justify himself in putting Moll away.

Ultimately, however, Moll is driven to abandon strategy. She resolves to tell her story to her husband. The decision is not made on moral grounds, for—as Moll tells us—she "had no great concern about [the incest] in point of Conscience" (98). Nor, since she has already trusted her mother with the truth, can her disclosure be accounted for as the effect of the intolerable pressure of unconfided secrecy.[7] Moll tells Humphrey, rather, because she is compelled to do so by an overpowering and implacable inner necessity to avoid cohabitation with her brother. She "could not bear the thoughts of coming between the Sheets with him," she writes, regardless of whether she "was right in point of Policy" (98).[8] Policy, or reserve, is Moll's characteristic mode of survival throughout her career; but while she will later allow Mother Midnight to assist her in concealing both a pregnancy and a child, the incest is a fact of life that she will not even conspire with her own mother to cover up.

Read literally, this narrative sequence unfolds according to a logic of progression. At the time of her incest, Moll has not yet reached that pitch of hardness and reserve that would enable her to carry off as formidable or sustained a feat of secrecy as concealment of her incest would require. Having undertaken to "Deceive the Deceiver"—man—in the courtship of her third husband (MF, 77), she now finds not only that she has been deceived herself but also that she is more unconditionally subject to the imperatives of self-disclosure than at any other time in her career. Only later, when Moll more fully understands prevailing sexual practices and codes, will she be able to work oppressive systems to her own ends. As John Richetti notes, Moll's "fully developed reserve . . . resists even her extravagant desire for Jemy," from whom she withholds her true identity to the very end.[9]

The sheer extraordinariness of what is rendered as the mere coincidence of Moll's incest, however, also encourages an emblematic reading that reveals another narrative logic at work as well. On this reading, Moll's response to her incest functions not simply as a narrative prelude or a logical antithesis to her eventual mastery of reserve as a hardened criminal (or, for that matter, as a dubious penitent) but also as the positive ideological ground on which her triumph as a cheat erects itself. Moll's self-disclosure, that is, is not simply chronologically but also logically prior to her self-concealment. For as I shall argue, in figuring incest as at once the most basic of all prohibitions and the one limit that Moll refuses to cross over willingly, the Virginia episode has the effect of both organizing and ultimately neutralizing the subversive force of Moll's subsequent transgressions against institutional authority. It is surely important to recognize the instrumentality of the incest in advancing Moll to the point where she is able at last to effect what Richetti has called "a synthesis of sexuality and profit" in her relationship with her Lancashire husband, Jemy Cole (119); but it is also essential to remain clear about the limiting ideological conditions of that imaginative synthesis. Ultimately, it is only within the terms established by Moll's rejection of incest that her life of crime becomes (in both the material and spiritual sense) "redeemable." What is rewarded at the end of

Moll Flanders is not simply a subversive female criminality but a criminality already constituted within a patriarchal ordering of feminine desire.

Although a number of critics have read Defoe's novel as a critique of bourgeois social relations that objectify women as property, the narrative figuring of individual freedom in the character of Moll Flanders does not necessarily preclude an essentializing view of women as objects of exchange in the formation of culture.[10] Marxist and feminist commentaries on Lévi-Strauss's account of kinship structures demonstrate clearly that it is entirely possible for an incisive analysis of social relations based on the exchange of women to stop short of a thoroughgoing critique of the underlying construction of sexuality that inscribes that gender-coded structure of exchange as a cultural necessity.[11] In *Moll Flanders,* Defoe offers precisely such an attenuated analysis. At one level, the account of Moll's triumphs challenges cultural codes that deny women agency in the realms of economic and symbolic exchange; at another it reinscribes women's status as a fundamental form of sexual currency whose circulation is a necessary condition of social order. Being both "speaker" and "spoken," Moll draws much of her appeal as a character from exactly the cultural tension that Lévi-Strauss identifies as the root of women's sexual mystique. Constructed by Defoe as the narrator of her own text, she is in Lévi-Strauss's terms "at once a sign and a value," both a self-made woman and the product of a discourse whose origins are external to her self.[12] Even "Flanders"—the one alias Moll privileges as the semiotic equivalent of herself—is simultaneously an identity that she dons independently (*MF,* 64) and one that she is *given* by her competitors in crime (214). The story of a woman's self-creation as "the greatest Artist of [her] time" (214), Moll's memoir is also the narrative of a woman's initiation into a specific cultural construction of womanhood.

The ideological significance of the tension between Moll's progressive mastery of social reserve on the one hand and her eventual surrender to an intense internal aversion to her incest on the other is best illuminated by considering Defoe's narrative as a text about exchange.[13] The narrative displays a pervasive preoccupation with Moll's position in relations of exchange.[14] In the context of this dominant thematic preoccupation, Moll's incest acquires emblematic meaning as an extension of her desire to short-circuit or withdraw from "normal" bourgeois relations in which women are circulated as objects among men. (What, after all, is Moll's mastery of reserve but a refusal to circulate in a male economy?) The inadvertence of the incest and Moll's appalled reaction to it, however, serve at the same time to inscribe Moll's desire for freedom from circulation negatively, or at least to inscribe it as a desire inherently divided from itself. For even as the incest concretizes Moll's impulses toward self-determination, it also figuratively equates that desire for autonomy with a forbidden form of sexuality. Circulation or incest: these are the narrative choices the text allows.

Three dominant forms of exchange are represented in the novel. The most visible, of course, is economic exchange: the exchange of money and commodities. It is something of a critical commonplace to say that *Moll Flanders* is a novel about money, that it represents with astonishing vividness and accuracy the workings of a culture in which goods are sovereign and social power (or class) a function not exclusively of heritage but also of the ability to acquire capital. The economic impulse of Moll's career—which is effectually fulfilled within the course of the narrative—is to master those processes of commercial exchange that will give her the status of gentility.[15]

Two other systems of exchange, however, become essential to Moll's quest. One of these is linguistic or symbolic exchange. Moll's relation to language (broadly conceived as the entire system of semiological exchange—made up of utterances, behavior, and physical appearances—by which social meanings are communicated and understood) is crucial at the level of plot; Defoe's heroine manifests an extraordinary gift for manipulating linguistic and social codes and for carrying off various forms of social masquerade. But language plays a critical role at the generic or narrative level, too, where as pseudo-autobiographer, Moll speaks in her own voice, sometimes in alignment and sometimes in tension with the moral subscript of Defoe's text. Indeed, one of the distinctive features of Defoe's narrative ventriloquism is its ability to produce within a single framed autobiographical utterance a colloquy of voices that ideologically complement even as they contest and demystify one another.

Subtly related to the economic and linguistic systems of exchange in which Moll is inextricably implicated is a third form of exchange: kinship or sexual exchange. Sexual exchange in England had traditionally worked to preserve a relatively fixed social hierarchy or kinship system in which power was a function more of lineage than of cash, but in the eighteenth century its role in the acquisition and transmission of property sustained it as an integral part of a social context characterized by class mobility as well. Women in commercial society not only continued to play a crucial role as reproducers in the orderly transmission of both real and personal property but, as Douglas Hay has noted, "the marriage settlement [now also became] . . . the sacrament by which land allied itself with trade."[16]

Positioned at the site where an emergent individualism articulated with the residual operation of feudal structures within the family, women thus occupied a contradictory cultural place within early modern capitalism. To recapitulate Juliet Mitchell's argument (cited in chapter 1): while capitalism rendered kinship structures archaic, it also preserved them in a residual way in the ideology of the biological family, which posits the nuclear family with its oedipal structure as a natural rather than a culturally created phenomenon. The ideology of the biological family comes into its own against the background of the remoteness of a kinship system but masks the persistence—in altered forms—of precisely those archaic patterns of kinship organization. "[M]en enter into the class-dominated structures of history," Mitchell writes, "while women (as women, whatever their actual work in production) remain defined by the kinship patterns of organization . . . harnessed into the family."[17]

By virtue of the way it organizes the relations among the categories of economic, linguistic, and sexual exchange, *Moll Flanders* works at once to articulate and to naturalize this contradiction. Written at the beginning of England's transition both to a market economy and to the conditions under which the visible presence of kinship structures would gradually recede, the novel contains dramas of class and kinship at the same time that it specifically elaborates the contradictory status of women in early capitalist society. Like the recessed but residually operative kinship structures that Juliet Mitchell alludes to in her account of economically advanced societies, moreover, the kinship drama staged in *Moll Flanders*—the heroine's incest—seems on the surface utterly incidental, while in fact it functions as the ideological and structural fulcrum of the text. The class drama in which Moll Flanders thrives as a woman, by means of her femaleness, is a more sustained focus of narrative interest than the drama of her incestuous coupling, but structurally and ideologically it is enclosed within and contingent on that less manifest sociosexual narrative. At one level, Moll's incest functions as a figure for the freedom of individual desire from the social imperatives of class; at another, it constitutes a narrative occasion for establishing sexual difference as the site of hierarchical structures of social organization. In *Moll Flanders,* that is to say, the heroine's inadvertently committed and ultimately repudiated incest operates as a necessary condition of possibility for Defoe's narrative of desiring womanhood.

The relationship among the three systems of exchange represented in Defoe's text is embodied in the figure of the heroine; it is her relation to each system that constitutes the locus of their narrative intersection. In exploring this complex intersection, I propose to examine Moll's relation to each type of exchange system—the economic, the linguistic, and the sexual—separately. My point of entry—to which I will repeatedly return—is the heroine's name, a feature of the text that gains metaphoric resonance by condensing into a single figure the interrelated narratives of Moll's relation to all three systems.

Moll Flanders is named for a species of forbidden merchandise, *Flanders* being the shorthand term for usually contraband Flemish lace.[18] The alias seems peculiarly apt for a fictional heroine who inherits a maternal legacy of cloth-stealing, her mother having been convicted of a felony for the theft of three pieces of fine Holland. (*Holland*—or Dutch linen—was also commonly contraband.) Moll's own first theft is of "a little Bundle wrapt in a white Cloth" containing, among other miscellanies, "a Suit of Child-bed Linnen . . . , very good and almost new, the Lace very fine" (*MF,* 191–92); her last (for which she is apprehended on the spot and returned to Newgate, where she was born) is of "two Pieces of . . . Brocaded Silk, very rich" from the home of a man who acts as a broker between weavers and mercers in the sale of woven goods (272). At a certain point in her career, Moll's preferred mode of criminal dealing consists of clandestinely informing customs officials of the location of illegally imported Flanders lace (210).

Moll's names tie her to the actual criminal underworld of Defoe's day. As Gerald Howson has pointed out, she is the namesake of the famous pickpocket Mary Godson (alias Moll King); and she clearly resembles such well-known female criminals as "Calico Sarah" and "Susan Holland," who were also nicknamed after commonly prohibited textiles.[19] But the logic of Defoe's choice in naming his heroine for illegally imported lace goes beyond the demands of historical verisimilitude. It follows from the ideological structure of his text.

In telling a story of a woman who cannot earn an honest livelihood as a seamstress and so becomes a prostitute and then a thief, *Moll Flanders* narratively addresses the problem of women's relation to a capitalist economy.[20] Moll's childhood desire is to support herself by honest needlework. It becomes clear very early, however, that the products of Moll's labor are not her own and that what she can earn for her handiwork (largely in economic transactions with other women) will hardly go far enough to maintain her at the level of subsistence. By setting aside the money that Moll earns, her nurse tries to honor Moll's innocent wish for self-sufficiency. But even at this early stage in her career, that wish cannot be "purely" realized, Moll's earnings being adequate to her needs only when they are supplemented by gifts from genteel ladies who patronize her out of amusement at her social innocence. An object of charity, the honest seamstress cannot clothe herself. As Lois Chaber notes, Moll's first guardian—"a fallen gentlewoman who nevertheless maintains a precarious independence as a teacher and weaver"—is tied to a mode of home-centered industry no longer viable in the London that Moll inhabits. Finally, neither she nor Moll's naive hope for *honest* self-sufficiency will survive.[21]

Forced by the death of her guardian into the very servitude she had so vehemently eschewed, Moll soon learns that in the economy in which she moves, the value of a woman's sexuality exceeds that of her industrial productivity. As the "Madam" who "mend[s] Lace, and wash[es] . . . Ladies Lac'd-heads" (*MF*, 14) as a front for prostitution demonstrates, material production by women is not as lucrative as the exchange of sexual favors in the world Defoe portrays. The gift of a single shilling from the mayor's wife, who condescendingly bids Moll "mind [her] Work" (13), may put money in her pocket; but however often that philanthropic gesture is repeated, it creates for Moll far less accumulated capital than the five guineas from the elder brother who interrupts Moll's sewing for another "kind of Work" (23). (It is this same man from whom Moll eventually acquires a plenitude of gold [26–29].) Moll's consciousness of her relation as a woman to capital will deepen over the course of her career. Schooled in the ways of marriage, she will come to understand the role of female sexuality in men's profit as well as pleasure, to recognize that a woman has social value not just as an object of male libidinal desire but also, in the higher classes, as a medium of exchange in the accumulation and transmission of property.

In the context of this education in the dynamics of exchange, Moll's turn to crime at forty-eight makes perfect sense both as an instance of Defoe's narrative realism and as an emblematic gesture on Moll's part. Occurring at the point when Moll's sexual appeal and reproductive capacity are in decline, it affirms woman's status as a sexual object not only by associating menopause with the loss of sexuality but also by depicting that loss as a desperate economic circumstance. (Moll describes her dismal condition at this point in her narrative as a sort of "bleeding to Death" [190].)[22] At the same time, however, Moll's turn to crime functions at a figurative level as an extension, or renewal, of her quest for economic solvency. In theft, and particularly in the theft of woven goods, she achieves unauthorized but nonetheless remunerative possession of the very goods she could not profit from by producing. Having turned her manual skills another way, Moll appropriates what, as a child, she naively assumed belonged to her: the power to dress herself by her own means. By the time Moll reaches sixty, that power has accrued a complex layering of meanings, for she has moved beyond the mere ability to support herself to become not only wealthy but an artist in the practice of disguise.

Thus, on one level, Moll's name contains in coded form the narrative of her relation to "material" production. Her quest for gentility is a quest both for economic self-sufficiency and for control over the products of her own labor. Lace is what Moll mends and what she steals, but it is a commodity to which she bears a consistently intermediate relation. In one sense, it is a fitting site for that conjunction of high and low for which Moll's career, indeed for which Moll herself, will come to stand. Lace, said Dr. Johnson, is like Greek; "every man gets as much of it as he can."[23] Its associations work upward as well as downward in the social order; as Levey notes, lace "was both one of the most expensive of all fashionable textiles and one of the cheapest of home-made trimmings."[24] At the same time that it suggests a certain indeterminacy of social class, however, lace functions in Defoe as a reminder of a particular set of economic power relations based on gender. Produced exclusively by women, it was purchased (no matter who did the actual buying or wearing) mainly by men. In another anecdote from Boswell, Dr. Johnson again gives an illustrative example: "when a gentleman told him he had bought a suit of laces for his lady, he said, 'Well, Sir, you have done a good thing and a wise thing!' 'I have done a good thing, (said the gentleman,) but I do not know that I have done a wise thing.' JOHNSON. 'Yes, Sir; no money is better spent than what is laid out for domestick satisfaction. A man is pleased that his wife is drest as well as other people; and a wife is pleased that she is drest.' "[25] Like Greek, and like gold, lace serves as a symbolic medium of value. For men it is a sign of social status, for women a symptom of dependency.

If Moll's name suggests the material conditions of her quest, however, it also suggests the means—those elaborate strategies of disclosure and concealment— by which she seeks to realize her desire. Moll's association with lace, that is, tells the story of her evolving relation to language. Covering and revealing at the same time, lace aptly objectifies the discursive logic of a narrative as intent as Moll's on self-exposure and anonymity. The product of a long education in the management of disguise, her memoir is at once confession and disavowal, a narrative space in which she both lays bare her vices and keeps herself covered in a certain artful obscurity. Linguistically, it achieves for Moll what she is eager to achieve in other ways throughout her life, the condition of being "Conceal'd and Discover'd both together" (*MF,* 175).

Beginning life as a naive interpreter both of experience and of discourse, Moll early becomes a victim of her own inability either to read or to exploit appearances. Her childish tendency to oversimplify the relationship of signifier to signified, first manifest in her excessively literal interpretation of the honor-ific "Madam," becomes socially catastrophic in her failure to read the "earnest-ness" of her seducer, the elder brother, as a cover-up for insincerity (21–22, 28). At the same time, Moll meets his dissembling with artless transparency (24–25). Even after the lesson of the elder brother has been learned and Moll assesses love a *"Cheat"* (60), resolving for the future to exercise greater physical and emotional reserve, she continues to be seduced by surfaces, guilelessly "selling herself," as she puts it, to a tradesman who is acceptable to her because he has the "look" of quality (60–61). Moll's gentleman-draper squanders her money and leaves her "to Rob [his] Creditors for something to Subsist on" (62).

At this point, Moll first adopts the name of "Flanders" and retires to the Mint in an episode that marks a critical transition in her life. It is here that she first undertakes the art of fraud. The hard-won knowledge she has acquired in the affair of the two brothers is a knowledge of the cultural codes that define her social value as a woman. By these, she has discovered, she is reduced—as all women are—at once to nothingness and to a form of currency, a mere means to ensure the patrilineal succession of property. As Moll's Colchester sister implied when she observed that on the marriage market a woman without money is "no Body" (20), a woman's fortune merely substitutes for her intrinsic worth-lessness. As Moll's experience with the elder brother has made clear, a poor woman is assumed to be a "Ware" that can be transferred rather casually among men (39–40, 47).

Moll, however, refuses to be reduced to a mere sign. By undertaking to ma-nipulate signs herself, she begins to resist her victimization by cultural codes that define her as a piece of merchandise whose worth is measurable only in relation to male desire. She learns not only how to read those codes correctly but also how to use them to control the way others construe her. Matrimony, she has perceived, is a game of chance—a mere "Lottery"—unless it is played with proper skill (75). That proper skill is entrepreneurial, a canny knowledge of how to market oneself profitably. Like winning in that other man's game of hazard that Moll will play much later on (260–62), or like maximizing one's profits as a shopkeeper by placing one's finger on the scale, winning here requires the ability to cheat.

The rumors Moll fabricates about the seafaring suitor of her friend from Redriff demonstrate that Moll's skill at deception is, at least at this stage, fundamentally linguistic. Her poetic courtship of her third husband makes the verbal dimension of her quest for social power clearer still. Having figured in social relations mainly as an object to be exchanged, Moll now resolves to establish herself as an exchanging subject by taking control of a romantic dialogue. Defoe's imagery is, characteristically, at once historically apt and rich in metaphoric implication. Writing on windows with jewelry or diamond-pointed pencils was customary in the eighteenth century.[26] As the site of a written dialogue, however, the pane of inscribed glass also functions emblematically as part of this episode's thematic preoccupation with the ambiguity and impermanence of meaning.

The surface on which Moll and her lover write is transparent, the instrument of inscription a diamond—an emblem of permanence that will etch a physically ineradicable text. Transparency and permanence, however, are belied not simply by the inherent fragility of glass but also by the exquisitely elusive nature of what Moll writes. Having acquired unpleasant knowledge of the instability of lovers' vows, Moll now shatters her lover's professions with disbelief. Indeed, she so challenges his sincerity (the transparency of his text), makes it so difficult for him to give his language force, that he is driven at last to physical violence—literally to holding her "fast" (*MF*, 79). The sexual passion involved in the lover's impatience makes his desire to switch at this point from ring to pen seem a desperate wish to assert masculine, phallic authority over Moll's teasing but impenetrable female elusiveness. But Moll continues to overturn his meanings while cunningly obfuscating all her own, until at last her man lays down his pen. By likening the pen to a cudgel, Moll reveals that, to her, his textual silence marks defeat, that this is a battle being fought on verbal grounds. It is now Moll who has her lover "fast"—not in her arms, but (yet more literally) "*in a word.*" Pinning him to his own text, she has "fore-closed all manner of objection" to her poverty on his part; feigning total openness, she has made a proper evaluation of her sincerity or her worth impossible (80). Language has become for Moll a weapon and a veil.

The image of the Mint is similarly situated both in and between realist and emblematic modes. At one level, it lends veracity to the fiction of a woman in debt; at another, it functions as a complex metaphor for Moll's behavior at this point in her career. An area in Southwark that provided legal sanctuary to debtors (so called because Henry VIII had kept a mint there), the Mint figures a place at once where money is manufactured and where Moll (like other debtors) is temporarily "freed" from the process of exchange.[27] Moll's hiding there thus neatly emblematizes her strategies of resistance as she emerges from its midst, a counterfeiter who hides behind her status as currency (impersonating a rich widow, she passes herself off as "a fortune") precisely in order to extricate herself from the debt nexus in which, as a woman, she seems doomed to circulate.

Moll's emergence from the Mint thus marks the point of her most centered and intense period of self-creation before her turn to crime. Having become the center of her own authority, she has learned to use resourceful lying to engineer a marriage that brings her what she has most aspired to obtain: a good husband and economic security. She is happily reunited with her mother. The same narrative sequence that figures this self-birth and Moll's return to her own blood, however, also figures the taint of blood in what Moll refers to at the end of her narrative as "the Blot" (*MF*, 342) of her incestuous coupling and reproduction with her brother. The moment in Defoe's narrative that signals Moll's fullest realization of the efficacy of her own desire as a female subject is also the point at which she is most contaminated and "undone."

Social theorists since St. Augustine have routinely ascribed to the incest taboo the positive social function of establishing relations of reciprocity between men; the very survival of the biological family has been understood to depend on such extended alliances.[28] "The prohibition of incest," writes Lévi-Strauss, "is less a rule prohibiting marriage with the mother, sister or daughter, than a rule obliging the mother, sister or daughter to be given to others."[29] Or as Talcott Parsons observes, "it is not so much the prohibition of incest in its negative aspect which is important as the positive obligation to perform functions for the subunit and the larger society by marrying out. Incest is a withdrawal from this obligation to contribute to the formation and maintenance of supra-familial bonds on which major economic, political and religious functions of the society are dependent."[30] Coming as it does at the pinnacle of her efforts to insert herself as a subject into a masculine economy, Moll's incest is constituted as a refusal of just the sort of cultural obligation such theorists describe. Like her assumption of linguistic mastery or her later appropriation of material goods, it emerges in the text as a narrative manifestation of her will to power. It even functions as an emblem (and a fulfillment) of Moll's desire for lucrative exchange with other women, the heroine's brother (by a different father) being nothing less than the conduit of a transaction with her own mother (in, of course, a reversal of the normal kinship pattern by which women become conduits for relations between men). Understood in terms of the positive function that socio-anthropological writing assigns to the incest prohibition, in other words, Moll's incest might be said to represent the ultimate threat to patriarchal authority—a refusal, to borrow Luce Irigaray's phrase, of the goods to go to market.[31] It is important, therefore (though probably not surprising), that Defoe should harness—or even cancel—the subversive force of Moll's desire for economic and symbolic agency by representing it as an inadvertent violation of a deeply internalized aversion that will make Moll not only hate herself but loathe the thought of sleeping with her husband.

There seems to be a kind of contradiction here. On the one hand, Moll's incest emerges in the plot as an extension (almost an allegorical emblem) of her quest for female power in the realms of economic and linguistic exchange. On the other hand, by virtue of its inadvertence and Moll's ultimate repudiation of it, the incest testifies to her lack of desire to extend that quest for female power beyond the limits of economic and linguistic exchange into the realm of sexual exchange, where, as Rubin and others have shown, the hierarchies of sexual difference originate. Moll's incest is, in this sense, both a manifestation of her transgressiveness and its limit. Through it, Defoe establishes that however determined Moll may be to acquire agency in the domains of material and symbolic production, she is even more forcefully driven *not* to challenge the basic kinship patterns on which the social order and, more importantly, the hierarchies of gender difference rest. It is thus all the more significant from a structural point of view that Moll does not actually enter into prostitution or hardened crime until *after* her incestuous liaison has been renounced. However transgressive those subsequent violations of social law may seem to be, the prior renunciation of her incest (as Defoe's narrative codes it symbolically) ensures that those transgressions are already inscribed within the limiting conditions of heteropatriarchal sexual exchange.

Moll's loathing of the fruits of her own desire thus triggers a countermovement or neutralizing subtext to the progress of her transgressive womanhood, propelling her back from America and its possibilities for self-generation to the social hierarchies of the Old World. Moll will be able to return to America and economic security only after she has taken her place within those hierarchies and, through her marriage to Jemy and the settlement of her estate upon her son, she is in a position to reenter the system of exchange in the "proper" role of wife and loving mother. As Jemy jests at the end of the book, Moll *has* become his "Fortune" after all—the very currency she has worked so hard throughout her life *not* to be (*MF,* 341). It is true that she has become that fortune largely through maternal inheritance, but even that inheritance carries with it vestigial reminders of patriarchal relations of dominance, having originally been the estate of her mother's master (88).

Moll confesses to a transient dream of endogamous bliss on her return to America; having been treated lavishly by her son, "as if," she writes, "I had been in a new World, [I] began secretly now to wish that I had not brought my *Lancashire* Husband from *England* at all" (335). But she dismisses that wish as "not hearty," as she had rejected her actual incest as not wholesome earlier. At the end of her text, we find Moll using her money to purchase clothes for her fallen gentleman—"two good long Wigs, two silver hilted Swords" (340), the semifeudal trappings of a male-centered system of gentility. This, it seems, is the fabric her text preserves, the social and symbolic order into which she is woven but which at last she does not make.

The name Moll Flanders thus tells the story of the heroine's relation to the production of gender as well as to the production of language and of goods. As a woman in this text, Moll is herself the essential form of foreign merchandise whose export is required in order to create the suprafamilial bonds that make other forms of trade or communication possible. Defoe's narrative represents her as spending her life attempting to work those other systems of exchange and as succeeding to a limited extent: she becomes wealthy; she writes an autobiographical memoir. At the same time, however, Moll can never escape the necessity of always having to circulate outside the circuit of her own authority in order for those very systems of economic and symbolic exchange to operate. Even Moll's own narrative is represented as needing to be "garbl'd," or purified for market, by a masculine editorial violence (3). As he represents it in the preface to his book, Defoe's task as editor is to "dress" the body of Moll's text in language fit for public consumption (1); "redressing" her act of authorship, he reauthorizes it for a social audience. When Moll does attempt to undo the categories of gender, when she tries to control her own circulation—to make *herself* contraband by expropriating herself out of the necessary condition of being an always dislocated entity—the result is incest, a violation of what Defoe represents as the most basic prohibition of them all. Why Defoe must figure the

alternative to female circulation as incest, or female self-sufficiency as an aber-
rant variety of heterosexual relations, is an ideological secret that his narrative
only mutely articulates.

If, as Juliet Mitchell has suggested, Defoe's *Moll Flanders* presents "a society
without a father," we would do well at the same time to recall Lacan's insistence
that the father's "effective presence is not always necessary for him not to be
missing."[32] Moll Flanders's female quest for economic and symbolic agency
leads her into the apparent lawlessness of incest, but it also returns her to the
very heteropatriarchal economic and symbolic order that it is the original aim
of her quest to either elude or undermine. This return is effected not by the
intervention of a threatening father figure or by some other externally repressive juridical force (the patriarch Humphrey, for instance, goes blind and mad
and eventually dies), but rather through the institution of an internal division
or split within the heroine herself. The scene of Moll's sibling incest—interestingly also figured as the heroine's return to a maternal plenitude of "Tenderness
and Affection" (*MF*, 85)—occupies the empty yet constitutive place of that divided desire, the narrative site where in a double movement the heroine simultaneously *turns away from* and *returns to* the law of masculine privilege. Troped
as a series of contradictions or logical impossibilities, that incest marks at once a
scene of uncommon filial "Felicity" (85) and of utter abjection; the revisiting of
a place of origin and a new beginning in a new world; a foray to Virginia, geographic repository of corruption inhabited and governed by convicted criminals, whose place-name nevertheless evokes an image of unadulterated law. As
such, it figures the logical impossibility of the division within which, as female
subject, Moll herself is constituted as both outside the law and a product of it.

At the same time, subtending the overlapping and sometimes conflicting
systems of sexual, symbolic, and commercial exchange that Moll traverses in
the course of her narrative, and within which she is positioned as a female
subject, is another economy of exchange. Like the figure of the father (whose
immanent force, as I have argued, asserts itself in Moll's relation to the imperatives of sexual exchange), this economy is more implicit than manifest in the
narrative, but it has its own immanent, constitutive force. I am referring to the
colonial or slave economy on which Moll's independence as the owner of a
profitable tobacco plantation in America itself depends and through whose
largely occluded presence her production as a gendered bourgeois subject is

implicitly racialized.[33] Race is not an express concern in this novel as it is in *Robinson Crusoe*—or in *Colonel Jack,* where the racial structure of American plantation culture is more overtly specified.[34] It would, nevertheless, be possible to argue that, in its representation of the female subject of early modern capitalism, and despite (if not because of) its virtual silence about race, *Moll Flanders* is engaged in the elaboration of a nationalist myth—just as engaged indeed as *Robinson Crusoe,* of which the later novel might be said to offer a female variant or counterpart.

The narrative's subtle articulation of gender and racial discourses informs the very passage in which Moll fantasizes an incestuous idyll with her son, a passage that in turn exposes the assumption of colonial sovereignty implicit in Defoe's representation of female sexuality. For it is not just being pampered by her son that makes Moll wish that she had left her Lancashire husband behind in England; it is also the specific terms of the pleasures that Humphrey provides—namely, his designation of his mother as the recipient of "all possible Respect" from his tenants and his gift, along with provisions for her supper, of "a Maid-Servant and a *Negro* boy to wait on [her]" (*MF,* 335). These are the constituents of those "new World" pleasures that prompt Moll's secret wish— her desire not to share the services of her "boy" (either her son or her slave) with a surrogate patriarch, whose existence threatens to return her to a merely intermediary position in a male homosocial economy. The fulfillment of that wish would mark the realization of her childhood determination to avoid the dependency of service by obviating her role as Jemy's caretaker and fortune, the prop to shore up his waning aristocratic superiority.[35]

The internal division of Moll's incestuous desire in this passage through her prompt rejection of that desire as only half-hearted both subtly replays the larger drama of her incestuous relation to her brother-husband and reveals the ambivalence and contradictions inherent in the position of the European colonial female subject as simultaneously the renderer and the recipient of service. This ambivalence is both enabled and resolved when Moll trades the dream of uncompromised female agency in the domestic realm for colonial supremacy abroad. Evading such a compromise would be impossible within the terms of intelligibility of the cultural bargain entailed in the constitution of white European female subjectivity as Defoe conceives it, where the privileges of colonial supremacy accrue only in exchange for the political concessions required by normative heterosexuality. This is the trade—and the trade-off—through which Moll finally acquires a certain paradoxical agency in the reproduction of patriarchal and colonial economies of exchange when, at the end of her narrative, she promises to send her son a white European wife from London with her next cargo of indentured servants and material goods.

If *Moll Flanders* is a narrative of the production of gender, language, and goods, then, it is also a story of that particular moment of cultural change when England moved from a domestic to a colonial, world economy. By the end of her narrative, the honest seamstress who cannot clothe herself is plentifully stocked with the material resources to attire not just herself but also her husband and a multitude of servants (*MF,* 340).[36] As the dream of honest self-sufficiency yields to the realities of a global colonial order, so too does Moll's quest to overcome the liabilities of sexual difference surrender to another priority: the need within that expanded global network to establish and secure her own sense of European cultural identity.

In a way, that need has been present from the very beginning of Moll's retrospective account of her origins, for which—significantly—she can produce only hearsay evidence. Because England, unlike other European nations, made no public provision for the orphaned children of condemned or transported criminals, Moll is left desolate, with "no Parish to have Recourse to" (*MF,* 8) as an infant and with no certain knowledge as an adult about how she managed to survive. The first account she reports being able to "Recollect, or could ever learn" of herself is that she "had wandred among a Crew of those People they call *Gypsies,* or *Egyptians*" (9). Here Moll is quick to observe that she must have lived with the Gypsies "but a very little while . . . , for I had not had my Skin discolour'd or blacken'd, as they do very young to all the Children they carry about with them" (9). Typically viewed as a vaguely criminal, vagabond, oriental "race" who wandered the European countryside and were wont to kidnap European children—whose faces were then blackened to prevent their being recognized as white, Gypsies frequently populated eighteenth- and nineteenth-century stories of displaced and orphaned children in search of origins.[37] But here again, as in other episodes, Moll's narrative functions in both literal and symbolic registers. In this instance, the narrator's anxious desire to assert a cultural identity clearly differentiated from that of the Gypsies through the figure of her unblackened face (or recognizable whiteness) takes on a certain overdetermined meaning in relation to the novel's colonial subtext. Ultimately, one might say, Defoe's novel both addresses and satisfies a cultural desire for the reaffirmation of systems of sexual and racial difference in a society where incest and miscegenation emerge as linked emblems of the dangers of increasing cultural dislocation and social mobility. That incest is inscribed in *Moll Flanders* as the inextricable accompaniment to Moll's ultimate fixing of her biological origin through reconnection with her mother simply points to another trade-off, or contingency, inherent in the novel's discursive articulation of sexuality and race; Moll's rejection of her incest works symbolically to normalize her relation to gender imperatives while, at the same time, that very incest—by returning her to biology—secures the symbolic purity of her racial identity. Endogamy is to be avoided except, as we have seen elsewhere, when required for the preservation of patriarchy or, as we see here, when it sustains empire by preserving the boundaries of cultural difference.

CHAPTER SIX

Ingesting Incest

Maternity, Textuality, and the Problem of Origins

> What you sacrifice by swallowing, like what you suppress by rejecting,
> nourishing mother or corpse, are merely pre-texts of the symbolic relation
> that links you to Meaning.　　　　　JULIA KRISTEVA, *Powers of Horror*

The year 1751 saw the publication of an anonymous pamphlet entitled *Eleanora; or a Tragical but True Case of Incest in Great-Britain*.[1] A story of mother-son and subsequent father-daughter as well as sibling incest, the narrative is based loosely on the thirtieth tale of Marguerite de Navarre's *L'Heptaméron* (1558), the same tale that would later inspire Horace Walpole's *Mysterious Mother* (1768) and that had provided the plot outline for two late-seventeenth-century plays: Robert Gould's *Innocence Distress'd; or, The Royal Penitents* (1737) and the anonymous *Fatal Discovery; or, Love in Ruines* (1698).[2] *Eleanora* distinguishes itself from these dramatic versions of the queen of Navarre's tale not just because it is a prose narrative but because—through exploration of the complex relationships among incest, textuality, and fictionality—it offers a sustained metanarrative reflection on the problem of origins. In fact, incest in *Eleanora* becomes a trope for the haunting of all textuality by the question of origins. Set in Scotland during the period of the Puritan Revolution and featuring a protagonist who fights for the cause of parliamentary liberty, *Eleanora* implicitly links political challenges to kingly authority with the violation of kinship imperatives—in particular, with the excesses of maternal desire attendant upon the death or absence of the father.

This chapter takes *Eleanora* as a point of departure for exploring a discursive phenomenon that emerges in the second half of the eighteenth century and that I shall refer to as *intercestuality*, a term by which I mean to invoke the complex intertextual logic whereby incest comes to signal the absence of origin that underpins modern representational regimes and whereby the narrative of maternal desire produces and structures, though it may be excluded from, stories about incestuous siblings or incestuous relations between fathers and daughters. When Manley turns in the second volume of *The New Atalantis* from narratives of incest between male guardians and female wards to the story of Polydore and Urania, the substitution of a female for a male guardian shifts the plot of incest from an intergenerational to a sibling relation. Similarly, the heroine's return to maternal plenitude in Defoe's *Moll Flanders* signals a scene of sibling rather than intergenerational incest. Why, in imagining the dangers of maternal desire (those dangers attendant on the Baroness's greed or Moll's mother's criminality and promiscuity), do these narratives displace the threat of incest from the parent-child to the sibling relation? One might speculate that the displacement works in both cases to foreclose the possibility of lesbian incest between mother and daughter (or maternal guardian and female ward); but such a theory neither entirely explains the narratives' simultaneous insistence upon circumventing the plot of incest between mother and son (or maternal guardian and male ward) nor fully accounts for Manley's representation of lesbian community in her New Cabal.

In the pages that follow, I consider the shift in plot configuration from parent-child to sibling incest that occurs with the introduction of the figure of the mother or maternal guardian by looking at how the entangled categories of representation, maternity, incest, and origins that are so central to modern symbolic systems and so starkly and paradigmatically rendered in *Eleanora* are reproduced and refracted in a range of texts produced around and after midcentury—most notably *Tom Jones, Tristram Shandy, David Simple,* and *Evelina*. My analyses identify a pervasive tension between the distancing and embrace of representation in these narratives, which, on the one hand, caution against the perils of unruly representation and, on the other, endorse an emergent ideal of the sentimental family that privileges affect over birth in the constitution of "true" family and thus opens the way to a valorizing of symbolic (or fictional) over biological kinship ties.[3] Structured as they are around this central instability between affect as performance, exteriority, or artifice and affect as feeling, interiority, or authenticity, incest narratives of the second half of the century share a certain intertextual (or intercestual) logic. But as I also seek to show here and in the following chapter, while such narratives as *Tom Jones* work to obscure the contradictions engendered by these opposing impulses surrounding representation, others, such as *Evelina* and *Mansfield Park*, undertake to target and expose them—even going so far as to exploit the unstable relation between artifice and authenticity to unsettle the discursive ground of emergent notions of psychological interiority.

Eleanora and the Intercestual Problem of Origins

The Heptameron tells the story of a rich and pious widow who decides to teach her adolescent son a lesson for soliciting the sexual favors of an innocent chambermaid. The maid having complained to her mistress about the son's unwanted attentions, the widow determines to verify the truth of the girl's allegations and, if necessary, to chastise her son by surprising him with her own presence in the bed where he would expect to find the helpless young virgin. Despite her intentions to reveal herself to her son upon his entry into the bed where she secretly lies, the mother (having vowed never to remarry and having observed the strictest virtue since her husband's death) finds that in the heat of the moment she is unable to resist the advances of the youth. Believing her to be the now willing maid, the widow's son thus consummates the sexual act with his own mother. After this encounter, and to avoid the son's discovery of her deceit by subsequent contact with the maid, the widow promptly arranges for him to be sent off to fight the wars in Italy. Having conceived a child by him, she later covertly gives birth to a very beautiful daughter, who is raised by the widow's bastard brother and eventually sent to live with Catherine, the queen of Navarre. When the son, now grown to full manhood, returns from Italy, he visits the court of Navarre, where he falls in love with and eventually marries the young woman, of whose true identity as his own daughter and sister he remains ignorant. His mother had instructed him "never to appear before her unless he was married to somebody he loved deeply,"[4] and having fulfilled her injunction, he now deems himself worthy to return home. The widow, of course, is horrified when she discovers the identity of the woman her son has married, whereupon she confesses her crime to the legate at Avignon, who advises her never to reveal the secret to her children, for they "had acted in ignorance and consequently had not sinned. But she, their mother, was to do penance for the rest of her life."[5] The narrative ends with the following account of the extraordinary mutual happiness-ever-after of the unwittingly incestuous pair and the attendant abject suffering of their mother: "Never was there such love between husband and wife, never were a husband and wife so close. For she was his daughter, his sister, his wife. And he was her father, brother and husband. They endured for ever in this great love, while the poor lady, their mother, in the extremity of her penitence, could not see them show their love but she would withdraw to weep alone" (321).

The queen of Navarre's tale is framed with comments by its narrator, Hircan, and his fellow storytellers, who reflect on the dangers of a woman's overconfidence in her own ability to avoid sin and of her failure to acknowledge her inherent weaknesses or to trust sufficiently in the superior power of God—concerns that, as we have seen, reemerge in the eighteenth century in Manley's story of Urania and Polydore. The widow, the storytellers speculate, "was one of those foolish, vainglorious women who had had her head filled with nonsense by the Franciscans . . . and thought she was so saintly that she was incapable of sin, as some of them would persuade us to believe that through our own efforts we actually can be" (322).[6] *Eleanora* supplants the religious dimension of the queen of Navarre's tale with a Sophoclean quest for knowledge, extends the story of multiple incest into a third generation, and significantly complicates the story's narrative frame, thus giving a distinctly Enlightenment turn to an account that, in its earlier version, took up essentially Reformation debates and themes. As I undertake to show in the following discussion, the inability of the widow's deception to realize her intentions functions in *Eleanora* both as a powerful emblem for the alienations of textuality and as a dramatization of the process whereby incest comes to signify the unspeakable and thus unthinkable ground of both narrative and history.

The preface to the anonymous 1751 narrative prepares the reader immediately for the ensuing story's intense preoccupation with questions of intentionality and desire. The story, to which the author/editor's late grandfather claimed to have been a witness "from the Intimacy he had with all the Actors in it"[7] and which, the grandson tells us, has been handed down orally from father to son for two generations, is now being brought into print for the first time, purportedly in his grandfather's "own Words," due to the happenstance discovery of a previously unknown manuscript in the grandfather's "own Hand" (ii). The authenticity of the narrative's truth claims and origins, however, are imme-

diately placed in doubt both by the dead grandfather's absence as an authoritative source of intention and by the grandson's own introduction of the possibility that textual origins may be obscured:

> I might have made some Alteration in the prefatory Part of the Narration, and have
> began the Story as from my self; but having advised with some Friends on that
> Head, have been persuaded to send it forth in his own Words, as he, I presume,
> intended to have published it, about the Year 1685, by a Date which appears on the
> Back of it. (ii)

Even as it points to an act of textual and historical preservation, the grandson's
invocation of the road not taken, in his claim to have chosen *not* to tamper with
the grandfather's manuscript by presenting it as his own, casts suspicion on the
credibility of the grandfather's earlier claim that the narrative "originates" with
him.

The grandson's inference of his grandfather's intention to publish the manuscript, moreover, flies directly in the face of the latter's assertion at the conclusion of his narrative that, being the sole witness of the tragic deaths of the
story's main actors (in this version, the incestuous widow's incestuously married children), he has chosen to suppress the tragedy's true cause by publicly
passing off their history of multiple incest as the story of a great romance (62).
The grandfather, that is, admits to producing two distinct narratives: the story
of incest that he reserves for his son, to be passed on to his grandson privately, and the "current Report" of tragic love that he circulates publicly "in the
World" (62).

If the admission of this cover-up does not in itself further impugn the story's
veracity (the grandfather, after all, is telling a story about his own invention of
stories), the grandson's preface ironically insinuates yet another complication
of the relation between authorial intention and editorial desire. The grandson
reports that it was his own ambitious quest to augment his patrimony that led
to his happening upon the undiscovered manuscript. Might not that same
spirit of enterprise have also motivated the project of publication?

> [My father] said, he had heard my Grandfather talk of printing the Account, as a
> Caution, against other persons falling into the like Dilemma; though I don't re-
> member, ever to have heard him mention the Manuscript of it.
>
> Now that might have possibly lain till Doomsday unobserved, had my self and
> my Descendants behaved with the same Equality of Temper as my Father and
> Grandfather did; for their Patrimony of three Hundred Pounds a Year, was trans-

mitted from one to the other, and from my Father to me, without either Addition or Diminution; till my active Genius, in Pursuit of an Augmentation, having involved me in some Difficulties, which obliged me to raise a Sum of Money upon it; on Inspection of my little Deeds for that Purpose, I there fell upon this Manuscript of my Grandfather's, written by his own Hand. (i–ii)

Indeed, might not the manuscript itself be an invention of the grandson's "active Genius," as he calls it—one of his "little Deeds for [the] Purpose" of raising the requisite monetary sum?

In the compressed space of the less than two pages occupied by its prefatory frame, the 1751 narrative is yet further hedged with doubt; a lack of material evidence makes its historical claims impossible to corroborate. Although the grandfather, we are told, knew all the names of the parties involved, those names have been lost to posterity, for in passing the story on to the grandson, the son referred to the actors only as "the Mother, the Son, and the Daughter" (i). The manuscript, moreover, declares its use of wholly "fictitious Names" (2), a gesture meant (or so we are told) to protect the parties' innocent descendents from knowledge of their impure origins. Most critically, the grandfather's claim to have arrived at knowledge of the facts through his intimacy with all the actors involved is significantly qualified, as it makes one exception—Arene, the widow's companion, who in this version, as we shall see, is the only character capable of verifying the truth of the narrative with any certainty.

Eleanora is set in Scotland in the time of Oliver Cromwell. In it, the eponymous young widow's son, Orestes, undertakes to debauch his mother's companion, Arene, during a vacation from his studies at Glasgow. Eleanora determines to overthrow her son's stratagems to molest Arene by devising a counterstratagem of her own: she will teach Orestes a lesson by substituting herself in bed in place of Arene, the text's ever-elusive object of desire. As in the queen of Navarre's tale, the mother fails to reveal her identity when her son enters the bed in which she lies, and incest ensues. Orestes returns to Glasgow. After some time, he obtains a position in the parliamentary army, where, after ten years, he is "honoured with the Commission of a Colonel" (15). During the time of her son's extended absence, Eleanora privately gives birth to a daughter, Cornelia, whom she places in the care of the widow of one of her tenant farmers in exchange for holding the farm rent free for the rest of the woman's life. But when the tenant becomes too ill to care for Cornelia any longer, Eleanora takes the girl in as her own ward. At the Restoration, Orestes, being "out of all Employ" (16), heads for London, where he spends three years searching, unsuccessfully, for a wife. He thus returns home, where he meets Cornelia and immediately falls in love with her.[8]

It is at this point that the 1751 narrative most significantly diverges from and expands upon its source. Wishing to marry Cornelia but fearing that, because she has no fortune, Eleanora would reject his suit, Orestes is thrown into a protracted struggle between love and duty. At first, he endeavors by various strategies to regulate his passion, but eventually he is "[n]o longer able to endure the preying Viper of Desire in his Breast" (19); like Aphra Behn's Oroonoko, who omits to inform the king, his grandfather, of his betrothal to Imoinda, Orestes finally allows the pressures of sexuality to take precedence over the imperatives of kinship obligation.[9] His "Impatience [being] so vehement, and his Love so predominant, as to over-balance even the Obligations of filial Regard" (25), he consummates his nuptials with Cornelia "without the least Suspicion of *Eleanora's*" (24).

Just as the narrative tells us that after Eleanora and Orestes' moment of incestuous enjoyment, "her Mouth was for ever stopped from reproaching him" (10), so after learning of the union of her children, Eleanora loses her powers of intelligible speech, a condition in which she continues, with some small improvement, for a matter of several years, in the course of which her son and daughter produce four children. It so happens that after a period of recovery in which Eleanora stops raving but continues to speak very little, Orestes travels away from home to assist in the political campaign of a close friend. His work takes him to a meeting of several ladies where he encounters, after many years, the former companion of his mother and object of his lust, Arene, whom he once again tries unsuccessfully to seduce and whose passing reference to someone having "supplied her Place" (34) during what he believed to have been their earlier encounter throws him into a state of painful apprehension. Thus begins Orestes' anguished quest for knowledge and identity. By turns entertaining and dismissing the possibility that Arene's proxy may have been his mother, he resolves by further recourse to Arene to make himself master of what appears to be an "unfathomable" mystery. Arene, however, proves impossibly elusive. Her residence being "undeterminable" (36) and her widowed name unknown, Orestes manages by riding "almost Night and Day" to overtake the York coach that Arene is reported to have taken to London, only to learn upon its arrival there that "she having little or no Baggage, had quitted the Stage for an Hack; and that no one knew whither she was gone to" (37–38).

Returning home, Orestes informs his mother of his brief reencounter with

Arene, whereupon Eleanora once again is rendered mute, this time never to speak again. When, during the three days that intervene before her death, Orestes presses his mother to signify in some fashion "whether he had been imposed upon in that Affair, by the Substitution of any other Person in [Arene's] Place" (42), Eleanora first strikes at him ("collecting her whole Force into one Arm . . . with incredible Fury" [43]) and then at last, through gestural signs, demands pen and paper, thereafter reverting solely to written communication.[10]

Eleanora's displacement into writing of what can not be spoken initiates an extended series of narrative deferrals. First, Orestes and all his mother's servants are sent away while Eleanora closets herself in her room for a period of nearly nine hours, from which confinement she emerges with the product of her labors, a sealed packet directed to Orestes, but with written instructions from her "not to be opened, till after I am interred; and subject to my every Curse upon his Failure" (*E*, 45). The packet having been delivered to Orestes, Eleanora sinks into a coma, in which she is heard to utter unintelligible sounds but from which she never recovers. Despite strong temptations to violate his mother's injunction to refrain from opening the packet until her interment, Orestes is ultimately compelled under the threat of her curse to put off unfolding its mystery, Eleanora's funeral being deferred to the fourth day after her death. Then, after her burial, when he hastens to uncase the letter, he hesitates for fear of what it holds: "O! that I could but find *Arene!*" he laments, "I would then, but just gain a Glimpse of the Solution of this Mystery, and go no further" (50). Besides, as he acknowledges, without confirmation from Arene, the mystery that plagues him can never positively be resolved: "why shall I aim at perplexing my self with Discoveries, of which, in *Arene*'s Absence, I can now never arrive to a Certainty; for should this Account of my Mother's, (as I suspect it is) be couched under Terms ambiguous, or obscure, I shall then be at a worse Plunge than ever; nay, may be inextricably mired in such Despondence, as I may never emerge from more" (50–51). In light of this indeterminacy of the letter, Orestes decides to cut his losses and burn the packet, but no fire being "at hand" (51), he instead tosses it aside onto a shelf, where it lies neglected for several months.

Happening upon the packet at a future date when he feels more the "Master of [his] Passions," Orestes decides to open it for what it can provide of "bare Amusement" (52).[11] But even after he has read its contents, he remains, as he had anticipated, plagued by doubt. Orestes, Eleanora asserts, is the father of her daughter Cornelia and "an Actor in the most abominable Sin of Incest" (53–

54).[12] But, Orestes protests, his mother being dead, there is no way to confirm the truth of her written text. What is more, she may well have been mad when she wrote the letter and her "Compositions [be] but an Exposure of the Defects of human Nature, at best" (53). At worst, Orestes' soul is condemned to an "irremidiable Difficulty" (54); for how, if his mother is asking him to believe that she has made him the victim of a "cursed Imposition" (55), can he ever be sure that her written confession of that prevarication is not a lie? Agonizingly torn between the drive to know and not to know—the desire, on the one hand, to tear out the eyes that "first transmitted to [his] Heart, a dishonourable Passion for *Arene*" (55) and that now take in the knowledge of possible incest with his mother and the contrary desire, on the other hand, to satisfy his curiosity by reading on, perhaps to discover (like Pandora in search of hope) some mitigating circumstance—Orestes is "just stepping for his Sword, to dispatch himself" (58) when Cornelia enters the room. Cornelia pleads with Orestes to unravel to her the cause of his sorrows, whereupon he gives her the letter. She reads it and expires on the spot. In the final, climactic moment, Orestes, declaring that "this Evidence of *Eleanora*'s . . . shall not be left behind to [the] Prejudice" of his innocent children, "first swallow[s] the Letter by Pieces, and then stab[s] himself, falling close at the Feet of *Cornelia*" (61–62).

The image of Orestes' introjection of the secret of incest seems a fitting emblem for British fiction's emergent interiorization of the drama of kinship at the moment when modernity is displacing a semiotics of surface with an epistemology of depth. By problematizing the ontological status of Eleanora's professed crime, the anonymous 1751 narrative approaches the problem of incest as, in effect, a problem of textuality. More powerfully than any other production of the age, *Eleanora* exposes the pivotal role that incest plays as the unspeakable truth that stands at the limits of representation, inhabiting and thereby displacing the conceptual void around which both subjectivity and narrative unfold.

When Orestes swallows his mother's letter, he removes from circulation and thus renders inaccessible to historical consciousness not simply "evidence" of his own posterity's impure origins but also the haunting possibility that seems implicit in the text's vertiginous ironies (and that is emphasized as well by its deferral of suppression of the widow's secret for a generation beyond that delineated by Marguerite de Navarre) that all human subjects may be the distant products of uncertain origins—"ignorant of the impure Mixture they proceed from" (2) or, like Orestes himself, "involuntarily involved in [some] bestial

Mixture" (54)—indeed, that the very idea of descent is inherently fraught with uncertainty. *Eleanora* records both the production of that possibility and the story of its erasure. By ingesting uncertain knowledge of incest, Orestes at once symbolically assimilates incest as an ever-present contingency at the level of consciousness and induces the condition of historical blindness and forgetfulness on which human sociality depends.[13] At the same time, by telling the story of that erasure, *Eleanora* exposes the ontological paradox whereby what is forgotten is precisely that which can never be known—is, indeed, precisely the impossibility of immanent knowledge. In this sense, the story of incest in *Eleanora* is also the story of the epistemological crisis of Enlightenment: a condition simultaneously predicated on the scientific search for positive knowledge of origins and haunted by the apprehension that such knowledge is finally always beyond reach. Origins in *Eleanora* are scandalously indeterminate and ineluctably impure. As such, they seem to presuppose the condition of original impurity that John Milton posited as a human certainty when he protested in *Areopagitica* that "Assuredly we bring not innocence into the world, we bring impurity much rather."[14] Like the eating of the apple of knowledge in Genesis or of the "little book" in Revelation, the ingestion of the story of incest and maternal desire in *Eleanora* marks both the origin and the end of history.[15]

In posing the enigma of its own origins, *Eleanora* at once points beyond itself to the possibility of a prior source (be it a textual model or a historical event) and establishes itself as a narrative without author or origin. It thus evinces a certain ontological instability, representing both the ultimate instance of a scandalous or unauthorized story and the embodiment of absolute authority, of a truth that has no positive ground or historical beginning because it stands outside of history. As such, it announces itself as a veritable paradigm of textuality—a purely symbolic and purely arbitrary and self-referential system of signs that, even as it gestures outside itself, ultimately betrays its own specular structure.

As a self-reflexive and groundless metanarrative of origins, *Eleanora* bears an interesting relation to the intertextual history of the *Heptameron*'s thirtieth tale—a history of which it is a part and that it seems to mirror synecdochically. The *Heptameron* tale circulated as a factual fiction so widely and in such diverse contexts during the sixteenth and seventeenth centuries that it was not always clear whether writers who reproduced it thought they were imitating life or art. On the one hand, as the British writer Steevens observes in an article about Walpole's *Mysterious Mother* that was prepared for the *Biographia Dramatica* of 1782 but eventually suppressed, even the queen of Navarre's story had its textual precedents, being traceable to a "collection of mock causes proposed for arguments at a Mooting in France, a custom anciently observed in our own seminaries of law"; and modern scholars have identified numerous additional pretexts and analogs.[16] On the other hand, Horace Walpole claims (apparently ingenuously) in the "Author's Postscript" to *The Mysterious Mother* to have "thought the story founded on an event in real life" that he had "heard when very young," involving a woman who had consulted the archbishop Tillotson. "Some time after I had finished the play on this ground-work," Walpole relates, "a gentleman to whom I had communicated it, accidentally discovered the origin of the tradition in the novels of the Queen of Navarre, Vol. II. No. 30; and to my surprise I found a strange concurrence of circumstances between the story as there related, and as I had adapted it to my piece."[17] In the history of Walpole's play and of the queen of Navarre's tale, as in the narrative of Eleanora, questions of authorship and origin are endlessly deferred.[18]

The role of reproduction and maternal desire is, of course, critical to the narrative's representation of textuality. Like Swift's *Tale of a Tub*, *Eleanora* figures the alienations of textuality in terms of authorial absence. In Swift's narrative, however, the figure of the absent author is the father, whose will becomes a site of hermeneutic instability upon his death.[19] *Eleanora* records not only the textual alienations occasioned by the death of the author (in this case the mother) but also the history of linguistic recuperation in the movement from speech to writing that occurs around the crisis of incest's enunciation. For, in *Eleanora*, it is also the very presence of the incestuous mother, her immanent corporeality, that threatens the dissolution of coherent meaning, the boundaries of identity and difference ("if Eleanora's words are to be credited" and the truth of their incestuous origins thus confirmed, the anguished Orestes tells Cornelia as he hands her the fatal letter, it is doubtful "if any Name can comprehend what thy self and I are" [60]). While the displacements of writing may register the uncertainties occasioned by authorial (maternal) absence in this text, in other words, they also—paradoxically—restore the maternal voice to intelligibility by shifting it from a physical to a purely symbolic ground (thereby obviating the need for maternal presence). The text of Eleanora's desire defers the son's relation to the mother by displacing the threatening materiality of her body; her letter becomes "legible"—that is, open to being read—only after her interment. In this context, Orestes' ingestion of his mother's words in the form of a letter opened only after her body is out of reach might be read as a figure for the simultaneous embrace and control of signification involved in any discursive act—what Julia Kristeva might call the subsumption or incorporation of the semiotic by the symbolic order, from within which the former always threatens to irrupt as "the effect of that which cannot be pinned down as sign."[20]

But if *Eleanora* imagines the history of the transformation into meaning-ful language of the undifferentiated speech associated (obviously long before Lacan) with the primitive fusion of mother and child (and represented here by Eleanora's ravings and aphasic vocalizations), it also exposes the process whereby the narrative of maternal desire is produced and assimilated as the repressed condition and sustaining ground of phallic order. In troping the ma-ternal text as an unauthorized birth over which its heroine labors in confine-ment for nearly nine hours, *Eleanora* (the narrative) gestures toward the pri-macy of female originary force in the production of the text of maternal desire (Eleanora's narrative). The story that frames that text's transmission from father to son and underwrites its public dissemination, however, ends with the incor-poration and containment of the mother's narrative (in something like a re-verse pregnancy) quite literally in the body of the son, who—however contami-nated by her desire—becomes, through its appropriation and suppression (his swallowing of the letter and subsequent suicide), the dead and absent father of the future. Is it any wonder that this son should be named Orestes, after the son of classic legend who commits matricide to avenge the death of his father at his adulterous mother's hand?

Significantly, Orestes ingests the letter "by Pieces"; the narrative goes out of its way to specify this, despite the probable physical impossibility of swallowing a letter whole. Such emphasis on the piecemeal consumption of the letter may signal metaphorically the son's psychological need to take in the horror of its contents by increments, a need dramatized in the narrative sequence of Orestes' protracted resistance to and rereading of its text. But I would like to suggest that the image of the son's tearing and cannibalization of his mother's narrative also registers another aspect of incest's symbolic structure: namely, the process whereby the heterosexual narrative of maternal desire, which com-prehends within itself the whole range of possible forms of heterosexual incest (mother-son, father-daughter, and sibling), multiplies and disperses in the mo-ment of its repression. I shall return to this idea of the narrative of maternal in-cest as a dismembered or fractured plot to suggest the totalizing symbolic force of paternal order, within which every story of heterosexual incest (whether it features a parent-child or a sibling incest plot) functions in some sense as a retelling of the same story—the story of maternal lawlessness and of the uncontrollability of the denatured and disembodied sign. These themes are already implicit in Marguerite de Navarre's tale, which explores the disastrous consequences that ensue when a mother, presuming—in her husband's absence—to act as the bearer of the law without invoking superior aid or answering to a higher authority, participates in the dangerous play of substitution. But *Eleanora* ties itself closely to the particular preoccupations of its historical moment when it introduces into this already extant narrative about the dangers of representation and maternal desire both the scene of maternal writing and those two classic figures of the paradigmatically alienated text: the found manuscript and the posthumous letter. Addressing the vagaries of textual production in a culture where writing was becoming increasingly detached from the imperatives of traditional authority; tackling Enlightenment problems of knowledge and language; and taking on, through its hero's position as a soldier in Cromwell's New Model Army, the politics of revolution and liberty, *Eleanora* engages nothing less than the advent—and threat—of modernity itself.

And what precisely is the nature of that threat if not the simultaneous erasure and proliferation of origins? Throughout the second half of the eighteenth century, narratives of incest repeatedly unfold across, and thus obscure, the conceptual void produced by this paradox. Incest becomes a figure for the absence of stable origin, for that which can never be known or, alternatively, for the very condition of epistemological and ontological groundlessness. A substitute for what is not really there, it comes to represent the scandal of fiction itself. Indeed, as we shall see in the ensuing reading of *Tom Jones*, even in the most canonical and authorized of texts, that which is exposed as the ultimate epistemic danger, obscuring identity and thus betokening the confusion of kinship categories, is not in and of itself incest but the maternal fiction that constitutes incest's condition of possibility. The exposure of Bridget Allworthy's lie about Tom's birth may dispel the threat of his having engaged in incestuous relations with Jenny Jones, but it does not fully neutralize or attenuate the structuring force of incest in the novel. In fact, I shall argue, while it may provide incidental relief from the scandal of incest, Fielding's exposure of the arbitrary relation between truth and the maternal word ultimately operates as little more than a pretext for obscuring the equally arbitrary and equally incestuous character of the logic that underwrites Tom's eventual legitimation. In the opening chapter of *Tom Jones*, Fielding's narrator presents his story as a metaphorical feast, for the edification and delectation of the reader; the process of its consumption, however, like that of Eleanora's letter, defers even as it resolves the question of origins.[21]

The Salve of Print: *Tom Jones* and *Tristram Shandy*

Perhaps the best known and most "canonical" example of an eighteenth-century prose fiction that invokes the threat of incest, *Tom Jones* illustrates how the early novel's concerns with class, kinship, and representation work themselves out in their "classic" form. While critics have long contended that the incest in Fielding's novel is merely "comic" and "incidental," I undertake to demonstrate that, on the contrary, it is in fact foundational. Incest not only pervades the plot of *Tom Jones*; it structures and legislates the novel's intelligible forms of subjectivity, regulating the hero's affective choices and organizing the narrative's licit as well as illicit forms of sexuality.[22]

From the novel's opening episodes, in which Squire Allworthy finds the infant Tom in his bed and bestows the foundling upon his sister as a "Present" and as an object of maternal care (1.4.44); to the author's later insinuations that Bridget's considerable attraction to the eighteen-year-old Tom renders him a rival to her suitors (3.6.139–40); to Tom's assumption of surrogate sonship at Squire Western's table, where his growing affection for his "playmate" Sophia Western takes on the character of sibling attraction as well as filial interloping; to the climactic episode in jail, where Tom is informed—to his horror—that the woman he slept with at Upton (in the famous inn scene occurring at the center of the text) is his own mother, incest hovers steadily over Fielding's plot, teasing us with its tabooed possibility. There is even a moment (in which Jenny Jones tells Allworthy that his "Sister was the Mother of that Child [he] found between [his] Sheets" [18.7.941]) when the reader is invited to imagine that Tom might have been incestuously conceived.[23] In the course of his coming of age, which is also cast as a quest for origins, Tom encounters several older women whose dangerous affections he must in one way or another overcome. Bridget Allworthy's exceptional fondness for Tom sows the seeds of envy in Thwackum, Square, and Blifil and thus helps to precipitate the protagonist's worst trial, his exile from Paradise Hall; the controlling, predatory, and sexually insatiable Lady Bellaston seduces Tom and keeps him emotionally and financially dependent; and through what one critic has called her "mammiform attack on Tom,"[24] Mrs. Waters (a.k.a. Jenny Jones) appears for a time to have lured the protagonist unwittingly into the most heinous of sexual crimes. The novel's denouement occurs when, believing that incest (along with parricide) has actually occurred, Tom takes responsibility for his past behavior, repudiates his lawless desires, and—with the subsequent unfolding of the secret of his birth—gains legitimacy, Sophia, and patriarchal inheritance.

Fielding's narrative, in other words, moves toward and away from incest according to precisely the Freudian logic that Peter Brooks proffers as a "model for narrative plot"—part of the reason, no doubt, that Terry Eagleton invokes it as a prime example of "classical narrative of the realist kind."[25] In Tom's circular quest for identity and social legitimacy, incest emerges as a version of what Brooks calls an "improper end" or "false erotic object-choice."[26] For Brooks, who characterizes narrative energy as "always . . . on the verge of premature discharge" or short circuit, "incest is only the exemplary version of a temptation of short-circuit from which the protagonist and the text must be led away, into *détour,* into the cure which prolongs narrative" (1042). The "cure" in Fielding's novel occurs when Tom comes to resist the "regressive pull" of female figures who seem to offer the illicit pleasures of lost maternal presence and is rewarded with Sophia, the ideal erotic object of desire.[27]

That Fielding's plot about the incestuous dangers inherent in alienation from parentage and identity is triggered entirely by Bridget's illicit pregnancy and its concealment (that is, by the dangerous combination of illicit female sexuality and maternal deception about origins) further establishes the novel as a product of its time in linking concerns about class with anxieties about both unlicensed sexual reproduction and the circulation of fraudulent histories. For some critics, the text's treatment of incest is essentially a function of class ideology and specifically of Fielding's positioning between landed and bourgeois interests and definitions of identity. Gary Gautier, for example, argues that because mother-son incest was a systemic possibility within a bourgeois social order that privileged merit and devalued birth and parentage as constitutive of human identity, it is a threat endemic to Tom's status as a foundling with no real knowledge of his origins. "Just as we become comfortable with the character's merit (despite indiscretions)," Gautier observes, "incest erupts into the picture," delimiting the narrative of merit by introducing the suppressed knowledge of Tom's birth.[28] But the problems of legitimacy that surround the protagonist of this text also surround its genre and tie the questions it raises about social authority to questions about literary authority as well. As Anita Levy explains, these were linked concerns in early modern discourses of cultural reproduction, which "like aristocratic kinship practices, looked back to notions of origin, authenticity, and the metaphysics of blood as purveyors of meaning and quality from the past to the present. Inasmuch as the authenticity of the cultural or social source could be verified, the futurity of texts and bodies was never in doubt and appeared immune to the incessant quantifying demands of print culture. Certainly the anxiety of illicit reproduction—readers copying books, words escaping original meanings, and bloodlines becoming sullied—was always present."[29] In the case of Tom Jones, both origin and authenticity remain unverifiable even at the end of the novel since, given Jenny's and Bridget's prior history of duplicity, their words regarding the foundling's parentage—whether spoken or written—will always remain tainted by uncertainty; and in any event, as Homer Brown points out, even if Tom really *is* Bridget's son, he will always be a bastard.[30] These same doubts about legitimacy inform discussions of the genre of the novel, which in its detachment from the domain of tradition was often figured as a bastard form, the product of a corrupt and monstrous maternity that, for writers like Swift and Pope, was emblematic of the debased proliferations of print culture itself.[31] Fielding invokes these very images in a well-known passage in the preface to book 11 of *Tom Jones,* where his narrator declares that, as a book is the author's offspring, "The Slander of a Book is, in Truth, the Slander of the Author: For as no one can call another Bastard, without calling the Mother a Whore, so neither can anyone give the Names of sad Stuff, horrid Nonsense, &c. to a Book, without calling the Author a Blockhead" (*TJ,* 11.1.569).

But if Fielding's novel raises the twin specters of textual and social illegitimacy (with incest figuring as the ultimate criminal possibility), it also dispels their threat through recourse to a logic of substitution and exchange in which incest also plays a central role—indeed, in which incest is constitutive of licit as well as illicit forms of sexuality. Sophia is Tom's ideal object of desire not simply because she is age-appropriate, but because of her sameness in difference from the text's excluded mother figures. Indeed, that she is also a displacement for the comforts of maternal presence is strongly suggested by an episode in book 4 in which, at the pubescent age of thirteen, she tends a little bird that Tom has given her as a present (much as Allworthy had given Tom to Bridget in an earlier episode).[32] Just as Tom is Allworthy's namesake, so the bird—Tommy—is Tom's. Fielding's account of the bliss of this little bird—taken from its nest and nursed up as a foundling, first by Tom and then by Sophia, whose "chief Business was to feed and tend it"—clearly evokes the pleasures of a maternal-infant plenitude: little Tommy, we are told, "was become so tame, that it would feed out of the Hand of its Mistress, would perch upon her Finger, and lie contented in her Bosom, where it seemed almost sensible of its own Happiness" (4.3.159). When Tommy is set free by a Blifil envious of the attention that Sophia gives the bird— in a scene that both duplicates the rivalry between Tom and Blifil over the attentions of their actual mother and foreshadows Tom's later separation from Sophia when he is forced to leave Paradise Hall—Sophia's association with lost maternal presence becomes yet more clear. The association has the quality of a chiastic opposition: just as Tom's voluntary turn away from forbidden mother figures marks his assumption of patriarchal power and responsibility, so his forced separation from Sophia at this point in the text signals that he is not yet in a position to take that challenge on. In other words, although Sophia is advanced as the *licit* alternative to the forbidden maternal object of desire, her very desirability as substitute remains grounded in the same incestuous libidinal economy that institutes paternal prohibition. Sophia is an object of incestuous desire, moreover, not simply because she is sometimes figured in maternal terms or because she has grown up with Tom as a surrogate sister (in a relation loosely analogous to that of Bridget and Thomas senior), but because, through her marriage to Tom, she becomes the linchpin of a complex system of male reciprocity in which her reproductive body serves the interests and desires not just of Tom but of her father and her father-in-law as well. Sophia is the ultimate reward that Allworthy bestows on Tom (18.9.954), along with status and inheritance, for the latter's filial duty and gratitude; and in turn she makes it possible for Tom to reward his uncle and his father-in-law with heirs for both their patrimonies and estates. She is Squire Western's gift to Tom, along with "his Family Seat, and the greater Part of his Estate" (18.13.981), in exchange for the young man's recently acquired power to consolidate the contiguous Western and Allworthy holdings; and Tom in turn devotes himself, along with Sophia, to the old man's pleasure—happily granting his father-in-law the same liberal access to Sophia that the elder man had much earlier granted Tom and loving Sophia all the more for her sense of duty and devotion to her father (18.13.981). In this arrangement, Squire Western's "violent Affection for [his] only Daughter" (5.3.221)—a violence that erupts in his overzealous support of Blifil's suit—at last seems happily pacified in the context of a sublime homosocial domesticity that at once affirms and destabilizes the opposition between reciprocity and incest on which the intelligibility of Fielding's plot seems to depend.

The threat of mother-son incest thus gets recontained by novel's end through legitimation of the incestuous heterosexuality of patriarchal marriage in which the husband serves as stand-in for the father by assuming the position of masculine authority. Fielding's narrative, that is, recuperates the threat of unlicensed reproduction posed by the figure of the "maternal sister" (represented both by Bridget and by Sophia at thirteen) through authorization of the figure of an idealized wife-substitute whose reproductive body is safely circumscribed within the order of patriarchal law. What is striking and modern in all of this, as others have remarked, is how the legal fiat of adoption transforms the effects of unlicensed sexuality into an occasion for the perpetuation of a patriarchal economy of sexual, material, and symbolic exchange. The ontological uncertainties surrounding Tom's identity and the ensuing possibilities of incest they open up are both sources of danger in Fielding's text; but they are also both recuperated as conditions of possibility for asserting the privilege of symbolic over biological origin. Tom's identity in the end is a function not of biological parentage but of his inscription within a symbolic order determined by the father's name and law.[33] That this circumstance is replicated in Fielding's declaration of a classical lineage for his "new Province of Writing" (2.1.77) (in a gesture that boldly *claims* lineage instead of being *adopted into* it) simply enhances our sense of the narrative's formal symmetries (though, as Homer Brown has shown and as I hope to have suggested here, it may not foreclose the possibility of also exploring the text's formal and ideological instabilities).

But Tom's coming of age within patriarchy is only partly a matter of being adopted into an external economy of power and property. It is also represented as a psychic process of achieving adulthood through the internalizing of sexual prohibition. It is about acquiring merit by coming to embrace the arbitrary logic of the patriarchy that has defined Tom's illegitimacy from the start, and about acquiring wisdom (Sophia) by coming to understand the laws of human desire. The unreliability of the maternal word that becomes emblematic of modern writing generally may threaten to undermine traditional institutions of cultural authority; but that authority reasserts itself when modern writing institutes incest within a patriarchal structure of desire as both the ultimate cultural transgression and the secret ground of truth—indeed, as the key to the mystery of "HUMAN NATURE" itself. That, in the end, is the "Provision" of Fielding's feast, the fare his novel serves up for the reader's consumption, edification, and delight (1.1.32). If in *Eleanora* the scene of maternal incest tragically portends the loss of language and intelligible meaning (a condition recuperable only through incorporation or interment), in *Tom Jones* it occasions a joyous reconnection with paternal tradition through the affirmation of symbolic origin. But as Tom's illegitimacy testifies, the symbolic order of patriarchy is in the end no more grounded in nature than the dangerous productivity of the mother's lie.

When Fielding uses the legal fiat of adoption to assert the priority of symbolic over biological origin in *Tom Jones,* thus privileging the denatured sign as the essence of origin, he paradoxically makes his novel an occasion for recuperating the threat to patriarchy that, in its very authorizing of the idea of originality, the novel genre itself has opened up. Through its authorization of multiple or discontinuous points of origin and its consequent proliferation of plural centers of linguistic authority, novel writing posed the danger of both endless and illicit reproduction and thereby threatened to unsettle patriarchal notions of authority and inheritance. But Fielding makes print a salve to the very wound that it inflicts on patriarchy when he figures fiction's dangerously reproductive power in the form of a deceitful maternity and institutes a distinction between his own narrative efforts and the fraudulent, feminine modern world of print. Fielding's distancing of his own writing from such promiscuous semiosis in order to establish his credibility as part of a masculine tradition grounded in the classics and their cultural inheritance nevertheless exposes (though it may not concede) the contingent relation of that writing to the threateningly "feminine" processes that it anxiously defines itself against.

Thus does Fielding undertake to recuperate the displacements of both adoption and textuality. If in Sophocles' *Oedipus the King,* adoption occasions a quest for identity and biological origin that ends catastrophically in the disclosure of incest and parricide, and in the protagonist's self-exile as a consequence of discovering the miasma that plagues his city in himself, in *Tom Jones* adoption resolves questions of identity by establishing the conditions for the hero's social legitimation and integration through a distancing of the prohibited maternal body and its allure. At the levels of plot and of narration respectively, the reproductive powers of women and of print in *Tom Jones* are at once debased and appropriated for more elevated cultural purposes.[34]

The same anxious relation among paternity, authorship, and cultural reproduction in modern print culture figures palpably in *Tristram Shandy,* where Laurence Sterne represents that ever-unrecuperable point of origin, the maternal body, as ultimately responsible for the writing subject's wounds and injuries. Tristram is the victim of dispersed animal spirits, the trauma of a head-first delivery, and the catastrophe of a bungled baptism occasioned by the conspiracy of fetal distress in the birth canal and that "leaky vessel" of a maid, Susannah, who cannot "carry Trismegistus in [her] head, the length of the gallery without scattering."[35] Sterne posits the proliferation of print both as a sign of and as an antidote to the state of human injury figured so pervasively throughout his text as generalized phallic vulnerability or anxiety about masculine generativity. Hence the setbacks produced when Tristram attempts to recuperate his losses through writing (the failures of linearity, sentences cut short, etc.) and the ironies that linger in his ludic deployment of print technology as a mode of laughter, a gesture of levity meant to counteract the gravity of mortal lack. But no moment in *Tristram Shandy* represents the precariousness of the project of mobilizing the redemptive powers of print at once more literally and more emblematically than the one in which Eugenius recommends "a soft sheet of paper just come off the press" (4:28.322) to be twisted around Phutatorius's penis as the best salve to take out the fire caused by the "fall" of a hot chestnut into his unbuttoned codpiece. Nor does any moment more archly expose the logical absurdity of trying to stabilize paternal authority by appealing to incest's legal instabilities.

If the precariousness of print's redemptive powers is not adequately affirmed by the questionable nature of Eugenius's cure (the work emanating from the press at the instant of the chestnut's fall happens to be the ninth chapter of Phutatorius's own treatise on concubines—a piece of "bawdry" ill-suited, as it turns out, to take the fire out), it is surely evinced by the irony of the occasion at which the incident occurs: a gathering of learned men convened by Walter Shandy to remedy an earlier "accident" by consulting the writings of church fathers and their distinguished commentators to determine if canon law will allow a change in the hero's Christian name. The falling chestnut's disruptive effect on Phutatorius's body as well as on the gravity of that dignified body of learned men just at the moment when they are attempting to ascertain Walter's own paternal prerogatives would seem to be enough to throw the reader's confidence in masculine authority into question. But the gentlemen's "jactitation" (their tossing up and down) of the arguments abets its cause.

Kysarcius begins by privileging the will and wishes of the father over the mother in the matter of an infant's name on the grounds of the well-established precedent that " '*the mother is not of kin to her child'* "; "Mrs Shandy, of all people," he maintains, "has the least to do in it" (4:29.324). Triptolemus attempts to extend that argument by appealing to the principle that in the law of kinship and succession, "things do not ascend, but descend"; "the parents are not begot by the child, but the child by the parents," he explains.[36] But, as Didius observes, in this endeavor Triptolemus "proves too much" (4:29.326) and thus, by imperiling the kinship of the father as well as the mother, undermines both Kysarcius's argument and paternal privilege. Exploiting the discrepancies between Leviticus and natural law, Didius in turn undertakes to salvage paternal privilege by proposing incest as a natural method whereby a father might acquire kinship to his child by confounding the expected order of descent; by begetting a child upon his grandmother, he proposes, a son can become the father of his own mother. Once again, however, the logic used to calm phallic anxiety proves abortive; for by virtue of the very principle of descent on which it is predicated, Didius's solution (in which the mother descends from the son) establishes nothing more securely than the kinship of the mother to the child.

Ironically, as Yorick's comments at last disclose, the collaborative male attempt to allay phallic anxiety by maternal silencing in the matter of naming ends by affirming maternal prerogative as well as, if not because of, the ever-only-presumptive status of paternity in general and of Walter's paternity of Tristram in particular:

> And pray, Yorick, said my uncle Toby, which way is this said affair of Tristram at length settled by these learned men? Very satisfactorily, replied Yorick; no mortal, Sir, has any concern with it—for Mrs Shandy the mother is nothing at all akin to him—and as the mother's is the surest side—Mr Shandy, in course, is still less than nothing—In short, he is not as much akin to him, Sir, as I am—
> —That may well be, said my father, shaking his head. (4:30.327)

"[B]utton up one cause of vexation!—and unbutton another!" (4:31.331). If the men have proved anything, it is the greater authority of the mother's word in the naming not only of the child but of the father.

The argument against the mother's kinship to the child, in other words, is finally exposed as a cover for anxiety about the "father's" paternity. Beneath his name and law, the father may in fact be "less than nothing," a mere substitute or representation of something that in fact is not really there.[37] The fear that paternity may be only nominal, moreover, points in turn to a more threatening possibility: that of the utter groundlessness of meaning in a world where the absurdity of attempting to mitigate the instability of paternal authority (i.e., paternal law) by exploiting the instability of incest law (i.e., paternal law) leads only to the further absurdity of trying to preserve the order of descent by its inversion. If nothing else, Sterne's episode exposes that, however ironically, the purely symbolic function of the father—what Judith Roof has called "the lie of the Father"[38]—is neither simply nor exclusively a function of the mother's lie.

The Lady in Labor with a Mask On

The figurative linkage between the female reproductive body and the productive powers of representation so central to the symbolic economies of both *Tristram Shandy* and *Tom Jones* has roots not only in the monstrous mothers of Swift and Pope but also in the work of women writers, who tend to deploy it to very different ends. Consider, for example, the striking image proffered by Manley at the beginning of volume 2 of *The New Atalantis*, when Mrs. Nightwork, the garrulous midwife who attends the laboring Harriat, is introduced as having once "brought a certain Lady to Bed with her Mask on."[39] In the context of the exchange about the moral ambiguities of scandal-mongering that takes place in this episode, the figure of a woman in labor with a mask on doubles as a trope for both female hypocrisy and the woman writer. Most immediately, it speaks to the "Mask of *Hypocrisy*" (2:9/1:541) that Harriat wears in her exposure of Urania's crime—a mask of virtue that is stripped of its force when (in an affirmation of the power of reality over representation) Harriat's body is delivered of the most material evidence of its own sexual transgressions. But when Lady Intelligence proceeds to railly Mrs. Nightwork for "ingrossing all the Scandal to [her] self" (2:12/1:544) and for violating tacit oaths of secrecy, the gossipy midwife's defense of her practices clearly gestures toward Manley's own self-appointed authorial role as midwife to scandalous truths through strategies of displacement and indirection.

Like the poets whom Lady Intelligence alludes to in an earlier digression about the degeneracy of modern writing in an "illiterate Age" (1:104/1:376) of print and who, as she informs an inquiring Astrea, can "speak Truth," but only "*Metaphorically*, or by way of *Allegory*" (1:105/1:377), Mrs. Nightwork is forsworn from telling secrets "*Directly*, but not *Indirectly*":

> as for Example, I must not say I delivered my Lady such a *One* of a lovely *Boy* in such a *Place*, and at such a *Time*. . . . But I may say, I did such a sort of Lady (describing her Person as well as I can) the good Office, but can't for my life imagin who she is. This is all under the Rose; and without this indirect *Liberty*, we should be but ill Company to most of our Ladies, who love to be amused with the failings of others, and would not always give us so favourable and warm a Reception, if we

had nothing of Scandal to entertain them with; not but that I'm extremely tender of an *Oath,* and would not break it for any thing but *Interest.* I never was so puzzl'd in all my Life, as in the Case of the Lady you know with the *Mask* on; I went to two *Divines,* and they could neither of 'em resolve me; at length a *Casuist* set me at rest, and shew'd me that as I had by Virtue of my first *Oath,* took the Ladies Mony and done her the *Service* required: The second *Oath* (which was forceably impos'd upon me) oblig'd me to take her *Lord*'s, and reveal all I knew touching the *First.* (2:13/1:545)

The analogy implicit here among the figures of Mrs. Nightwork, Lady Intelligence, and Manley herself, all of whom display the same inability to "delay divulging what [they] know, tho' at the expence of Danger" (2:9/1:541), plays on traditional misogynous associations of women with uncontrolled speech and thus raises questions about scandal's underlying morality. For while Intelligence may protest that the exposure of "pretenders to *Vertue . . .* who rail at all the World" is more just than criminal (2:9/1:541), Mrs. Nightwork (ironist though she may be) clearly displays signs of sophistry, self-interest, and moral hypocrisy. At the same time, the storytelling midwife's unabashedly mercenary determination to keep her public happy by privileging the entertainment-value over the truth-value of representation also points to the possibility of freeing the sign from the body's material liabilities. The image of the lady in labor with a mask on lends itself as readily to being read as a figure for the power of the denatured sign to displace the body's generative force and thus empower women's public engagement in symbolic and commercial interchange as it does to being read as a sign of the masked female body whose sexuality always ultimately undermines its performative agency. Indeed, it may be read as a figure for scandal itself, which, as Catherine Gallagher has suggested, also becomes a trope in Manley for the peculiar pleasures of fictionality.[40]

In its play on the correspondences and tensions between biological and semiological reproduction, Manley's use of the figure of the lady in labor with a mask on as a complex representation of representation recalls Aphra Behn's earlier depiction of the performative powers of the pregnant Silvia as well, perhaps, as Behn's use of the defaced and decaying corpse of the pregnant Imoinda in *Oroonoko* as a symptom of the unregenerate violence of Whig corruption and hypocrisy.[41] By contrast, while they often remain thematically linked to maternal figures, representations of the dangerous powers of representation in the work of women writing at and after midcentury tend to lack strong metaphorical associations with pregnancy. This change may be in part a function of the emergent moral emphases of the didactic, sentimental novel, but it also clearly signals the growing attractions for women writers of pure significitation—of representation freed from the demands of the body or of truth. Representations of female fabulists produced after 1740 are by no means entirely positive renderings; the pernicious figures of Livia in Sarah Fielding's *David Simple* and Jane Austen's eponymous Lady Susan come to mind. Nevertheless, there is a significant difference between Manley's story of Polydore and Urania, in which Harriat distorts or twists the truth by exposing an actual incest between her cousins in order hypocritically to establish her own moral virtue, and Sarah Fielding's account of Camilla and Valentine, in which the corrupt stepmother Livia victimizes her husband's children by inventing and disseminating an entirely spurious incest narrative.

We encounter in *David Simple*, as we do with variations in *Evelina*, the recurring figure of the corrupt maternal substitute who, like Manley's venal Baroness (a figure essentially inseparable from her scandal-mongering daughter, Harriat), is associated simultaneously with the scene of sibling incest and the public circulation of factitious truths. As claims of truth and the body are entirely taken up into signification in later narratives, however, the stark opposition that Sarah Fielding establishes between the dissembling of the maternal surrogate and the authenticity of the dutiful daughter becomes increasingly problematic and unstable. Indeed, as we shall see in the ensuing discussion of *Evelina*, and even more decidedly as we turn to *Mansfield Park*, the dangers of supplementarity, imitation, and surrrogacy that at midcentury seem to be shifting from paternal to maternal "guardians" eventually come to center on embodiments of dutiful daughterhood.

While this shift in focus might appear to return us to the performative tactics of Aphra Behn's Silvia, the relationship between the categories of kinship and performance by now has changed. As we shall see in my concluding discussion of *Mansfield Park*, the performative strategies that move Silvia *beyond* incest— positioning her finally outside the outside of her father's house and thus outside the logic of male oedipal rivalry—establish Fanny Price as a permanent fixture at Mansfield Park, where "[a]fter settling her at Thornton Lacey with every kind attention to her comfort," Fanny's surrogate-father-turned-father-in-law, Sir Thomas Bertram, makes it the "object of almost every day . . . to see her there, or to get her away from it."[42] The final movement of Fanny and her cousin Edmund into the vacant parsonage formerly occupied by the Grants and Crawfords (the original *other* family at Mansfield Park), a movement whereby the young couple at once displace and themselves become the *others within* the Bertram family, evinces the increasingly complex and unstable articulations of interiority that were emerging by 1814, as the British colonial project extended its scope and influence abroad and thus paradoxically increased the porousness of its national boundaries. Distance or apartness from familial law are by then no longer located, as they are for Silvia or Moll Flanders, in Brussels or Paris or the New World but unfold instead inside the private terrain of domestic space and individual consciousness. As we shall see, it is this remapping or reterritorialization of kinship that will make it possible for writers like Burney and Austen to exploit the unstable borders of the intercestual regime through their representation of dutiful daughters as cultural sites of supplementarity and, therefore, power.

Pure Invention: *David Simple* and *Evelina*

Like Manley's Polydore and Urania, Sarah Fielding's sentimental siblings Camilla and Valentine are forced into a mutual dependency by the jealous ambitions of an evil mother substitute. Motivated by material greed, self-interest, and jealousy over both her husband's fortunes and affections, Livia—like Manley's Baroness—places class imperatives above familial obligation. As Camilla reports of her stepmother, "she thought her Interest incompatible with ours; and that the only way to spend all her Husband's Fortune, was to make him believe we were his greatest Enemies."[43] Livia thus concocts the fiction that her stepchildren are engaged in an incestuous liaison.[44] While giving the appearance of wishing to protect familial sanctity, she succeeds so thoroughly in alienating the loving siblings from their father's affections that "no Nearness of Blood, or any Tye whatever" could protect them from his anger or prevent their expulsion from his house.[45] Envious of her husband's "Partiality, and Fondness" for his daughter (139), Livia makes "no scruple of inventing any thing" (161) to persuade others of the siblings' "criminal Conversation" (162–63). Even their refuge at the home of a potentially sympathetic aunt is destroyed by her determination to make them "appear guilty of some monstrous Villany" (149). As Camilla tells David, "*Livia* took care to make the Story that we were run from home, that we might have a better Opportunity to carry on our Intrigues, fly like Lightening through all our Relations and Acquaintance. So that, altho' we tried to speak to several of them, it was in vain" (164–65).

Livia's strategies are those of the classic fabulist. Like Defoe's Moll Flanders or

Richardson's Lovelace before her, she succeeds in her designs by "act[ing] a Part" (161): playing the injured party, feigning reluctance to reveal her step-children's crime, and pretending openness to confirm the truth of her asser-tions (163). Presuming on her own "good Character" (160) to ruin theirs, she hypocritically trades on the sort of "good Breeding, whose Politeness consists in nothing more, than an Art of hurting others, without making Use of Vulgar terms," to say "all the most shocking Things she could think of" (152) about Camilla and Valentine. Livia, in short, understands the power of representa-tion, knowing very well, as Camilla says, that "there could be no more than our bare Words against her's" (163).

Valentine represents the antithesis of Livia's selfish individualism. He is dis-tinguished, for example, from such brothers as James Harlowe, who worry more about their estates and reputation than the welfare of their kin (154). Indeed, as "all the Comfort" (147) that Camilla has left her after the death of her mother and Livia's corruption of her father's trust, Valentine functions for Camilla as a sort of substitute for maternal plenitude. Camilla dates "all the Miseries of [her] Life" from the moment of her mother's death (137). Initially, she takes comfort in replacing her mother herself, making it "the business of [her] Life to obey and please [her] Father"; to "obey him," she confesses, "was all the Pleasure [she] had in Life" (136–7). Possessing an "inexpressible Fondness" for her father, she goes so far as to resolve "never to marry, for it was impossible for [her] to change [her] Situation for a happier" (137). Within this context, Valentine figures as a sort of double displacement: a substitute for both the idealized mother figure (the perfect embodiment of familial obligation) and for her dangerous supple-ment (the evil stepmother, who falsely represents the father's most faithful representative). Once again, as in Manley's tale, the introduction of a female "guardian" into the space of representation—the space, in short, of surrogacy and supplementarity—signals a shift in the scene of incest from the parent-child to the sibling bond. Although in this case incest, being purely fictional, is entirely taken up into signification, it nevertheless remains a function of the unreliability of the now fully denatured "maternal" word.

Frances Burney's *Evelina* is a reverse adoption story in which a displaced and abandoned daughter reclaims her rightful identity as her father's legal heir when the truth of her biological origins is brought to light. The novel's ep-onymous heroine is a natural embodiment of true gentility and of "merit which ought not to be buried in obscurity,"[46] but she has been brought up in retirement as the ward of a country clergyman because her upper-class father, Sir John Belmont, long ago abandoned his pregnant wife, who subsequently died giving birth to Evelina. "Disappointed of the fortune he expected" (15) in marrying Evelina's mother, Caroline Evelyn, Belmont denied the marriage and burned the only material evidence of their legal kinship—their marriage certificate, thus leaving his daughter, as Evelina puts it, "motherless, [and] worse than fatherless" (218). But in a powerful scene of recognition in which the sixteen-year-old Evelina finally comes *"face to face"* (159) with her biological father, the truth of her identity can no longer be denied. Appearing before her father "without any other certificate of [her] birth, [than] that which [she carries] in [her] countenance," Evelina displays such a striking resemblance to her injured mother that, as her guardian anticipates, her genesis "cannot admit of a doubt" (337). Ultimately, the heroine is restored to legitimacy and inheritance through what seems an irrefutable affirmation of origins.

The most damaging falsehood circulating in Burney's novel thus appears to be Belmont's denial of the truth of his daughter's legal claim on him. In fact, however, the double dispossession of Caroline Evelyn and her daughter has other roots in, significantly, the machinations and lies of several maternal figures. The first of these is Evelina's maternal grandmother, the "ungovernable" (163) Madame Duval, whose own prior abandonment of her daughter is ultimately responsible for the young woman's involvement with the unscrupulous Sir John. It is Madame Duval's negligence and her ambitious scheme to marry her daughter to a distant relation (her husband's nephew) that pushes Caroline into Belmont's arms. As a child, Caroline is left by her father (Madame Duval's first husband) in the care of his own former tutor, Reverend Villars. Her troubles begin when she turns eighteen and her remarried mother summons her to Paris, where, in order to escape from a forced marriage, the young woman is driven into a clandestine union with a "known" libertine (15). In an ominous recapitulation of the adventures of Caroline, Madame Duval now reappears to *"make something"* of Evelina (121). Determined to prove her granddaughter's birthright, she launches a scheme to take Evelina with her to Paris to demand justice from Sir John—her motive, the profitable marriage of Evelina to Madame Duval's own relation, the decidedly unappealing and ill-bred young Branghton. No wonder that Villars should write to Lady Howard that "Madame Duval is by no means a proper companion or guardian" for Evelina! (13).

But Madame Duval is not the only maternal figure in *Evelina* who contributes to the creation of confusion and calumny or who exposes her children to social and moral dangers. By suppressing the truth of her son's paternity, Mr. Macartney's mother (also abandoned by Sir John) creates the tragic conditions that cause her son to fall in love with his own sister (or so for a time it seems). The opportunistic wet nurse Dame Green, assured of Reverend Villars's intention to educate the abandoned heroine, fraudulently substitutes her own infant daughter, Polly, for Evelina when, at Caroline's death, a repentant Sir John decides to do justice to his late wife's memory by taking in his newborn child and giving her his name. Dame Green's deception leads not only to Evelina's exclusion from paternal protection and inheritance but also to the confusion that engenders Macartney's misery and near suicide upon learning of his actual origins.[47] Thus, while Belmont's profligacy may be the most manifest target in Burney's story, its effects are mitigated by the greater responsibility that these three women bear for the parental omissions and confusions of identity and kinship categories that pervade the narrative. The lies and schemes of Dame Green and Mrs. Macartney incur the dangers of sibling incest attendant on mistaken or displaced identities more certainly than do Belmont's sexual crimes. And as Evelina's words to Villars late in the novel evince, Madame Duval is more guilty than Sir John of the crime of parental neglect, which in his case "was not the effect of insensibility or unkindness, but of imposition and error," so that "at the very time we concluded I was unnaturally rejected, my deluded father meant to show me the most favour and protection" (*Evelina*, 375). The scene of recognition between Evelina and her father thus functions as more than a triple *éclaircissement*. It not only resolves the mystery of Evelina's birth, dispels the threat of sibling incest by returning people to their rightful places, and clears Caroline Evelyn's sullied reputation; it also redeems the figure of the vitiated and irresponsible father who seemed to harbor such "strange indifferency" (122) to the welfare of his child.

Just as the plot of *Evelina* centers on full disclosure of the truth, so its protagonist is figured as an embodiment of artless transparency. In contrast to Madame Duval, who is of low birth but flaunts citified fashion and affects French manners, Evelina is—despite (if not, indeed, because of) her upper-class origins, the certainty of which she carries in her countenance (374)—free of affectation or artifice. As Orville declares in a statement that mobilizes the full range of meanings that link and distinguish nature and nurture in relation to the condition of being "bred," the heroine's "elegant face can never be so vile a mask" as to allow for the possibility of her ill-breeding, despite her obvious cultural illiteracy (35). In a world of fashion where the high style of the ladies is almost as entertaining as a theatrical performance (38), the woman without knowledge of how to "act" is the quintessential embodiment of genuineness and "natural" quality.

Evelina's ignorance of how to act at her first ball also demonstrates, however, that artlessness can be a form of power. As Sir Clement Willoughby playfully but astutely observes upon being informed that Evelina had burst out laughing in the foppish Lovel's face, "there's some *genius*" in being innocent of the rules of propriety. And as Orville acknowledges, it is impossible to know whether Evelina's freedoms mark her as "ignorant, or mischievous" (36); ignorance of the law may simply be a pretext for transgression. Like epistolarity itself— which, as Julia Epstein has demonstrated, represents the very essence of artful artlessness[48]—or like Burney's dedication and preface, in which humility threatens simultaneously to mask and disclose the monster of egotism, Evelina's naïveté partakes of a certain instability. In one who expresses "raptures" at the ease and artlessness of Garrick's performance just days before attending her first public assembly (*Evelina*, 26), might not innocence be an *imitation* of authenticity?[49]

As Brian McCrea has recently demonstrated, the unstable opposition between nature and art in *Evelina* plays out interestingly around the competing demands of biological and fictive forms of kinship,[50] a theme that converges as well with Burney's exploration of the unstable virtues of "belonging" to family. To whom and with whom does the heroine belonging "to nobody" (*Evelina*, 340) most belong? Are her primary ties of kinship biological or affective? Villars, she declares, is "the Parent [her] heart acknowledges" (350), and, as "the creature of [his] own forming," she is his true child (336). At the same time, her biological father must "own" her (must acknowledge publicly that she *belongs* to him) in order for her to marry and for her quest for identity and legitimacy to be resolved. But Evelina's tie to her biological father, whose name she carries only fleetingly, finally emerges as decidedly perfunctory, particularly since Orville has already declared his intent to marry her whether or not Belmont will publicly acknowledge her. For all its importance in the narrative as that which drives the heroine's quest for identity, the daughter's relation to the "real" father—to the immanence of paternal origin—is in the end more arbitrary and less authentic than her relation to her ersatz father—the paternal substitute.

Tensions between the demands of internal or affective and external or social identity similarly inform questions of familial obligation. When Willoughby attempts to discover Evelina's relation to the insolent Madame Duval, who accosts her granddaughter at the opera in a rage because the young woman has "'dare[d] to disobey'" (84) her by attending the opera in others' company, he wonders "*why* [Evelina] should scruple to treat [the woman] as she deserves" (86). The question of what Madame Duval "deserves" here carries the full ironic weight of the tension between kinship obligation and intrinsic merit—or between biology and performance, what Michael McKeon in another connection has called "birth" and "worth."[51] Evelina knows that, as kin, her grandmother "deserves" to be treated with filial respect, but the older woman's outrageous behavior has hardly earned that deference, and Evelina is too ashamed to "own" the filial connection.[52] The porous border between inside and outside or between private and public imperatives that characterizes the letter form pervades Burney's text, complicating the boundaries between self and other as well as the very concepts of place and family in a world where strangers (like the Scotsman Macartney or that "supposed foreigner," Madame Duval [*Evelina*, 52]) turn out to be relations and where substitutes take priority over their prototypes.

Strikingly, but in keeping with this problematic, the uncertainty surrounding Evelina's artlessness and the construct of the letter also pervades the moment of truth or recognition that takes place between the heroine and her father. As a hermeneutic fable in which a quest for truth is staged as a young woman's desire to be owned, Burney's narrative constitutes the interview between Evelina and Sir John (very much as *Eleanora* constitutes Orestes' reading of his mother's letter) as a moment of immanence in a world predicated on that project's inherent impossibility. Because the narrative restores Evelina to her father and her true identity while at the same time problematizing the grounds of truth, the name-of-the-father is ultimately exposed as arbitrary, whether applied to surrogate or to "real" paternity. Susan Greenfield astutely observes that when Evelina appears before her father with maternal letter in hand, body and text come together as if to restore stable meaning in a world where biological kinship seems to have become alienated from its semiological force.[53] Paradoxically, however, as we have seen, the interview also powerfully exposes the purely nominal nature of paternity, an effect all the more powerful when one considers that the doubt surrounding Evelina's simplicity may extend as well to the credibility of her mother. According to Villars, Caroline Evelyn's "credulity had been no match for [Belmont's] art" in her attempts to procure proofs of their legal marriage. For this reason and "from the guiltless tenor of her unspotted youth," we are told, "[e]very body *believed* her innocent" (15, emphasis added) of having borne an illegitimate child. But while Caroline may indeed have been legally married to Sir John, there is in reality no material evidence of Evelina's biological parentage beyond a striking physical resemblance to her *mother* and the force of that mother's posthumous written word. Could Evelina, as Greenfield hints,[54] be—like Tom Jones—a merely symbolically legitimated "natural" child? For all his "art," after all, Belmont—who "never doubted the veracity of the nurse" (*Evelina,* 374)—is also capable of credulity.[55]

The very form in which the narrative's moment of revelation and return occurs, moreover, contaminates it as a moment of immanence by establishing it as an effect of substitution. Evelina is acknowledged by Sir John because she bears both the prosthetic object of a posthumous letter and an uncanny resemblance to her mother; she is herself a representation. (In their interview, Belmont declares her "the representative of the most injured of women!" [384] and addresses her as "thou representative of my departed wife" [385]). But as Irene Fizer demonstrates, even as the daughter's likeness to the mother confirms her connection to Caroline, it also has the effect of destabilizing her identity as a daughter by blurring the distinction between the two women, thus giving the fleeting and unbearable interview between father and daughter its strong erotic charge and necessitating the immediate intervention of further substitutions. Belmont's violent reaction to Evelina's presence—in which he embraces her, rages at her, banishes her from his sight, and finally (in a recapitulation of his earlier actions) leaves her to the protection of another (this time Orville)—suggests the extent of this contaminating force.[56] Evelina is restored to "true" identity when she is brought inside the law, but there is something left over, left outside, an excess, even in this moment of truth, in which as a mere substitute, the representative of the mother evokes the desire of the father and thus threatens the legitimating moment's own legitimacy (if not by virtue of that desire, then by virtue of the uncertainty of the daughter's true paternal origin). Very much as in *Eleanora,* where in order for her moment of revelation to take place, the mother must absent herself to a place beyond corporeality, so here the revelation of Evelina's true identity occurs in the mother's absence, though in the presence of her posthumous written word. Could it be that what engenders Sir John's horror and so shakes his equanimity at the appearance of the living specter of his "departed" wife is his recognition not simply of Evelina but of the referential void lurking beneath the surface of that knowledge?

Once Evelina sets foot in the world outside of Berry Hill, an event coterminus with her passage into writing, she enters not simply London but also a world of fraud and duplicity (*Evelina,* 116) where there can be no moment of absolute truth, where certainty and veracity are always plagued by doubt. Within this context, the name-of-the-father that determines meaning is an inherently unstable ground. Incest occupies the place of that instability, at once enabling and threatening familial identity. Because, as Fizer notes, the father's desire must be acknowledged in order for the daughter to become transferable,[57] Belmont's authority over Evelina is constituted in the moment of its transmission. I would thus take issue with Brian McCrea's assessment that *Evelina* is about "patriarchal weakness" rather than, as he observes that the authors of a 1991 special issue on *Evelina* all contend, "patriarchal constraint";[58] for as we have seen in previous chapters, the precariousness of the father's authority as constituted within modernity is precisely a function of his privilege. Rather than resolving that instability, Burney exposes it, unsettling conventional binaries and problematizing the distinction between the immanence of truth and the emptiness of signs. In *Mansfield Park*, as we shall see, Austen also problematizes the distinction between artifice and authenticity so as to trouble the ground of truth and expose the arbitrary nature of the paternal prohibition that structures licit as well as illicit forms of sexuality. As is evident in Evelina's eventual marriage to Lord Orville, who is alternately cast in the role of father and of brother to his bride, even heterosexual marriage—the most sanctioned of sexual relations—is constituted within the substitutive structure of an incest economy.

To suggest, as I do above, that incest plots of different types invoke and refract one another reiteratively and intertextually is by no means to argue that such narratives invariably foreclose the possibility of subversive or transformative textual or authorial agency. My readings of Behn and Manley should already have made that clear. Although the trope of textual ingestion in *Eleanora* suggests the containment and effacement of maternal excess, the mother's narrative of maternal desire is not necessarily silenced by its incorporation into the order of cultural intelligibility. It is possible, as Judith Butler has argued in another connection, for "the unspeakable nevertheless [to make] itself heard through borrowing and exploiting the very terms that are meant to enforce its silence."[59]

Kaja Silverman has discussed the trope of eating the book—what Lacan in *Seminar VII* calls "incorporat[ing] the signifier"—as a figure for the sacrifice of "being" entailed in the act of signification in connection precisely with the retroactive rearticulations of artistic creation. If, as Heidegger argues, the subject experiences a death or fading of "being" in the process of its constitution as a meaningful entity, Silverman undertakes to show, that process also gives rise to the subject's "insatiable urge" to recuperate its experience of loss through symbolization:

> To eat the book means to embrace signification, and thereby not merely to experience but also to affirm the eclipse of "being." The eclipse of "being" is itself the condition for something much more important—for Being, or what Lacan calls the "properly apocalyptic creation." . . . And once again, this sublation from "being" to Being is something which befalls the creator. . . . The creator becomes what she creates.
>
> Lacan is very precise about the terms of this transformation, which he elaborates in the form of an autobiographical parable: "When I ate the book, I didn't thereby become the book, any more than the book became flesh," he explains. "The book became *me* so to speak." . . . The difference between the first of these possibilities and the last . . . is the difference between a simple self-expropriation and what Heidegger would call an "expropriative appropriati[on]"; between the dispiriting apprehension of the otherness of one's self, and the ecstatic rediscovery, at the site of the other, of one's utmost "ownness."[60]

In this chapter I have considered some of the ways in which the narrative of maternal desire is reproduced and appropriated (or incorporated) by writers at and after the middle of the eighteenth century. The narrative of incest and maternal desire that is so paradigmatically represented in *Eleanora* is variously elaborated after 1740 in narratives as diverse as *David Simple, Tristram Shandy,* and *Tom Jones.* In *Evelina,* it is rendered increasingly problematic. Like Orestes, who effaces his mother's narrative by making it his own, Burney expropriates the narrative of incest and maternal desire for her own purposes while subjecting the very idea of "ownness" to scrutiny at the limits of the intercestual regime.

CHAPTER SEVEN

Incest and Liberty

Mansfield Park

> To articulate the past historically does not mean to recognize it "the way it really was." . . . It means to seize hold of a memory as it flashes up at a moment of danger. . . . The danger affects both the content of the tradition and its receivers. The same threat hangs over both: that of becoming a tool of the ruling classes.
>
> WALTER BENJAMIN, "Theses on the Philosophy of History"

> There seems something more speakingly incomprehensible in the powers, the failures, the inequalities of memory, than in any other of our intelligences. The memory is sometimes so retentive, so serviceable, so obedient—at others, so bewildered and so weak—and at others again, so tyrannic, so beyond controul!—We are to be sure a miracle every way—but our powers of recollecting and of forgetting, do seem peculiarly past finding out.   JANE AUSTEN, *Mansfield Park*

> We need a *critique* of moral values, *the value of these values themselves must first be called in question—*
>
> FRIEDRICH NIETZSCHE, *On the Genealogy of Morals*

Jane Austen's *Mansfield Park,* a novel that pointedly joins the problem of incest and the problem of slavery, provides an opportunity to explore the complex articulations of late-eighteenth-century discourses of sexual and civil liberty— in particular, British defenses of close kindred marriage and of the political freedoms of African slaves transported from the British colonies to English soil. In a climate of global expansion, growing antislavery sentiment, and increasing geographical and class mobility, contingent definitions of incest and the naturalized notions of gender asymmetry they presupposed were sometimes mobilized in the interest of securing racial boundaries and naturalizing ideologies of racial difference. Considering *Mansfield Park*'s deployment of the articulated themes of incest and liberty in the context of historical concerns about miscegenation and the sexual rights of English men that surrounded the famous

Mansfield decision of 1772 (a decision resonant, as many have argued, in the novel's title), this chapter seeks to illuminate two important and in some ways competing dimensions of Austen's work: on the one hand, her vexed relationship to prevailing ideals of British liberty and, on the other, her distinct contribution to the discursive production of modern epistemological structures that give incest a central role in the constitution of human subjectivity.

To accomplish this two-pronged goal, I begin by situating the novel's preoccupation with the definitional contingencies surrounding incest within the larger framework of its preoccupation with instabilities surrounding definitions of virtue generally. Through extended semantic play, Austen internally and intertextually problematizes the categories of honesty (or honor) and good breeding—concepts that function in turn as productive points of contact between the novel's incest plot and its colonial subtext. An analysis of the semantic and moral ambiguities surrounding these categories provides the point of departure for my subsequent effort to illuminate Austen's complex representation of the relationship between incest and liberty. As we have seen, the question of incest had been implicated in discourses of British nationalism at least since Henry VIII's break with Rome—a rupture precipitated by debates surrounding the status of Henry's marriage to his brother's widow, Catherine of Aragon. Austen's narrative engages the intricated discourses of incest and liberty that had long figured so importantly in the production of British national identity and that by the 1770s had become further inflected by antislavery rhetoric associated with the Atlantic trade. In *Mansfield Park*'s deployment of tropes of incest and slavery, it is possible to discern the discursive mechanisms whereby incipient notions of desire that install incest at the center of an emerging modern logic of psychic interiority worked to mitigate the threatening effects of encroaching moral and epistemological instability by providing the stable or natural ground on which traditional gender hierarchies could be reproduced and anxieties about racial mixing could be both acknowledged and defused. At the same time, through her penetrating analysis of historical memory, Austen subtly unsettles those founding assumptions about gender and desire through which heteropatriarchal kinship structures and their multiple cultural exclusions were sustained.

What Good Men Judge to be Honest

> In contracting Marriage we are not only to have regard to our own
> Conscience . . . but to Succession also, and to Inheritances. And
> therefore . . . that is to be done, both which good Men judge to be honest,
> and is allowed by lawful Governours.
>
> SIMON PATRICK, *A Commentary Upon the Historical Books of the Old Testament*

> ANHALT. Why do you force from me, what it is villanous to own?—I love
> you more than life—Oh, Amelia! Had we lived in those golden times, which
> the poets picture, no one but you——But, as the world is changed, your
> birth and fortune make our union impossible—To preserve the character,
> and, more, the feelings of an honest man, I would not marry you without
> the consent of your father—And could I, dare I, propose it to him?
> AMELIA. He has commanded me never to conceal or disguise the truth.
>
> ELIZABETH INCHBALD, *Lovers' Vows*

That Western definitions of incest in the seventeenth and eighteenth centuries were the contingent products of the dynamics of several interlocking
economic systems is nowhere more succinctly evinced than in the words of
Bishop Simon Patrick cited above. Commenting on Leviticus, Patrick acknowledges that moral determinations concerning the legitimacy of close kindred
marriages are not solely matters of conscience but are also intimately tied to the
vagaries of inheritance and property, as well as to prevailing definitions of
honor—or, as it was sometimes also termed, honesty. What "good men judge to
be honest" or honorable (and therefore, by extension, what they deem incestuous), Patrick observes, is contingent simultaneously on scriptural injunctions, economic interests, and the moral consensus of those in power.

No early work of British prose fiction more deftly explores such contingent
relations among overlapping economies of material, sexual, and symbolic exchange or more shrewdly exposes definitions of incest (and of honesty) as the
contingent products of the dynamics of those relations than Jane Austen's
Mansfield Park. From the moment that Mrs. Norris hatches the project of bringing her poor relation, Fanny Price, into the Bertram household from outside, we
enter a world of categorical instabilities and circumstantial uncertainties that
cause the family patriarch, Sir Thomas, to debate and hesitate. Fanny's importation to Mansfield promises mutual material benefits to the Price and
Bertram families: in exchange for the "benevolence" of relieving Mrs. Price

"from the charge and expense of one child,"[1] Sir Thomas will receive not only "the credit of projecting and arranging so expensive a charity" (9) but also, as we soon see, Fanny's services as a companion to his wife. The full profit to be accrued by raising Fanny, however, depends not merely on the operations of a labor economy in which Mrs. Price is able to trade her daughter's services for the "trouble and expense" (7) of the girl's maintenance; it is contingent as well on Fanny's potential value within the male homosocial economy of marriage.[2] The ultimate value of Fanny's "services"—her marketability as an object of sexual exchange—is a matter of speculation at this point in the narrative. Indeed, as Mrs. Norris reassures her brother-in-law, the degree to which Sir Thomas invests in Fanny's education and upbringing will determine his eventual ability to circulate her profitably outside the family: "Give a girl an education, and introduce her properly into the world," she insists, "and ten to one but she has the means of settling well, without farther expense to any body" (*MP*, 7).

That despite such glib assurances Norris's project involves a significant element of risk is evinced in part by Sir Thomas's generalized anxiety about class. It is not just that Fanny might fail to marry "well" and thus become a lifelong drain on resources but also that her dependent presence in the family has as much chance of diluting as of setting off the Bertram's class superiority. Such "credit" as might be gained by taking the girl in, after all, might just as readily be forfeited should one of Sir Thomas's own sons marry down.

But while the dangers of class contamination certainly play an important role in Sir Thomas's doubts about Norris's plan, Norris's allusions to her brother-in-law's "delicacy" and "propriety" (7) indicate that his scruples also pertain to the moral character of close kindred marriages. Although its respectability was much debated, cousin marriage in and of itself was not illegal;[3] nevertheless, when nine-year-old Fanny enters the material and sexual economies of the Bertram family, she enters its symbolic economy as well. Mrs. Norris invokes the surrogate siblinghood of Fanny and her cousins ("brought up, as they would be, always together like brothers and sisters") as insurance against the perils of "cousins in love, &c." (*MP*, 7); but, as Sir Thomas seems to understand, it is also precisely Fanny's *representative* status as a Bertram sibling that renders the idea of cousin-love incestuous.

At this point in the narrative, the interrelated moral and class anxieties that Fanny's liminal status as an outsider inside the Bertram family arouses in Sir Thomas are mutually sustaining and point toward the same solution: on the grounds of both class and kinship, Fanny is unsuitable—indeed "undesirable"—

as a match for the Bertram sons. She herself acknowledges, in the afterglow of
the gratitude she feels for Edmund's gift of a gold chain, that a more than familial affection for her cousin is, or ought to be, unthinkable. And in her case, as in
Sir Thomas's, it is not at all clear whether the evil of such unthinkable excess
would proceed more from the violation of kinship or of class imperatives:

> To think of him as Miss Crawford might be justified in thinking, would in her be
> insanity. To her, he could be nothing under any circumstance—nothing dearer
> than a friend. Why did such an idea occur to her even enough to be reprobated and
> forbidden? It should not have touched on the confines of her imagination. She
> would endeavour to be rational, and to deserve the right of judging of Miss Craw-
> ford's character and the privilege of true solicitude for him by a sound intellect and
> an honest heart. (181)

That by the end of the novel Sir Thomas (in the interest of expediency and
under the pressure of altered prospects of his own) has managed to turn the
liabilities of Fanny's presence into an asset and has come to see the "moral
impossibility" of her marriage to Edmund as a "more than possibility" (320)—as
"not only morally possible, but morally necessary"[4]—only underscores the contingent nature of his morality and of the codes of conduct that he in turn
expects his dependents to observe.

What exactly does Fanny mean when she resolves to endeavor to maintain
an "honest heart"? If we understand the term *honest,* as she clearly intends it
here, in its archaic sense of "honorable" or "decent," then an "honest heart"
is one that will not admit unauthorized (and therefore immodest) thoughts
or feelings to cross into or even "touch on" its boundaries. Austen, however,
plays older against newer meanings of the term, ironically setting the heart that
will not admit (in the paradoxical sense of neither allowing nor acknowledging
the entry of) unauthorized material in tension with a heart like Mary Crawford's, whose unregulated candor and sometimes refreshing irreverence for
shallow codes of honor and decorum earn her the imputation of "blunted
delicacy and a corrupted, vitiated mind" (*MP,* 310). Which is the more honest,
which the more pretentious or more pretending heart? Mary's tendency to own
her thoughts without self-censorship loses her Edmund's, and perhaps also the
reader's, high regard, while Fanny understands that self-censorship has the
power to earn her certain rights and privileges. She will "deserve the right" to
judge Mary's character and "the privilege" of being thought to have (and of

thinking of herself as having) a disinterested and therefore "true," as opposed to selfish or mercenary, interest in her cousin. In this sense, Fanny makes what Pierre Bourdieu has characterized as a particular kind of cultural investment— one that "secures profits which do not need to be pursued as profits" and that therefore brings to investors "the supplementary profit of being seen (and seeing themselves) as perfectly disinterested, unblemished by any cynical or mercenary" motive.[5] Such investments are the enabling condition of what Austen calls delicacy and Bourdieu refers to as the "distinction" of good taste.

Austen's problematizing of the concept of honesty finds intertextual reinforcement in her use of Elizabeth Inchbald's *Lover's Vows* as the play that the young Bertrams and Crawfords select for "home representation" in volume 1 of *Mansfield Park* (97).[6] In the passage from Inchbald's play that serves as one of the epigraphs to this chapter, the poor clergyman Anhalt responds to a declaration of love by his pupil, the wealthy heiress Amelia, by in turn declaring the impossibility of their union. Anhalt and Amelia's love predominantly violates distinctions of rank, but Austen's implicit use of it as an intertextual analog to the love between Fanny and her clergyman-mentor Edmund (with all its Abelardian overtones) may insinuate an incestuous charge as well. When Anhalt is forced by Amelia's declaration to commit the villainy of owning (i.e., admitting) his forbidden passion for her, he endeavors—like Fanny in the passage from *Mansfield Park* discussed above—to "preserve the character, and . . . the feelings" (353) of *honesty* by resisting those passions and deferring to the codes of duty and honor that privilege and sustain paternal authority. Amelia, however, undercuts his resistance by disclosing the contradiction inherent in this ideal of honesty: her father, she insists, has enjoined her "never to conceal or disguise the truth" (364).

In addition to exposing honesty as an unstable signifier with this retort, Amelia (fittingly played by Mary Crawford in the Mansfield theatricals) also somewhat irreverently lifts the veil over the operations of paternal privilege. If definitions of honesty (like definitions of incest) are unstable, that is because they are contingent on the arbitrary exercise of paternal desire; as rulers of their families, only fathers have the freedom and authority to legislate virtue or to extenuate the law. In professing to police desire, patriarchal definitions of honesty simply obscure their own status as always already a function of it.

Playing off Richardson's *Sir Charles Grandison*, Austen joins a long line of literary predecessors in her ironic portrayal of the contingent or suspect morality of such "good men" as Sir Thomas Bertram. Henry Fielding genially mocked the foibles of good men in the figures of Heartfree, Squire Allworthy, Captain Booth, and Parson Adams.[7] But the edge in Austen's satire is closer in spirit to Sarah Fielding's much bleaker vision of male virtue, represented on one side by the sad fate of her guileless hero, David Simple, and his utopian "little Community" and on the other by the "good Man" David meets early in his adventures at the Royal-Exchange, whose epithet has been earned only because he is "worth a Plumb," or one hundred thousand pounds.[8] In some ways, Austen's ironic portrayal of male virtue seems to reach as far back for models as the libertine world of Manley's Intelligence, where "there can be no Laws contriv'd, how binding soever, in Intention and Appearance, but what [the race of men] can extenuate" and where whatever "crafty, long-sighted Lawyer" is most adept at untying "the *Gordian*" of a new law is deemed "an *extraordinary* Person, an *excellent* Man, a *worthy* Councellor, deserving not only treble Fees, but all the Honours of the Gown."[9] In other ways, it recalls the even more distant world of Aphra Behn's fiction, where so unregenerate a figure as Philander, having been imprisoned for regicide, can "at last [be] pardoned, [kiss] the King's Hand, and [come] to Court in as much Splendour as ever, being very well understood by all good Men."[10] Austen's satire, of course, is far more subtle than Behn and Manley's; Tory though she was, she was not directly engaged, as they were, in the public sphere of party politics. Indeed, as I shall argue at greater length below, the objects of Austen's critique ultimately expand beyond the limits of a particular class, gender, or political group to posit the play of prohibited desire in all moral choice. Austen nevertheless participates in a well-established tradition when, as Jan Fergus observes, she "requires us to register the irony that a generally good man like Sir Thomas" will both participate in colonial slavery and encourage young women to sell themselves in marriage, while "discard[ing] the daughter who sold herself when she becomes damaged goods,"[11] or when, as Claudia Johnson notes, she mocks Fanny's determination to see Edmund as " 'an example of everything good and great' " despite the fact that he "shares his father's tendency to invest personal desires with the dignity of moral imperatives."[12]

Margaret Kirkham calls our attention in this connection to another important intertext in *Mansfield Park,* Shakespeare's *Henry VIII,* which Henry Crawford discovers Fanny has been reading to Lady Bertram in chapter 3 of volume 3. At this point in the novel, as Kirkham notes, Fanny has become the object of Sir Thomas's wrath and will soon be sent away by her uncle, in a circumstance mirroring that in which Queen Katherine will be cast off by her husband in the third act of Shakespeare's play.[13] But while Kirkham rightly observes that both women are being forced to submit to the arbitrary authority of (supposedly) good men, she overlooks the importance of the problem of incest in Austen's choice of Shakespearean intertext. Fanny surely fits the model of obedience that Katherine invokes to characterize herself as she struggles to understand why she, a "poor woman, and a stranger,"[14] should suddenly be cast off by a man whose will she has sought so fervently to uphold: "When was the hour / I ever contradicted your desire? / Or made it not mine too?" (2.4.27–29). And Sir Thomas can easily be read as a version of the angry monarch threateningly invoked by Cardinal Wolsey to elicit cooperation from the queen: "The hearts of princes kiss obedience, / . . . but to stubborn spirits / they swell and grow, as terrible as a storm" (3.1.162–64). In order to appreciate the full force of these intertexts, however, we must read them in light of the instability of Sir Thomas's position regarding Fanny's marriage into the Bertram family. Katherine, it will be recalled, is cast off when Henry—in quest of an heir by the already pregnant Anne Bullen and having, as Katherine ironically comments, "grown . . . desperate to be honest" (3.1.86)—deploys contingent definitions of incest to have their marriage (contracted twenty years prior under a papal dispensation) annulled. That this annulment, which effectually cancels Henry's earlier marital vows, demonstrates rather inconstancy than honesty reverberates ironically in *Mansfield Park,* not only when Fanny reads from Shakespeare's play in a chapter that also makes much of the question of another Henry's constancy, but also at the end of the novel, when the inconstant nature of Sir Thomas's moral principles is exposed. What Shakespeare's Queen Katherine cannily observes upon the approach of the Cardinals Campeius and Wolsey may surely be applied to both Sir Thomas and Henry Crawford: "they should be good men . . . / But all hoods make not monks" (3.1.22–23).[15] Nevertheless, when Austen intertextually activates a long tradition of ironic portrayals of good men by alluding to Shakespeare's play, she also invokes a long history of contingent determinations of incest. Like Henry VIII, it turns out, Sir Thomas is a person of false scruples. That Austen makes Crawford rather than Sir Thomas the king's namesake merely extends the field of possible analogies, suggesting through the shared Henrician association that the distinction between Crawford's profligacy and capriciousness on the one hand and the sturdiness of the settled patriarch on the other may not be very stable after all.

Breeding Distinctions

> The so-called modern domestic family has largely been constructed
> through narratives of absence and figures of pathological deficiency . . . ; it
> has been always already dysfunctional, in crisis, *en miettes,* porous, and
> open to the outside.   RODDEY REID, *Families in Jeopardy*

Critical understanding of Sir Thomas Bertram's domestic morality has been
much enriched in recent years by studies that have sought to understand the
contingent relationship between Mansfield Park's moral economy and the material economy of colonial expansion and the slave trade.[16] Not only do the
comforts and security of the Mansfield estate depend on profits from Sir Thomas's Antiguan sugar plantation, which is in economic trouble in the wake of
abolition and a drop in sugar prices, but Fanny Price's position in the Bertram
family serves as an analog of slavery itself. Moira Ferguson notes that Fanny's
original transportation to Mansfield Park from her native Portsmouth is described "in terms often reserved for epiphanic moments in the narrative of
slavery,"[17] while Joseph Lew characterizes her later exile to Portsmouth for
resisting exchange on the market in the form of marriage to Henry Crawford as
"a domestic equivalent to the colonial practice of starving slaves into submission."[18] Mrs. Norris, it has been observed, shares the name of one of the
cruelest of colonial overseers alluded to in Thomas Clarkson's *Abolition of the
Slave Trade,* which Austen read before composing *Mansfield Park;*[19] Fanny is
compelled, at Norris's whim and at the risk of her own health, to "[stoop] in a
hot sun" (*MP*, 52); and so on.

Even the comforts of Mansfield that Fanny enjoys at her most ascendant
moments belie oppression. It is true that Portsmouth's punitive character as a
place of exile for Fanny proceeds, in part, from the change in status that, as a
woman, she experiences on her return there. At Mansfield, as she reflects nostalgically, "every body had their due importance; every body's feelings were
consulted. If tenderness could be ever supposed wanting, good sense and good
breeding supplied its place" (*MP*, 266). By contrast, when after nine years she
arrives at Portsmouth, where Mrs. Price's "daughters never had been much to
her" (264) and Mr. Price talks "only to his son" (258) and "only of the dockyard"
(264), Fanny's brothers rudely ignore her while conversing about ships. Where
at Mansfield Park, women are preeminently interesting topics of conversation
(are they "out"? are they "*not* out"? whom are they destined to marry? [36–38]),

the only subject of interest at Portsmouth—indeed, the "one subject [that swallows] up all the rest" (260)—is the Thrush: her beauty, her destination, her "coming out" (258). But Austen ironically insinuates identity as well as difference between Portsmouth and Mansfield Park. If women have no direct role in the "manoeuvring business" (34) of commerce and conquest that animates Portsmouth, the place of importance they occupy in that other sort of trade conducted by men at Mansfield Park does not, as Sir Thomas's treatment of his niece surely testifies, guarantee more genuine regard for their feelings and welfare than is evident in Mr. Price's benign neglect. It might even be argued that, because Portsmouth restricts its commerce primarily to the exchange and plunder of material goods, it has a moral edge over Mansfield Park, which, in trafficking women at home and exploiting slave labor abroad, is no less guilty of the commodification of human beings than the urban ports of Bristol and Liverpool that dominated the trade in human flesh.[20] Women may have a certain status and "due importance" as "interesting objects" at Mansfield Park, but such distinction commands a price; and Fanny chafes under the obligations that accompany her acquisition of "consequence" there on more than one occasion, perhaps most memorably at the ball her uncle sponsors in her honor, where she is unable to perform the "hard duty" of being at the center of attention ("introduced here and there . . . , and forced to be spoken to, and to curtsey, and speak again") without looking longingly—and, we cannot help feeling, enviously—"at William, as he [walks] about at his ease in the back ground of the scene" (MP, 187). Like Maria's escape from her father's house into a marriage in which, like the starling, she subsequently feels caged ("I cannot get out, as the starling said" [71]), the female adventure of "coming out" at Mansfield Park, as Fanny's appearance at the ball suggests both literally and figuratively, entails bearing a cross and chain.

The metaphoric link between women and slaves as forms of property also positions Fanny metonymically in an analogical relationship to the Antiguan estate itself. Like her, Sir Thomas Bertram's West Indian property occupies the place at Mansfield Park of a dangerous supplement that will prove either an asset or a liability to the family fortune, depending on the extent to which it is able to be improved; and in both instances, improvement is a function of good breeding. Just as the question of whether Fanny will be a source of family "credit" or a drain on resources is contingent on the success of the Bertrams' "breeding [her] up" (8) so as to maximize her reproductive value on the marriage market, so is Sir Thomas's ability to turn a profit on his Antiguan plantation in the wake of abolition dependent on the replenishment of his labor force by means other than *buying* slaves. As critics have noted previously, the increased demand on West Indian planters to improve living and working conditions on their plantations in order to ensure the health, survival, and reproduction of their slaves after 1807 (when slave-trading, though not slaveholding, became illegal) is precisely the sort of economic exigency that might have called an absentee owner like Sir Thomas Bertram away from home, though as Moira Ferguson and Maaja Stewart also suggest, Sir Thomas's role in the reproduction of his labor force may be even more direct than that, given the common practice among planters of fathering children by their female slaves.[21]

It is clear, in any event, that Austen is interested in the semantic and moral ambiguities inherent in the category of good breeding, which, like the term *honesty,* is tinged with impurity. Sometimes in *Mansfield Park* the aims of cultural and biological reproduction overlap, as when Fanny's breeding (or education) serves to regulate her breeding (or reproductive life) by ensuring that she marry into a certain class and adhere to the laws of proper sexual circulation. But at other moments those aims diverge, producing an ironic gap or slippage between manners and morals. Such slippage is evident, for example, in the passage cited above in which Fanny, exiled to Portsmouth, reflects wistfully on Mansfield Park as a place where good breeding always "supplied the place" of a lack of tenderness (one thinks perhaps most readily here of the Bertram daughters' behavior toward their father); but it emerges even more pointedly in a comment Mary Crawford makes to her brother in a discussion of his suitability as a husband for Fanny Price. In this conversation, Mary disagrees with Henry that their uncle, Admiral Crawford, is "a very good man." Henry's filial relationship with his uncle, she insists, has "blinded" him to the latter's faults, but fortunately an early marriage would rescue him from the admiral's corrupting influence. There "could not be two persons in existence, whose characters and manners were less accordant" than Henry and Admiral Crawford, she affirms; but she follows with an assertion that, though intended as a "reflection on the Admiral," ultimately betrays her own combination of familial blindness and moral shallowness:

> Henry, I think so highly of Fanny Price, that if I could suppose the next Mrs. Crawford would have half the reason which my poor ill used aunt had to abhor the very name, I would prevent the marriage, if possible; but I know you, I know that a wife you *loved* would be the happiest of women, and that even when you ceased to love, she would yet find in you the liberality and good-breeding of a gentleman. (*MP,* 202)

That the "liberality and good-breeding of a gentleman" can accommodate the sort of discreet adulterous breeding that Fanny might expect from a husband like Henry Crawford once he had ceased to love her not only indicts Henry Crawford but seems to reach out to incriminate Sir Thomas Bertram as well, in whose marriage, we have been assured, "good breeding" will always substitute for a lack of tenderness. Austen's irony at once allows the slippage between manners and morals and realigns the divergent aims of legitimate culture and unlicensed biological reproduction: the good breeding of Mansfield Park is supported by the patriarch's breeding of slaves abroad (some of which breeding may very well be adulterous), while at home it comes to depend on another suspect type of breeding when Sir Thomas finally decides that he has in fact "been bringing up [a] wife for his younger son" (191).

Incest, Liberty, and National Identity

> In the growth of virtuous females all human happiness depends.
>
> JOHN ALLEYNE, *The Legal Degrees of Marriage Stated and Considered*

Regulatory discourses about incest had been implicated in the evolving discourse of British liberty from the time that Henry VIII broke with Rome. In fact, as we have seen, the question of incest had rested squarely at the heart of British nationalism since its inception. By the 1770s, however, incest discourses, which had long partaken of the rhetoric of slavery and freedom associated with England's resistance to the ecclesiastical authority of the Roman Empire, became additionally resonant with those new forms of antislavery rhetoric associated with the Atlantic trade. Thus, in the second edition of *The Legal Degrees of Marriage Stated and Considered*, John Alleyne invokes such "illustrious decisions" as the Mansfield Judgment and the principles of "political freedom" and "domestic liberty" established by them to justify his defense of close kindred marriages. Since *Mansfield Park* also mobilizes the linked discourses of incest and liberty as they were inflected by late-eighteenth-century antislavery arguments, it is worth looking more closely for a moment at the nuances of Alleyne's deployment of the concept of "domestic" liberty in order to better understand the vagaries of the relationship between those two discourses over time.

Alleyne represents ecclesiastical restraints on certain varieties of close kindred marriage (primarily marriage to the deceased wife's sister) as a form of slavery. Prohibitions against marriage with a parent or, by analogy, with an "elder kinsman, immediately connected with the parent—as the uncle or the aunt" he deems necessary to the preservation of "due respect and authority";[22] sensual love between brothers and sisters, he further grants, should be avoided, lest "every house. . . become a brothel" in a society where "in the growth of virtuous females all human happiness depends" (10). But beyond these relations, there is none whose good effects are not in his opinion enhanced by a "more intimate union" (11) (siblings, in other words, represent the outer limit on intrafamilial marriage). Religious restraints on such unions constitute nothing less for Alleyne than an infringement of the civil liberty of British subjects "in a nation whose constitution nearly has reached perfection,—wherein political freedom, has been secured by the most illustrious decisions; wherein the rights of nature, have been asserted by manifest actions, and vindicated by the most consummate reasoning; wherein domestic liberty hath been acknowledged, and the very air pronounced too pure for slavery to exist in" (vi).

It is surely more than historical accident that only two years prior to the publication of the first edition of *The Legal Degrees of Marriage,* Alleyne had made his first appearance in Westminster Hall as a counsel in defense of liberty in the Somerset case, in which Chief Justice Mansfield pronounced his famous ruling denying Captain Charles Stewart proprietary rights over James Somerset, an African whom Stewart had purchased as a slave in Virginia and brought to England in 1769.[23] When after two years Somerset deserted his master, Stewart had had him apprehended and locked in irons for forcible shipment to Jamaica to be sold; but Stewart's agents were brought to court on a writ of habeas corpus. At the conclusion of a lengthy trial, Lord Mansfield ruled in a reluctant and controversial decision that the positive laws of England did not support Stewart's right to Somerset's forcible detainment for sale and that "therefore the black must be discharged."[24] Echoing Blackstone and, before him, legal precedents from as far back as the reign of Queen Elizabeth, the counsels for Somerset's defense had repeatedly sounded the same refrain: "England was too pure an air for Slaves to breathe in."[25] Although Lord Mansfield himself later equivocated about the intended scope of his ruling, the Somerset case—coming as it did in the wake of several earlier rulings that had favored the rights of white Britons to abduct Africans in England for sale abroad—was hailed as a major victory for the cause of universal liberty. In the words of Thomas Clarkson, Somerset had finally settled the "great question . . . hitherto studiously avoided": " 'Whether an African slave coming into England became free?' "[26]

It matters little whether Austen knew of Alleyne or his work, although Alleyne is certainly mentioned in Clarkson's *History,* a work that we know Austen read and much admired.[27] What is striking is the extent to which her extended exploration of the ideal of domestic liberty in *Mansfield Park* discursively activates the same nexus of concerns. Like Alleyne, Austen joins the problem of incest and the problem of slavery: in a novel whose title alludes to Lord Mansfield's landmark decision, she produces a heroine who, according to R. F. Brissenden, comes to represent English liberty in its purest form through an endogamous refusal to circulate against her will in a mercenary marriage scheme.[28] As Margaret Kirkham observes, moreover, *Mansfield Park* echoes the favorite phrase of Somerset's counsels in its frequent references to the "free air and liberty" of the English countryside, suggesting that Austen was likely to have been familiar with the phrase, if only from her reading of Clarkson's history.[29] Be that as it may, when Fanny Price—vindicated at last in her rebellious refusal of Henry Crawford's suit—returns near the end of Austen's novel from the "closeness . . . noise, . . . confinement, bad air [and] bad smells" of Portsmouth to the "liberty, freshness, fragrance, and verdure" (*MP,* 293) of Mansfield Park and its "modern, airy" house (303), she enters the Bertram family for the second time on very different terms from those that characterized her original appearance there. She is no longer an outsider and an inferior, but a soon-to-be-fully-integrated member of the Bertram clan as daughter to her uncle and wife to her cousin and foster brother. It is a plot turn that seems to mark her liberation into full and equal membership in the Mansfield community in much the same way that the Mansfield decision seemed to free James Somerset into full English subjecthood—the proverbial "family of man." A further look at Alleyne's treatise and the history of the Mansfield Judgment, however, may provide the context for a better understanding of the ironies through which Austen's novel in fact problematizes the very ideal of English liberty that it appears to authorize.

When Alleyne appropriates the phrase about the purity of the English air from the Somerset trial for his defense of another type of "domestic" liberty, that of English subjects to marry their extended kin, he draws an implicit parallel between colonial and ecclesiastical oppressions. At the level of metaphor, that is, he represents the vindication of James Somerset and of close kindred marriages as two versions of the same humanitarian project with the same broad emancipatory aims. In chapter 2, I observe that, despite such universalized representations, the concepts of domestic liberty and natural rights deployed by Alleyne in fact presuppose clear sexual and racial hierarchies. That some of the same liberatory arguments that Henry VIII had deployed to ratify restrictions on kindred marriage are here used by Alleyne in defense of their reduction, furthermore, suggests that what was at stake historically in debates over the validity of specific marriage prohibitions was not so much the inherent nature of individual laws as the changing role played by those laws in period-specific struggles for power among groups of men competing for access to women.[30] Produced in a cultural context where political rights to liberty and property were measured in terms of such access, Alleyne's project undertakes to extend the rights of English men by reducing restrictions on their freedom of sexual access to their female kin.

But which groups of men were vying for rights of sexual access to the female kin of Englishmen? In her fine reading of *Mansfield Park,* Maaja Stewart argues that concerns over the sexual behavior of Sir Thomas Bertram's daughters during his absence from England is a displacement of anxieties about his own sexual transgressions abroad. "The discourse of female virtue and domesticity in England and the commodification of the slave women's sexuality in the West Indies," Stewart writes, "are both expressions of the imperial adventurer's fear and the displacement of his own transgressive sexuality."[31] But while Stewart perceptively identifies "Fanny's final triumph in marrying her cousin" as "the triumph of the familiar over the alien in a novel that touches so much foreign material," she defines the category of "the foreign" almost exclusively in terms of the non-European women with whom English planters came in contact in the West Indies (127). Although she refers to the Mansfield decision in another connection, she makes no mention of concern about the corresponding circumstance: that of English women's exposure to the presence of non-European men at home.

That fears about the growing population of blacks in London haunted the popular imagination from the 1770s on is clear from a range of contemporary commentary. Predictably, concern about what David Brion Davis calls "the domestic implications of 'outlawing slavery' " emerged most emphatically in the opinions of those hostile to the Somerset cause.[32] For example, in his *Considerations on the Negroe Cause* (1772)—excerpts of which appeared in *The London Chronicle* in 1772 and in *The Gentleman's Magazine* in the following year—Samuel Estwick observes that at the time of the Somerset trial "there were already fifteen thousand Negroes in England; and scarce is there a street in London that does not give many examples of that." Calling for legislation to prohibit "the importation of them . . . to this country," he hopes to "preserve the race of Britons from stain and contamination."[33] Edward Long's *Candid Reflections upon the Negroe Cause* (1772)—excerpted alongside Estwick in *The London Chronicle*—follows suit:

We must agree with those who have declared, that the public good of this kingdom requires that some restraint should be laid on the unnatural increase of *blacks* imported into it. . . . The lower class of women in *England,* are remarkably fond of the blacks, for reasons too brutal to mention; they would connect themselves with horses and asses, if the laws permitted them. By these ladies they generally have a numerous brood. Thus, in the course of a few generations more, the English blood will become so contaminated with this mixture, and . . . this alloy may spread so extensively, as even to reach the middle, and then the higher orders of the people, till the whole nation resembles the *Portuguese* and *Moriscos* in complexion of skin and baseness of mind. This is a venemous and dangerous ulcer, that threatens to disperse its malignancy far and wide, until every family catches infection from it.[34]

These are the express concerns of the opponents of Somerset's cause. Less expected may be the worry about miscegenation displayed by Somerset's own counsels at his trial. Sergeant Davy, who himself introduced the phrase about the purity of the English air in his opening arguments, also acknowledged the need for a law to regulate the influx of individuals of African descent to England, "for now and then we have some Accidents of Children born of an Odd Colour." Without such a law, Davy declared, "I don't know what our Progeny may be, I mean of what Colour—a Freeman of this country may in the course of time be the grandfather of half a Score of Slaves for what we know."[35] In the meantime, Davy assured the court, the existence of plantation laws preventing slaves from escaping to England or denying freedom to such fugitives (in contrast to slaves brought to England by their masters) guaranteed that a positive ruling for Somerset would not open the floodgates to the immigration of a vast number of West Indian slaves.

Like his trope of the English air as "too pure for a slave to breathe in," which in a telling slippage suggests simultaneously that England is too pure to countenance the institution of slavery *and* that its air, being too pure for a slave to breathe, is apt to be contaminated by the presence of too many immigrant Africans,[36] Davy's position demonstrates clearly that antislavery sentiments and racist concerns about miscegenation in the 1770s were by no means politically inconsistent attitudes. It is thus entirely possible that the rhetorical move in which Alleyne presents his defense of close kindred marriage as a parallel development to his defense of the rights of enslaved Africans who had set foot on English soil may obscure what was in fact a more complex historical and ideological relationship. Rather than setting a precedent or model for later arguments in favor of close kindred marriages (as Alleyne's rhetoric suggests it does), the Somerset case may in fact have *prompted* those arguments as a sort of limiting ideological countermove—a policing mechanism in the renegotiation of interior and exterior borders necessitated by the climate of global expansion and of class and geographical mobility that characterized the age and whose threat to the stable boundaries between metropole and colony was so starkly represented by the Somerset trial. In fact, I would argue, the historically and ideologically convergent discourses of racial and sexual liberation deployed by John Alleyne were not so much analogs of one another as they were mutually constitutive and mutually regulatory—even complementary formations, one of which promised to consolidate boundaries that the other one had threatened to disperse. As such, they exemplify precisely the relationship that Ann Laura Stoler posits as generally characteristic of early modern discourses of sexuality and race in her observation that "Europe's eighteenth-century discourses of sexuality . . . were refracted through the discourses of empire and its exigencies, by men and women whose affirmations of a bourgeois self, and the racialized contexts in which those confidences were built, could not be disentangled."[37]

The point is certainly not that the growing population of free blacks to which writers like Estwick, Long, and Davy allude was in fact vying for rights to the women of white Englishmen. In this sense, Maaja Stewart is right to see mechanisms of projection and displacement at work in connection with cultural anxieties about the domestic effects of British colonialism in the West Indies—even indeed the displacement of anxiety about the sexual transgressions of European men. But if women, both free Europeans and enslaved Africans, were the sites of such displacements, so surely were those freed African men whose mobility and attractiveness—as these were construed in the white European imagination—appeared to pose a threat to the exclusive proprietary control of Englishmen over their female kin. If male freedom in England was tacitly understood in terms of the privilege of access to women for purposes of breeding (as Alleyne's assertion that "all human happiness depends" on "the growth [or breeding, in the sense of multiplying as well as cultivating] of virtuous females" implies it was), then the manumission of Somerset would at some level have to be understood in those terms as well—that is, as potentially allowing Africans freed from the feminized position of commodities to move into the "field of men." Stewart explores the "problematics of authority" in *Mansfield Park* through an analysis of the novel's images of hunting and a discussion of English game laws (which worked "to contain the gifts of nature for the exclusive enjoyment of a few legally qualified men"),[38] linking the operation of such laws at the level of society to the ideology of property informing the laws of primogeniture at the level of the family. This ideology, she suggests, provided the underlying justification for the " 'right of acquiring property' in human beings" (120), and she further observes that the progressive positions of Blackstone and Mansfield on game laws and the Somerset case, respectively, turn critically on the distinction between natural and positive law. She might profitably have mentioned incest laws and Alleyne's progressive views about them here as well; for as we have seen, such laws were grounded in the same proprietary ethos as game laws and primogeniture, and they were a site where the distinction between natural and positive law was perennially exploited in the negotiation and maintenance of political, class, and racial boundaries.[39] Eurocentrically understood, the legalization of close kindred marriage would extend legitimate access to female kin more broadly not only to white Englishmen but theoretically to freed Africans as well, thus expanding the options for legitimate "inbreeding" in both populations and thereby presumably curtailing the threatening effects of interracial sexuality. Naturalized notions of gender asymmetry were the enabling condition of this paradoxical and internally self-regulating logic, which in addition to projecting a British model of kinship onto an immigrant African population also presupposed a certain cross-cultural reciprocity or homosocial bond on the part of men: white Englishmen, or so they seemed to believe, could abolish the commodification of immigrant blacks, acknowledging the freedom of black men *as men,* while at the same time neutralizing any consequent threat to the stability of racial—and thus, by extension, national—boundaries by exploiting the long-standing instability of intrafamilial boundaries (i.e., incest laws) grounded in the presumably natural and universal commodification of women. In this sense, as Austen seems to understand, the traffic in women functioned as the enabling ground of British liberty.

That an inverse relation between incest prohibitions and miscegenation anxiety persisted well into the nineteenth century, when indeed the link between liberalization of the prohibited degrees of marriage and fears about racial mixing became explicit, is clear from comments surrounding the "Wife's Sister Bill," whose passage in 1907 finally ended a long history of parliamentary debate over that "perennial legislative problem"—marriage to the deceased wife's sister—that had begun with the passage of Lord Lyndhurst's Act regulating such marriages in 1835.[40] Nancy F. Anderson recounts the case of a supporter of the bill, writing in the *Westminster Review* in 1875, who "defended cousin marriages on the grounds that it was natural to want to marry someone similar to oneself":

> If there is, he said, an "innate horror of intermarriage with relations," there is "an equally universal and much better founded dislike of marriage with foreigners . . . 'God made white men, and God made black men, but the Devil made half-castes.'" The tone of this argument suggests that, at least for this author, anxiety about miscegenation, surely a common occurrence in the nineteenth-century British colonial empire, was greater than incest anxiety.[41]

Like the discourse of race that emerges in the context of New World slave rebellions and the British antislavery movement of the late eighteenth century as an attempt to ground racial difference in nature at a time when the political and geographical bases of that difference were being challenged, incest discourse questioning the scope of the prohibited degrees of marriage relies on naturalized notions of gender asymmetry to reinforce racial boundaries. One of the various "progressive projects" to which racial thinking tacitly "harnesse[d] itself" in the late eighteenth century, incest discourse defending close kindred marriages also qualifies as one of those "deeply sedimented discourses on sexual morality" that, in another connection, Stoler suggests "could redraw the 'interior frontiers' of national communities, frontiers that were secured through—and sometimes in collision with—the boundaries of race."[42]

"Not in a state of utter barbarism": Desire and the Scandal of Recognition

> "My dear Miss Price," said Miss Crawford. . . . "Selfishness must always be forgiven you know, because there is no hope of a cure."
>
> JANE AUSTEN, *Mansfield Park*

> Fanny looked on and listened, not unamused to observe the selfishness which, more or less disguised, seemed to govern them all.
>
> JANE AUSTEN, *Mansfield Park*

Understanding *Mansfield Park*'s deployment of the articulated themes of incest and slavery in the context of cultural anxieties regarding the sexual rights of English men may help to explain not only the narrative's subtly racialized descriptions of the Crawfords (Mary has a "dark eye" and "clear brown complexion"; Henry is "black and plain" and has "so much countenance, and his teeth were so good, and he was so well made, that one soon forgot he was plain" [*MP*, 33]) but also the underlying nature of Edmund's moral dilemma over acting in the Mansfield theatricals. Edmund's quandary about whether to act or not to act turns on his assessment of the relative risks of refusing to act on moral grounds and thereby forcing the young players to go *outside* of Mansfield for a man to fill the part of Anhalt, or agreeing (against his better judgment) to play the part of Anhalt himself and thereby keep the "business" of acting (108) *inside* the "family circle" (110). His dilemma is to determine which is the lesser evil of the two. Ultimately, of course, in a decision that prefigures Sir Thomas's later change of heart about cousin marriage, Edmund chooses to compromise his own moral scruples rather than incur the dangers attendant on allowing a stranger, Charles Maddox, "the *more* than intimacy—the familiarity" of being "domesticated among us—authorized to come at all hours—and placed suddenly on a footing which must do away all restraints" (108). There are several ironies surrounding Edmund's choice. His insistence on the necessity of making such a compromise so as to protect his sister's "delicate" situation (89) and to prevent Miss Crawford's subjection to the "unpleasantness" of "acting with a stranger" (108), of course, belies the fact that, by preventing Maddox from playing opposite Mary, Edmund is protecting his own self-interest against the incursions of a potential rival for her favors. His final decision to *go in* with the crowd by installing himself (as an insider) in the role of Anhalt, moreover, ensures precisely the circumstance that he claims to be endeavoring to forestall: namely, Mary Crawford's "acting with a stranger." For as Edmund himself has previously suggested to his brother, Tom, what makes the private theatricals so dangerous in this context to begin with (so "highly injudicious" as the two families "are circumstanced" [89]) is that the Bertram "family circle" has already been infiltrated from outside, has already extended its boundaries to include not "only brothers and sisters" but also "intimate friends" (91). In fact, the Crawfords have no more relation to the Bertrams by blood or affinity than does John Yates, though their connection to and residence with the rather aptly named Grants has *granted* them precisely the privileged access to the Mansfield children that makes Charles Maddox such a threat in Edmund's eyes. Like James Somerset, on whom a change of place had conferred a change of status, the Crawfords are accorded freedoms merely by virtue of their habitation within a given domestic space, when in fact, despite the way things "seem" to Edmund later on, the city-bred siblings no more "belong" to Sir Thomas's "own domestic circle" or have any legitimate "claim" (135) to its privileges than an African slave transplanted to England after the Mansfield decision would have had a claim to the full privileges of English subjecthood.

My point is not to suggest a simple racial allegory in *Mansfield Park* whereby the deracinated, nomadic—indeed gypsylike—Crawfords come to stand for freed Africans and Maria Bertram's adultery with Henry Crawford for a metaphorical form of miscegenation. Nor is it to suggest that the novel's racialized depiction of the Crawfords signals Austen's anxious concern with interracial sexuality per se. It is, rather, to recapitulate what my discussion of Alleyne's writing has sought to show: that discourses of incest and domestic liberty as they were constituted in the early nineteenth century were always already inflected by racial thinking, so that when *Mansfield Park* deploys those discourses, it also mobilizes their racial implications. The Crawfords' racial marking functions less as a sign of their national or racial identity, that is, than as an index of their discursive function in the narrative as embodiments of what is foreign, somehow not-English, or culturally Other. Like the presence of free blacks in England, their presence at Mansfield Park creates a circumstance in which the boundaries between outside and inside, strangers and "intimate friends," or acceptable and unacceptable partners (in life or on stage) become difficult, if not impossible, to sustain.

If this condition of indeterminacy accounts for the difficulties inherent in Edmund's moral choice in the theatricals episode, it also explains the horror with which Fanny encounters the news of Maria's adulterous elopement with Henry Crawford, an "event . . . so shocking" to Fanny that, as the narrator confides,

> there were moments even when her heart revolted from it as impossible—when she thought it could not be. A woman married only six months ago, a man professing himself devoted, even *engaged,* to another—that other her near relation—the whole family, both families connected as they were by tie upon tie, all friends, all intimate together!—it was too horrible a confusion of guilt, too gross a complication of evil, for human nature, not in a state of utter barbarism, to be capable of!— yet her judgment told her it was so. (299)

One of the first to note the "anxiety of boundary-confusion" in *Mansfield Park* in her important essay on the novel, Ruth Bernard Yeazell relates Fanny's horror at Maria and Henry's affair to a repudiation of adultery as "the greatest of crimes, the most threatening violation of domestic purity" on the part of a novel that at the same time manifests "a certain bias toward incest." According to Yeazell, Austen's novel displays an "insistent endogamy" grounded not in the historical specificity of an early-nineteenth-century ideal of domesticity but in the timeless and finally irrational impulses of "primitive morality."[43] That *Mansfield Park* becomes a veritable proving ground for anthropological theory on this reading may suggest as much about Yeazell's own historically situated willingness to reify anthropological concepts of the primitive as it does about Austen's narrative per se.[44] Nevertheless, one might be tempted, for the sake of historical argument, to appropriate Yeazell's theory about the novel's privileging of incest over adultery as a bulwark against the dissolution of familial boundaries. Such an appropriation would plausibly align Austen, after all, with such defenders of close kindred marriage as John Alleyne, who explicitly follows John Fry's arguments in *The Case of Marriages Between Near Kindred* (1756) and Fry's radical precursors of the 1640s in taking the position that the Levitical prohibitions were directed not in fact against incest but against adultery.[45]

Ultimately, however, to read *Mansfield Park* as privileging incest over adultery within the binary alternatives of what Susan Stewart in another connection has called "the overly propinquitous and the overly alterior" seems to me to oversimplify the case, to close questions that Austen goes out of her way to leave undecided, and to posit antinomies that she takes some pains to subtly destabilize.[46] In fact, I would argue, Fanny's shock and disbelief at the "confusion of guilt" and "complication of evil" represented by Henry and Maria's adultery has less to do with the *difference* between adultery and incest than with the fact that, in a circumstance in which alterity has already been so domesticated that adultery ends up violating internal *as well as* external boundaries, it has become impossible to clearly distinguish between the two. That the marriage of Edmund and Fanny that resolves *Mansfield Park*'s comic plot should possess the same ambiguous character as Maria's adultery, being predicated as it is on *going out* and *going in* at the same time (the family interloper having become acceptable as a conjugal partner for her cousin only because she has taken on the status of a sister), is one of the novel's brutal ironies. Only a complex, doubly negative locution like the one Austen uses to characterize Fanny's experience of that "too horrible a confusion of guilt, too gross a complication of evil for human nature, not in a state of utter barbarism to be capable of"—which asserts that it simply *is not possible* for humans *not* in a primitive state to be capable of such vice—could be worthy of such an irony, for despite Fanny's conviction of its impossibility, Henry and Maria *have* committed precisely such a barbarous deed. Austen, I would argue, is not so much invested in endorsing incest over adultery as she is in exposing the inherently interested and thus contingent nature of all moral choices in a world where the presence of *outsiders within* has always already disturbed the possibility of domestic purity. Within a global context of increasing geographic and class mobility where distinctions between inside and outside were becoming historically blurred, the "incestuous" marriage of Fanny and Edmund is less a solution to than itself a symptom of such cultural contingency.

The Wimpole Street scandal sends home to Fanny the truth that what she has assumed must be unthinkable might not be so impossible after all. Not only has the event unsettled her ability to rely on a stable distinction between civilization and barbarity by exposing the barbarousness of civilized human beings; it has also, as a consequence of that epistemological disturbance, given new scope to her own unruly and unauthorized desires, not the least of which is her desire for Edmund to regard her as something more than a sister or a friend. Why otherwise should it be so "dangerous" for Fanny to contemplate the scandal's "consequence"? Could that desire, with the irrepressible glee that attends it and threatens to erupt just below the surface of her horror, be—above all—what produces her sense of shock? One might as well be privy to the thoughts of an intractable being like Emma Woodhouse in the passage that details Fanny's reflections on the news:

> What would be the consequence? Whom would it not injure? Whose views might it not affect? Whose peace would it not cut up forever? Miss Crawford herself—Edmund; but it was dangerous, perhaps, to tread such ground. She confined herself, or tried to confine herself to the simple, indubitable family-misery which must envelope all. (*MP*, 300)

As her own refusal of Henry will now be vindicated and "Edmund must be for ever divided from Miss Crawford" (307), the Bertram family scandal is destined to affect Fanny's own "views," or romantic prospects, in ways that make it difficult for her (however she might *try*) to respond to it as a source of unqualified misery. And indeed, before long, we learn explicitly (in words that serve by repetition and revision only to highlight the urgency of Fanny's affective wishfulness) that, on being called back to Mansfield by Sir Thomas three days after her discovery of the affair, "She was, she felt she was, in the greatest danger of being exquisitely happy, while so many were miserable" (301).[47]

In this sense, Fanny's experience of astonishment at the news of her cousin's adultery is not unlike the experience of wonder that Stephen Greenblatt has identified as characteristic of European encounters with other cultures—that mixture of pleasure and pain, longing and horror that immobilizes the human subject at the apprehension of something at once unbelievable and true and that thereby forces a suspension of categories and a revision of assumptions as to what is possible and what is only fabulous.[48] Insofar as Fanny sees in Henry and Maria's adultery the possibility of what has to her always seemed unthinkable (for example, her thinking of Edmund as only Miss Crawford might have been justified in thinking of him), her experience of surprise at the scandalous news of her cousin's affair signals another critical aspect of those New World encounters that Greenblatt describes: namely, a recognition of the other in herself. It has often been noted that Fanny's response to Maria and Henry's elopement involves "feelings of sickness" and "shudderings of horror" (MP, 299) that seem more appropriate to the crime of incest than adultery; but that response may seem more fitting if we read it not only in connection with Maria and Henry's adultery but also in light of the consummation of Fanny's desire for Edmund, to which, in fact, their crime opens the way.

In this context, Edmund's passionate declaration upon first reuniting with his cousin at Portsmouth—when Fanny finds herself "pressed to his heart with only these words . . . , 'My Fanny—my only sister—my only comfort now'" (MP, 302)—registers considerable irony. By virtue of Maria and Henry's crime, Edmund has lost a sister and a prospective wife, both of which losses it may now be possible for Fanny to supply. Edmund's insistence on Fanny's purely sisterly function as a source of comfort to him—an insistence underscored by his (perhaps unconsciously defensive) insertion of the qualifier "my only sister" into a phrase that, unqualified, might have allowed for something more—suggests both Edmund's own determined obtuseness to Fanny's desire and Fanny's inevitable disappointment at his having uttered "only these words" when, just moments before, she had been "ready to sink" at the thought of Edmund's being "so near her, and in misery" (302). Those who invoke this passage as evidence of the novel's privileging of sisterly regard over sexual passion miss Austen's irony,[49] which subtly establishes that what Fanny feels for Edmund is not at all "warm and sisterly regard"—the reassuring illusion of which Edmund at last submits to believing he may be able to settle for—but rather a full-fledged passion of which he remains as yet obstinately and somewhat comically unaware (MP, 319). Fanny, that is to say, has precisely the sort of tenacious desire for Edmund that Edmund is moved to repudiate as tainted and self-serving in Mary Crawford—a passion indeed that saturates and contaminates the very moment of "modest loathing" by which Austen tempts us to distinguish her from Mary (308).[50]

That Mary, in her way, understands the irony of Edmund's position is suggested by the bitter reflection she makes in her last, painful interview with him. Edmund is shocked at Mary's equanimity in the face of what he calls "the dreadful crime committed by her brother and my sister." His own sudden recognition of Mary's cultural "difference" from him—a difference that up to this point "it had not entered [his] imagination to conceive"—produces in him an astonishment that mirrors Fanny's earlier sense of shock in the face of what she had deemed unthinkable. (Ironically, of course, what is unthinkable in Mary here also mirrors what Fanny finds so disturbing in her own response to the affair: her failure to properly "[consider] its ill consequences.") Although he laments Mary's cruelty, Edmund himself cruelly appropriates the moral high ground in this exchange, insisting that he would rather mourn the loss of the Mary he thought he loved than have to acknowledge the desire underlying her impulse to minimize the Bertram scandal's social consequence ("could I have restored her to what she had appeared to me before," he reports having been determined to confess to her, "I would infinitely prefer any increase of the pain of parting, for the sake of carrying with me the right of tenderness and esteem"). It never occurs to Edmund that Mary's impulse to play down the enormity of the affair may proceed from her own desire to avoid the necessity of having to separate from him. In any event, although Edmund sees himself as the only sufferer in this exchange ("I had not supposed it possible, coming in such a state of mind into that house, as I had done, that any thing could occur to make me suffer more, but . . . she had been inflicting deeper wounds in almost every sentence"), his diatribe prompts Mary's own astonishment, wounded laughter, and these words: "A pretty good lecture upon my word. Was it part of your last sermon? At this rate, you will soon reform every body at Mansfield and Thornton Lacey; and when I hear of you next, it may be as a celebrated preacher in some great society of Methodists, or as a missionary into foreign parts" (310–11). Mary seems to intuit the colonial desire underlying Edmund's domestic morality when she implies here that his zealous intolerance of difference must in time extend beyond the boundaries of his own domestic space. Indeed, as Johanna Smith suggested some time ago when she argued that Fanny actually manipulates Edmund into the decision to marry her, this may be the same zealous passion that underlies Edmund's blind insistence on construing Fanny's "tenderness" as nothing more formidable or threatening than sisterly regard (319).[51] It may be the same impulse, that is, by which he sustains the illusion that Fanny is not a desiring subject but the perfect mirror of his own best self—the figure who guarantees his freedom by representing a domestic "otherness" marked not by alterity, alliance, or exteriority but by sameness, kinship, and interiority. Much the same gesture of jettisoning difference through substitution that governs Fanny's displacement of Mary in Edmund's affective economy characterizes the final move whereby the "married cousins" at last displace the Grants and Crawfords as the "other" family in Sir Thomas's domestic economy when, at the very moment that they are ready to reproduce, Fanny and Edmund take up residence in the recently vacated Mansfield parsonage (*MP*, 321).

Austen's critique of Edmund and Sir Thomas Bertram's colonial impulse to appropriate and reduce all difference to sameness with the self, nevertheless, remains part of her more general satire on human nature and the inconsistency of all human motives, including those of even so virtuous a character as Fanny Price. Such inconsistencies, Austen implies, are inherent in the very structure of human desire, which, when prohibited from attaining its object, will satisfy itself with more lawful—or less "impossible"—substitutes. As Mrs. Grant at one point casually but also resonantly observes, "if one scheme of happiness fails, human nature turns to another; . . . we find comfort somewhere" (34). What does it mean for Austen to posit a substitutive model of human interiority at a moment of epistemological crisis precipitated by the privileging of class over kinship and characterized by the consequent disturbance of a clear distinction between being and representing family? If Fanny replaces Mary in Edmund's affective economy, what does it mean that Edmund functions in Fanny's as a substitute for that more primary love object, her brother William Price? I address Austen's treatment of the foundational status of sibling love in more detail in the following pages. What I hope to have intimated here is that in *Mansfield Park* Austen at once participates in and interrogates the emergent production of an incestuous notion of human subjectivity that, by reproducing the gender asymmetries of traditional kinship systems at once as natural and as saturated with desire, also provides the soil and sustaining ground for naturalized notions of racial purity.

Too Close for Comfort: Kinship, Politics, and the Erasures of History

It is always through replacement that values are created.

JEAN-JOSEPH GOUX, *Symbolic Economies*

Oedipus is always colonization pursued by other means, it is the interior colony . . . our intimate colonial education.

DELEUZE AND GUATTARI, *Anti-Oedipus*

It is far less the father than the brother that modern literature calls to account; less the mother than the sister who must be recognized and given her due as the real rather than the imaginary "other" necessary to found male identity and group life; less the son than the younger brother, the son-not-heir who can appear in a new symbolic.

JULIET FLOWER MACCANNELL, *The Regime of the Brother*

R. F. Brissenden locates *Mansfield Park*'s "greatness," its "psychological depth," in its understanding of the liberatory role that incestuous love plays in the "complex, dynamic and vital web of motivations, desires, compulsions and affections by which the main characters are linked to each other."[52] Fanny's marriage to her cousin and surrogate brother, he observes, "can be seen as fulfilling the forbidden incestuous dream of giving complete sexual expression to the feelings of love and affection we have for the closest members of our own family" (166). A similar view of the emancipatory value of Fanny's love for Edmund and consequent rejection of marriage to Henry Crawford emerges even in an interpretation as nuanced as Susan Fraiman's 1995 reading of the novel, which argues that when Fanny crosses Sir Thomas and "declines to enrich her family by sacrificing herself," she "tacitly asserts her right to reject and also to love where she will," thereby taking a stand against the gender givens of her day.[53] In assessing Fanny's refusal to *marry out* in the absence of a counterbalancing discussion of the gender implications of her desire to *marry in*, however, Fraiman's account of Fanny's "significant rebellion" against "the sexual politics of marriage" (812) ultimately occludes Austen's simultaneous critique of the sexual politics of kinship. Such a critique, I shall argue, is implicit in the novel's deployment of the concept of place and in its extended meditation on the displacements of historical memory.

In chapter 1, I looked at the role that incest narratives play in establishing the spatial and temporal boundaries of cultural intelligibility. As Judith Butler observes, such narratives mobilize a distinction between what is "before" and "during" culture and between what is "inside" and "outside" of normativity and the law.[54] In this chapter, I have focused thus far on the ways in which *Mansfield Park* exposes the contingent and mutually regulatory relation between the exercise of liberty inside and outside the family. I conclude now by looking in a more sustained fashion at how, through the narrative manipulation of spatial and temporal perspectives, Austen also interrogates the privileged place of fraternal love in her heroine's psychic economy. Contrary to the prevailing critical consensus that *Mansfield Park* privileges the love between brother and sister as primary and foundational, I argue that the novel in fact constitutes the bond between siblings of the opposite sex as an essentially arbitrary and thus unstable moral ground.[55]

The Place of the Brother

"The place of all places, the envied seat, the post of honour, was unappropriated. To whose happy lot was it to fall?" (*MP*, 58). One could easily imagine such a question being asked at the end of the penultimate chapter of *Mansfield Park*. The adultery of Maria Bertram and the imprudent elopement of her sister Julia have vacated the position of favored daughter in Sir Thomas Bertram's household, and Mary Crawford's "blunted delicacy" (310) has ousted her from the affections of her suitor, Edmund Bertram. Both a daughter and a wife are thus "wanted" at Mansfield Park (320). By the end of the novel, both "post[s] of honour" will fall to the "happy lot" of Fanny Price, who will occupy the "place of all places" in her dual status as wife to her cousin Edmund and daughter to her uncle-guardian.

Of course, the "envied seat" in question here is not literally Fanny's position at Mansfield Park but the empty seat next to Henry Crawford on his barouche-box. The uncertainty as to who (whose fanny?) will occupy this wished-for spot arises in volume 1, as a select party of Mansfield women are preparing to "take their places" (58) in Crawford's barouche for a trip to Mr. Rushworth's ancestral estate at Sotherton. Up to this point in the narrative, Henry has been dallying with the affections of both Bertram sisters, "with no object but of making them like him" (33). Each sister now covets the affirmation of consequence that her place by Henry's side would signify and the opportunity to engage his full attentions. Well trained by their Aunt Norris's example to mask desire with the pretense of self-sacrifice, each thus meditates "how best, and with the most appearance of obliging . . . others" to secure the coveted object of desire (58).

The figural relation of the barouche-box seat to Fanny's final position of consequence as niece, daughter, wife, and sister at Mansfield Park nevertheless establishes identity as well as difference between the heroine and her female cousins and thus raises questions about her motives and character. Does the text's conclusion vindicate Fanny "without qualification" as an embodiment of "true moral consciousness amid the selfish manoeuvring and jostling of society," as Tony Tanner has argued,[56] or has the all-enduring Fanny Price herself undertaken, like her cousins, to secure a place of consequence with the mere "appearance of obliging . . . others"? Consciously or not, as Michael Heyns observes, Fanny displays a "surprising elasticity of principle."[57] Does she also therein disclose symptoms of Aunt Norris's monstrous selfishness? In *Mansfield Park*'s world of overstated impossibilities, is the Fanny Price who "cannot act" (*MP*, 102) an emblem of moral virtue and authenticity, or as David Marshall and Joseph Litvak so compellingly demonstrate, is she always already implicated in the play of signs and appearances?[58]

If the barouche-box episode raises possible doubts about Fanny's character, moreover, its sustained exploration of what we might call the novel's situational contingencies of value[59] also suggests questions about the relative comfort of her ultimate position of importance at Mansfield Park. This is not simply because the coveted attentions of Henry Crawford (here figured, like Fanny's fate, by the barouche-box) are insincere and ultimately selfishly bestowed, thus insinuating the hypocrisy and selfishness of the Bertrams. It is also because the earlier episode so firmly establishes the principle that what one sees depends on where one sits. Edmund has suggested use of the barouche-box as a way of opening a space for Fanny to join the party to Sotherton, provided it will entail no hardship or unpleasantness for the other ladies. On the contrary, Maria insists, as the barouche-box commands the best view of the country, it would be "the favourite seat" (*MP*, 56). This assessment of the relative comforts of riding inside the carriage or on the barouche-box is borne out when Mrs. Grant assigns the vacant spot to Julia, and Maria is condemned to remain "within," where despite the more fitting accommodations, she has "very little real comfort" because "her prospect always [ends] in Mr. Crawford and her sister sitting side by side full of conversation and merriment" (58). That gloomy prospect brightens temporarily when the party comes within view of Sotherton and Maria is reminded of those other sorts of "prospects" represented by her impending marriage to Mr. Rushworth. But the "dreadful" situation of the house at Sotherton (59), which (we soon learn) excludes "the possibility of much prospect from any of the rooms" (61), already foreshadows the discomforts and disappointments that Maria's loveless marriage to Rushworth will entail despite the present promise of wealth and consequence.

Such extended play on the idea of place as both a status and a physical location, with its corollary play on "prospects" as both spatial and social phenomena, lends resonance and irony to the novel's concluding assessment of the perfection of Fanny's "place" at Mansfield Park, qualified as that assessment is by phrases delimiting the frames or perspectives through which Austen's characters and readers look or see.[60] Although formerly an object of restraint and alarm to Fanny, the parsonage into which she and Edmund move with the acquisition of Mansfield living upon the death of Dr. Grant, we are told, "soon grew as dear to her heart, and as thoroughly perfect in her eyes, as every thing else, within the view and patronage of Mansfield Park, had long been" (*MP*, 321). Clearly, to attribute perfection to everything within the view and patronage of Mansfield Park is to assign value from a decidedly limited vantage point.[61] Persecuted as Fanny has been by the demands and "interest" of her uncle, it may be difficult to imagine such willful blindness on her part; but Fanny's character is nothing if not painfully other-directed in its determination to see the world from the point of view of masculine power. Whether that inclination has taken the form of thinking and feeling as Edmund would have her think and feel (indeed, as he himself thinks and feels) or of attempting to please her benefactor, Sir Thomas, by assuming an interest first and foremost in all that interests him, Fanny's eyes have tended to view Mansfield from within a man's field of vision—indeed, from "within the view of Mansfield" itself.

In other words, as in the scene of the barouche-box, what one sees at the end of Austen's novel and how one assesses the "picture of good" presented there depends upon one's prospect or point of view—on whether or not one stands (with Fanny) morally and ideologically "within the view of Mansfield Park." Austen's art resides precisely in her unrelenting exploration of the effects of spatial and status positions on epistemology and morals, and on her gift for opening (and thereby exposing the conditions and contingencies of) multiple and shifting horizons of possibility. Value in Austen's novel never exists within an open perceptual field but always emerges as an effect of moral and spatial boundaries and of the displacements and substitutions that the mapping of such boundaries requires.

Austen's interest in such contingencies of value has much to do with her own historical situatedness at a moment of crisis in traditional notions of place and identity. Within the classical episteme, identity was coded as function of place—of the subject's position within a social hierarchy. The discursive order of the Enlightenment, on the other hand, enacts a disassociation of place *from* identity (what Francis Barker has called an "imaginary desocialization of subjectivity")—a transformation manifested, as Duckworth notes, in a broad cultural shift "from ontology to psychology, from public orders to private worlds" that establishes the sovereignty of a morally autonomous subject as the site of an essential interiority.[62] But as Juliet MacCannell implies in the passage quoted as an epigraph above, the modern subject is a *gendered* subject in a "new symbolic" that is neither politically nor ideologically innocent.[63] The place of the sovereign subject in the Enlightenment program to overthrow "the cult of the ancestor" (11) ("to forget the dead, to install the rule of the contemporary, the same generation, over the rule by the dead, the elders" [18]) is occupied not by just *any* subject but specifically by the figure of the brother.

In her treatment of sibling love in *Mansfield Park*, Austen simultaneously posits and problematizes the foundational status of such fraternal privilege within the modern episteme. Key to her analysis is a sequence of conversations about place that occur almost exactly midway through the novel and that invoke the privilege of fraternal access to the sister as a necessary condition for the founding of male identity and the negotiation of social relations between men. In the first exchange, the Bertrams have accepted an invitation to the Grants', where they are enjoying a game of speculation and an extended conversation about place begun when Henry recounts having happened upon Thornton Lacey the day before. Henry insists that, with judicious improvement, Edmund's intended living may be raised "into a *place*" (rather than "a mere gentleman's residence" [*MP*, 167]) and advances a proposal, which is promptly but politely rejected, to move quite literally into Edmund's "place" by renting Thornton Lacey for the coming winter. The object of Henry's scheme, as he explains to Fanny, is to establish year-round residence in the Mansfield neighborhood, so that he might "come at any time" and thereby "find himself continuing, improving and *perfecting* that friendship and intimacy with the Mansfield Park family which was increasing in value to him every day" (169).

Henry desires, in other words, to move into Edmund's place socially as well as physically, for residence at Thornton Lacey would afford him the privilege of sustained access to Fanny that Edmund—as a surrogate brother—already has. As Henry's language pointedly suggests, he wishes to *improve* his place in the Mansfield community.

The foundational status of privileged fraternal access to the sister emerges again in a related exchange about place that immediately follows this brief interlude. Here William picks up the thread of a side conversation he has had about visiting his cousin Maria at Beachy Head—a "smart" place where, being a "poor scrubby midshipman," he claims not to expect much of a welcome (168). This self-effacing quip about the liabilities of his own place, or rank, is taken up now privately, when Fanny asks her brother whether he regrets not being present at the Portsmouth Assembly and William responds by saying that he does not regret it at all since, as a midshipman, he is not likely to attract the interest of the "Portsmouth girls." "One might as well be nothing as a midshipman," he laments. "One *is* nothing indeed." In her rejoinder to William's blanket assumption that his entire worth and identity are subsumed by his social place, Fanny insists upon a more complex ontology—one that posits an essential, authentic self or identity anterior to and independent of social determinations. "But never mind it, William. . . . ," she declares, "It is no reflection on *you;* it is no more than the greatest admirals have all experienced, more or less, in their time."[64] As the conversation unfolds, however, it becomes apparent that what Fanny takes for granted as William's intrinsic worth is in fact a function of his position, or place, in the gendered structures of familial privilege. When, in a gesture that acknowledges her brother's class dependency even as it insists on his inherent consequence, Fanny presumptuously assures William that Sir Thomas "will do everything in his power to get you made" (171),[65] the Price siblings fall under the supervisory gaze of their uncle and find it necessary to talk of something else. But the change of subject is no more than a shift of register—from talk of social and professional status to talk of domestic consequence—as William alludes to another status, this time one that he no longer occupies: that of Fanny's childhood dancing partner.

The subtle movement that occurs here between spatial and temporal frames, as it does earlier in Fanny's allusion to rank as a function of time ("it is no more than the greatest admirals have all experienced . . . in their time"), is one to which I shall have occasion presently to return. For the moment, I would simply observe that the siblings' choice of altered topic in this conversation seems hardly the most likely or best suited to defuse the threat of paternal discipline. Prompted by the thought of his "nothingness" among the Portsmouth girls and to compensate for his sense of class and professional inferiority, William entertains the nostalgic wish for a return to the childhood consequence he once enjoyed as Fanny's brother—a pleasure he proposes to recapture by dancing with her at Mansfield Park, where no one would know his real identity ("I'd dance with you if you *would*, for nobody would know who I was here, and I should like to be your partner once more"). In an obverse reenactment of the mimetic freedoms of the private theatricals that gave Maria Bertram and Henry Crawford license to trade passionate words and gestures under the pretense of representing family (specifically, Agatha and her son, Frederick), William's scheme of dancing with Fanny while impersonating a stranger would allow him for a blissful moment to defy the laws of sexual exchange that require the surrender of his privileged status as his sister's primary object of interest. Strikingly, although Fanny anticipates "some very grave reproof" from her uncle for such talk, Sir Thomas is "by no means displeased" (172) by his nephew's incestuous fantasy (no more displeased, indeed, than he was by Henry's earlier expression of desire to cultivate a greater intimacy with the Mansfield family ["Sir Thomas heard and was not offended" (169)]). On the contrary, he "prolong[s] the conversation on dancing" (172) as precisely the founding moment for his niece's introduction into social circulation. For Sir Thomas, it would appear, the thought of Fanny's dancing with her brother presages his ward's entry into the very system of substitution and exchange that might enable him at last to reap the profits of his "charitable" investment in her.[66]

That the same verbal exchange phantasmatically gratifies both William's incestuous longings and Sir Thomas's patriarchal and material speculations underscores the dialectical and mutually sustaining relationship between incest and exchange within a heteropatriarchal sexual economy. Constituted as both the model and the limit of desire, incestuous love between brother and sister functions in this economy as the zero degree point or horizon of possibility that at once necessitates and mobilizes desire's substitutive movement at the level of the sign; as Terri Nickel observes in another connection, "sibling affection here is the ground for any exogamous love."[67] It is fitting, therefore, that the Price siblings' conversation should be interrupted and finally eclipsed by the more insistent question of which "stranger" will ultimately come to stand in William's place of consequence, as Henry—having been foiled in his earlier attempt to gain access to Fanny by moving into Edmund's "place"—now proceeds by other means, imperiously seizing that metonymic sign of Fanny herself, her shawl, from Edmund's grasp, so that Fanny (in a pointedly redundant iteration of her condition of pure lack) is "obliged to be indebted to his more prominent attention" (*MP,* 173). It is a gesture that sets the stage for the drama of the ensuing two chapters, where Fanny must decide whether to support William's cross with Edmund's or Henry's chain and where her introduction to the "trade of *coming out*" (183)—a trade in which, as Mary Crawford casually acknowledges, "[a]ll are supplanted sooner or later" (190)—only exacerbates her "longing to be with" her brother (187).[68]

Memory's Horizon: or, The Brother's Time

Fanny's marriage to her cousin Edmund simultaneously defers and fulfills this fraternal longing. At the same time, in her status as a fully assimilated outsider at *Mansfield Park,* Fanny performs an essentially inoculative function. Through her resistance to Henry and her subsequent marriage to Edmund, she not only seals the Mansfield estate off from the external intrusion of such threatening influences as the Crawfords and their tainted morality; she also steps into the breach that opens inside the family when the sexuality of a woman like Maria Bertram eludes male control and thereby threatens what John Alleyne had called "the general system of [human] happiness."[69] She thus occupies the simultaneously discomfiting and comforting position of excessive closeness that enables Mansfield Park to be self-sustaining and to withstand change.

But if, as we have seen, the recuperative value of Fanny's marriage to Edmund is rendered problematic by Austen's manipulation of spatial perspectives and metaphors, it is just as powerfully destabilized by the narrative's exploration of temporal contingencies. On the one hand, Fanny functions as a guardian of cultural memory.[70] In contrast to the Miss Bertrams, who arrogantly "exercise their memories" on "the chronological order of the kings of England" (*MP,* 16–17)—including, presumably, Henry VIII—but, like Mary Crawford, show little genuine interest in the history of Sotherton and its former inhabitants (except, in Maria's case, to gratify her vanity), Fanny attends "with unaffected earnestness to all that Mrs. Rushworth could relate of the family in former times, its rise and grandeur, regal visits and loyal efforts, delighted to connect any thing with history already known, or warm her imagination with scenes of the past" (61). Against the Crawfords' passion for improvements that obscure historical memory and deliberately erase all visible signs of change,

Fanny's sense of attachment and obligation to the past makes her wish always to be reminded of origins—of what is being, or what has been, lost. She relishes the idea of seeing Sotherton "in its old state" (41) and, in contrast to Mary Crawford, who insists that, had she an estate to improve, she "should never look at it, till it was complete," expresses delight at the idea, in such a circumstance, of "seeing the progress of it all" (42). Indeed, Fanny seems a veritable object lesson in the deleterious effects of unregulated desire on memory and familial obligation, for, on more than one occasion, she herself becomes the victim of others' "forgetfulness" (54) and neglect—not least of all that of her cousin Edmund, who twice abandons her while in the grip of infatuation with the "careless" (178) and irreverent Mary Crawford.

And yet, as Fanny herself expostulates while sitting with Mary in Mrs. Grant's shrubbery, the faculty of memory is as much an extension of as a defense against desire. Just as spatial positioning always implies a horizon beyond which one cannot see, the act of remembering has its own internal limits and entails its own forgetfulness. Struck by the "growth and beauty" of Mrs. Grant's shrubbery, which only three years earlier had been "nothing but a rough hedgerow" and now (in an arc of improvement that mirrors Fanny's own) is "converted into a walk" that might as readily be deemed "an ornament" as "a convenience," Fanny observes in wonder that "perhaps in another three years we may be forgetting—almost forgetting what it was before" (143). In the self-editing that here transforms "forgetting" into "almost forgetting," Fanny seems to intuit that in the moment one acknowledges forgetting, one begins remembering. Her ensuing meditation on the mysteries of memory nevertheless suggests that, even in the most devoted historian, recollection is imperfect, limited by the scope of human understanding and distorted by desire. The marvel of memory, she observes, resides not simply in what it is able to retain but also in what it has the power to shut out or to exclude: " 'If any one faculty of our nature may be called *more* wonderful than the rest, I do think it is memory. There seems something more speakingly incomprehensible in the powers, the failures, the inequalities of memory, than in any other of our intelligences. The memory is sometimes so retentive, so serviceable, so obedient—at others, so bewildered and so weak—and at others again, so tyrannic, so beyond controul!—We are to be sure a miracle every way—but our powers of recollecting and of forgetting, do seem peculiarly past finding out' " (143).

Mrs. Norris's assumption that her nine-year-old niece's inability to recite the chronological order of the English kings or the Roman emperors probably means that Fanny has no memory "at all" may be designed to show the aunt's arrogant stupidity (16), but it by no means guarantees that Fanny's memory is without deficiencies. Just as the Miss Bertrams "cannot remember the time when [they] did not know a great deal" about Western history, and just as one may be apt to forget that a walk was once a mere hedgerow, so Fanny is inclined to forget aspects of her own experience. At Mansfield, she recalls her Portsmouth home nostalgically as a place of warmth and affection that "would heal every pain that had since grown out of the separation" from her family (251), only to be wounded upon her return there with reminders of her parents' indifference and neglect; at Portsmouth she indulges in much the same version of what Fraiman calls "idealizing retrospection,"[71] when she remembers Mansfield Park as a place of "peace and tranquillity" where "every body had their due importance; every body's feelings were consulted" and "no tread of violence was ever heard" (*MP*, 266).

Given the clear inclination of Fanny's memory to edit out both her Portsmouth family's and the Bertrams' abusive treatment of her, how are we to assess the degree of blindness and forgetting entailed in her recollection of the "felicity" of childhood attachment to her brother, an attachment whose "precious remains," we are told (perhaps ironically), would feel "the influence of time and absence only in its increase"? Grounded in the pleasures of shared recollection ("a strengthener of love, in which even the conjugal tie is beneath the fraternal" [161]), sibling love certainly does seem to be presented by Austen's narrator as the moral fulcrum of *Mansfield Park*—the privileged "model not only for affection within the original family but for the formation of new homes and families."[72] Through her penetrating analysis of historical memory, however, Austen introduces the possibility that Fanny's assessment of an "unchecked, equal, fearless intercourse" (*MP*, 161) with her brother might entail its own element of the familiar wishfulness—that the idyll of sibling love might, like both Portsmouth and Mansfield Park, be yet another of the novel's deficient plenitudes.[73]

Like Edmund at Mansfield Park, William is the only member of Fanny's Portsmouth family who takes an interest in her in what is otherwise an environment of emotional deprivation. There is thus an element of ironic understatement in the narrator's assertion that Fanny "had never known so much felicity in her life" as in her intercourse with him, a certain painful suggestion that Fanny's "felicity" may be inspired as much by gratitude for whatever crumb of attention or affection she may be able to command as by a genuine fraternal reciprocity.

William is described as "opening all his heart to [his sister], telling her all his hopes and fears, plans, and solicitudes respecting that long thought of, dearly earned, and justly valued blessing of promotion" while, with the exception of the "hardships of her home, at Mansfield—" (which are, significantly, minimized as "little"), his interest in Fanny consists largely of curiosity about other people (her parents, the Bertrams, Mrs. Norris [*MP,* 161]).[74] Like Edmund's, in other words, William's interest in Fanny is decidedly self-referential. Later, when William and Fanny are riding to Portsmouth, "the pleasant talk between the brother and sister" is confined once again exclusively to William's concerns (praise of the Thrush, naval encounters, speculations upon prize money, his next promotion, and—only after all of these—"the little cottage comfortable, in which he and Fanny were to pass all their middle and latter life together" [254]), while those of his sister (with whose feelings about Mr. Crawford William is expressly unable to empathize) make "no part of their conversation" (254).[75] Such asymmetrical relations are perhaps unsurprising between children whose "first associations and habits" are established in "the same family" (*MP,* 161)— one where "William's concerns must be dearest—they always had been—and he had every right" (260).

Pace Brissenden, *Mansfield Park*'s "psychological depth" and "range of social and moral significance" consist not in its recognition of incestuous love as the natural ground of cultural reproduction (the original, prohibited pleasure that drives the processes of substitution and exchange),[76] but rather in its subtle exposure and interrogation of the founding presuppositions about gender and desire through which kinship structures and their multiple cultural exclusions are reproduced. Far from sounding the depths of the human heart, as Brissenden suggests she does, Austen deftly discloses the mechanisms whereby power relations are affectively instituted at the level of the individual subject, unmasking the processes whereby what Foucault has called "the deployment of alliance" installs itself in the order of sexuality.[77] As the ground of consciousness or subjectivity, Fanny's endogamous "no" to Sir Thomas functions as *both* an escape from the imperatives of family, gender, and exchange *and* as the occasion for reinscribing the cultural value of those very imperatives. For if the "domestic liberty" figured by her rebellion against paternal desire marks the space of incestuous freedom, it does so in a turn to the brother that, while seeming to challenge gender hierarchies, in fact enables and obscures the institution of fraternal privilege.

If sibling love is *Mansfield Park*'s psychic horizon of possibility, in other words, there is no reason to assume that that horizon is any less problematized as the effect of bounded human perception in a world of space and time, or any less subject to the erasures of history, than the novel's other psychic and moral certainties. To borrow a phrase from another context, such certainties may be the very "grounds of being,"[78] the founding conditions of the subject's cultural intelligibility; but they exist as *certainties* only so long as they appear to be natural and without historical provenance—so long as the conditions of their emergence (their *Entstehung*) are screened from view and the trace of privilege or tread of violence displaced from the reach of cultural or of personal memory.[79] If, as Michael Seidel has written, the work of satire is to unmask the sanctifications of violence that the operations of history cover up, then Austen—true to her genre—"blows history's cover" by disturbing those settled "grounds" upon which cultural and narrative traditions sustain and reproduce themselves.[80]

Whether in becoming Edmund's wife and the beneficiary of Sir Thomas's forgetfulness of his "early opinion" (320) of cousin love, Fanny Price has forgotten her own class origins and thus fulfills the threat alluded to by Walter Benjamin in the epigraph that heads this chapter—"that of becoming a tool of the ruling classes";[81] or whether, on the contrary, she remembers her history of suffering with a vengeance and retains a private sense of *ressentiment* or performative agency remains undecided at the end of *Mansfield Park*. What does seem clear is that Austen understands the "speakingly incomprehensible" dimension of all historical narrative—that telling contradiction whereby every recollection of the past and every prospect for the future of civilization entails erasures at once brutal and consoling. It is a contradiction that Benjamin also acknowledges when he writes that "[t]here is no document of civilization which is not at the same time a document of barbarism" (256); and it is registered in *Mansfield Park*'s record of the process whereby the Bertrams' civilizing project of cultural preservation in the assimilation of Fanny Price secures for British men the domestic liberty *of* internal access and *from* external intrusion through acts of honesty, good breeding, and occluded memory.

Notes

ONE: Modernity, Incest, and Eighteenth-Century Narrative

1. Incest plots appear as well in a variety of short fiction of the period, including Aphra Behn, "The Dumb Virgin or, The Force of Imagination" (1700); Delarivier Manley, "The Perjur'd Beauty" (1720); Eliza Haywood, *The Force of Nature; or, The Lucky Disappointment* (1725); Mary Davys, *The Reform'd Coquette* (1724); and the anonymous *Illegal Lovers* (1728) and *Eleanora; or A Tragical but True Case of Incest in Great-Britain* (1751). For some suggestive recent analyses of incest in a variety of genres, see Ellen Pollak, ed., *Constructions of Incest in Restoration and Eighteenth-Century England,* a special issue of *The Eighteenth Century: Theory and Interpretation* 39.3 (fall 1998).

2. The prevalence of incest plots in eighteenth-century English fiction is noted in J. M. S. Tompkins, *The Popular Novel in England, 1770–1800* (London: Constable & Co., 1932; reprint, Lincoln: University of Nebraska Press, 1961), 62–66; Margaret Anne Doody, *Frances Burney: The Life in the Works* (New Brunswick, N.J.: Rutgers University Press, 1988), 277; and Julia Epstein, "Burney Criticism: Family Romance, Psychobiography, and Social History," *Eighteenth-Century Fiction* 3.4 (1991): 279–80. Within the last decade, several critics have begun to offer more sustained article or chapter-length treatments. See, e.g., Caroline Gonda, *Reading Daughters' Fictions, 1709–1834: Novels and Society from Manley to Edgeworth* (Cambridge: Cambridge University Press, 1996), chap. 1; George E. Haggerty, *Unnatural Affections: Women and Fiction in the Later Eighteenth Century* (Bloomington: Indiana University Press, 1998), esp. pt. 1; T. G. A. Nelson, "Incest in the Early Novel and Related Genres," *Eighteenth-Century Life,* n.s., 16.1 (1992): 127–62; Terri Nickel, "'Ingenious Torment': Incest, Family, and the Structure of Community in the Work of Sarah Fielding," *The Eighteenth Century: Theory and Interpretation* 36.3 (1995): 234–47; and Brian McCrea, *Impotent Fathers: Patriarchy and Demographic Crisis in the Eighteenth-Century Novel* (Newark: University of Delaware Press, 1998), esp. chap. 7. In the case of incest in Renaissance literature, several full-length studies have appeared in roughly the last decade: e.g., Marc Shell, *The End of Kinship: 'Measure for Measure,' Incest, and the Ideal of Universal Siblinghood* (Stanford, Calif.: Stanford University Press, 1988); Bruce Boehrer, *Monarchy and Incest in Renaissance England: Literature, Culture, Kinship, and Kingship* (Philadelphia: University of Pennsylvania Press, 1992); and Richard A. McCabe, *Incest, Drama, and Nature's Law, 1550–1700* (Cambridge: Cambridge University Press, 1993).

3. Peter L. Thorslev Jr., "Incest as Romantic Symbol," *Comparative Literature Studies* 2 (1965): 56, 56 n. 2. In the same spirit, Jean H. Hagstrum writes: "It has been thought that during the eighteenth century the theme [of incest] remained out of sight. This is not

true. No less than five of Dryden's plays make it prominent, and Defoe and Fielding chose not to avoid it. But of course it did not become prominent and obsessive, nor did it receive powerful literary treatment, until that soaring—or searing—of the spirit that we call Romanticism or at least until respect for institutional control declined as the French and American revolutions became imminent" (*Sex and Sensibility: Ideal and Erotic Love from Milton to Mozart* [Chicago: University of Chicago Press, 1980], 58).

4. McCabe, *Incest, Drama, and Nature's Law*, 291.

5. Nelson, "Incest in the Early Novel," 160. Interestingly, Nelson reverts to this phantasmatic mode of explanation at about the same point in his article at which he raises the question of the relation of incest plots to social reality, a question he links to the observation that when women write about father-daughter incest, they tend to do so in sensationalist or romantic instead of realistic ways. As I hope to suggest in the course of the following investigation, Nelson's implication that imagined father-daughter incest has the same seductive draw for female as for male writers fails adequately to account for the complicating effects of ideological context on the oppositional coding of romance and realism in early modern England. In particular, it fails to acknowledge the potentially counterhegemonic effects of the romance genre in a literary culture where realism participated so critically in the work of naturalizing a heteropatriarchal model of desire.

6. In a related move, W. Austin Flanders invokes both Freud and Lévi-Strauss to corroborate the view that fictional violations (or near violations) of incest prohibitions in eighteenth-century texts constitute "a mode of imaginative liberation of individual desires" (*Structures of Experience: History, Society, and Personal Life in the Eighteenth-Century British Novel* [Columbia: University of South Carolina Press, 1984], 131–35). Emphasizing the "authenticity of [the] work [of eighteenth-century novelists] in seizing and reporting experience," Flanders accords the early novel a certain ideological innocence and epistemological privilege as a form of proto-anthropology, a project in support of which he quotes the French critic Claude Labrosse, who writes: "Somewhere between music and scientific study, the language of the novel, through its own way of clarifying our fundamental situation, seems like an anthropology in the process of formation and serves an immediate and broad function needed by societies in beginning a self-interpretation" (4–5). This study takes a similar position from the vantage point of the other side of a critique of anthropology.

7. A similar Enlightenment bias characterizes such psychobiographical accounts as Martin C. Battestin's nevertheless interesting discussion of incest in the works of Henry and Sarah Fielding. See "Henry Fielding, Sarah Fielding, and 'the dreadful Sin of Incest,'" *Novel* 13 (1979): 6–18; Martin C. Battestin with Ruthe R. Battestin, *Henry Fielding: A Life* (London: Routledge, 1989), 23–30, 541–42. The classic application of psychobiographical methods of analysis to literary incest as a way of corroborating the universality of the findings of psychoanalysis is Otto Rank, *The Incest Theme in Literature and Legend: Fundamentals of a Psychology of Literary Creation*, trans. Gregory C. Richter (Baltimore: Johns Hopkins University Press, 1992).

8. I use the term *Enlightenment* here, as it is defined by John Bender in "A New History of the Enlightenment?" *Eighteenth-Century Life*, n.s., 16.1 (1992), not to refer to a "strict historical period but rather as a marker to signify a large somewhat rough-edged phase in European culture . . . structured by its production of and operation within certain characteristic diadic oppositions such as reason vs. sentiment, practical vs. aesthetic, public vs. private, the masculine vs. the feminine, and so forth" (5), many of whose categorical

assumptions were consolidated and institutionalized during the Romantic period (8). I would add to Bender's illustrative inventory of productive Enlightenment oppositions two more dyads: romance vs. realism (already invoked above in note 5) and exchange vs. incest (whose importance is the subject of this study). Bender's article also appears as "Eighteenth-Century Studies" in *Redrawing the Boundaries: The Transformation of English and American Literary Studies,* ed. Stephen Greenblatt and Giles Gunn (New York: MLA, 1992), 79–99. Roy Porter makes a compelling case for an "English Enlightenment" in *The Creation of the Modern World: The Untold Story of the British Enlightenment* (New York: Norton, 2001).

9. For a useful brief account of the history of the term *sciences of man,* and particularly of its relation to the history of anthropology since the seventeenth century, see George W. Stocking Jr., "Paradigmatic Traditions in the History of Anthropology," in *The Ethnographer's Magic and Other Essays in the History of Anthropology* (Madison: University of Wisconsin Press, 1992), 342–61. For more extended accounts of the seventeenth- and eighteenth-century roots of nineteenth- and twentieth-century anthropology, see William Y. Adams, *The Philosophical Roots of Anthropology* (Stanford, Calif.: Center for the Study of Language and Information, 1998), esp. chap. 4; Margaret T. Hodgen, *Early Anthropology in the Sixteenth and Seventeenth Centuries* (Philadelphia: University of Pennsylvania Press, 1964); and Michel Foucault, *The Order of Things: An Archaeology of the Human Sciences,* a translation of *Les mots et les choses* (New York: Vintage Books, 1973).

10. The concept of knowledge as a discursive form of power is, of course, Michel Foucault's, most notably in *Discipline and Punish: The Birth of the Prison,* trans. Alan Sheridan (New York: Pantheon Books, 1978); and in *The History of Sexuality, Volume I: An Introduction,* trans. Robert Hurley (New York: Vintage Books, 1980).

11. Because of the power of this naturalized construct in our culture, it may be necessary to reiterate for the sake of clarity and emphasis that the object of analysis in this study is not the social practice of incest but a particular historical construction or representation of incest that emerges in the early modern period and that presents itself as grounded in nature. That there are crucial connections between this representation and social practice, and that these connections have serious practical consequences in the culture, particularly for women, are matters that I address below (see text accompanying notes 45–48). My aim here, in other words, is not to reify but to historicize the cultural construction of incest as liberatory and as a ground of truth.

12. Since the very idea of incest depends on the institution of prohibition (an idea I discuss at further length in the ensuing section), I refer to incest and its prohibition throughout this study as aspects of a single narrative formation or cultural binary. This binary will sometimes also appear in the following pages as incest and sexual exchange—a process thought to ensure, and be ensured by, incest's prohibition.

13. Gayle Rubin, "The Traffic in Women: Notes on the 'Political Economy' of Sex," in *Toward an Anthropology of Women,* ed. Rayna R. Reiter (New York: Monthly Review Press, 1975), 157–210.

14. The term *gender-instituting* is Judith Butler's in *Gender Trouble: Feminism and the Subversion of Identity* (New York: Routledge, 1990), 38.

15. Rubin, "Traffic in Women," 200.

16. Jacques Lacan, *Speech and Language in Psychoanalysis,* trans. Anthony Wilden (Baltimore: Johns Hopkins University Press, 1968), 48.

17. Ibid., 126. See also "The Freudian Thing," where Lacan writes that "in establish-

ing . . . the Oedipus Complex as the central motivation of the unconscious, [Freud] recognized this unconscious as the agency of the laws on which marriage alliance and kinship are based" (*Ecrits: A Selection*, trans. A. Sheridan [London: Tavistock, 1977], 141–42).

18. Nor does Lacan conceive the Oedipus complex as either universal or ideologically innocent ("I do not think that the Oedipus complex appeared with the origin of man . . . but rather at the dawn of history, of 'historical' history, at the limit of 'ethnographic' cultures" [Lacan, *Speech and Language*, 126]; and "The Symbolic order in its initial functioning is androcentric. That is a fact" [quoted in Ellie Raglan-Sullivan, *Jacques Lacan and the Philosophy of Psychoanalysis* (Urbana: University of Illinois Press, 1986), 289]). The term *structural defect in being* is Ragland-Sullivan's (*Jacques Lacan*, 281).

19. Lacan, *Speech and Language*, 40. While it is impossible to argue with Ellie Ragland-Sullivan's account of Lacan's move from an instinctual to a linguistic register ("from the realm of the Freudian sexual triangle to that of symbolic effect") in his reworking of the Oedipus, it does not necessarily follow, as she further argues, that he therefore "leaves the scene of the incest taboo to dramatists and anthropologists" (*Jacques Lacan*, 267). The privilege that Lacan himself accords to the figure of incest makes that clear.

20. "I felt as if I had been guilty of incest," from *The Confessions of Jean-Jacques Rousseau*, quoted in Jacques Derrida, *Of Grammatology*, trans. Gayatri Chakravorty Spivak (Baltimore: Johns Hopkins University Press, 1976), 95.

21. Spivak, "Translator's Preface," in Derrida, *Of Grammatology*, lxv.

22. Derrida, *Of Grammatology*, 262–65.

23. Ibid., 105–6. For Lévi-Strauss on anthropology's debt to Rousseau, see his "Jean-Jacques Rousseau, Founder of the Sciences of Man" in *Structural Anthropology*, vol. 2, trans. Monique Layton (New York: Basic Books, 1976), 33–43.

24. Derrida, *Of Grammatology*, 266.

25. Claude Lévi-Strauss, *The Elementary Structures of Kinship*, rev. ed., trans. James Harle Bell, John Richard von Sturmer, and Rodney Needham (Boston: Beacon Press, 1969), 12, 25; Derrida, *Of Grammatology*, 267. Diane R. Fourny argues that the Rousseau of *Of Grammatology* is in fact "a Rousseau of Derrida's invention." Derrida reads Rousseau through Freud, Fourny argues, while Rousseau's conception of human desire in fact is more consistent with a Girardian model of triangular desire. See Fourny, "The Festival at the Water Hole: Rousseau, Freud, and Derrida on Incest," *The Eighteenth-Century: Theory and Interpretation* 31.2 (1990): 138.

26. Teresa de Lauretis, *Alice Doesn't: Feminism, Semiotics, Cinema* (Bloomington: Indiana University Press, 1984), 112.

27. Judith Roof, *Come As You Are: Sexuality and Narrative* (New York: Columbia University Press, 1996), 64.

28. De Lauretis, *Alice Doesn't*, 120–21.

29. Butler, *Gender Trouble*, 76.

30. Rubin, "Traffic in Women," 180.

31. "The object of repression," writes Butler, "is not *the desire* it takes to be its ostensible object but the multiple configurations of power itself, the very plurality of which would displace the seeming universality and necessity of the juridical or repressive law. In other words, desire and its repression are an occasion for the consolidation of juridical structures; desire is manufactured and forbidden as a ritual symbolic gesture whereby the juridical model exercises and consolidates its own power" (*Gender Trouble*, 75–76).

32. Terry Eagleton, *Literary Theory: An Introduction* (Minneapolis: University of Minnesota Press, 1983), 187.

33. Anita Levy makes a similar argument with respect to nineteenth-century fiction in "Blood, Kinship, and Gender," *Genders* 5 (summer 1989): 70–84. "Paradoxically," she writes, "it is precisely to fiction that we must look to recapture the historical dimension that has been lost in the human sciences" (81).

34. On the decline of kinship, see Lawrence Stone, *The Family, Sex, and Marriage in England, 1500–1800* (New York: Harper & Row, 1977), esp. chap. 4; Randolph Trumbach, *The Rise of the Egalitarian Family: Aristocratic Kinship and Domestic Relations in Eighteenth-Century England* (New York: Academic Press, 1978); and Alan Macfarlane, *Marriage and Love in England: Modes of Reproduction, 1300–1840* (Oxford: Basil Blackwell, 1986). I am particularly indebted in the following discussion to Linda J. Nicholson, *Gender and History: The Limits of Social Theory in the Age of the Family* (New York: Columbia University Press, 1986).

35. Locke is quoted in Nicholson, *Gender and History,* 152, and discussed by Nicholson throughout chapter 5. The terms "Conjugal" and "Political" power are used by Locke in *Two Treatises of Civil Government,* ed. Peter Laslett, 2d ed. (Cambridge: Cambridge University Press, 1963), bk. 1, chap. 5, sec. 48, lines 11–16.

36. On the idea of discourse production as a mechanism of social discipline, see Foucault, *Discipline and Punish* and *History of Sexuality.* On the emergence of early print culture, see Jürgen Habermas, *The Structural Transformation of the Public Sphere: An Inquiry into a Category of Bourgeois Society,* trans. Thomas Burger with Frederick Lawrence (Cambridge, Mass.: MIT Press, 1991). Carole Patemen usefully considers the presuppositions about gender and kinship in early modern contract theory in *The Sexual Contract* (Stanford, Calif.: Stanford University Press, 1988). For a nuanced account of some of the difficulties in determining the extent to which historiographical claims of a shift in family structure in this period may themselves participate in the production of what was, even at its inception, "essentially a semiotic event," see Christopher Flint, *Family Fictions: Narrative and Domestic Relations in Britain, 1688–1798* (Stanford, Calif.: Stanford University Press, 1998), 1–20.

37. See, e.g., Nancy Armstrong, *Desire and Domestic Fiction: A Political History of the Novel* (New York: Oxford University Press, 1987); Jacques Donzelot, *The Policing of Families,* trans. Robert Hurley (New York: Pantheon Books, 1979); and Bender, "New History."

38. Nicholson, *Gender and History,* 165.

39. Juliet Mitchell, *Psychoanalysis and Feminism* (New York: Vintage Books, 1975), 406. Nicholson makes a similar point when she writes that "women's lives, particularly over the past two centuries, . . . have . . . acutely expressed the conflict between an expanding individualism and an older conception of the family" (*Gender and History,* 165).

40. Habermas, *Structural Transformation,* 55; Juliet Flower MacCannell, *The Regime of the Brother: After the Patriarchy* (London: Routledge, 1991), 12, 16.

41. Foucault, *History of Sexuality,* 108. Feminist theorists have critiqued Foucault's treatment of gender but have also significantly appropriated, extended, and reconfigured his formulations about sexuality. For some of the most notable contributions to this effort, see Nancy Armstrong, "Some Call It Fiction: On the Politics of Domesticity" in *The Other Perspective in Gender and Culture: Rewriting Women and the Symbolic,* ed. Juliet Flower MacCannell (New York: Columbia University Press, 1990), 59–84; Butler, *Gender Trouble,*

Bodies That Matter: On the Discursive Limits of "Sex" (New York: Routledge, 1993), and *The Psychic Life of Power: Theories in Subjection* (Stanford, Calif.: Stanford University Press, 1997); and the collection *Feminism & Foucault: Reflections on Resistance,* ed. Irene Diamond and Lee Quinby (Boston: Northeastern University Press, 1988).

42. Foucault, *History of Sexuality,* 108.

43. Gilles Deleuze and Félix Guattari, *Anti-Oedipus: Capitalism and Schizophrenia,* trans. Robert Hurley, Mark Seem, and Helen R. Lane (Minneapolis: University of Minnesota Press, 1983), 50.

44. Butler, *Gender Trouble,* 42.

45. The assertion is made by Lévi-Strauss in *Kinship,* 491.

46. Butler, *Gender Trouble,* 42. In this connection, I would argue that theories of natural aversion to incest, which date back at least to the eighteenth century and are articulated in the twentieth century most notably by such writers as Edward Westermarck and Havelock Ellis, simultaneously challenge and complement Freudian theories of a primary incestuous desire. Rather than understanding these two opposing schools of thought as mutually exclusive, I would suggest that they represent two sides of a single ideological formation within which, as Butler's analysis suggests, they are mutually constitutive and interdependent. For an interesting discussion of the Freud-Westermarck debate that illuminates the complementary nature of such opposing theories, though to different ends from mine, see Robin Fox, *The Red Lamp of Incest: An Enquiry into the Origins of Mind and Society* (Notre Dame, Ind.: University of Notre Dame Press, 1983), esp. chaps. 1 and 2. Early versions of this modern debate between theories of natural attraction on the one hand and natural aversion on the other pervade eighteenth-century fiction, as Ruth Perry observes in "Incest as the Meaning of the Gothic Novel," *The Eighteenth Century: Theory and Interpretation* 39.3 (1998), where she suggests that "[i]nstantaneous and inexplicable repugnance to sexual contact with blood kin in fiction" of the period constituted the "flip side of '*cri du sang*' magnetism between members of the same family" (271).

47. See, e.g., Florence Rush, *The Best-Kept Secret: Sexual Abuse of Children* (Blue Ridge Summit, Pa.: TAB Books, 1980); Judith Lewis Herman, *Father-Daughter Incest* (Cambridge, Mass.: Harvard University Press, 1981); and Diana E. H. Russell, *The Secret Trauma: Incest in the Lives of Girls and Women* (New York: Basic Books, 1986).

48. Herman's work is discussed at further length in chapter 2.

49. Although sustained discussion of this episode is not within the scope of this study, it has been fruitfully and suggestively undertaken by Ros Ballaster in *Seductive Forms: Women's Amatory Fiction from 1684–1740* (Oxford: Clarendon Press, 1992), 136–42; and Catherine Gallagher in *Nobody's Story: The Vanishing Acts of Women Writers in the Marketplace, 1670–1820* (Berkeley: University of California Press, 1994), 137–44.

50. Christine van Boheemen, *The Novel as Family Romance: Language, Gender, and Authority from Fielding to Joyce* (Itahca, N.Y.: Cornell University Press, 1987), 31.

51. Juliet Mitchell, introduction to *The Fortunes and Misfortunes of the Famous Moll Flanders,* by Daniel Defoe, ed. Juliet Mitchell (Harmondsworth: Penguin, 1978), 12.

52. Van Boheemen, *Novel as Family Romance,* 32.

53. See text accompanying notes 20–25 and 44–48 above.

54. The phrase is Judith Butler's in *Antigone's Claim: Kinship between Life and Death* (New York: Columbia University Press, 2000), where it is used to characterize the terms in which Antigone's association with kinship has been read by Hegel, Lacan, and Irigaray— i.e., as articulating a "prepolitical opposition to politics" (2).

TWO: Incest and Its Contingencies

1. Jeremy Taylor, *Ductor Dubitantium, or The Rule of Conscience,* part 1, ed. Alexander Taylor, vol. 9 of *The Whole Works of the Right Rev. Jeremy Taylor,* ed. Reginald Heber, rev. and corrected by Charles Page Eden (London: Longman, Brown, Green & Longmans, 1855), bk. 2, chap. 2, rule 3, sec. 17, p. 371.

2. On Taylor's precursors, see C. J. Stranks, *The Life and Writings of Jeremy Taylor* (London: S.P.C.K., 1952), 202–3.

3. Taylor, *Ductor Dubitantium,* bk. 2, chap. 2, rule 3, sec. 17, p. 371.

4. Prior to the thirteenth century, the range of marriage prohibitions had extended as far as the seventh degree. In 1215, however, the Fourth Lateran Council reduced these prohibitions to the fourth degree. For detailed accounts of the two different methods used historically within the church to compute degrees of consanguinity (the Roman and the Germanic), see Jack Goody, *The Development of the Family and Marriage in Europe* (Cambridge: Cambridge University Press, 1983), 134–46; Frances Gies and Joseph Gies, *Marriage and the Family in the Middle Ages* (New York: Harper & Row, 1987), 84–87; and Bruce Thomas Boehrer, *Monarchy and Incest in Renaissance England: Literature, Culture, Kinship, and Kingship* (Philadelphia: University of Pennsylvania Press, 1992), 163 n. I am indebted in the following pages to all three of these studies for their useful discussions of the history of marriage prohibitions in Europe. For William Blackstone's account of the canonical method of reckoning degrees of consanguinity that was adopted by British law and on the differences in methods of computing degrees within the civil law on the one hand and the canon and common laws on the other with respect to determining hereditary successions, see his *Commentaries on the Laws of England: A Facsimile of the First Edition of 1765–1769,* with an introduction by A. W. Brian Simpson (Chicago: University of Chicago Press, 1979), vol. 2, chap. 14.

5. "Collateral" affinity exists when two persons of the same generation (e.g., brother-in-law and sister-in-law) are related by marriage. Affinity in the "direct" line obtains between persons of different generations (as between son-in-law and mother-in-law). Collateral consanguines are relations descending from the same stock or ancestor but not from each other. Kindred relations between two persons of whom one is descended in a direct line from the other are called "lineal."

6. All quotations from the Bible are from the King James Version. For detailed accounts of Henry's repudiation of his marriage to Catherine and its political implications, see Bishop Gilbert Burnet, *History of the Reformation of the Church of England,* 6 vols. (London: 1820), vol. 1, pt. 1, bk. 2; Agnes Strickland, *The Lives of the Queens of England,* 6 vols., rev. ed. (London: George Bell & Sons, 1901), 2:97–175; and J. J. Scarisbrick, *Henry VIII* (Berkeley: University of California Press, 1968), chaps. 6–11.

7. Scarisbrick, *Henry VIII,* chap. 7; Boehrer, *Monarchy and Incest,* 32.

8. Scarisbrick, *Henry VIII,* 167–68.

9. Boehrer, *Monarchy and Incest,* 39–40; Gies and Gies, *Marriage and the Family,* 87, 40.

10. Scarisbrick, *Henry VIII,* 164.

11. Goody, *Development of the Family,* 174.

12. Taylor, *Ductor Dubitantium,* bk. 2, chap. 2, rule 3, sec. 17, p. 371.

13. Scarisbrick, *Henry VIII,* 160–61. The role of intercourse in establishing affinity played a part in debates about Henry's divorce in another way, since Catherine claimed that her marriage to Arthur had never been consummated and that therefore no actual

affinity between her and Henry existed. On the controversy over whether an unconsummated marriage could create affinity, see Sybil Wolfram, *In-Laws and Outlaws: Kinship and Marriage in England* (London: Croom Helm, 1987), 27–28; and Scarisbrick, *Henry VIII,* 183–97.

Burnet cites one writer, Sanders, who claims that Anne was Henry's daughter, the king having had an affair with her mother, but Burnet dismisses the account as a boldfaced lie designed to discredit Queen Elizabeth (*History of the Reformation,* vol. 1, pt. 1, bk. 2, pp. 64–65).

14. Goody, *Development of the Family,* 172–73.

15. Although the question of the legitimacy of marriage to the deceased wife's sister was much discussed throughout the eighteenth century, it was not until 1842 that a formal bill providing for the legalization of such marriages was introduced into Parliament. The "Deceased Wife's Sister Bill" was formally debated and repeatedly defeated throughout the second half of the nineteenth century and finally passed in 1907. For the history of parliamentary debates over this issue, see Cynthia Fansler Behrman, "The Annual Blister: A Sidelight on Victorian Social and Parliamentary History," *Victorian Studies* 11.4 (1968): 483–502; Nancy F. Anderson, "The 'Marriage with a Deceased Wife's Sister Bill' Controversy: Incest Anxiety and the Defense of Family Purity in Victorian England," *Journal of British Studies* 21.2 (spring 1982): 67–86; and Margaret Morganroth Gullette, "The Puzzling Case of the Deceased Wife's Sister: Nineteenth-Century England Deals with a Second-Chance Plot," *Representations* 31 (1990): 142–66.

16. For a good explanation of the "parity of reason" interpretation of Leviticus, which argues that prohibitions on marriages between relatives not literally mentioned in Leviticus can be assumed on the basis of their "parity" with those mentioned, see Wolfram, *In-Laws and Outlaws,* 26–27.

17. John R. Gillis, *For Better, For Worse: British Marriages, 1600 to the Present* (New York: Oxford University Press, 1985), 102.

18. *Little Non-Such or, Certaine New Questions Moved out of Ancient Truths* (London, 1646), 7.

19. Thomas Edwards, *Gangraena* (London, 1647); *The Counter Buffe; or, Certaine Observations upon Mr. Edwards his* Animadversions (London, 1647).

20. Quoted in Keith Thomas, "The Puritans and Adultery: The Act of 1650 Reconsidered," in *Puritans and Revolutionaries,* ed. Donald Pennington and Keith Thomas (Oxford: Clarendon Press, 1978), 275.

21. C. H. Firth and R. S. Rait, eds., *Acts and Ordinances of the Interregnum, 1642–1660,* 3 vols. (London: H. M. Stationery Office, printed by Wyman & Sons, Ltd., 1911), 2:387–89.

22. In 1883, Sir James F. Stephen wrote the following in *A History of the Criminal Law of England,* 3 vols. (London: Macmillan & Co., 1883): "the only reason which I can assign why incest in its very worst forms is not a crime by the laws of England is that it is an ecclesiastical offence, and is even now occasionally punished as such. It is, I believe, the only form of immorality which in the case of the laity is still punished by ecclesiastical courts on the general ground of its sinfulness" (2:430). Wolfram usefully summarizes the legal history of the prohibited degrees through the nineteenth century, chronicling the process of legalizing marriage to first-degree collateral affines. When the Matrimonial Causes Act of 1857 transferred jurisdiction over matrimonial cases to the temporal courts, she notes, it failed to make any provision for the punishment of incest. Thus, "no

one could be in trouble for incest between 1857 and 1908" (*In-Laws and Outlaws,* 43). When the Punishment of Incest Act was passed in 1908, making incest a criminal offence, the range of prohibited relatives was much narrower than it had been before 1857; viz., mother, sister, half-sister, daughter, granddaughter, and blood relatives in the second degree.

23. Christopher Hill, *Society and Puritanism in Pre-Revolutionary England,* 2d ed. (New York: Schocken Books, 1967), 315, 353, 355, 376–77. Even Martin Ingram, who rejects Hill's position that the church courts were obsolete before the civil war, concedes that their "role and standing . . . had been profoundly affected" by the events of the forties and fifties (*Church Courts, Sex, and Marriage in England, 1570–1640* [Cambridge: Cambridge University Press, 1987], 372).

24. Goody, *Development of the Family,* 182. See also Ingram, *Church Courts,* 245–49. Such a paucity of prosecutions was the case as well under Puritan rule, when incest was officially a felony. Indeed, as Keith Thomas observes, the Puritan ordinance of 1650 was largely a dead letter act with "primarily symbolic" significance, "a public assertion of offences to be abominated. . . . not an effective part of the criminal code" ("Puritans and Adultery," 280). In this sense, the relatively lenient measures of the church courts were actually more in keeping with popular attitudes than the harsher strictures of the Puritan regime.

25. Polly Morris, "Incest or Survival Strategy? Plebian Marriage within the Prohibited Degrees in Somerset, 1730–1835," *Journal of the History of Sexuality* 2.2 (October 1991): 252.

26. Ibid., 239, 261–63. In his *Serious Inquiry into that Weighty Case of Conscience, Whether a Man may Lawfully Marry his Deceased Wife's Sister* (London, 1703), facsimile reprint in *The Marriage Prohibitions Controversy: Five Tracts,* ed. Randolph Trumbach (New York: Garland, 1985), the minister John Quick recounts the following case, which he says he has seen cited in a work by Luther: "A certain Ship-Carpenter, who lived near a great Town in the West of *England* had begot a Child upon the Body of his own unmarried Daughter, and when the Minister of that Parish was taxed for baptizing this Infant, born of incestuous Parents, who testified no Remorse, nor had undergone any publick Pennance for their scandalous and most abominable Crime, he replyed in his own Defence, that he was no Bishop to injoyn them Pennance, nor was the Discipline of the Church committed unto him, who was a Priest only, but no Prelate" (34–35).

John Fry observes a similar laxity among the clergy in *The Case of Marriages Between Near Kindred Particularly Considered, With Respect to The Doctrine of Scripture, The Law of Nature, and The Laws of England* (London, 1756), facsimile reprint in Trumbach, *Marriage Prohibitions Controversy,* when he writes that "Clear and plain Instances might be given of *many of the Canons* that are very little regarded even by the Generality of the Clergy" (133–34).

27. Ingram, *Church Courts,* 374.

28. John Vaughan, *The Reports and Arguments of that Learned Judge, Sir John Vaughan* (London: Edward Vaughan, 1677), 302–29.

29. William Salkeld, *Reports of Cases Adjudged in the Court of King's Bench,* 2d ed. (London, 1722), 2:548.

30. Vaughan, *Reports and Arguments,* 312. According to the *OED,* which quotes *Termes de la Ley* (1641) for its definition of this legal term, "Consultation is a writ whereby a cause being formerly removed by prohibition, out of the Ecclesiasticall Court or Court Chris-

tian, to the Kings Court, is returned thither againe." A similar definition is included in *The Gentleman's Magazine* of August 1749, which also offers this legal definition of "Prohibition" from *Jacob's Law Dictionary:* "a writ issuing out of the Chancery, King's Bench, or Common Pleas, to forbid the Spiritual court, Admirality court, &c. to proceed in a cause there depending; upon suggesting that the cognisance thereof belongs not to the said courts, but to the common law courts" (354).

For interpretive discussion of the Levitical injunction against taking a wife's sister "to vex her . . . in her life time" (Lev. 18:18), see also Simon Patrick, *A Commentary upon the Historical Books of the Old Testament,* 2 vols. (London, 1727); and *The Gentleman's Magazine* 16 (August 12, 1746), 410; (September 8, 1746), 461; (October 1746), 544–45; and (January 1750), 13.

31. Fry, *Case of Marriages,* 138.

32. Thomas Salmon, *A Critical Essay Concerning Marriage,* 2d ed. (London, 1724), 167; James Johnstoun, *A Juridical Dissertation Concerning the Scripture Doctrine of Marriage Contracts, and the Marriages of Cousin-Germans* (London, 1734; facsimile reprint in Trumbach, *Marriage Prohibitions Controversy*), iii–iv; John Alleyne, *The Legal Degrees of Marriage Stated and Considered, in a Series of Letters to a Friend,* 2d ed. (London, 1775; facsimile reprint in Trumbach, *Marriage Prohibitions Controversy*), 42.

33. Boehrer, *Monarchy and Incest,* 152. Boehrer elaborates: "Henry used Parliament—as in the 1540 cousin-marriage statute—to determine what is and is not incest; and while matrimonial cases remained within the purview of the church courts throughout the Renaissance, it was clear from Henry on that church law did not have exclusive authority over such matters" (152).

34. Martin Luther, *The Estate of Marriage,* trans. Walther I. Brandt, in *The Christian in Society,* ed. Walther I. Brandt, vol. 45 of *Luther's Works,* ed. Helmut T. Lehmann (Philadelphia: Muhlenberg Press, 1962), 24; and Martin Luther, *The Babylonian Captivity of the Church,* trans. A. T. W. Steinhauser, revised by Frederick C. Ahrens and Abdel Ross Wentz, in *Word and Sacrament,* ed. Abdel Ross Wentz, vol. 36 of *Luther's Works,* ed. Helmut T. Lehmann (Philadelphia: Muhlenberg Press, 1959), 97.

35. Henrician Statute 32, H. VIII, chap. 38, quoted in Fry, *Case of Marriages,* 97.

36. Johnstoun, *Juridical Dissertation,* 31.

37. Fry, *Case of Marriages,* 62–65. Bishop Patrick, however, points to Mohammed and the prohibition of marriages between mothers and sons in the Alcoran to make a different point—i.e., as proof that parent-child incest was against nature, since even pagans prohibited it: "Mohamet as lewd and impudent as he was, had not the boldness to controul these Laws; but in the fourth Chapter of his *Alcoran* expressly forbids his Followers to marry their *Mothers,* their *Mothers-in-Law,* etc. and a great many of the rest which here follow" (*Commentary,* Lev. 18:7).

38. For accounts of this tradition, see Leo Strauss, *Natural Right and History* (Chicago: University of Chicago Press, 1953); Otto Gierke, *Natural Law and the Theory of Society: 1500–1800,* trans. Ernest Barker (Boston: Beacon Press, 1957); Stephen Buckle, *Natural Law and the Theory of Property: Grotius to Hume* (Oxford: Clarendon Press, 1991); and Knud Haakonssen, *Natural Law and Moral Philosophy: From Grotius to the Scottish Enlightenment* (Cambridge: Cambridge University Press, 1996).

39. Edward Surtz and Virginia Murphy, eds., *The Divorce Tracts of Henry VIII* (Angers, France: Moreana, 1988), 205; see also 49. As Bishop Burnet put it, Henry's canonists held

that "the Pope could not dispense in this case of the first degree of affinity, which they esteemed forbidden by a divine, moral, and natural law" (*History of the Reformation*, 71).

40. Boehrer, *Monarchy and Incest*, 28–36.

41. For other discussions of the dissociation between theology and natural law theory in the seventeenth and eighteenth centuries, particularly with respect to questions of incest, see Alfred Owen Aldridge, "The Meaning of Incest from Hutcheson to Gibbon," *Ethics* 61 (1951): 309–13; Susan Staves, *Players' Scepters: Fictions of Authority in the Restoration* (Lincoln: University of Nebraska Press, 1979), chap. 5; Bruce Boehrer, " 'Nice Philosophy': *'Tis Pity She's a Whore* and The Two Books of God," *Studies in English Literature* 24 (1984): 355–71; and W. Daniel Wilson, "Science, Natural Law, and Unwitting Sibling Incest in Eighteenth-Century Literature," *Studies in Eighteenth-Century Culture* 13 (1984): 249–70.

42. Hugo Grotius, *The Law of War and Peace (De Jure Belli ac Paci Libri Tres)*, trans. Francis W. Kelsey (Indianapolis: Bobbs-Merrill, 1925), bk. 2, chap. 5, sec. 12, par. 1, p. 239.

43. Samuel Pufendorf, *The Law of Nature and Nations. Eight Books*, trans. Basil Kennett, 3d ed. (London, 1717), bk. 6, chap. 1, sec. 28, p. 354.

44. Grotius, *Law of War and Peace*, bk. 2, chap. 5, sec. 12, par. 2, p. 240; Pufendorf, *Law of Nature and Nations*, bk. 1, chap. 1, sec. 32, pp. 359–61.

45. Grotius, *Law of War and Peace*, bk. 2, chap. 5, sec. 13, par. 1, p. 242.

46. Taylor, *Ductor Dubitantium*, bk. 2, chap. 2, rule 3, sec. 24, pp. 375–77. One writer in *The Gentleman's Magazine* criticizes Taylor for borrowing from Grotius so extensively without adequately crediting his source (July 1749, 300).

47. Taylor, *Ductor Dubitantium*, bk. 2, chap. 2, rule 3, secs. 30–89, pp. 380–404.

48. Samuel Dugard, *The Marriages of Cousin Germans, Vindicated from the Censures of Unlawfullnesse, and Inexpediency* (Oxford, 1673). On the reference to Taylor, see *Dictionary of National Biography*, s.v. "Dugard, Samuel."

49. Fry cites Taylor no less than nine times within the scope of fifty pages (see Fry, *Case of Marriages*, e.g., 28, 43, 60–61, 65, 68, 69–70, 73, 77, 86).

50. Taylor, *Ductor Dubitantium*, bk. 2, chap. 2, rule 3, sec. 17, p. 371; Dugard, *Marriages of Cousin Germans*, "Epistle to the Reader."

51. Randolph Trumbach, *The Rise of the Egalitarian Family: Aristocratic Kinship and Domestic Relations in Eighteenth-Century England* (New York: Academic Press, 1978), 19.

52. Quick, *Serious Inquiry*, dedication; Alleyne, *Legal Degrees of Marriage*, 54. For Fry's position, see his *Case of Marriages*, xi–xii.

53. Alleyne, *Legal Degrees of Marriage*, 50, v–vi. *The Gentleman's Magazine*, Aug. 1746, 545.

54. Fry, *Case of Marriages*, xi; Quick, *Serious Inquiry*, 2–4.

55. Quick, *Serious Inquiry*, 14.

56. Vaughan, *Reports and Arguments*, 221.

57. Bernard Mandeville, *The Fable of the Bees: or, Private Vices, Publick Benefits*, 2d ed., enlarged with many additions (London, 1723), 379.

58. Vaughan, *Reports and Arguments*, 222.

59. Francis Hutcheson, *A System of Moral Philosophy* (London, 1755), 173.

60. Henry St. John Bolingbroke, "Fragments or Minutes of Essays," in *The Works of Lord Bolingbroke*, 4 vols. (Philadelphia: Carey & Hart, 1841), 4:228.

61. Fry, *Case of Marriages*, x.

62. Gillis, *For Better, For Worse,* 103–4.

63. Alleyne, *Legal Degrees of Marriage,* 19.

64. A letter from an S. Stennett appearing in the appendix of the 1775 edition of Alleyne's treatise refers to a reprinting of Fry's treatise two or three years prior—that is, around 1772 or 1773 (ibid., appendix, 16).

65. Ibid., 4. A letter to Alleyne from a Mr. Tremlet, of Exeter, questions even this limit in a manner reminiscent of Vaughan and Bolingbroke:

> "Nature," you say, "certainly forbids such connections between persons related in an ascending or descending line." I know not in what law of *nature* this prohibition is certainly expressed, or implied.
>
> The discovery would be new to me, and I believe to the world in general— "Increase and multiply" *is the voice of nature. . . .*
>
> . . . the impulse of nature, which is *wild morality,* will *rebel,* and maintain a constant war against the usurpation of artificial policy—such a condition cannot generally produce happiness. . . . The proper remedy seems to be, the removal of all impediments put upon nature . . . (ibid., appendix, 2–3)

66. Alleyne quotes, and claims to be heavily influenced by, both Montesquieu and Hume.

67. By 1800, cousin marriage was legal, as it had been under Henry VIII, and marriage to the deceased wife's sister and the deceased husband's brother continued to be prohibited.

68. Alleyne, *Legal Degrees of Marriage,* 59.

69. Boehrer, *Monarchy and Incest,* 22.

70. Bolingbroke, *Works,* 4:230.

71. Goody, *Development of the Family,* 167.

72. These observations regarding women's function in patrilineal and patronymic kinship systems have been made, of course, by others. See Claude Lévi-Strauss, *The Elementary Structures of Kinship,* rev. ed., trans. James Harle Bell, John Richard von Sturmer, and Rodney Needham (Boston: Beacon Press, 1969), 478–90; Gayle Rubin, "The Traffic in Women: Notes on the 'Political Economy' of Sex," in *Toward an Anthropology of Women,* ed. Rayna R. Reiter (New York: Monthly Review Press, 1975), 173–74; and Carole Pateman, *The Sexual Contract* (Stanford, Calif.: Stanford University Press, 1988), 111.

73. While inadvertency sometimes absolved incestuous couples from blame, it did not necessarily mitigate the law with respect to legal inheritance.

74. Trumbach, *The Rise of the Egalitarian Family,* 19.

75. One notable exception is David Herlihy, who, in *Medieval Households* (Cambridge: Harvard University Press, 1985), briefly postulates that the rules of exogamy in the late Middle Ages worked to prevent the disproportionate accumulation of women, and therefore property, in a few powerful households (61, 135–36). "The woman must marry out," he writes, "and she inevitably takes some property with her. The circulation of women thus also produced a circulation of capital" (136). Herlihy's study, however, extends only to 1500.

76. Alleyne, *Legal Degrees of Marriage,* 7.

77. The claim that the air in England was "too pure for a slave to breathe in" sounded as a frequent refrain in the Somerset case of 1772, in which Lord Mansfield ruled that James Somerset, who had been a slave in Virginia, must be discharged from slavery upon

being brought to England. Alleyne himself had been a council for Somerset's defense. But although Blackstone had written that "the spirit of liberty is so deeply implanted in our constitution" that a slave, the moment he lands in England, is free; and although the Mansfield Judgment was widely understood as freeing slaves in England, British courts still recognized colonial slavery. It was not until 1792 that the House of Commons voted in favor of "gradual" abolition and not until 1807 that the slave trade became illegal by act of Parliament (J. H. Baker, *An Introduction to English Legal History,* 3d ed. [London: Butterworths, 1990], 540–43). At the time of the Somerset case, Britain's share of the existing slave traffic in the Atlantic constituted approximately one-half of the total trade. For more sustained discussion of John Alleyne and the Somerset case, see chap. 7.

78. Judith Lewis Herman, *Father-Daughter Incest* (Cambridge, Mass.: Harvard University Press, 1981); Florence Rush, *The Best-Kept Secret: Sexual Abuse of Children* (Blue Ridge Summit, Pa.: TAB Books, 1980).

79. Herman, *Father-Daughter Incest,* 61.

80. The German philosopher Johann David Michaelis put the logic of the levirate this way: "the widow who [has] had sons, has in a manner repaid the price which she cost; while she who has yet had no sons, still continues a part of the inheritance, and belongs to the next brother" (*Commentaries on the Laws of Moses,* trans. Alexander Smith, 4 vols. [London, 1814], 2:27–28).

81. Consider, for example, the opinion of Thomas de Vio, Cardinal Cajetan, "That the marrying a brother's wife was simply unlawful; but that, in some circumstances, it might be good, if a much greater good should follow on such a marriage than that provided for [*sic*] *Deut.* v. of continuing the name of a brother dead without children" (translation quoted in *The Gentleman's Magazine,* July 1749, 299).

82. Bolingbroke, *Works,* 4:229.

83. Patrick, *Commentary,* Num. 27:4, 11.

84. Taylor, *Ductor Dubitantium,* bk. 2, chap. 2, rule 3, sec. 53, p. 389.

85. Bolingbroke, *Works,* 4:185–86.

86. Patrick, *Commentary,* Lev. 18:30.

87. Other biblical marriages that were commonly invoked as instances of divinely sanctioned kindred unions include those of Abraham and Sarah, Jacob and Rachel, Ruth and Boaz, and Tamar and Amnon. These exceptions typically operate according to the principle of a "greater good" constituted by some specific, alternative deployment of female reproductive power: to continue the name of a brother dead without children, to perpetuate the lineage of the future Messiah, to produce a heritage of great Jewish leaders, etc.

88. Flavius Josephus, *Antiquities of the Jews,* vol. 1 of *The Works of Flavius Josephus,* trans. William Whiston (Philadelphia, 1844), bk. 12, chap. 4, sec. 6; Humphrey Prideaux, *The Old and New Testament Connected in the History of the Jews,* pt. 2 (London: for Knaplock & Tonson, 1718). The latter work was better known as *Prideaux's Connections.*

89. See Exod. 34:16; Deut. 7:3; I Kings 11:2; Ezra 9:11–12; Neh. 10:30, 13:25.

90. Prideaux, *Old and New Testament,* bk. 2, p. 112.

91. Ibid., 112–13. For an argument similar to Prideaux's, see Dugard, who attempts to justify first-cousin marriage on the grounds that many Hebrew writers believed that "*Unkles* and *Neeces,* who are one degree nearer then *Cousin Germans,* are not forbid *Levit.* 18" (*Marriages of Cousin Germans,* 82). Dugard cites several other instances in Josephus where fathers give their daughters to close male relatives (84–86). For the standard argu-

ment against marriages between uncles and nieces, which relies on the parity-of-reason interpretation of Leviticus, see *The Gentleman's Magazine,* Sept. 1749, 357.

92. For a study of this intersection that focuses on the complex cultural relation between physical and spiritual incest, see Marc Shell, *Children of the Earth: Literature, Politics, and Nationhood* (Oxford: Oxford University Press, 1993). On incest and miscegenation, see also Werner Sollers, *Neither Black nor White yet Both: Thematic Explorations of Interracial Literature* (Cambridge, Mass.: Harvard University Press, 1997), chap. 10.

93. *The Gentleman's Magazine,* June 1746, 289; July 1746, 362.

94. Ibid., July 1746, 362.

95. I retain the original spelling and capitalization of the names of the letter-writers in *The Gentleman's Magazine.*

THREE: Beyond Incest

1. For further discussion of the Berkeley-Ford affair, see Maureen Duffy, *The Passionate Shepherdess: Aphra Behn, 1640–89* (New York: Avon Books, 1977), 221–24; Angeline Goreau, *Reconstructing Aphra: A Social Biography of Aphra Behn* (New York: Dial Press, 1980), 273–78; and Janet Todd, *The Secret Life of Aphra Behn* (New Brunswick, N.J.: Rutgers University Press, 1997), 299–306. For an account of the trial, see *Cobbett's Complete Collection of State Trials* (London, 1811), 9:127–86. For the probable identification of Dryden's Caleb as Grey, see Cecil Price, *Cold Caleb: The Scandalous Life of Ford Grey, First Earl of Tankerville, 1655–1701* (London: Andrew Melrose, 1956), 71.

2. Ros Ballaster discusses the effect on Behn of conventions regarding "appropriate" female forms in *Seductive Forms: Amatory Women's Fiction from 1684–1740* (Oxford: Clarendon Press, 1992), 73–81.

3. Susan Staves, *Players' Scepters: Fictions of Authority in the Restoration* (Lincoln: University of Nebraska Press, 1979), chap. 5. For other discussions of the dissociation between theology and natural law theory in the seventeenth and eighteenth centuries, see Bruce Boehrer, " 'Nice Philosophy': *'Tis Pity She's a Whore* and the Two Books of God," *Studies in English Literature* 24 (1984): 355–71; Alfred Owen Aldridge, "The Meaning of Incest from Hutcheson to Gibbon," *Ethics* 61 (1951): 309–13; and W. Daniel Wilson, "Science, Natural Law, and Unwitting Sibling Incest in Eighteenth-Century Literature," *Studies in Eighteenth-Century Culture* 13 (1984): 249–70.

4. Aphra Behn, *Love-Letters between a Nobleman and his Sister,* vol. 2 of *The Works of Aphra Behn,* ed. Janet Todd (Columbus: Ohio State University Press, 1993), 11–12. All further references are to this edition, abbreviated *L-L* where necessary for clarity. Page numbers are inserted parenthetically in the text. For the ease of reading, I have omitted extensive use of italics in some passages of *Love-Letters* and, where necessary, use quotation marks instead of italics to indicate dialogue in Behn's sections of third-person narration.

5. Sybil Wolfram, *In-Laws and Outlaws: Kinship and Marriage in England* (London: Croom Helm, 1987), 43. On the status of the in-law relationship with respect to incest in England, see also Jack Goody, "A Comparative Approach to Incest and Adultery," *British Journal of Sociology* 7 (1956): 291; and Staves, *Players' Scepters,* 304. Behn's Mertilla in effect assumes affinal as well as consanguineal ties in the in-law relation when she suggests to Silvia that the existence of her child by Philander strengthens his connections to Silvia both by relation and by blood. Philander, she writes, "has lain by thy unhappy sister's

side so many tender years, by whom he has a dear and lovely off-spring, by which he has *more fixed himself to thee by relation and blood"* (*L-L,* 70; emphasis added). The doctrine of "one flesh" that underlay the British concept of marriage became the basis also for arguments regarding the illegality of sexual relations between stepson and stepmother. See, e.g., Jeremy Taylor, who argues that "she that is one flesh with my father is as near to me as my father, and that's as near as my own mother" (*Ductor Dubitantium: or The Rule of Conscience,* part 1, ed. Alexander Taylor, vol. 9 of *The Whole Works of the Right Rev. Jeremy Taylor,* ed. Reginald Heber, rev. and corrected by Charles Page Eden [London: Longman, Brown, Green & Longmans, 1855], bk. 2, chap. 2, rule 3, n. 29).

6. Perry makes her point in *Women, Letters, and the Novel* (New York: AMS Press, 1980), 24. The Behn quotations are in *L-L,* 35 and 36.

7. René Girard, *Violence and the Sacred,* trans. Patrick Gregory (Baltimore: Johns Hopkins University Press, 1977), 74.

8. Such an association of seditious rebellion with incest was not unusual in Royalist discourse of the Restoration. Like sorcery, incest was associated with the sanctioning of alternative (and therefore illegitimate) sources of authority. Thus, for example, when George Hickes undertook in 1678 to recount the trial and conviction of the seditious conventicle preacher James Mitchell for his attempt on the life of the archbishop of St. Andrews, there seemed reason enough to feature Mitchell's tenuous association with the unsavory figure of Thomas Weir by appending to the record of Mitchell's trial the story of Weir's own earlier trial and execution for adultery, incest, sorcery, and bestiality. See *Ravillac Redivivus: being a Narrative of the late Tryal of Mr. James Mitchel . . . , To which is Annexed, An Account of the Tryal of that most wicked Pharisee Major Thomas Weir . . .* (London, 1678). Weir had been tried and executed in 1670. Hickes, a nonjuror, was personal chaplain to the duke of Lauderdale. An expanded second edition of his narrative was published in 1682. In 1710, Curll also brought out an amplified version under the title "The Spirit of Fanaticism exemplified." On the association of incest and sorcery (both of which figure significantly in *Love-Letters*), see Mary Douglas, *Purity and Danger: An Analysis of the Concepts of Pollution and Taboo* (London: Routledge & Kegan Paul, 1966), 107–13; David M. Schneider, "The Meaning of Incest," *Journal of the Polynesian Society* 85.2 (1976): 149–69; and Judith Lewis Herman, *Father-Daughter Incest* (Cambridge, Mass.: Harvard University Press, 1981), 50.

9. Grey, his Whig allegiances notwithstanding, was also of Royalist birth. "Consider my Lord," writes Silvia, "you are born Noble, from Parents of untainted Loyalty" (*L-L,* 39).

10. See, e.g., Goreau, *Reconstructing Aphra,* 272–73; Ballaster, *Seductive Forms,* 78–79; Robert Markley, " 'Be impudent, be saucy, forward, bold, touzing, and leud': The Politics of Masculine Sexuality and Feminine Desire in Behn's Tory Comedies," in *Cultural Readings of Restoration and Eighteenth-Century English Theatre,* ed. Douglas J. Canfield and Deborah C. Payne (Athens: University of Georgia Press, 1995), 114–15; and Robert Markley and Molly Rothenberg, "Contestations of Nature: Aphra Behn's 'The Golden Age' and the Sexualizing of Politics" in *Rereading Aphra Behn: History, Theory, and Criticism,* ed. Heidi Hutner (Charlottesville: University Press of Virginia, 1993), 301–21. For a more general examination of Tory feminism, particularly in the works of Margaret Cavendish and Mary Astell, see Catherine Gallagher, "Embracing the Absolute: The Politics of the Female Subject in Seventeenth-Century England," *Genders* 1 (1988): 24–39.

11. Janet Todd, *The Sign of Angellica: Women, Writing, and Fiction, 1660–1800* (New

York: Columbia University Press, 1989), 83; Maureen Duffy, introduction to *Love-Letters between a Nobleman and His Sister*, by Aphra Behn (New York: Virago, 1987), xi–xii.

12. Perry, *Women, Letters, and the Novel*, 25.

13. On self-preservation in seventeenth-century natural law theory, see Maximillian E. Novak, *Defoe and the Nature of Man* (London: Oxford University Press, 1963).

14. Todd, *Angellica*, 79–82.

15. Judith Kegan Gardiner, "The First English Novel: Aphra Behn's *Love Letters*, the Canon, and Women's Tastes," *Tulsa Studies in Women's Literature* 8.2 (fall 1989): 201–22.

16. For discussion of oedipal models of the novel's origins, especially Ian Watt's, see also Laurie Langbauer, *Women and Romance: The Consolations of Gender in the English Novel* (Ithaca, N.Y.: Cornell University Press, 1990), 28–30.

17. See, e.g., Judith Butler, "Prohibition, Psychoanalysis, and the Heterosexual Matrix," in *Gender Trouble: Feminism and the Subversion of Identity* (New York: Routledge, 1990), chap. 2.

18. This question, in the form of debate about whether Henrietta Berkeley had been a consenting party in leaving her father's house, was also an important issue in Grey's trial. See *Cobbett's Complete Collection* (1811), 9:127–86; and Price, *Cold Caleb*, 98–100.

19. For a theoretical consideration of such destabilizing narrative strategies in twentieth-century women's writing, see Rachel Blau DuPlessis, *Writing beyond the Ending: Narrative Strategies of Twentieth-Century Women Writers* (Bloomington: Indiana University Press, 1985).

20. Others have fruitfully discussed Behn's characteristic multiplying of subject positions. See, most notably, Ballaster, *Seductive Forms*, chap. 3; and Jessica Munns, " 'I By A Double Right Thy Bounties Claim': Aphra Behn and Sexual Space," in *Curtain Calls: British and American Women and the Theatre, 1660–1820*, ed. Mary Anne Schofield and Cecilia Macheski (Athens: Ohio University Press, 1991), 193–210.

21. Gardiner, "First English Novel," 212–13.

22. For another reading of Philander's impotence as a symptom of syphilis and thus "a tell-tale signal" of his sexual promiscuity, see Duffy, *Passionate Shepherdess*, xii; and Todd, *Angellica*, 81. While it is true that Behn is exploiting a long tradition of representations of impotent love that goes as far back as Ovid (indeed, Behn herself invoked the tradition in her famous poem "The Disappointment" [1680]), context here gives the topos a unique twist. Philander himself alludes to "Tales" of disappointed love in a series of disjointed assertions that raise the question of his sincerity and leave his referents ambiguous and his meanings open to interpretation: "Oh, what can *Silvia* say? What can she think of my fond passion? She'll swear 'tis all a cheat, I had it not. No, it could not be, such Tales I've often heard, as often laught at too; of disappointed Lovers; wou'd *Silvia* wou'd believe (as sure she may) mine was excess of Passion: What!" (*L-L*, 57). The possibility of feigned impotence is explicitly invoked, moreover, in a later episode, when Silvia—yet unaware that Brilljard has substituted himself for Octavio—speculates that the latter's illness upon encountering Antonet in bed may in fact have been a ruse (217).

23. Although I use it in a different sense, I borrow the impulse to characterize gender performance and cross-dressing as potential "put-ons" from Kristina Straub's work on female theatrical cross-dressing and the parodic performance of masculinity in the career and writing of Charlotte Charke: *Sexual Suspects: Eighteenth-Century Players and Sexual Ideology* (Princeton, N.J.: Princeton University Press, 1992), chap. 7; a version of this chapter, entitled "The Guilty Pleasures of Female Theatrical Cross-Dressing and the

Autobiography of Charlotte Charke," also appears in *Body Guards: The Cultural Politics of Gender Ambiguity,* ed. Julia Epstein and Kristina Straub (New York: Routledge, 1991), 142–66.

24. Gardiner simplifies what Behn makes problematic when she reads these assertions by Silvia as "subversive of traditional gender roles" in that they characterize the heroine as a desiring subject who "glories in her new desires" ("First English Novel," 213).

25. This is not to deny Philander's account of his garden escapade either its comic hilarity or its status as Behn's satire of Philander/Grey. One cannot help but agree with Gardiner that Perry (who bases her reading solely on part 1 of the narrative) is wrong in her assertion that "there is no gaiety about [the] truancy" of Philander and Silvia (ibid.; Perry, *Women, Letters, and the Novel,* 25). But is the gaiety of the episode generated solely, or even primarily, by Behn's wicked delight in humiliating Philander/Grey? Or is there some other, competing source of comedy at work? There is a question of audience at issue here, since Philander (to the extent that he functions as a character rather than a mere surrogate for Behn) controls the narration, which he offers as entertainment to Silvia. What is at stake for Philander in this relation? He claims a simple, practical motive—that of feeding Silvia information that Melinda will need to cover for him with the count. But if Philander were so utterly ashamed of the impotence that Gardiner sees reenacted in the scene, why would he bother to give so elaborate an account of those events to Silvia? Surely, if Beralti's garden tryst with the disguised Philander is a parodic repetition of the youthful upstairs encounter between Philander and Silvia, its effect is less to burlesque Philander than the count.

26. That Silvia and "the maid" are surrogates for one another is suggested at several other points; e.g., when Silvia claims to be inditing for Melinda or when she puts (or at least attempts to put) Antonett to bed in her place with Octavio.

27. Once again, my reading here diverges from that of Gardiner, who insists that because Philander is Silvia's brother "in law," as opposed to her father or her brother, he "has no authority over her," despite the fact that he is "politically more powerful" than she is ("First English Novel," 218).

28. Eve Kosofsky Sedgwick, *Between Men: English Literature and Male Homosocial Desire* (New York: Columbia University Press, 1985), 24.

29. Quoted in ibid., 23.

30. Another such instance occurs when Philander attempts to secure control over Silvia by staging a plot in which Brilljard, in effect, cuckolds him.

31. Sedgwick, *Between Men,* 49–51.

32. On the function of cross-dressing in the eighteenth century, see Pat Rogers, "The Breeches Part" in *Sexuality in Eighteenth-Century Britain,* ed. Paul Gabriel Boucé (Manchester, Eng.: Manchester University Press, 1982), 244–58; Lynne Friedli, " 'Passing women': A Study of Gender Boundaries in the Eighteenth Century," in *Sexual Underworlds of the Enlightenment,* ed. G. S. Rousseau and Roy Porter (Chapel Hill: University of North Carolina Press, 1988), 234–60; and Straub, *Sexual Suspects.* For a more theoretical approach to the relationship between femininity and masquerade, see Mary Ann Doane's now-classic essay "Film and the Masquerade: Theorising the Female Spectator," *Screen* 23 (1982): 74–87. For another instance in Behn's text where female cross-dressing serves a specular and homosocial function, see Philander's reaction to Calista in male attire; drag increases Calista's likeness to Octavio and therefore enhances Philander's attraction to her (*L-L,* 308–9).

33. Samuel Richardson, *Clarissa, or The History of a Young Lady,* ed. Angus Ross (Harmondsworth: Penguin, 1985), 1233.

34. Behn seems to comment indirectly on the ideological link between an ethics of sincerity and such a superabundance of father figures in her somewhat ironic portrayal of Octavio's initiation into a fraternal order of religious fathers.

35. The figure of Hermione interestingly reinvokes the theme of incest, since she is the former mistress of Cesario's father, the king.

36. Nor is it insignificant that in her last cross-dressing escapade in the novel, Silvia assumes a name, Bellumere, with an onomastic association to, among other things, maternity; the name suggests both a beautiful sight or luminary (Belle-lumière) and a beautiful mother (Belle-mère). Gardiner faults Behn for her inadequate treatment of maternity in the novel in terms that seem to me to make a number of essentialist assumptions about female experience ("First English Novel," 215–16).

FOUR: Guarding the Succession of the (E)state

1. John Fry, *The Case of Marriages Between Near Kindred Particularly Considered, With Respect to the Doctrine of Scripture, the Law of Nature, and the Laws of England* (London, 1756), facsimile reprint in *The Marriage Prohibitions Controversy: Five Tracts,* ed. Randolph Trumbach (New York: Garland, 1985), 67. Fry appends an "Advertisement" to his preface, indicating that his treatise was written some years before it was published (xii). On the "parity of reason" interpretation of Scripture, see chap. 2, note 16. Fry's reference to "Fathers and Mothers-in-law" in this context denotes stepparents.

2. William Blackstone, *Commentaries on the Laws of England: A Facsimile of the First Edition of 1765–1769,* with an introduction by A. W. Brian Simpson (Chicago: University of Chicago Press, 1979), vol. 1, chap. 17, p. 448.

3. This subject is treated in depth by Cheryl L. Nixon in "Creating the Text of Guardianship: 12 Car.II.c.24 and *Cutter of Coleman Street*," *Restoration: Studies in English Literary Culture, 1660–1700* 19.1 (1995): 1–28. See also by Nixon, "Fictional Families: Guardianship in Eighteenth-Century Law and Literature" (Ph.D. diss., Harvard University, 1995).

4. Jürgen Habermas, *The Structural Transformation of the Public Sphere: An Inquiry into a Category of Bourgeois Society,* trans. Thomas Burger with Frederick Lawrence (Cambridge, Mass.: MIT Press, 1991), chaps. 1–8. W. J. T. Mitchell briefly but usefully discusses the structural relations and complex interactions between aesthetic and political notions of representation in his essay "Representation" in *Critical Terms for Literary Study,* eds. Frank Lentricchia and Thomas McLaughlin, 2d ed. (Chicago: University of Chicago Press, 1995), 11–22. "Since antiquity . . . ," he observes, "representation has been the foundational concept in aesthetics . . . and semiotics. . . . In the modern era (i.e., in the last three hundred years) it has also become a crucial concept in political theory, forming the cornerstone of representational theories of sovereignty, legislative authority, and relations of individuals to the state" (11). Manley is deeply engaged in exploring the complicated relation between art and politics that was emerging in her culture, and she would no doubt concur with Mitchell's statement that "representation, even purely 'aesthetic' representation . . . , can never be completely divorced from political and ideological questions" (15). For a fascinating discussion of the legal concept of representation and its relation to the law of succession in Matthew Hale's *De Successionibus apud Anglos: The Law*

of Hereditary Descents, see Brian McCrea, *Impotent Fathers: Patriarchy and Demographic Crisis in the Eighteenth-Century Novel* (Newark: University of Delaware Press, 1998), 20–25.

5. I am indebted in the following pages to Cheryl Nixon's important work on guardianship, both in the article mentioned above and in a longer unpublished manuscript by the same title that she has generously shared with me.

6. Blackstone, *Commentaries,* vol. 2, chap. 5, p. 62; vol. 2, chap. 6, p. 88.

7. Joel Hurstfield, *The Queen's Wards: Wardship and Marriage under Elizabeth I* (Cambridge, Mass.: Harvard University Press, 1958), 7–10. See also Nixon, "Creating the Text," 9.

8. Nixon, "Creating the Text," manuscript version.

9. Nixon, "Creating the Text," 8; Hurstfield, *Queen's Wards,* 179–80, 338–46; and H. E. Bell, *An Introduction to the History and Records of the Court of Wards and Liveries* (Cambridge: Cambridge University Press, 1953), 57–58.

10. On the relative infrequency of kin guardianship, see Bell, *History and Records,* 116–17; and Scott L. Waugh, *The Lordship of England: Royal Wardships and Marriages in English Society and Politics, 1217–1327* (Princeton, N.J.: Princeton University Press, 1988), 195–97. For other arguments advanced against maternal guardianship, see Nixon, "Creating the Text," 13–15; and Frederick Pollock and Frederic William Maitland, *The History of English Law before the Time of Edward I,* 2d ed. (Cambridge: Cambridge University Press, 1923), vol. 1, bk. 2, chap. 1, sec. 8, p. 326.

11. Quoted in Blackstone, *Commentaries,* vol. 2, chap. 5, p. 77. For the text of Parliament's "Ordinance for removing the Court of Wards" on February 24, 1645/6, see C. H. Firth and R. S. Rait, eds., *Acts and Ordinances of the Interregnum, 1642–1660* (London: H. M. Stationery Office, printed by Wyman & Sons, Ltd., 1911), 1:833. For the text of Charles's statute, see *The Statutes of the Realm (1225–1713)* (London: G. Eyre & A. Strahan, 1810–22), vol. 5, chap. 24, sec. 8, p. 260.

12. Blackstone, *Commentaries,* vol. 2, chap. 6, p. 88.

13. Nixon, "Creating the Text," 9.

14. Nixon, "Creating the Text," manuscript version.

15. Bell, *History and Records,* 114.

16. Nixon, "Creating the Text," manuscript version.

17. Nixon, "Creating the Text," 5.

18. Delarivier Manley, *Secret Memoirs and Manners of Several Persons of Quality of Both Sexes. From the New Atalantis, an Island in the Mediteranean,* 2 vols. (London, 1709; reprinted, 2 vols. in 1, in *The Novels of Mary Delariviere Manley,* ed. Patricia Köster [Gainesville, Fl.: Scholars' Facsimiles & Reprints, 1971]), 1:50/1:322. As Köster's pagination differs from that of the original text, I include parenthetically in my text two sets of volume and page citations separated by a slash, the first set to the 1709 edition and the second set to the reprint edition. For my bracketed identifications of Manley's characters, most of whom are based on historical figures, I rely primarily on the index at the end of Köster's two-volume edition.

19. My reading differs here from that of Ros Ballaster, who gives a sort of prototypical or representative status not to Delia's story but to Charlot's, calling the latter a "landmark story in Manley's text, . . . an exemplary tale of seduction and betrayal to or from which all subsequent stories in the novel correspond or diverge" (*Seductive Forms: Women's Amatory Fiction from 1684–1740* [Oxford: Clarendon Press, 1992], 132).

20. Volume 1 of *The New Atalantis* was published in May of 1709; volume 2 was published in October of the same year. The Tories did not rise to power until August of 1710, almost a year after Manley's account of Anne's "delivery" was published. See Gwendolyn B. Needham, "Mary de la Rivière Manley, Tory Defender," *Huntington Library Quarterly* 12 (1948–49): 263–64.

21. The classic account of this well-known trope is Ernst H. Kantorowicz, *The King's Two Bodies: A Study in Mediaeval Political Theology* (Princeton, N.J.: Princeton University Press, 1957).

22. In the introduction to her 1992 edition of *The New Atalantis*, Ros Ballaster follows Edmund Curll's 1725 edition of Manley's autobiographical *Adventures of Rivella* in dating Manley's birth around 1671 (Delarivier Manley, *The New Atalantis*, ed. Ros Ballaster [London: Penguin, 1992], vi). In "Mistress Delariviere Manley's Biography," *Modern Philology* 33 (1935–36), Paul Bunyan Anderson rejects the date of 1663 proposed in a revised version of the original *Dictionary of National Biography* article and instead accepts the *DNB*'s original designation of 1672 (264 n). Thus, even by the most conservative estimate, Delarivier could not have been younger than seventeen when she married her cousin in 1689.

23. Ballaster contends that "the story of Delia is an unabashed attempt at whitewashing Manley's complicity in her bigamous marriage" (*Seductive Forms*, 151).

24. In a sense, the allegorical dimension of Manley's text itself acknowledges the status of representation as a corrupt derivative of truth. Indeed, Manley's allegorical representations of historical figures might be seen as occupying the same position of dangerous supplementarity in relation to the truth as guardians occupy in relation to fathers or as courtiers occupy in relation to kings; that is, they embody an inherent potential for misrepresentation. For further discussion of the complex relationship between representation and referentiality in *The New Atalantis*, see Catherine Gallagher's important work *Nobody's Story: The Vanishing Acts of Women Writers in the Marketplace, 1670–1820* (Berkeley: University of California Press, 1994), 88–144.

25. Kantorowicz, *King's Two Bodies*, 378.

26. For discussion of the developing emphasis on economic over nonmaterial considerations in contracting marriages, see H. J. Habakkuk, "Marriage Settlements in the Eighteenth Century," *Transactions of the Royal Historical Society*, 4th ser., 32 (1950), 24–25. For an important corrective to some of the errors in the theories of Habakkuk and some of his followers, see Eileen Spring, "Law and the Theory of the Affective Family," *Albion* 16.1 (spring 1984): 1–20, and "The Heiress-at-Law: English Real Property from a New Point of View," *Law and History Review* 8.2 (fall 1990): 273–96.

27. According to Geoffrey Bullough, when Henry VIII failed to produce an heir by his brother's widow, both Luther and the pope urged him to commit bigamy rather than divorce his queen; and when Charles II's Portuguese queen proved infertile, the question of polygamy's legitimacy and expediency arose again. To Gilbert Burnet, polygamy was— like the levirate marriage—a sacred obligation in certain circumstances (Bullough, "Polygamy among the Reformers," in *Renaissance and Modern Essays*, ed. G. R. Hibbard [London: Routledge & Kegan Paul, 1966], 8–15). To Bolingbroke and Hume, whose perspectives otherwise differed markedly, it constituted a natural liberty (Alfred Owen Aldridge, "Polygamy and Deism," *Journal of English and Germanic Philology* 48 [1949]: 356–57). For analysis of the sexual and colonial politics of discussions of polygamy in the eighteenth

century, see Felicity Nussbaum, *Torrid Zones: Maternity, Sexuality, and Empire in Eighteenth-Century English Narratives* (Baltimore: Johns Hopkins University Press, 1995), chap. 3.

28. The specificities of this sexual as well as Whig double standard are clearly articulated in the remarks that Hernando makes to trick Wilmot into "upholding the [male] Sex's Charter" (1:220/1:492) before Louisa:

> [Hernando] introduc'd a learned Discourse of the lawfulness of double Marriages; indeed, he own'd that in all Ages, Women had been appropriated, that for the benefit and distinction of Children, with other necessary Occurrences, Polygamy had been justly deny'd the Sex, since the coldness of their Constitution, the length of time they carry'd their Children and other Incidents seem'd to declare against them; but for a Man who possess'd an uninterrupted Capacity of propagating the Specie, and must necessarily find all the Inconveniencies above-mention'd, in any one Wife; the Law of Nature, as well as the Custom of many Nations, and most Religions, seem'd to declare for him; . . . The *Turks,* and all the People of the World, but the *Europeans,* still preserved the privilege; that . . . their Manners . . . were less adulterated than ours . . . ; that in pretending to reform from their Abuses, Europe had only refin'd their Vices; Pleasures that were forbidden had a better *Gusto,* and tho' they had ty'd themselves out of Policy to one Wife, to make particular Families great, and maintain distinction; yet there was scarce a Man (but himself) that had Capacity to uphold his Pleasures abroad, but went in search of 'em. (1:219–20/ 1:491–92)

29. This cautionary note about the dangers of female reliance on individual judgment is sounded as well in *Eleanora* and discussed in chapter 6.

30. John Vaughan, *The Reports and Arguments of that Learned Judge, Sir John Vaughan* (London: Edward Vaughan, 1677), 224–25. For the roots of this idea in the seventeenth century, see, e.g., Maximillian E. Novak, *Defoe and the Nature of Man* (Oxford: Oxford University Press, 1963), 3–13.

31. Pierre Bourdieu, *Distinction: A Social Critique of the Judgement of Taste,* trans. Richard Nice (Cambridge, Mass.: Harvard University Press, 1984), 6.

FIVE: *Moll Flanders,* Incest, and the Structure of Exchange

1. On this aspect of Moll's character, see John J. Richetti, "The Family, Sex, and Marriage in Defoe's *Moll Flanders* and *Roxana," Studies in the Literary Imagination, Daniel Defoe: The Making of His Prose Fiction* 15.2 (1982): 19–35, and *Defoe's Narratives: Situations and Structures* (Oxford: Clarendon Press, 1975), chap. 4; James H. Maddox, "On Defoe's *Roxana," ELH* 51 (1984): 669–91; Miriam Lerenbaum, "Moll Flanders: 'A Woman on her own Account,'" in *The Authority of Experience: Essays in Feminist Criticism,* ed. Arlyn Diamond and Lee R. Edwards (Amherst: University of Massachusetts Press, 1977), 101–17; and Michael Shinagel, "The Maternal Theme in *Moll Flanders:* Craft and Character," *Cornell Library Journal* 7 (1969): 3–23.

2. René Girard, *Violence and the Sacred,* trans. Patrick Gregory (Baltimore: Johns Hopkins University Press, 1977), 74.

3. For a comparison of Moll Flanders and Roxana with respect to the question of kinship, see Richetti, "Family, Sex, and Marriage." Maddox develops a parallel argument

about the differences between the two heroines, with a particularly interesting analysis of Moll's brother-husband's function as a scapegoat onto whom Moll's negative feelings about her incest are displaced ("On Defoe's *Roxana*," 686–88).

4. Michael Seidel, *Exile and the Narrative Imagination* (New Haven, Conn.: Yale University Press, 1986), 28.

5. Even child-murder gets justified in the interest of the survival of the (female) self. On Moll's indirect involvement in child-murder, see Maddox, "On Defoe's *Roxana*," 683–86.

6. Daniel Defoe, *The Fortunes and Misfortunes of the Famous Moll Flanders,* ed. G. A. Starr (Oxford: Oxford University Press, 1981), 88. Subsequent quotations are from this edition; page references are inserted parenthetically in my text, with the abbreviation *MF* where needed for clarity.

7. Moll refers to the oppressive weight of secrets on pages 88 and 325; and in a note on 396, Starr points to several other instances in which Defoe discusses the irresistible force of conscience.

8. See W. Daniel Wilson's argument that Moll's response to her incest operates not "on the level of morality, but of impulse and gut feeling," in "Science, Natural Law, and Unwitting Sibling Incest in Eighteenth-Century Literature," *Studies in Eighteenth-Century Culture* 13 (1984): 257. For earlier comment on the incest in Defoe's text, and other interpretations, see Maximillian E. Novak, *Defoe and the Nature of Man* (London: Oxford University Press, 1963), 108–10, and "Conscious Irony in *Moll Flanders:* Facts and Problems," *College English* 26 (1964): 201; G. A. Starr, *Defoe and Casuistry* (Princeton, N.J.: Princeton University Press, 1971), 134–35; and J. Paul Hunter, ed., *Moll Flanders* (New York: Thomas Y. Crowell Co., 1970), 74 n.

9. Richetti, *Defoe's Narratives,* 118.

10. For readings that emphasize the novel's status as a critique of bourgeois values and institutions, see Richetti, "Family, Sex, and Marriage," esp. 24–25; Maddox, "On Defoe's *Roxana*," 688; Juliet McMaster, "The Equation of Love and Money in *Moll Flanders*," *Studies in the Novel* 2.2 (1970): esp. 142; and Lois Chaber, "Matriarchal Mirror: Women and Capital in *Moll Flanders*," *PMLA* 97.2 (1982): esp. 213, 223.

11. See, e.g., Gayle Rubin, "The Traffic in Women: Notes on the 'Political Economy' of Sex," in *Toward an Anthropology of Women,* ed. Rayna R. Reiter (New York: Monthly Review Press, 1975), 157–210; Sebastiano Timpanaro, *On Materialism,* trans. Lawrence Garner (London: Verso, 1980), chap. 4; Teresa de Lauretis, *Alice Doesn't: Feminism, Semiotics, Cinema* (Bloomington: Indiana University Press, 1984), esp. chap. 5; and Judith Butler, *Gender Trouble: Feminism and the Subversion of Identity* (New York: Routledge, 1990), chap. 2.

12. On woman's dual nature as a sign and a generator of signs, see Claude Lévi-Strauss, *The Elementary Structures of Kinship,* rev. ed., trans. James Harle Bell, John Richard von Sturmer, and Rodney Needham (Boston: Beacon Press, 1969), 496. See also Rubin, "Traffic in Women," 201.

13. Reading the novel as a narrative about exchange eliminates the dichotomy between the subjective and the social that Douglas Brooks finds it necessary to insist upon in his "*Moll Flanders:* An Interpretation," *Essays in Criticism* 19.1 (1969): 46–59. Brooks attempted to refute the popular belief that Defoe's novel lacks formal unity by analyzing the incest motif as the key to the structural logic of the text. By privileging an economic reading, he argued, previous criticism had minimized or obscured the importance of the

psychological drama surrounding Moll's incest. To him, the novel is not so much about "money, poverty, aspirations to gentility" as about personal pathology (46). That a critical tradition that rigidly insisted on reading Defoe in socioeconomic terms had remained blind to the text's more subjective meaning is testimony, Brooks suggests, to the danger of assuming " 'too close an identification of literature with society' " (57). In many ways, I consider Brooks's analysis groundbreaking; he was the first to subject the incest episode in the novel to sustained scrutiny, and many of the details of his reading are highly suggestive. I differ, however, with the underlying theoretical assumptions of his article. Brooks argues the centrality of the incest episode in order to foreground the personal dimension of Defoe's text, those aspects of the narrative that he sees as eluding socioeconomic analysis. By contrast, I treat the subjective and the social as ideologically continuous. My aim is to explore how Moll's incest functions narratologically at once to organize her desire and to elaborate the social implications of her text.

14. Nancy K. Miller touches on the importance of this thematic preoccupation in *The Heroine's Text: Readings in the French and English Novel, 1722–1782* (New York: Columbia University Press, 1980), 20.

15. For studies that especially emphasize this aspect of the narrative, see Ian Watt, *The Rise of the Novel: Studies in Defoe, Richardson, and Fielding* (Berkeley: University of California Press, 1957), chap. 4; Michael Shinagel, *Daniel Defoe and Middle-Class Gentility* (Cambridge, Mass.: Harvard University Press, 1968), esp. chap. 7; and McMaster, "Equation."

16. Douglas Hay, "Property, Authority, and the Criminal Law," in *Albion's Fatal Tree: Crime and Society in Eighteenth-Century England,* by Douglas Hay, Peter Linebaugh, John G. Rule, E. P. Thompson, and Cal Winslow (New York: Pantheon Books, 1975), 22.

17. Juliet Mitchell, *Psychoanalysis and Feminism* (New York: Vintage Books, 1975), 406.

18. On the smuggling of Flemish lace in the seventeenth century, and on lace's fascination as a forbidden object, see Santina M. Levey, *Lace: A History* (London: Victoria and Albert Museum, 1983), 40, 44. According to Levey, Flanders was the prime offender when, in 1697, the English Parliament passed an act to tighten controls on the importation of foreign lace (44). Defoe's novel is, of course, set in the seventeenth century; Moll claims to have written it in 1683 at the age of almost seventy (*MF,* 342–43). Useful, too, is Starr's note on "the thriving trade in smuggled lace" (380).

19. Gerald Howson, "Who Was Moll Flanders?" in *Moll Flanders, an Authoritative Text: Backgrounds and Sources; Criticism,* ed. Edward Kelly (New York: Norton, 1973), 312–19.

20. I refer here, of course, to early capitalism and not to the large-scale industrialization of the later part of the eighteenth century. For relevant discussions of the effects of commercialization on the economic position of women in the late seventeenth and early eighteenth centuries, see Ellen Pollak, *The Poetics of Sexual Myth: Gender and Ideology in the Verse of Swift and Pope* (Chicago: University of Chicago Press, 1985), 22–39; Alice Clark, *Working Life of Women in the Seventeenth Century* (London: Routledge, 1919); and Susan Cahn, *Industry of Devotion: The Transformation of Women's Work in England, 1500–1660* (New York: Columbia University Press, 1987).

21. Chaber, "Matriarchal Mirror," 219.

22. Although, as Hay has pointed out, it was conventional in the eighteenth century to liken the circulation of gold to the circulation of the blood ("Property," 19), it is interesting that Defoe should choose to have Moll use the image of bleeding to death at this particular point in her career, since gold and blood are also conventionally tied to

women, childbirth, and taboo. Consider, e.g., the lyrics to Air 5 of John Gay's *Beggar's Opera* (*The Beggar's Opera and Companion Pieces*, ed. C. F. Burgess [Arlington Heights, Ill: AHM Publishing Corp., 1966]):

> A maid is like the golden ore;
> . . . A wife's like a guinea in gold,
> Stampt with the name of her spouse;
> Now here, now there; is bought, or is sold;
> And is current in every house. [act 1, sc. 5])

If Moll's education during the novel is in "reserve," which is ordinarily a male preroga-tive, it is somehow fitting that her criminal career should begin at this moment of her "death" as a woman. For what is criminal about Moll's thievery is precisely that it enables her to accumulate wealth without reinvesting it (she keeps it in reserve)—without, that is, participating in normal relations of exchange. The one other time in the narrative when Moll describes her poverty as "*bleeding to Death*" is when she spends the "Season" at Bath, just after fleeing her incestuous marriage. Bath, she points out, is the wrong place for a woman to turn her sexuality to profit, for men sometimes find mistresses there but "very rarely look for a Wife" (*MF*, 106).

23. James Boswell, *Boswell's Life of Johnson,* ed. George Birkbeck Hill, revised by L. F. Powell, 6 vols. (Oxford: Clarendon Press, 1934–64), 4:23.

24. Levey, *Lace*, 1.

25. Boswell, *Life of Johnson,* 2:352. I am grateful to David B. Morris for helping me to make the connections here between lace, gender, and social class.

26. See Defoe, *Moll Flanders,* ed. Starr, 361 n. 1 to p. 79; and Kelly, *Moll Flanders, an Authoritative Text,* 63 n.

27. On the Mint, see Defoe, *Moll Flanders,* ed. Hunter, 52 n; and E. P. Thompson, *Whigs and Hunters: The Origin of the Black Act* (New York: Pantheon Books, 1975), 248–49.

28. Augustine, *The City of God,* trans. Marcus Dods (New York: Modern Library, 1950), 4:500. See also Lévi-Strauss's statement of the "very simple fact" that "the biological family . . . must ally itself with other families in order to endure" (*Kinship,* 485).

29. Lévi-Strauss, *Kinship,* 481.

30. Talcott Parsons, "The Incest Taboo in Relation to Social Structure," in *The Family: Its Structures and Functions,* ed. Rose Laub Coser (New York: St. Martin's Press, 1964), 56.

31. "*But what if the 'goods' refused to go to market?*" writes Irigaray. "What if they maintained among themselves 'another' kind of trade?" (Luce Irigaray, "When the Goods Get Together," trans. Claudia Reeder, in *New French Feminisms,* ed. Elaine Marks and Isabelle de Courtivron [Amherst: University of Massachusetts Press, 1980], 110). For a slightly different translation, see also Luce Irigaray, *This Sex Which Is Not One,* trans. Catherine Porter with Carolyn Burke (Ithaca, N.Y.: Cornell University Press, 1985), 196.

32. Juliet Mitchell, introduction to *The Fortunes and Misfortunes of the Famous Moll Flanders,* by Daniel Defoe, ed. Juliet Mitchell (Harmondsworth: Penguin, 1978), 12. The passage from Lacan is quoted by Jacqueline Rose in Juliet Mitchell and Jacqueline Rose, eds. *Feminine Sexuality: Jacques Lacan and the école freudienne,* trans. Jacqueline Rose (New York: Norton; London: Pantheon Books, 1985), 39.

33. For relevant theoretical discussion of the "implicit racial grammar [that] under-wrote the sexual regimes of bourgeois culture" identified by Foucault, see Ann Laura

Stoler, *Race and the Education of Desire: Foucault's* History of Sexuality *and the Colonial Order of Things* (Durham, N.C.: Duke University Press, 1995), 12.

34. Daniel Defoe, *Colonel Jack* (London, 1722).

35. It is fitting that the wish for endogamy here should emerge as a counterpoint to marriage with Jemy, whose Irishness significantly designates him as a colonized subject with whom marriage would constitute a form of figurative miscegenation. At the same time, however, Jemy's aristocratic origins guarantee that such a crossing of national boundaries is counterbalanced by its simultaneous figuration of a form of class allegiance associated with the British imperial project. In this connection, see Aparna Dharwadker, "Nation, Race, and the Ideology of Commerce in Defoe," *The Eighteenth-Century: Theory and Interpretation* 39.1 (1998): 63, who quotes Richard Helgerson's observation (in *Forms of Nationhood: The Elizabethan Writing of England* [Chicago: University of Chicago Press, 1992]) that British imperial expansion brought merchant and gentry classes into a common enterprise.

36. On the relative condition of servants and slaves in colonial Virginia, and the use of the term *servant* to designate both categories, see Defoe, *Moll Flanders*, ed. Starr, 361–62 n. 2 to p. 86. See also Edmund S. Morgan, *American Slavery, American Freedom: The Ordeal of Colonial Virginia* (New York: Norton, 1975; reprint, New York: Norton, 1995).

37. See in this connection Deborah Epstein Nord, " 'Marks of Race': Gypsy Figures and Eccentric Femininity in Nineteenth-Century Women's Writing," *Victorian Studies* 41.2 (1998): 189–210. On the role of Asia in Defoe and Defoe's "Orientalism," see Dharwadker, "Nation, Race," 78–82.

SIX: Ingesting Incest

1. London, 1751. Only three extant copies of the London printing of *Eleanora* are recorded in library holdings, two in North America (at the Library of Congress and the Lewis Walpole Library, Yale University) and one at the British Library. A 1751 Dublin printing is also held at SUNY Stonybrook.

2. Although Gould's play was written in 1698, it was printed posthumously. For sustained discussion of both plays, including their performance and publication histories and an account of questions surrounding attribution of authorship, see J. Douglas Canfield, "Mother as Other: The Eruption of Feminine Desire in Some Late Restoration Incest Plays," *The Eighteenth Century: Theory and Interpretation* 39.3 (fall 1998): 209–19.

3. For helpful discussions of the privileging of affect over birth in connection with the sentimental family, see Terri Nickel, " 'Ingenious Torment': Incest, Family, and the Structure of Community in the Work of Sarah Fielding," *The Eighteenth Century: Theory and Interpretation* 36.3 (1995): 234–47; Caroline Gonda, *Reading Daughters' Fictions, 1709–1834: Novels and Society from Manley to Edgeworth* (Cambridge: Cambridge University Press, 1996); and Brian McCrea, *Impotent Fathers: Patriarchy and Demographic Crisis in the Eighteenth-Century Novel* (Newark: University of Delaware Press, 1998).

4. Marguerite de Navarre, *The Heptameron*, trans. P. A. Chilton (London: Penguin, 1984; reprint, 1988), 320.

5. Ibid., 321. The question of the sinfulness of unwitting incest was, of course, a perennial one among casuists in the seventeenth century. See W. Daniel Wilson, "Science, Natural Law, and Unwitting Sibling Incest in Eighteenth-Century Literature," *Stud-*

ies in Eighteenth-Century Culture 13 (1984): 249–70; and G. A. Starr's note in Daniel Defoe, *The Fortunes and Misfortunes of the Famous Moll Flanders,* ed. G. A. Starr (Oxford: Oxford University Press, 1981), 363 n.

6. For an interesting feminist reading of the *Heptameron,* see Patricia Francis Chola-kian, *Rape and Writing in the* Heptaméron *of Marguerite de Navarre* (Carbondale: Southern Illinois University Press, 1991).

7. *Eleanora; or A Tragical but True Case of Incest in Great-Britain* (London, 1751), i. Further references are cited by parenthetical page numbers in the text, using the abbreviation *E* where needed for clarity.

8. As a member of Cromwell's New Model Army, Orestes participates in the battle of Naseby (*E,* 14), at which the royalist army was defeated in 1645, leaving Charles with no recourse but to surrender. This was the decisive victory of the first phase of the English Civil War, in which the intervention of Scotland on the side of Parliament helped to turn the tide against the king. In a later phase of the war, the victors quarreled and Cromwell parted ways with the Scots and Presbyterians.

9. Of course, as a soldier in Cromwell's army, Orestes clearly represents a more revolu-tionary model of resistance to the imperatives of sovereign and familial authority than Behn's figure of beleaguered royalty.

10. For another narrative that explores the thematic relations among incest, speech-lessness, and gestural signifying, see Aphra Behn, "The Dumb Virgin, or The Force of Imagination" (1700). *Eleanora's* plot, in which knowledge of incest silences the mother, curiously reverses Behn's story, in which the discovery of sibling incest releases the dumb virgin's tongue but silences the narrator.

11. This moment constitutes a sort of protoversion of the grandson's happening upon his grandfather's manuscript and deciding to publish, as mere entertainment, what he had been led to believe the grandfather had meant to be a cautionary tale. It thus replicates at the level of plot the tension between intention and desire that structures the story's frame.

12. Eleanora, however, goes on to qualify the crime. "Incest in me, my Son," she writes to Orestes, "while thou art (though not free from Fornication) involuntarily in-volved in that bestial Mixture" (*E,* 54). Her assertion echoes the reasoning of such com-mentators as Bishop Patrick, who had, for example, differentially identified the crime in the biblical case of Judah and Tamar as "incest in her tho only fornication in him" (see text accompanying note 87 in chap. 2). Her allusion to the "abominable Sin of Incest" echoes the words of Sarah Fielding in *The Adventures of David Simple* (Oxford: Oxford University Press, 1987), where Livia "launch[es] out into a long Harangue on the crying and abominable Sin of Incest" (160) as part of her plot to alienate her stepchildren, Camilla and Valentine, from their father's love and defraud them of their rightful inheri-tance. Interestingly, both texts also echo the opening sentence of the Puritan act of 1650, which made "the abominable and crying sins of Incest, Adultery, and Fornication" fel-onies punishable by death. The story of Camilla and Valentine is discussed later in this chapter. For discussion of the Puritan act of 1650, see the first section of chap. 2.

13. For the concept of "blindness and forgetting" I am indebted to Scott J. Juengel's remarkable essay "Oroonoko's Scar," which suggestively identifies "the limits of vi-sion and memory [as] the enabling conditions of modernity's relation to the other" (manuscript).

14. John Milton, *Complete Poems and Major Prose,* ed. Merritt Y. Hughes (New York: Odyssey Press, 1957), 728.

15. See, in connection with Orestes' ingestion of the letter, Kaja Silverman's chapter entitled "Eating the Book" in *World Spectators* (Stanford, Calif.: Stanford University Press, 2000), 29–50.

16. The statement by Steevens appears on p. 249 of several canceled leaves of *The Biographia Dramatica* that are bound with Walpole's *Mysterious Mother* and a copy of *Eleanora* in the Lewis Walpole Library, Yale University. For an account of pretexts and analogs, Cholakian cites Nicole Cazauran, "La trentième nouvelle de *L'Hemptaméron* ou la méditation d'un 'Exemple,'" (in *Mélange Jeanne Lods* [Paris: Ecole Normale Supérieure de Filles, 1978], 617–52) (Cholakian, *Rape and Writing,* 146, 263–64 n).

17. Horace Walpole, *The Mysterious Mother, a Tragedy* (London: printed for J. Dodsley, 1781), "Author's Postscript," 94–96. Marguerite's story is also retold in John Quick's *Serious Inquiry into that Weighty Case of Conscience, Whether a Man may Lawfully Marry his Deceased Wife's Sister* (London, 1703), facsimile reprint in *The Marriage Prohibitions Controversy: Five Tracts,* ed. Randolph Trumbach (New York: Garland, 1985). Quick reports having also seen it elsewhere "in Print both in French and English" (31).

18. This effect is even further enhanced in *Eleanora* by the author's anonymity.

19. See Terry J. Castle, "Why the Houyhnhnms Don't Write: Swift, Satire, and the Fear of the Text," *Essays in Literature* 7 (1980): 31–44.

20. Julia Kristeva, "Signifying Practice and Mode of Production," *Edinburgh Review* 1: 68, quoted by Elizabeth Grosz in *Jacques Lacan: A Feminist Introduction* (London: Routledge, 1990), 152.

21. Henry Fielding, *The History of Tom Jones, a Foundling,* ed. Fredson Bowers (Middletown, Conn.: Wesleyan University Press, 1975), bk. 1, chap. 1. Subsequent quotations are from this edition; book, chapter, and page references are inserted parenthetically in my text, with the abbreviation *TJ* where needed for clarity.

22. For discussion of work that has minimized the importance of incest in Fielding's work and in eighteenth-century fiction generally, see chap. 1 of this volume, notes 2–4 and accompanying text. For work that does devote serious critical attention to the incest in Fielding's novel, see Martin C. Battestin, "Henry Fielding, Sarah Fielding, and 'the dreadful Sin of Incest,'" *Novel* 13 (1979): 6–18; Christine van Boheemen, *The Novel as Family Romance: Language, Gender, and Authority from Fielding to Joyce* (Ithaca, N.Y.: Cornell University Press, 1987), chaps. 1–4; Douglas Brooks-Davies, *Fielding, Dickens, Gosse, Iris Murdoch, and Oedipal Hamlet* (London: Macmillan, 1989), chap. 1; Minaz Jooma, "The Alimentary Structures of Incest: Eating and Incest in Eighteenth-Century English Narrative" (Ph.D. diss., Michigan State University, 1995), chap. 4; T. G. A. Nelson, "Incest in the Early Novel and Related Genres," *Eighteenth-Century Life,* n.s., 16.1 (1992): 127–62; William Park, "Tom and Oedipus," *Hartford Studies in Literature: A Journal of Interdisciplinary Criticism* 7 (1975): 207–15; Ronald Paulson, *The Life of Henry Fielding: A Critical Biography* (Oxford: Blackwell, 2000), 238–39. Incest, of course, also emerges as a tabooed possibility in Fielding's *Joseph Andrews,* where the hero believes for a time that his beloved Fanny is his sister.

23. Indeed, Bridget's affair with Summer itself has incestuous overtones. As Jenny Jones observes, Summer, the son of Allworthy's friend, had been educated, bred up, and buried by the squire "as if he had been [Allworthy's] own Son" (18.7.940). Bridget's

relation to her lover would thus have been that of a surrogate aunt, precisely the relation she is, for much of the novel, believed to bear to Tom.

24. Jooma, "Alimentary Structures of Incest," 225.

25. Peter Brooks, "Freud's Masterplot," in *The Critical Tradition: Classic Texts and Contemporary Trends,* 2d ed., ed. David H. Richter (Boston: Bedford Books, 1998), 1036; Terry Eagleton, *Literary Theory: An Introduction* (Minneapolis: University of Minnesota Press, 1983), 186.

26. Brooks, "Freud's Masterplot," 1039.

27. Although Brooks does not mention *Tom Jones* in his discussion and Eagleton does not mention incest, the crucial link between the novel's averted incest and the "classic" nature of its plot seems implicit in both discussions and is more explicitly addressed in the readings of van Boheemen and Brooks-Davies. The idea of Tom's attraction to maternal figures as a "regressive pull" is from Brooks-Davies (*Fielding, Dickens,* 49).

28. Gary Gautier, *Landed Patriarchy in Fielding's Novels: Fictional Landscapes, Fictional Genders,* Studies in British Literature, vol. 35 (Lewiston, N.Y.: Edwin Mellen Press, 1998), 165, 172, quotation on 172. See also Homer Obed Brown's comment that "transgression of the incest taboo at once marks a limit to possible narrative drift and serves as a threshold to the revelation of a proper name," in *"Tom Jones:* The 'Bastard' of History," *boundary 2* 7 (1979): 204. Brown's important and subtly argued essay appears as chapter 3 of his book *Institutions of the English Novel: From Defoe to Scott* (Philadelphia: University of Pennsylvania Press, 1997), which more generally addresses some of the same thematic and formal issues of genealogy, succession, and patriarchal inheritance that concern me here.

29. Anita Levy, "Reproductive Urges: Literacy, Sexuality, and Eighteenth-Century Englishness," in *Inventing Maternity: Politics, Science, and Literature, 1650–1865,* ed. Susan C. Greenfield and Carol Barash (Lexington: University Press of Kentucky, 1999), 197–98.

30. Brown, *"Tom Jones,"* 202.

31. See Marilyn Francus, "The Monstrous Mother: Reproductive Anxiety in Swift and Pope," *ELH* 61 (1994): 829–51.

32. My reading of the episode of the little bird Tommy is much indebted to the work of Catherine Swender in "The Mediating Mother: Desire and Control in *Tom Jones*" (manuscript). See also Paulson, *Life of Henry Fielding,* 239.

33. Van Boheemen, *Novel as Family Romance,* 48, 85, 93. Van Boheemen suggests that, as a representative fiction, Fielding's novel "enacts what we might well call the plot of plot . . . , the 'plot,' by which our culture constitutes the subjective self" (49–50); in this sense, she writes, "[f]iction embodies the plot of patriarchy" (99).

34. William B. Warner incisively explores the contingent relation of "elevated" eighteenth-century novels to the work of women writers in *Licensing Entertainment: The Elevation of Novel Reading in Britain, 1684–1750* (Berkeley: University of California Press, 1998).

35. Laurence Sterne, *The Life and Opinions of Tristram Shandy,* ed. Graham Petrie (Harmondsworth: Penguin Books, 1967), vol. 4, chap. 14, p. 287. All further references to this edition are parenthetically cited by volume, chapter, and page number in my text.

36. Triptolemus also appeals here to the doctrine of "one flesh": "the father, the mother, and the child, though they be three persons, yet are they but (*una caro*) one flesh; and consequently no degree of kindred" (4:29.326).

37. In context, of course, the phrase that Walter may be "less than nothing" points ironically to the novel's frequent hints that Tristram may be illegitimate.

38. Judith Roof, *Reproductions of Reproduction: Imaging Symbolic Change* (New York: Routledge, 1996), 17.

39. Delarivier Manley, *Secret Memoirs and Manners of Several Persons of Quality of Both Sexes. From the New Atalantis, an Island in the Mediteranean,* 2 vols. (London, 1709; reprinted, 2 vol. in 1, in *The Novels of Mary Delarivière Manley,* ed. Patricia Köster [Gainesville, Fla.: Scholars' Facsimiles & Reprints, 1971]), 2:10 in the 1709 ed., 1:542 in the reprint ed. The parenthetical references include both sets of volume and page-number citations.

40. See Catherine Gallagher, *Nobody's Story: The Vanishing Acts of Women Writers in the Marketplace, 1670–1820* (Berkeley: University of California Press, 1994), 130–44.

41. For a fascinating discussion of Behn's "portrait" of the defaced Imoinda as a figure for representation, which, however, does not treat the matter of her pregnancy, I am indebted to Juengel, "Oroonoko's Scar."

42. Jane Austen, *Mansfield Park: Authoritative Text, Contexts, Criticism,* ed. Claudia L. Johnson (New York: Norton, 1998), 320.

43. Sarah Fielding, *David Simple,* 142.

44. For a psychobiographical approach to the episode, see Battestin, "Henry Fielding, Sarah Fielding." For two suggestive critical readings of incest in *David Simple,* see also Nickel, "Ingenious Torment"; and George E. Haggerty, *Unnatural Affections: Women and Fiction in the Later Eighteenth Century* (Bloomington: Indiana University Press, 1998), chap. 1. Nickel argues that sibling incest is a theme "through which [Fielding] frames competing models of the family." Because "[i]ncest registers the demand for sympathetic identification . . . while at the same time marking the inevitable self-destruction of such empathy . . . , Fielding uses the incest-motif to mark the boundaries of the family" (235). Acccording to Hagggerty, the story of Camilla and Valentine constitutes a sort of parable about how, in heteropatriarchal culture, familial relations that do not "assure the ascendancy of the father" (30) are "written into a discourse of the 'unnatural' " (31).

45. Sarah Fielding, *David Simple,* 153.

46. Frances Burney, *Evelina, or the History of a Young Lady's Entrance into the World,* ed. Edward A. Bloom and Lillian D. Bloom (Oxford: Oxford University Press, 1982), 123. Further page references are inserted parenthetically in the text, with the abbreviated title *Evelina* added where needed for clarity.

47. For a time, as Irene Fizer notes, Macartney's affections for Evelina also have "incestuous overtones" ("The Name of the Daughter: Identity and Incest in *Evelina,*" in *Refiguring the Father: New Feminist Readings of Patriarchy,* ed. Patricia Yaeger and Beth Kowaleski-Wallace [Carbondale: Southern Illinois University Press, 1989], 83).

48. Julia Epstein, *The Iron Pen: Frances Burney and the Politics of Women's Writing* (Madison: University of Wisconsin Press, 1989), chap. 3. See also Julia Epstein, "Jane Austen's Juvenilia and the Female Epistolary Tradition," *Papers in Language and Literature* 21 (1985): 399–416.

49. As we shall see, Austen explores this possibility in the figure of Fanny Price. She uses epistolarity to a similar end in *Lady Susan,* most notably in the single letter written by the heroine's daughter, Frederica, who ends up marrying Sir James Martin, her mother's former beau. Read through the lens provided by Epstein in "Jane Austen's Juvenilia and

the Female Epistolary Tradition," Frederica's letter constitutes a model of artful artlessness. One wonders, in this connection, whether in marrying Frederica to Sir James, Austen may have been remembering the moment in *Evelina* when Madame Duval's cicisbeo, Monsieur Dubois, declares his undying affection for the artless Evelina.

50. McCrea, *Impotent Fathers*, 141–53.

51. Michael McKeon, "Generic Transformation and Social Change: Rethinking the Rise of the Novel," *Cultural Critique* 1 (1985): 173. McKeon's analysis of the emergent novel's implication in the shift from a traditional, status-based culture to a modern, class-based culture is, of course, much more fully elaborated in his *Origins of the English Novel, 1600–1740* (Baltimore: Johns Hopkins University Press, 1987). While the influence of this important work with respect to the narrative effects of epistemological and moral change in the early modern period will be apparent at various points throughout my study, McKeon's insistence on understanding issues of sex and gender in the early English novel as, in essence, epiphenomena of class issues limits its usefulness to my study of the way incest is constructed in the genre. Even if we were to assent to McKeon's assertion in the introduction to the recently published fifteenth anniversary edition of *Origins* that "gender difference has not yet been sufficiently separated out from status difference to receive direct attention" during the first half of the eighteenth century, it does not necessarily follow—as I hope this study demonstrates—that the gender implications of class ideologies will not be usefully illuminated by an analytic approach that interrogates those implications rather than taking them on their own terms (Michael McKeon, *The Origins of the English Novel, 1600–1740,* 15th anniversary ed. [Baltimore: Johns Hopkins University Press, 2002], xxv). McKeon provides a subtly articulated account of his understanding of the relationship between the categories of class, gender, sexuality, and (to some extent) race in "Historicizing Patriarchy: The Emergence of Gender Difference in England, 1660–1769," *Eighteenth-Century Studies* 28.3 (1995): 295–322.

52. It is debatable whether Burney rewards or punishes Evelina for this omission, for although the heroine eventually does concede to attend the opera with her grandmother and the Branghtons, her embarrassment at being associated with them eventually leads to her disastrous decision to allow Sir Clement to escort her to the Mirvans. In attempting to prevent Sir Clement from being "witness of Madame Duval's power over" her, in other words, Evelina ironically and treacherously (in both senses of the term) places herself in his (*Evelina,* 94–99).

53. Susan C. Greenfield, " 'Oh Dear Resemblance of Thy Murdered Mother': Female Authorship in *Evelina,*" *Eighteenth-Century Fiction* 3.4 (1991): 311–12.

54. Although she acknowledges the "tenuousness" of the association between Evelina's face and the certainty of her lawful kinship to Sir John, Greenfield does not read that tenuousness as a problem that is acknowledged by Burney's text: "There is no avowal of the tenuousness of this association—no admission that Evelina's resemblance to her mother does not necessarily prove that she is Belmont's legitimate child. *It is simply assumed* that since Evelina looks just like her mother, who was a virtuous woman, Belmont must be the father. Accordingly, when he sees Evelina for the first time, Belmont senses that she is his real daughter and suspects that the girl he raised is a fraud. Echoing Villars, Evelina explains that 'the certainty I carried in my countenance, of my real birth, made him . . . suspect . . . the imposition' " (ibid., 311; my emphasis). I am suggesting that Burney leaves that assumption open to being read as simply that—an assumption with implications for the meaning and the structure of her text. In *Mothering Daughters: Novels*

and the Politics of Family Romance, Frances Burney to Jane Austen (Detroit: Wayne State University Press, 2002), which appeared just as this book was going to press, Greenfield goes on to develop a compelling case that the assumption of Evelina's legitimacy on the basis of her exclusively maternal resemblance reflects Burney's feminist appropriation of contemporary theories about pregnancy, maternal imprinting, and physiognomic legibility (chap. 1).

55. So, of course, is Madame Duval. As Evelina reports to Villars while recounting her mortifying application to two prostitutes to protect her in Mary-bone Gardens: "As to Madame Duval, she was really for some time so strangely imposed upon, that she thought they were two real fine ladies. Indeed it is wonderful to see how easily and how frequently she is deceived" (*Evelina,* 236). The irony, however, is at the expense of Evelina, who has just reported making the very same error.

56. Fizer, "Name of the Daughter," 91–95.

57. Ibid., 95–97.

58. McCrea, *Impotent Fathers,* 150. McCrea is alluding to *Eighteenth-Century Fiction* 3.4 (1991).

59. Judith Butler, *Antigone's Claim: Kinship between Life and Death* (New York: Columbia University Press, 2000), 78.

60. Silverman, *World Spectators,* 48–49.

SEVEN: Incest and Liberty

1. Jane Austen, *Mansfield Park: Authoritative Text, Contexts, Criticism,* ed. Claudia L. Johnson (New York: Norton, 1998), 7. Further references are cited by parenthetical page numbers in the text, using the abbreviation *MP* where needed for clarity.

2. For an excellent analysis of Fanny's value as an investment, see Eileen Cleere, "Reinvesting Nieces: *Mansfield Park* and the Economics of Endogamy," *Novel* 28.2 (1995): 113–30.

3. Samuel Dugard wrote that "*Cousin Germans have more reason to know one anothers Tempers and Humours from their dayley converse, and Education oftentimes together.* And so being thoroughly acquainted, their Marriages are not so much Lotteryes as others are" (*The Marriages of Cousin Germans, Vindicated from the Censures of Unlawfullnesse, and Inexpediency* [Oxford, 1673; facsimile reprint in *The Marriage Prohibitions Controversy: Five Tracts,* ed. Randolph Trumbach, New York: Garland, 1985], 106–7). On the other hand, John Alleyne, who generally concurred with Dugard's views, quotes the following relevant words from Montesquieu's *Spirit of Laws:* "There are nations . . . amongst whom cousin-germans are considered as brothers, because they commonly dwell in the same house: there are others where this custom is not known. Among the first, the marriage of cousin-germans ought to be regarded as contrary to nature; not so among the others" (*The Legal Degrees of Marriage Stated and Considered, in a Series of Letters to a Friend,* 2d ed. [London, 1775; facsimile reprint in *The Marriage Prohibitions Controversy: Five Tracts,* ed. Randolph Trumbach, New York: Garland, 1985], appendix, 43).

4. David Kaufmann, "Closure in *Mansfield Park* and the Sanctity of the Family," *Philological Quarterly* 65.2 (1986): 214.

5. Pierre Bourdieu, *Distinction: A Social Critique of the Judgement of Taste,* trans. Richard Nice (Cambridge, Mass.: Harvard University Press, 1984), 86.

6. Inchbald's play was loosely based on August Friedrich Ferdinand von Kotzebue's

"Das Kind der Liebe" (1791). My references to *Lover's Vows* are to the 1798 text reprinted in Claudia Johnson's edition of *Mansfield Park,* 329–75.

7. For studies that specifically examine Austen's debts to Samuel Richardson and Henry Fielding, see Jocelyn Harris, *Jane Austen's Art of Memory* (Cambridge: Cambridge University Press, 1989); and Jo Alyson Parker, *The Author's Inheritance: Henry Fielding, Jane Austen, and the Establishment of the Novel* (Dekalb: Northern Illinois University Press, 1998).

8. Sarah Fielding, *The Adventures of David Simple* (Oxford: Oxford University Press, 1987), 26–30.

9. Delarivier Manley, *Secret Memoirs and Manners of Several Persons of Quality of Both Sexes. From the New Atalantis, an Island in the Mediteranean,* 2 vols. (London, 1709; reprinted in vol. 1 of *The Novels of Mary Delarivière Manley,* ed. Patricia Köster [Gainesville, Fla.: Scholars' Facsimiles & Reprints, 1971]), 2:194–95 in the 1709 ed., 1:726–27 in the reprint ed.

10. Aphra Behn, *Love-Letters between a Nobleman and his Sister,* vol. 2 of *The Works of Aphra Behn,* ed. Janet Todd (Columbus: Ohio State University Press, 1993), 439.

11. Jan Fergus, *Jane Austen: A Literary Life* (New York: St. Martin's Press, 1991), 149.

12. Claudia L. Johnson, *Jane Austen: Women, Politics, and the Novel* (Chicago: University of Chicago Press, 1988), 115.

13. Margaret Kirkham, *Jane Austen, Feminism, and Fiction* (Sussex: Harvester Press, 1983), 114–16.

14. William Shakespeare, *The Famous History of the Life of King Henry the Eighth,* in *The Riverside Shakespeare* (Boston: Houghton Mifflin, 1974), 2.4.15.

15. After having provoked Sir Thomas's ire by her refusal of Henry Crawford, we are told, Fanny "was willing to hope . . . that her uncle's displeasure was abating, and would abate farther as he considered the matter with more impartiality, and felt, as a good man must feel" (*MP,* 220).

16. See, e.g., Frank Gibbon, "The Antiguan Connection: Some New Light on *Mansfield Park,*" *Cambridge Quarterly* 11.2 (1982): 298–305; Edward W. Said, *Culture and Imperialism* (New York: Alfred A. Knopf, 1993), 80–97; Moira Ferguson, *Colonialism and Gender Relations from Mary Wollstonecraft to Jamaica Kincaid* (New York: Columbia University Press, 1993), chap. 4; Maaja A. Stewart, *Domestic Realities and Imperial Fictions: Jane Austen's Novels in Eighteenth-Century Contexts* (Athens: University of Georgia Press, 1993), chap. 4; Ruth Perry, "Austen and Empire: A Thinking Woman's Guide to British Imperialism," *Persuasions* 16 (1994): 95–106; Joseph Lew, " 'That Abominable Traffic': *Mansfield Park* and the Dynamics of Slavery," in *History, Gender, and Eighteenth-Century Literature,* ed. Beth Fowkes Tobin (Athens: University of Georgia Press, 1994), 271–300; Susan Fraiman, "Jane Austen and Edward Said: Gender, Culture, and Imperialism," *Critical Inquiry* 21 (1995): 805–21; Brian Southam, "The Silence of the Bertrams: Slavery and the Chronology of *Mansfield Park,*" *Times Literary Supplement,* February 7, 1995, 13–14; and Michael Steffes, "Slavery and *Mansfield Park:* The Historical and Biographical Context," *English Language Notes* 34.2 (1996): 23–41.

17. Ferguson, *Colonialism and Gender Relations,* 71.

18. Lew, " 'That Abominable Traffic,' " 290.

19. Ferguson, *Colonialism and Gender Relations,* 70–71.

20. As Joseph Lew notes, "Bristol and Liverpool (the former especially) dominated the British share of the trade, distantly followed by other ports on the west coast of England.

Portsmouth was largely untainted by the slavers' interest" (" 'That Abominable Traffic,' " 275).

21. Ferguson, *Colonialism and Gender Relations,* 77; Stewart, *Domestic Realities,* 109. For an informative discussion of the time frame of events in *Mansfield Park* in relation to the history of the slave trade, see Southam, "Silence of the Bertrams."

22. Alleyne, *Legal Degrees of Marriage,* 11.

23. With the help of Guy Holborn, librarian of the Lincoln's Inn Library; A. S. Adams, librarian of the Society of the Middle Temple; and the Middle Temple printed admission registers, I have been able to confirm that the only barrister by the name of John Alleyne in the early 1770s was John Alleyne, son and heir of Thomas Alleyne, of Queen Street, City of Westminster, Esq., who was admitted to the Middle Temple on April 27, 1767, and called to the bar on May 8, 1772. The Somerset case was heard on May 14, 1772, when, according to F. O. Shyllon, "Mr. Alleyne . . . was making his first appearance in Westminster Hall" (*Black Slaves in Britain* [London: Oxford University Press, 1974], 99). Alleyne also appeared as counsel in the case of *Campbell v. Hall* (1774) 20 State Tr. 239 concerning the island of Grenada, which was also before Chief Justice Mansfield. An eighteenth-century ledger of accounts shows that John Alleyne paid his dues as a barrister member from Easter 1772 until Trinity 1777, during which latter term he died on July 2. As the title page of the second edition of *The Legal Degrees of Marriage* identifies its author as a "Barrister at Law" and the prefatorial advertisement of the third edition of 1810 notes that "The second edition of this work [1775] was published during the lifetime of its highly respectable author," it appears that the John Alleyne of the Somerset trial is indeed the same John Alleyne who authored *The Legal Degrees of Marriage,* although no published source that I have been able to find explicitly connects the two. This was also presumably the same John Alleyne with whom Benjamin Franklin corresponded in 1768 on the subject of early marriage (Benjamin Franklin, *Writings,* ed. J. A. Leo Lemay [New York: Library of America, 1987], 835–37). A letter from Franklin, dated Oct. 15, 1773, on the subject of marriage to the deceased wife's sister, also appears in the second edition of *The Legal Degrees of Marriage,* appendix, 1–2.

24. *English Reports* 98 (King's Bench Division 27), Easter Term, 12 Geo. 3, 1772, K.B.: Somerset against Stewart, May 14, 1772.

25. Shyllon, *Black Slaves in Britain,* 92. For discussion of the Somerset trial, see also David Brion Davis, *The Problem of Slavery in the Age of Revolution, 1770–1823* (Ithaca, N.Y.: Cornell University Press, 1975), chap. 10.

26. Thomas Clarkson, *The History of the Abolition of the African Slave-Trade,* 2 vols. (London, 1808), 1:76. For a nuanced account of the legal and political dimensions of Lord Mansfield's ruling in the Somerset case, see James Oldham, *The Mansfield Manuscripts and the Growth of English Law in the Eighteenth Century* (Chapel Hill: University of North Carolina Press, 1992), vol.2, chap. 21.

27. "The eloquence displayed . . . by those who were engaged on the side of liberty," writes Clarkson, "was perhaps never exceeded on any occasion; and the names of the counsellors Davy, Glynn, Hargrave, Mansfield, and Alleyne, ought always to be remembered with gratitude by the friends of this great cause" (Clarkson, *History,* 1:77–78). For Austen's admiration for Clarkson, see Kirkham, *Jane Austen,* 117.

28. R. F. Brissenden, "*Mansfield Park:* Freedom and the Family" in *Jane Austen: Bicentenary Essays,* ed. John Halperin (Cambridge: Cambridge University Press, 1975), 156–71.

29. Kirkham, *Jane Austen,* 118–19.

30. See chap. 2, the section titled "Untying the Gordian Knot."

31. Stewart, *Domestic Realities,* 109.

32. Davis, *Problem of Slavery,* 494.

33. Samuel Estwick, *Considerations on the Negroe Cause Commonly So Called, Addressed to the Right Honourable Lord Mansfield, Lord Chief Justice of the Court of King's Bench. . . . ,* 2d ed. (London, 1773), quoted in Shyllon, *Black Slaves in Britain,* 151.

34. Edward Long, *Candid Reflections upon the judgement lately awarded by the Court of King's Bench in Westminster-Hall on what is commonly called the Negroe-Cause. By a Planter* (London: Printed for T. Lowndes, 1772), 46–49. Exploring metaphors of infection in antitheatrical literature of the late eighteenth and early nineteenth centuries in his excellent essay on *Mansfield Park,* Joseph Litvak draws a link between the "poison of theatricality" and "the poison of foreignness"—emphasizing particularly British xenophobic reaction to "the revolutionary doctrines threatening to spread to England from the continent," including those of Kotzebue and Inchbald ("The Infection of Acting: Theatricals and Theatricality in *Mansfield Park,*" *ELH* 53 [1986]: 338). My reading attempts to suggest another type of "poisonous" foreignness as well. A later version of Litvak's piece also appears as the first chapter of his *Caught in the Act: Theatricality in the Nineteenth-Century English Novel* (Berkeley: University of California Press, 1992).

35. Quoted in Davis, *Problem of Slavery,* 495. The obverse concern about how to distinguish between insiders and outsiders (focusing, significantly, on the contaminations of incest rather than miscegenation) occurred in the colonies, where a slave owner could not always be sure whether in raping his female slave he might not be having sex with his own daughter.

36. In other words, the figure of contamination through dispersal of infection via interracial sexuality that is made explicit by Long and Estwick is also in some sense already implicit in the very trope that Davy uses to advocate the freedom of immigrant slaves. Davis makes a related point when he observes that Davy "was not inviting more slaves to come and breathe the freedom-giving air. He made it clear that the air of England was also too pure for a Negro to breathe in" (Davis, *Problem of Slavery,* 495).

37. Ann Laura Stoler, *Race and the Education of Desire: Foucault's* History of Sexuality *and the Colonial Order of Things* (Durham, N.C.: Duke University Press, 1995), 7.

38. Stewart, *Domestic Realities,* 116, 117.

39. See Teresa Michals, " 'That Sole and Despotic Dominion': Slaves, Wives, and Game in Blackstone's *Commentaries,*" *Eighteenth-Century Studies* 27.2 (1993–94): 195–216. For an analysis of the relations between incest tropes and game laws, see Minaz Jooma, "The Alimentary Structures of Incest: Eating and Incest in Eighteenth-Century English Narrative" (Ph.D. diss., Michigan State University, 1995), chap. 4.

40. Cynthia Fansler Behrman, "The Annual Blister: A Sidelight on Victorian Social and Parliamentary History," *Victorian Studies* 11.4 (1968): 483.

41. Nancy F. Anderson, "The 'Marriage with a Deceased Wife's Sister Bill' Controversy: Incest Anxiety and the Defense of Family Purity in Victorian England," *Journal of British Studies* 21.2 (spring 1982): 84.

42. Stoler, *Race and the Education of Desire,* 9, 7–8.

43. Ruth Bernard Yeazell, "The Boundaries of Mansfield Park," *Representations* 7 (1984): 137, 140, 151 n. 21.

44. Others have observed that Yeazell's identification of nineteenth-century anxiety over the ontological boundaries of the family ultimately begs the question of history and

ideology. See, e.g., Paula Marantz Cohen, *The Daughter's Dilemma: Family Process and the Nineteenth-Century Domestic Novel* (Ann Arbor: University of Michigan Press, 1991), 67; and Fraser Easton, who writes: "Yeazell leaves out the historical perspective on boundaries. . . . The bodily fear of external 'infection' and the xenophobic sense of others as 'foreign'—as well as the often noticed endogamy of the novel—are as much about the defence of a property line as a blood line. It is a modern impulse—not a primitive one—and far from writing 'against the tide of history,' Austen writes with a fully historical understanding of the making of domestic isolation" ("The Political Economy of *Mansfield Park:* Fanny Price and the Atlantic Working Class," *Textual Practice* 12.3 [1998]: 468–69).

45. These arguments are addressed above, in the text accompanying notes 18–19 and 61–63 in chap. 2.

46. Susan Stewart, *Crimes of Writing: Problems in the Containment of Representation* (Durham, N.C.: Duke University Press, 1994), 198. In contrast to Yeazell, Johanna M. Smith takes the position that Austen is critiquing endogamy (" 'My Only Sister Now': Incest in *Mansfield Park*," *Studies in the Novel* 19.1 [1987]: 1–15). Alternatively, Cleere suggests that "the construction of adultery as incest" in Fanny's account "permit[s] endogamy to pass for normative heterosexuality when Fanny finally marries Edmund. The incest potential that has always been in the Bertram family is ultimately naturalized by this conversion of adultery into a *'family misery* which must envelope all' " ("Reinvesting Nieces," 128). Cohen offers an interesting analysis of incest and adultery as counterpoints both in the novel and in social theory (*Daughter's Dilemma,* 78).

47. Earlier, at the ball thrown in her honor, when Edmund is vexed and disappointed by Mary's behavior, we encounter a similar intimation of barbarity: "Fanny, not able to refrain entirely from observing them, had seen enough to be tolerably satisfied. It was barbarous to be happy when Edmund was suffering. Yet some happiness must and would arise, from the very conviction, that he did suffer" (*MP,* 191).

48. "Wonder—," Greenblatt writes, "thrilling, potentially dangerous, momentarily immobilizing, charged at once with desire, ignorance, and fear—is the quintessential human response to what Decartes [*sic*] calls a 'first encounter' " (*Marvelous Possessions: The Wonder of the New World* [Chicago: University of Chicago Press, 1991], 20). Here are Austen's words describing Fanny's first response to the announcement of the Rushworth's "matrimonial *fracas*" (*MP,* 298): " 'It is a mistake, Sir,' said Fanny instantly; 'it must be a mistake—it cannot be true—it must mean some *other* people.' . . . The truth rushed on her; and how she could have spoken at all, how she could have breathed—was afterwards matter of wonder to herself" (299, emphasis added).

49. See, e.g., Glenda A. Hudson, "Incestuous Relationships: Mansfield Park Revisited," *Eighteenth-Century Fiction* 4.1 (1991): esp. 61–66. See also Glenda A. Hudson, *Sibling Love and Incest in Jane Austen's Fiction* (New York: St. Martin's Press, 1992).

50. Compare Fanny's suspicious overreaction to Maria's affair to her earlier horror at the idea of acting: "it would be so horrible to her to act that she was inclined to suspect the truth and purity of her own scruples" (*MP,* 107).

51. Smith, "My Only Sister Now," 11–12.

52. Brissenden, "*Mansfield Park*," 168.

53. Fraiman, "Jane Austen and Edward Said," 812, 811.

54. Judith Butler, *Gender Trouble: Feminism and the Subversion of Identity* (New York: Routledge, 1990), 77–78. See chap. 1 above, the section titled "Gender, Incest, and Narrative in Twentieth-Century Theory."

55. Claudia Johnson makes the following observation, primarily in connection with novels other than *Mansfield Park*: "Brothers are treated with great respect in Austenian criticism, certainly with much more than they deserve if *Northanger Abbey* and *The Watsons* are considered with due weight. Because it is assumed that Austen's feelings for her brothers—about which we actually know rather little—were fond and grateful to the point of adoration, the sceptical treatment brother figures receive in her fiction has been little examined" (*Jane Austen*, 37).

56. Tony Tanner, *Jane Austen* (Cambridge, Mass.: Harvard University Press, 1986), 143, 171.

57. Michael Heyns, "Shock and Horror: The Moral Vocabulary of 'Mansfield Park,'" *English Studies in Africa* 29.1 (1986): 15.

58. Litvak, "Infection of Acting," 334; David Marshall, "True Acting and the Language of Real Feeling: *Mansfield Park*," *Yale Journal of Criticism* 3.1 (1989): 87–106. See also Kingsley Amis, who calls Fanny "untiringly sychophantic" and "a monster of complacency and pride" ("What Became of Jane Austen? [*Mansfield Park*]," in *Jane Austen: A Collection of Critical Essays*, ed. Ian Watt [Englewood Cliffs, N.J.: Prentice-Hall, 1963], 141–44); and Nina Auerbach, who finds Fanny monstrous, "a killjoy, a blighter of ceremonies and divider of families" ("Jane Austen's Dangerous Charm: Feeling As One Ought about Fanny Price," in *Jane Austen: New Perspectives*, ed. Janet Todd, vol. 3 of *Women and Literature*, new series (New York: Holmes & Meier, 1983), 211.

59. The phrase is from Barbara Herrnstein Smith, *Contingencies of Value: Alternative Perspectives for Critical Theory* (Cambridge, Mass.: Harvard University Press, 1988).

60. On the idea of place in Mansfield Park, see Duckworth, *Improvement of the Estate*, chap. 1; on the word *prospect*, see Maaja Stewart, *Domestic Realities*, 34.

61. Easton offers an illuminating discussion of what is screened from view at Mansfield Park ("Political Economy," 465–69).

62. Francis Barker, *The Tremulous Private Body: Essays on Subjection* (London: Methuen, 1984), 39; Duckworth, *Improvement of the Estate*, 24.

63. Juliet Flower MacCannell, *The Regime of the Brother: After the Patriarchy* (London: Routledge, 1991), 39.

64. A similar distinction between a man and his office occurs in an exchange about the clergy in which Mary Crawford proclaims to Edmund that a "clergyman is nothing" (*MP*, 66).

65. Fanny's language here tellingly suggests the manufactured nature of the public self, thus implicitly coding the private self as natural.

66. Cleere calls the scene at the ball that Sir Thomas throws for Fanny a "homosocial negotiation of [Fanny's] sexual worth" ("Reinvesting Nieces," 125).

67. Terri Nickel, "'Ingenious Torment': Incest, Family, and the Structure of Community in the Work of Sarah Fielding," *The Eighteenth Century: Theory and Interpretation* 36.3 (1995): 239.

68. The figure of the shawl is critical here both in rendering Fanny as a promised source of comfort to the man who gains access to her and in unfolding the heterosexual trade-off whence, by submitting to male protection, women at once sustain masculine identity and secure colonial privilege. Henry admires Fanny as a source of warmth and an object of beauty when he encounters the ardent interest with which she envelops her brother William (*MP*, 161–62, 200). As nurturer and later also surrogate daughter to be brought "out" at Mansfield Park, Fanny functions—like a shawl—as both convenience

and ornament. Edward Said and Susan Fraiman, moreover, invoke the figure of the shawl in connection with the colonial subtext of Austen's novel. In her depiction of the indolent imperiousness with which Lady Bertram insists that "William must not forget [her] shawl, if he goes to the East Indies" (in fact, like a naval commander, Lady Bertram gives William "a commission" for two shawls, along with "any thing else that is worth having" [*MP*, 208]), Austen levels a critique of colonial expansion, representing Europe "as the leisured consumer . . . kept in luxury by the backbreaking labor of colonial workers"; the shawl, Fraiman suggests, is "a figure for the consumerism of the pampered and feminized West" ("Jane Austen and Edward Said," 819). As both exploited labor and imported merchandise at Mansfield Park, Fanny too suggests such colonial relations of production and consumption; the product of a "foreign" culture, she is domesticated, assimilated, and rendered utterly serviceable—more reassuringly so, perhaps, than that human "cargo" transported to the West Indies to support the Bertrams' English life of luxury and now eligible for freedom should they make their way to British shores.

69. Alleyne, *Legal Degrees of Marriage*, 7.

70. If, as Alistair Duckworth has argued, the estate is "a metonym of an inherited culture endangered by forces from within and from without" (*Improvement of the Estate*, 71), then in her role as cultural icon who guarantees the continuity of the masculine estate, Fanny Price functions as the guardian of cultural memory. See also Frederick M. Keener, who offers the following observations: "The quasi-orphan Fanny is a daughter of Mnemosyne"; "This is a Book of Memory"; and "memory seems to give Fanny her personal identity, her lifeline" (*The Chain of Becoming: The Philosophical Tale, the Novel, and a Neglected Realism of the Enlightenment: Swift, Montesquieu, Voltaire, Johnson, and Austen* [New York: Columbia University Press, 1983], 279 and 281).

71. Fraiman, "Jane Austen and Edward Said," 809.

72. Smith, " 'My Only Sister Now,' " 2.

73. While Smith (ibid.) critiques the asymmetrical "sibling" relation of Fanny and Edmund as ultimately flawed and constricting, she does not extend her critique to the relationship between Fanny and William; nor does she explore the operations of memory in connection with Fanny's account of that relationship. The problem seems to be that Edmund fails to fulfill the model represented by William and Fanny's bond. Hudson, in "Incestuous Relationships," also accepts the sibling bond as the novel's moral center. For a fascinating recent treatment of memory in Austen's fiction that does not, however, address *Mansfield Park*, see Margaret Anne Doody, "'A Good Memory Is Unpardonable': Self, Love, and the Irrational Irritation of Memory," *Eighteenth-Century Fiction* 14.1 (2001): 67–94.

74. Austen's placement of a comma after "home," with the characteristically pregnant dash after "Mansfield" (in William's reference to "the little hardships of her home, at Mansfield—") seems sly.

75. In an on-line exchange regarding sibling relations in *Mansfield Park*, Ellen Moody writes: "Austen . . . makes a kind of fond joke showing the kind of irony she usually 'subjects' both Fanny and William to. While William and Fanny are riding to Portsmouth, what does William dream? He dreams of a cottage he and Fanny are going to have and share and live a blissful life together for the rest of their lives just as soon as he gets his next promotion. Austen expects us to laugh sympathetically at William here" (see "18th Century Siblings and Some Johnsonian Reflections," at *www.jimandellen.org/mp/18thCenturySiblingsandSomeJohnsonianReflections.html*, July 6, 2002).

76. Brissenden, *"Mansfield Park,"* 168.

77. Michel Foucault, *The History of Sexuality, Volume I: An Introduction,* trans. Robert Hurley (New York: Vintage Books, 1980), 106–13.

78. The phrase is from the title of Duckworth's first chapter, *"Mansfield Park:* Jane Austen's Grounds of Being" (*Improvement of the Estate*).

79. I use the term *Entstehung* (from Nietzsche's *Genealogy of Morals*) in the sense in which Michel Foucault defines it in "Nietzsche, Genealogy, History," in *Language, Counter-Memory, Practice,* trans. Donald F. Bouchard and Sherry Simon (Ithaca, N.Y.: Cornell University Press, 1977), 148–52.

80. Michael Seidel, *Satiric Inheritance, Rabelais to Sterne* (Princeton, N.J.: Princeton University Press, 1979), 18–19.

81. Walter Benjamin, "Theses on the Philosophy of History," in *Illuminations,* ed. Hannah Arendt (New York: Schocken Books, 1969), 255.

Bibliography

Adams, William Y. *The Philosophical Roots of Anthropology.* Stanford, Calif.: Center for the Study of Language and Information, 1998.

Aldridge, Alfred Owen. "The Meaning of Incest from Hutcheson to Gibbon. *Ethics* 61 (1951): 309–13.

———. "Polygamy and Deism." *Journal of English and Germanic Philology* 48 (1949): 343–60.

Alleyne, John. *The Legal Degrees of Marriage Stated and Considered, in a Series of Letters to a Friend.* 2d ed. London, 1775; facsimile reprint in *The Marriage Prohibitions Controversy: Five Tracts,* ed. Randolph Trumbach, New York: Garland, 1985.

Amis, Kingsley. "What Became of Jane Austen? [*Mansfield Park*]." In *Jane Austen: A Collection of Critical Essays,* ed. Ian Watt, 141–44. Englewood Cliffs, N.J.: Prentice-Hall, 1963.

Anderson, Nancy Fix. "The 'Marriage with a Deceased Wife's Sister Bill' Controversy: Incest Anxiety and the Defense of Family Purity in Victorian England." *Journal of British Studies* 21.2 (spring 1982): 67–86.

Anderson, Paul Bunyan. "Mistress Delariviere Manley's Biography." *Modern Philology* 33 (1935–36): 261–78.

Armstrong, Nancy. *Desire and Domestic Fiction: A Political History of the Novel.* New York: Oxford University Press, 1987.

———. "Some Call It Fiction: On the Politics of Domesticity." In *The Other Perspective in Gender and Culture: Rewriting Women and the Symbolic,* ed. Juliet Flower MacCannell, 59–84. New York: Columbia University Press, 1990.

Auerbach, Nina. "Jane Austen's Dangerous Charm: Feeling As One Ought about Fanny Price." In *Jane Austen: New Perspectives,* ed. Janet Todd, vol. 3 of *Women and Literature,* new series, 208–23. New York: Holmes & Meier, 1983.

Augustine. *The City of God.* Trans. Marcus Dods. New York: Modern Library, 1950.

Austen, Jane. *Lady Susan, The Watsons, Sanditon.* Ed. Margaret Drabble. Harmondsworth: Penguin Books, 1974.

———. *Mansfield Park: Authoritative Text, Contexts, Criticism.* Ed. Claudia L. Johnson. New York: Norton, 1998.

Baker, J. H. *An Introduction to English Legal History.* 3d ed. London: Butterworths, 1990.

Ballaster, Ros. Introduction to *The New Atalantis,* by Aphra Behn. London: Penguin, 1991.

———. *Seductive Forms: Women's Amatory Fiction from 1684–1740.* Oxford: Clarendon Press, 1992.

Barker, Francis. *The Tremulous Private Body: Essays on Subjection.* London: Methuen, 1984.

Battestin, Martin C. "Henry Fielding, Sarah Fielding, and 'the dreadful Sin of Incest.'" *Novel* 13 (1979): 6–18.

Battestin, Martin C., with Ruthe R. Battestin. *Henry Fielding: A Life*. London: Routledge, 1989.

Behn, Aphra. "The Dumb Virgin." In *The Works of Aphra Behn,* vol. 3, ed. Janet Todd, 335–60. Columbus: Ohio State University Press, 1995.

——. *Love-Letters between a Nobleman and his Sister*. Vol. 2 of *The Works of Aphra Behn*. Ed. Janet Todd. Columbus: Ohio State University Press, 1993.

Behrman, Cynthia Fansler. "The Annual Blister: A Sidelight on Victorian Social and Parliamentary History." *Victorian Studies* 11.4 (1968): 483–502.

Bell, H. E. *An Introduction to the History and Records of the Court of Wards and Liveries*. Cambridge: Cambridge University Press, 1953.

Bender, John. *Imagining the Penitentiary: Fiction and the Architecture of Mind in Eighteenth-Century England*. Chicago: University of Chicago Press, 1987.

——. "A New History of the Enlightenment?" *Eighteenth-Century Life,* n.s., 16.1 (1992): 1–20.

Benjamin, Walter. *Illuminations*. Ed. Hannah Arendt. Trans. Harry Zohn. New York: Schocken Books, 1969.

Benrekassa, G. "Loi naturelle et loi civile: L'idéologie des Lumières et la prohibition de l'inceste. *Studies in Voltaire and the Eighteenth Century* 87 (1972): 115–44.

Bhabha, Homi K. *The Location of Culture*. London: Routledge, 1994.

Blackstone, William. *Commentaries on the Laws of England: A Facsimile of the First Edition of 1765–1769*. With an introduction by A. W. Brian Simpson. 4 vols. Chicago: University of Chicago Press, 1979.

Boehrer, Bruce. *Monarchy and Incest in Renaissance England: Literature, Culture, Kinship, and Kingship*. Philadelphia: University of Pennsylvania Press, 1992.

——. " 'Nice Philosophy': *'Tis Pity She's a Whore* and The Two Books of God." *Studies in English Literature* 24 (1984): 355–71.

Bolingbroke, Henry St. John. *The Works of Lord Bolingbroke*. 4 vols. Philadelphia: Carey & Hart, 1841.

Boswell, James. *Boswell's Life of Johnson*. Ed. George Birkbeck Hill. Revised by L. F. Powell. 6 vols. Oxford: Clarendon Press, 1934–64.

Bourdieu, Pierre. *Distinction: A Social Critique of the Judgement of Taste*. Trans. Richard Nice. Cambridge, Mass.: Harvard University Press, 1984. Originally published as *La distinction: Critique sociale du jugement* (Paris, 1979).

Brissenden, R. F. "*Mansfield Park:* Freedom and the Family." In *Jane Austen: Bicentenary Essays,* ed. John Halperin, 156–71. Cambridge: Cambridge University Press, 1975.

Brooks, Douglas. "*Moll Flanders:* An Interpretation." *Essays in Criticism* 19.1 (1969): 46–59.

Brooks, Peter. "Freud's Masterplot." In *The Critical Tradition: Classic Texts and Contemporary Trends,* 2d ed., ed. David H. Richter, 1036–44, Boston: Bedford Books, 1998.

Brooks-Davies, Douglas. *Fielding, Dickens, Gosse, Iris Murdoch, and Oedipal Hamlet*. London: Macmillan, 1989.

Brown, Homer Obed. *Institutions of the English Novel: From Defoe to Scott*. Philadelphia: University of Pennsylvania Press, 1997.

——. "*Tom Jones:* The 'Bastard' of History." *boundary 2* 7 (1979): 201–33.

Buckle, Stephen. *Natural Law and the Theory of Property: Grotius to Hume*. Oxford: Clarendon Press, 1991.

Bullough, Geoffrey. "Polygamy among the Reformers." In *Renaissance and Modern Essays,* ed. G. R. Hibbard, 5–23. London: Routledge & Kegan Paul, 1966.

Burnet, Gilbert. *History of the Reformation of the Church of England.* 6 vols. London, 1820.

Burney, Frances. *Evelina, or the History of a Young Lady's Entrance into the World.* Ed. Edward A. Bloom and Lillian D. Bloom. Oxford: Oxford University Press, 1982.

Butler, Judith. *Antigone's Claim: Kinship between Life and Death.* New York: Columbia University Press, 2000.

——. *Bodies That Matter: On the Discursive Limits of "Sex."* New York: Routledge, 1993.

——. *Gender Trouble: Feminism and the Subversion of Identity.* New York: Routledge, 1990.

——. *The Psychic Life of Power: Theories in Subjection.* Stanford, Calif.: Stanford University Press, 1997.

Cahn, Susan. *Industry of Devotion: The Transformation of Women's Work in England, 1500–1660.* New York: Columbia University Press, 1987.

Canfield, J. Douglas. "Mother as Other: The Eruption of Feminine Desire in Some Late Restoration Incest Plays." *The Eighteenth Century: Theory and Interpretation* 39.3 (fall 1998): 209–19.

Castle, Terry J. "Why the Houyhnhnms Don't Write: Swift, Satire, and the Fear of the Text," *Essays in Literature* 7 (1980): 31–44.

Chaber, Lois. "Matriarchal Mirror: Women and Capital in *Moll Flanders.*" *PMLA* 97.2 (1982): 212–26.

Cholakian, Patricia Francis. *Rape and Writing in the* Heptaméron *of Marguerite de Navarre.* Carbondale: Southern Illinois University Press, 1991.

Clark, Alice. *Working Life of Women in the Seventeenth Century.* London: Routledge, 1919.

Clarkson, Thomas. *The History of the Abolition of the African Slave-Trade.* 2 vols. London, 1808.

Cleere, Eileen. "Reinvesting Nieces: *Mansfield Park* and the Economics of Endogamy." *Novel* 28.2 (1995): 113–30.

Cobbett's Complete Collection of State Trials and Proceedings for High Treason and Other Crimes and Misdemeanors from the Earliest Period to the Present Time. Vols. 9, 13. London, 1811–12.

Cohen, Paula Marantz. *The Daughter's Dilemma: Family Process and the Nineteenth-Century Domestic Novel.* Ann Arbor: University of Michigan Press, 1991.

The Counter Buffe; or, Certaine Observations upon Mr. Edwards his Animadversions. London, 1647.

Dalke, Anne. "Original Vice: The Political Implications of Incest in the Early American Novel." *Early American Literature* 23.2 (1988): 188–201.

Davies, Mary. *The Reform'd Coquette.* London, 1724; reprinted in *Popular Fiction by Women, 1660–1730: An Anthology,* ed. Paula R. Backscheider and John J. Richetti, Oxford: Clarendon Press, 1996.

Davis, David Brion. *The Problem of Slavery in the Age of Revolution, 1770–1823.* Ithaca, N.Y.: Cornell University Press, 1975.

Defoe, Daniel. *Colonel Jack.* Ed. Samuel Holt Monk. London: Oxford University Press, 1970.

——. *The Fortunes and Misfortunes of the Famous Moll Flanders.* Ed. G. A. Starr. Oxford: Oxford University Press, 1981.

——. *Moll Flanders.* Ed. J. Paul Hunter. New York: Thomas Y. Crowell, 1970.

De Lauretis, Teresa. *Alice Doesn't: Feminism, Semiotics, Cinema.* Bloomington: Indiana University Press, 1984.

Deleuze, Gilles, and Félix Guattari. *Anti-Oedipus: Capitalism and Schizophrenia.* Trans. Robert Hurley, Mark Seem, and Helen R. Lane. Minneapolis: University of Minnesota Press, 1983.

Derrida, Jacques. *Of Grammatology.* Trans. Gayatri Chakravorty Spivak. Baltimore: Johns Hopkins University Press, 1976. Originally published as *De la grammatologie* (Paris, 1967).

——. "Structure, Sign, and Play in the Discourse of the Human Sciences." In *The Structuralist Controversy: The Languages of Criticism and the Sciences of Man,* ed. Richard Macksay and Eugenio Donato, 247–65. Baltimore: Johns Hopkins University Press, 1972.

Dharwadker, Aparna. "Nation, Race, and the Ideology of Commerce in Defoe." *The Eighteenth-Century: Theory and Interpretation* 39.1 (1998): 63–84.

Diamond, Irene, and Lee Quinby, eds. *Feminism & Foucault: Reflections on Resistance.* Boston: Northeastern University Press, 1988.

Doane, Mary Ann. "Film and the Masquerade: Theorising the Female Spectator." *Screen* 23 (1982): 74–88.

Donzelot, Jacques. *The Policing of Families.* Trans. Robert Hurley. New York: Pantheon Books, 1979. Originally published as *La police des familles* (Paris, 1977).

Doody, Margaret Anne. *Frances Burney: The Life in the Works.* New Brunswick, N.J.: Rutgers University Press, 1988.

——. " 'A Good Memory Is Unpardonable': Self, Love, and the Irrational Irritation of Memory." *Eighteenth-Century Fiction* 14.1 (2001): 67–94.

Douglas, Mary. *Purity and Danger: An Analysis of the Concepts of Pollution and Taboo.* London: Routledge & Kegan Paul, 1966.

Duckworth, Alistair. *The Improvement of the Estate.* Baltimore: Johns Hopkins University Press, 1971.

Duffy, Maureen. Introduction to *Love-Letters between a Nobleman and His Sister,* by Aphra Behn. New York: Virago, 1987.

——. *The Passionate Shepherdess: Aphra Behn, 1640–89.* New York: Avon Books, 1977.

Dugard, Samuel. *The Marriages of Cousin Germans, Vindicated from the Censures of Unlawfullnesse, and Inexpediency.* Oxford, 1673; facsimile reprint in *The Marriage Prohibitions Controversy: Five Tracts,* ed. Randolph Trumbach, New York: Garland, 1985.

DuPlessis, Rachel Blau. *Writing beyond the Ending: Narrative Strategies of Twentieth-Century Women Writers.* Bloomington: Indiana University Press, 1985.

Eagleton, Terry. *Literary Theory: An Introduction.* Minneapolis: University of Minnesota Press, 1983.

Easton, Fraser. "The Political Economy of *Mansfield Park:* Fanny Price and the Atlantic Working Class." *Textual Practice* 12.3 (1998): 459–88.

Edwards, Thomas. *Gangraena.* London, 1647.

Eleanora; or A Tragical but True Case of Incest in Great-Britain. London, 1751.

English Reports. Edinburgh: W. Green & Sons, 1900–1932.

Epstein, Julia. "Burney Criticism: Family Romance, Psychobiography, and Social History." *Eighteenth-Century Fiction* 3.4 (1991): 277–82.

——. *The Iron Pen: Frances Burney and the Politics of Women's Writing.* Madison: University of Wisconsin Press, 1989.

——. "Jane Austen's Juvenilia and the Female Epistolary Tradition." *Papers in Language and Literature* 21 (1985): 399–416.

——, ed. *Special* Evelina *Issue. Eighteenth-Century Fiction* 3.4 (1991).

Epstein, Julia, and Kristina Straub, eds. *Body Guards: The Cultural Politics of Gender Ambiguity.* New York: Routledge, 1991.

Fergus, Jan. *Jane Austen: A Literary Life.* New York: St. Martin's Press, 1991.

Ferguson, Moira. *Colonialism and Gender Relations from Mary Wollstonecraft to Jamaica Kincaid.* New York: Columbia University Press, 1993.

Fielding, Henry. *The History of Tom Jones, a Foundling.* Ed. Fredson Bowers. Middletown, Conn.: Wesleyan University Press, 1975.

Fielding, Sarah. *The Adventures of David Simple.* Oxford: Oxford University Press, 1987.

Firth, C. H., and R. S. Rait, eds. *Acts and Ordinances of the Interregnum, 1642–1660.* 3 vols. London: H. M. Stationery Office, printed by Wyman & Sons, Ltd., 1911.

Fizer, Irene. "The Name of the Daughter: Identity and Incest in *Evelina.*" In *Refiguring the Father: New Feminist Readings of Patriarchy,* ed. Patricia Yaeger and Beth Kowaleski-Wallace, 78–107. Carbondale: Southern Illinois University Press, 1989.

Flanders, W. Austin. *Structures of Experience: History, Society, and Personal Life in the Eighteenth-Century British Novel.* Columbia: University of South Carolina Press, 1984.

Flint, Christopher. *Family Fictions: Narrative and Domestic Relations in Britain, 1688–1798.* Stanford, Calif.: Stanford University Press, 1998.

Foucault, Michel. *Discipline and Punish: The Birth of the Prison.* Trans. Alan Sheridan. New York: Pantheon Books, 1978. Originally published as *Surveiller et punir: Naissance de la prison* (Paris, 1975).

——. *The History of Sexuality. Volume I: An Introduction.* Trans. Robert Hurley. New York: Vintage Books, 1980. Originally published as *La volenté de savoir* (Paris, 1976).

——. "Nietzsche, Genealogy, History." In *Language, Counter-Memory, Practice,* trans. Donald F. Bouchard and Sherry Simon, 139–64. Ithaca, N.Y.: Cornell University Press, 1977.

——. *The Order of Things: An Archaeology of the Human Sciences.* New York: Vintage Books, 1973. Originally published as *Les mots et les choses* (Paris, 1966).

Fourny, Diane R. "The Festival at the Water Hole: Rousseau, Freud, and Derrida on Incest." *The Eighteenth-Century: Theory and Interpretation* 31.2 (1990): 137–60.

Fox, Robin. *The Red Lamp of Incest: An Enquiry into the Origins of Mind and Society.* Notre Dame, Ind.: University of Notre Dame Press, 1983.

Fraiman, Susan. "Jane Austen and Edward Said: Gender, Culture, and Imperialism." *Critical Inquiry* 21 (1995): 805–21.

Francus, Marilyn. "The Monstrous Mother: Reproductive Anxiety in Swift and Pope." *ELH* 61 (1994): 829–51.

Franklin, Benjamin. *Writings.* Ed. J. A. Leo Lemay. New York: Library of America, 1987.

Friedli, Lynne. " 'Passing women': A Study of Gender Boundaries in the Eighteenth Century." In *Sexual Underworlds of the Enlightenment,* ed. G. S. Rousseau and Roy Porter, 234–60. Chapel Hill: University of North Carolina Press, 1988.

Fry, John. *The Case of Marriages Between Near Kindred Particularly Considered, With Respect to The Doctrine of Scripture, The Law of Nature, and The Laws of England.* London, 1756; facsimile reprint in *The Marriage Prohibitions Controversy: Five Tracts,* ed. Randolph Trumbach, New York: Garland, 1985.

Gallagher, Catherine. "Embracing the Absolute: The Politics of the Female Subject in Seventeenth-Century England." *Genders* 1 (1988): 24–39.

——. *Nobody's Story: The Vanishing Acts of Women Writers in the Marketplace, 1670–1820.* Berkeley: University of California Press, 1994.

Gallop, Jane. *The Daughter's Seduction: Feminism and Psychoanalysis.* Ithaca, N.Y.: Cornell University Press, 1982.

Gardiner, Judith Kegan. "The First English Novel: Aphra Behn's *Love Letters,* the Canon, and Women's Tastes." *Tulsa Studies in Women's Literature* 8.2 (fall 1989): 201–22.

Gautier, Gary. *Landed Patriarchy in Fielding's Novels: Fictional Landscapes, Fictional Genders.* Studies in British Literature, vol. 35. Lewiston, N.Y.: Edwin Mellen Press, 1998.

Gay, John. *The Beggar's Opera and Companion Pieces.* Ed. C. F. Burgess. Arlington Heights, Ill: AHM Publishing Corp., 1966.

Gentleman's Magazine. Vols. 16–29. London, 1746–50.

Gibbon, Frank. "The Antiguan Connection: Some New Light on *Mansfield Park.*" *Cambridge Quarterly* 11.2 (1982): 298–305.

Gierke, Otto. *Natural Law and the Theory of Society: 1500–1800.* Trans. Ernest Barker. Boston: Beacon Press, 1957.

Gies, Frances, and Joseph Gies. *Marriage and the Family in the Middle Ages.* New York: Harper & Row, 1987.

Gillis, John R. *For Better, For Worse: British Marriages, 1600 to the Present.* New York: Oxford University Press, 1985.

Girard, René. *Violence and the Sacred.* Trans. Patrick Gregory. Baltimore: Johns Hopkins University Press, 1977. Originally published as *La violence et le sacré* (Paris, 1972).

Gonda, Caroline. *Reading Daughters' Fictions, 1709–1834: Novels and Society from Manley to Edgeworth.* Cambridge: Cambridge University Press, 1996.

Goody, Jack. "A Comparative Approach to Incest and Adultery." *British Journal of Sociology* 7 (1956): 286–305.

——. *The Development of the Family and Marriage in Europe.* Cambridge: Cambridge University Press, 1983.

Goreau, Angeline. *Reconstructing Aphra: A Social Biography of Aphra Behn.* New York: Dial Press, 1980.

Goux, Jean-Joseph. *Symbolic Economies: After Marx and Freud.* Trans. Jennifer Curtiss Gage. Ithaca, N.Y.: Cornell University Press, 1990.

Greenblatt, Stephen. *Marvelous Possessions: The Wonder of the New World.* Chicago: University of Chicago Press, 1991.

Greenfield, Susan C. *Mothering Daughters: Novels and the Politics of Family Romance, Frances Burney to Jane Austen.* Detroit: Wayne State University Press, 2002.

——. "'Oh Dear Resemblance of Thy Murdered Mother': Female Authorship in *Evelina.*" *Eighteenth-Century Fiction* 3.4 (1991): 301–20.

Grosz, Elizabeth. *Jacques Lacan: A Feminist Introduction.* London: Routledge, 1990.

Grotius, Hugo. *The Law of War and Peace (De Jure Belli ac Paci Libri).* Trans. Francis W. Kelsey. Indianapolis: Bobbs-Merrill, 1925.

Gullette, Margaret Morganroth. "The Puzzling Case of the Deceased Wife's Sister: Nineteenth-Century England Deals with a Second-Chance Plot." *Representations* 31 (1990): 142–66.

Haakonssen, Knud. *Natural Law and Moral Philosophy: From Grotius to the Scottish Enlightenment.* Cambridge: Cambridge University Press, 1996.

Habakkuk, H. J. "Marriage Settlements in the Eighteenth Century." *Transactions of the Royal Historical Society,* 4th ser., 32 (1950): 15–30.

Habermas, Jürgen. *The Structural Transformation of the Public Sphere: An Inquiry into a Category of Bourgeois Society*. Trans. Thomas Burger with Frederick Lawrence. Cambridge, Mass.: MIT Press, 1991. Originally published as *Strukturwandel der Öffentlichkeit* (Darmstadt, 1962).

Haggerty, George E. *Unnatural Affections: Women and Fiction in the Later Eighteenth Century*. Bloomington: Indiana University Press, 1998.

Hagstrum, Jean H. *Sex and Sensibility: Ideal and Erotic Love from Milton to Mozart*. Chicago: University of Chicago Press, 1980.

Harris, Jocelyn. *Jane Austen's Art of Memory*. Cambridge: Cambridge University Press, 1989.

Hay, Douglas. "Property, Authority, and the Criminal Law." In *Albion's Fatal Tree: Crime and Society in Eighteenth-Century England*, by Douglas Hay, Peter Linebaugh, John G. Rule, E. P. Thompson, and Cal Winslow, 17–63. New York: Pantheon Books, 1975.

Haywood, Eliza. *The Force of Nature; or, The Lucky Disappointment*. London, 1725.

Helgerson, Richard. *Forms of Nationhood: The Elizabethan Writing of England*. Chicago: University of Chicago Press, 1992.

Herlihy, David. *Medieval Households*. Cambridge: Harvard University Press, 1985.

Herman, Judith Lewis. *Father-Daughter Incest*. Cambridge, Mass.: Harvard University Press, 1981.

Heyns, Michael. "Shock and Horror: The Moral Vocabulary of 'Mansfield Park.' " *English Studies in Africa* 29.1 (1986): 1–18.

Hickes, George. *Ravillac Redivivus: being a Narrative of the late Tryal of Mr. James Mitchel . . . , To which is Annexed, An Account of the Tryal of that most wicked Pharisee Major Thomas Weir. . . .* London, 1678.

Hill, Christopher. *Society and Puritanism in Pre-Revolutionary England*. 2d ed. New York: Schocken Books, 1967.

Hodgen, Margaret T. *Early Anthropology in the Sixteenth and Seventeenth Centuries*. Philadelphia: University of Pennsylvania Press, 1964.

Howson, Gerald. "Who Was Moll Flanders?" In *Moll Flanders, an Authoritative Text: Backgrounds and Sources; Criticism*, ed. Edward Kelly, 312–19, New York: Norton, 1973.

Hudson, Glenda A. "Incestuous Relationships: Mansfield Park Revisited." *Eighteenth-Century Fiction* 4.1 (1991): 53–68.

———. *Sibling Love and Incest in Jane Austen's Fiction*. New York: St. Martin's Press, 1992.

Hurstfield, Joel. *The Queen's Wards: Wardship and Marriage under Elizabeth I*. Cambridge, Mass.: Harvard University Press, 1958.

Hutcheson, Francis. *Inquiry into the Original of our Ideas of Beauty and Virtue*. London, 1725.

———. *A System of Moral Philosophy*. London, 1755.

The Illegal Lovers. London, 1728.

Ingram, Martin. *Church Courts, Sex, and Marriage in England, 1570–1640*. Cambridge: Cambridge University Press, 1987.

Irigaray, Luce. "When the Goods Get Together." Trans. Claudia Reeder. In *New French Feminisms*, ed. Elaine Marks and Isabelle de Courtivron, 107–10. Amherst: University of Massachusetts Press, 1980. Originally published as "Des marchandises entre elles," in *Ce sexe qui n'en est pas un* (Paris, 1977).

———. *This Sex Which Is Not One*. Trans. Catherine Porter with Carolyn Burke. Ithaca, N.Y.: Cornell University Press, 1985. Originally published as *Ce sexe qui n'en est pas un* (Paris, 1977).

Johnson, Claudia L. *Jane Austen: Women, Politics, and the Novel*. Chicago: University of Chicago Press, 1988.

Johnstoun, James. *A Juridical Dissertation concerning the Scripture Doctrine of Marriage Contracts, and the Marriages of Cousin-Germans*. London, 1734. Facsimile reprint in *The Marriage Prohibitions Controversy: Five Tracts*, ed. Randolph Trumbach. New York: Garland, 1985.

Jooma, Minaz. "The Alimentary Structures of Incest: Eating and Incest in Eighteenth-Century English Narrative." Ph.D. diss., Michigan State University, 1995.

Josephus, Flavius. *Antiquities of the Jews*. Vol. 1 of *The Works of Flavius Josephus*. Trans. William Whiston. Philadelphia, 1844.

Juengel, Scott J. "Oroonoko's Scar." Manuscript.

Kantorowicz, Ernst H. *The King's Two Bodies: A Study in Mediaeval Political Theology*. Princeton, N.J.: Princeton University Press, 1957.

Kaufmann, David. "Closure in *Mansfield Park* and the Sanctity of the Family." *Philological Quarterly* 65.2 (1986): 211–29.

Keener, Frederick M. *The Chain of Becoming: The Philosophical Tale, the Novel, and a Neglected Realism of the Enlightenment: Swift, Montesquieu, Voltaire, Johnson, and Austen*. New York: Columbia University Press, 1983.

Kirkham, Margaret. *Jane Austen, Feminism, and Fiction*. Sussex: Harvester Press, 1983.

Kristeva, Julia. *Powers of Horror: An Essay on Abjection*. New York: Columbia University Press, 1982.

Lacan, Jacques. *Ecrits: A Selection*. Trans. A. Sheridan. London: Tavistock, 1977.

———. *Speech and Language in Psychoanalysis*. Trans. Anthony Wilden. Baltimore: Johns Hopkins University Press, 1968.

Langbauer, Laurie. *Women and Romance: The Consolations of Gender in the English Novel*. Ithaca, N.Y.: Cornell University Press, 1990.

Lerenbaum, Miriam. "Moll Flanders: 'A Woman on her own Account.' " In *The Authority of Experience: Essays in Feminist Criticism*, ed. Arlyn Diamond and Lee R. Edwards, 101–17. Amherst: University of Massachusetts Press, 1977.

Levey, Santina M. *Lace: A History*. London: Victoria and Albert Museum, 1983.

Lévi-Strauss, Claude. *The Elementary Structures of Kinship*. Trans. James Harle Bell, John Richard von Sturmer, and Rodney Needham. Rev. ed. Boston: Beacon Press, 1969. Originally published as *Les structures élémentaires de la parenté* (1949).

———. "Jean-Jacques Rousseau, Founder of the Sciences of Man." In *Structural Anthropology*, vol. 2, trans. Monique Layton, 33–43. New York: Basic Books, 1976.

Levy, Anita. "Blood, Kinship, and Gender," *Genders* 5 (summer 1989): 70–84.

———. "Reproductive Urges: Literacy, Sexuality, and Eighteenth-Century Englishness." In *Inventing Maternity: Politics, Science, and Literature, 1650–1865*, ed. Susan C. Greenfield and Carol Barash, 193–214. Lexington: University Press of Kentucky, 1999.

Lew, Joseph. " 'That Abominable Traffic': *Mansfield Park* and the Dynamics of Slavery." In *History, Gender, and Eighteenth-Century Literature*, ed. Beth Fowkes Tobin, 271–300. Athens: University of Georgia Press, 1994.

Little Non-Such or, Certaine New Questions Moved out of Ancient Truths. London, 1646.

Litvak, Joseph. *Caught in the Act: Theatricality in the Nineteenth-Century English Novel*. Berkeley: University of California Press, 1992.

———. "The Infection of Acting: Theatricals and Theatricality in *Mansfield Park*," *ELH* 53 (1986): 331–55.

Locke, John. *Two Treatises of Civil Government.* Ed. Peter Laslett. 2d ed. Cambridge: Cambridge University Press, 1963.

Long, Edward. *Candid Reflections upon the judgement lately awarded by the Court of King's Bench in Westminster-Hall on what is commonly called the Negroe-Cause. By a Planter.* London: Printed for T. Lowndes, 1772.

Luther, Martin. *The Babylonian Captivity of the Church.* Trans. A. T. W. Steinhauser. Revised by Frederick C. Ahrens and Abdel Ross Wentz. In *Word and Sacrament,* ed. Abdel Ross Wentz. Vol. 36 of *Luther's Works,* ed. Helmut T. Lehmann. Philadelphia: Muhlenberg Press, 1959.

——. *The Estate of Marriage.* Trans. Walther I. Brandt. In *The Christian in Society,* ed. Walther I. Brandt. Vol. 45 of *Luther's Works,* ed. Helmut T. Lehmann. Philadelphia: Muhlenberg Press, 1962.

MacCannell, Juliet Flower. *The Regime of the Brother: After the Patriarchy.* London: Routledge, 1991.

Macfarlane, Alan. *Marriage and Love in England: Modes of Reproduction, 1300–1840.* Oxford: Basil Blackwell, 1986.

Maddox, James H. "On Defoe's *Roxana.*" *ELH* 51 (1984): 669–91.

Mandeville, Bernard. *The Fable of the Bees: or, Private Vices, Publick Benefits.* 2d ed., enlarged with many additions. London, 1723.

Manley, Delarivier [Mary]. "The Perjur'd Beauty." In *The Power of Love: In Seven Novels.* London, 1720.

——. *Secret Memoirs and Manners of Several Persons of Quality of Both Sexes. From the New Atalantis, an Island in the Mediteranean.* 2 vols. London, 1709. Reprinted, 2 vols. in 1, in *The Novels of Mary Delarivière Manley,* ed Patricia Köster, Gainesville, Fla.: Scholars' Facsimiles & Reprints, 1971.

Markley, Robert. " 'Be impudent, be saucy, forward, bold, touzing, and leud': The Politics of Masculine Sexuality and Feminine Desire in Behn's Tory Comedies." In *Cultural Readings of Restoration and Eighteenth-Century English Theatre,* ed. Douglas J. Canfield and Deborah C. Payne, 114–40. Athens: University of Georgia Press 1995.

Markley, Robert, and Molly Rothenberg. "Contestations of Nature: Aphra Behn's 'The Golden Age' and the Sexualizing of Politics." In *Rereading Aphra Behn: History, Theory, and Criticism,* ed. Heidi Hutner, 301–21. Charlottesville: University Press of Virginia, 1993.

Marshall, David. "True Acting and the Language of Real Feeling: *Mansfield Park.*" *Yale Journal of Criticism* 3.1 (1989): 87–106.

McCabe, Richard A. *Incest, Drama, and Nature's Law, 1550–1700.* Cambridge: Cambridge University Press, 1993.

McCrea, Brian. *Impotent Fathers: Patriarchy and Demographic Crisis in the Eighteenth-Century Novel.* Newark: University of Delaware Press, 1998.

McKeon, Michael. "Generic Transformation and Social Change: Rethinking the Rise of the Novel." *Cultural Critique* 1 (1985): 159–81.

——. "Historicizing Patriarchy: The Emergence of Gender Difference in England, 1660–1769." *Eighteenth-Century Studies* 28.3 (1995): 295–322.

——. *The Origins of the English Novel, 1600–1740.* Baltimore: Johns Hopkins University Press, 1987. Reprint with a new introduction, Baltimore: Johns Hopkins University Press, 2002.

McMaster, Juliet. "The Equation of Love and Money in *Moll Flanders.*" *Studies in the Novel* 2.2 (1970): 131–44.

Michaelis, Johann David. *Commentaries on the Laws of Moses.* Trans. Alexander Smith. 4 vols. London. 1814.

Michals, Teresa. " 'That Sole and Despotic Dominion': Slaves, Wives, and Game in Blackstone's *Commentaries.*" *Eighteenth-Century Studies* 27.2 (1993–94): 195–216.

Miller, Nancy K. *The Heroine's Text: Readings in the French and English Novel, 1722–1782.* New York: Columbia University Press, 1980.

Milton, John. *Complete Poems and Major Prose.* Ed. Merritt Y. Hughes. New York: Odyssey Press, 1957.

Mitchell, Juliet. Introduction to *The Fortunes and Misfortunes of the Famous Moll Flanders,* by Daniel Defoe, ed. Juliet Mitchell. Harmondsworth: Penguin, 1978.

———. *Psychoanalysis and Feminism.* New York: Vintage Books, 1975.

Mitchell, Juliet, and Jacqueline Rose, eds. *Feminine Sexuality: Jacques Lacan and the école freudienne.* Trans. Jacqueline Rose. New York: Norton; London: Pantheon Books, 1985.

Mitchell, W. J. T. "Representation." In *Critical Terms for Literary Study,* ed. Frank Lentricchia and Thomas McLaughlin, 1–22. 2d ed. Chicago: University of Chicago Press, 1995.

Moody, Ellen. "18th Century Siblings and Some Johnsonian Reflections." *www. jimandellen.org/mp/18thCenturySiblingsandSomeJohnsonianReflections.html,* July 6, 2002.

Morgan, Edmund S. *American Slavery, American Freedom: The Ordeal of Colonial Virginia.* New York: Norton, 1975. Reprint, New York: Norton, 1995.

Morris, Polly. "Incest or Survival Strategy? Plebian Marriage within the Prohibited Degrees in Somerset, 1730–1835." *Journal of the History of Sexuality* 2.2 (October 1991): 235–65.

Munns, Jessica. " 'I By A Double Right Thy Bounties Claim': Aphra Behn and Sexual Space." In *Curtain Calls: British and American Women and the Theatre, 1660–1820,* ed. Mary Anne Schofield and Cecilia Macheski, 193–210. Athens: Ohio University Press, 1991.

Navarre, Marguerite de. *The Heptameron.* Trans. P. A. Chilton. London: Penguin, 1984.

Needham, Gwendolyn B. "Mary de la Rivière Manley, Tory Defender." *Huntington Library Quarterly* 12 (1948–49): 253–88.

Nelson, T. G. A. "Incest in the Early Novel and Related Genres." *Eighteenth-Century Life,* n.s., 16.1 (1992): 127–62.

Nicholson, Linda J. *Gender and History: The Limits of Social Theory in the Age of the Family.* New York: Columbia University Press, 1986.

Nickel, Terri. " 'Ingenious Torment': Incest, Family, and the Structure of Community in the Work of Sarah Fielding." *The Eighteenth Century: Theory and Interpretation* 36.3 (1995): 234–47.

Nietzsche, Friedrich. *On the Genealogy of Morals.* Trans. Walter Kauffman and R. J. Hollingdale. Published with *Ecce Homo.* New York: Vintage, 1989.

Nixon, Cheryl L. "Creating the Text of Guardianship: 12 Car.II.c.24 and *Cutter of Coleman Street.*" *Restoration: Studies in English Literary Culture, 1660–1700* 19.1 (1995): 1–28.

———. "Fictional Families: Guardianship in Eighteenth-Century Law and Literature." Ph.D. diss., Harvard University, 1995.

Nord, Deborah Epstein. " 'Marks of Race': Gypsy Figures and Eccentric Femininity in Nineteenth-Century Women's Writing." *Victorian Studies* 41.2 (1998): 189–210.

Novak, Maximillian E. "Conscious Irony in *Moll Flanders:* Facts and Problems." *College English* 26 (1964): 198–204.

———. *Defoe and the Nature of Man*. London: Oxford University Press, 1963.

Nussbaum, Felicity. *Torrid Zones: Maternity, Sexuality, and Empire in Eighteenth-Century English Narratives*. Baltimore: Johns Hopkins University Press, 1995.

Oldham, James. *The Mansfield Manuscripts and the Growth of English Law in the Eighteenth Century*. 2 vols. Chapel Hill: University of North Carolina Press, 1992.

Park, William. "Tom and Oedipus." *Hartford Studies in Literature: A Journal of Interdisciplinary Criticism* 7 (1975): 207–15.

Parker, Jo Allyson. *The Author's Inheritance: Henry Fielding, Jane Austen, and the Establishment of the Novel*. Dekalb: Northern Illinois University Press, 1998.

Parsons, Talcott. "The Incest Taboo in Relation to Social Structure." In *The Family: Its Structures and Functions*, ed. Rose Laub Coser, 48–70. New York: St. Martin's Press, 1964.

Pateman, Carole. *The Sexual Contract*. Stanford, Calif.: Stanford University Press, 1988.

Patrick, Simon. *A Commentary upon the Historical Books of the Old Testament*. 2 vols. London, 1727.

Paulson, Ronald. *The Life of Henry Fielding: A Critical Biography*. Oxford: Blackwell, 2000.

Perry, Ruth. "Austen and Empire: A Thinking Woman's Guide to British Imperialism." *Persuasions* 16 (1994): 95–106.

———. "Incest as the Meaning of the Gothic Novel." *The Eighteenth Century: Theory and Interpretation* 39.3 (1998): 261–78.

———. *Women, Letters, and the Novel*. New York: AMS Press, 1980.

Pollak, Ellen. *The Poetics of Sexual Myth: Gender and Ideology in the Verse of Swift and Pope*. Chicago: University of Chicago Press, 1985.

———, ed. *Constructions of Incest in Restoration and Eighteenth-Century England*. A special issue of *The Eighteenth Century: Theory and Interpretation* 39.3 (1998).

Pollock, Frederick, and Frederic William Maitland. *The History of English Law before the Time of Edward I*. 2d ed. Vol. 1. Cambridge: Cambridge University Press, 1923.

Porter, Roy. *The Creation of the Modern World: The Untold Story of the British Enlightenment*. New York: Norton, 2001.

Price, Cecil. *Cold Caleb: The Scandalous Life of Ford Grey, First Earl of Tankerville, 1655–1701*. London: Andrew Melrose, 1956.

Prideaux, Humphrey. *The Old and New Testament Connected in the History of the Jews*. Part 2. London: For Knaplock & Tonson, 1718.

Pufendorf, Samuel. *The Law of Nature and Nations. Eight Books*. Trans. Basil Kennett. 3d ed. London, 1717.

Quick, John. *Serious Inquiry into that Weighty Case of Conscience, Whether a Man may Lawfully Marry his Deceased Wife's Sister*. London, 1703. Facsimile reprint in *The Marriage Prohibitions Controversy: Five Tracts*, ed. Randolph Trumbach, New York: Garland, 1985.

Raglan-Sullivan, Ellie. *Jacques Lacan and the Philosophy of Psychoanalysis*. Urbana: University of Illinois Press, 1986.

Rank, Otto. *The Incest Theme in Literature and Legend: Fundamentals of a Psychology of Literary Creation*. Trans. Gregory C. Richter. Baltimore: Johns Hopkins University Press, 1992. Originally published as *Das Inzest-Motiv in Dichtung und Sage* (Vienna, 1912).

Reid, Roddey. *Families in Jeopardy: Regulating the Social Body in France, 1750–1910*. Stanford, Calif.: Stanford University Press, 1993.

Richardson, Samuel. *Clarissa, or The History of a Young Lady.* Ed. Angus Ross. Harmondsworth: Penguin, 1985.

Richetti, John J. *Defoe's Narratives: Situations and Structures.* Oxford: Clarendon Press, 1975.

——. "The Family, Sex, and Marriage in Defoe's *Moll Flanders* and *Roxana.*" *Studies in the Literary Imagination, Daniel Defoe: The Making of His Prose Fiction* 15.2 (1982): 19–36.

Rogers, Pat. "The Breeches Part." In *Sexuality in Eighteenth-Century Britain,* ed. Paul Gabriel Boucé, 244–58. Manchester, Eng.: Manchester University Press, 1982.

Roof, Judith. *Come As You Are: Sexuality and Narrative.* New York: Columbia University Press, 1996.

——. *Reproductions of Reproduction: Imaging Symbolic Change.* New York: Routledge, 1996.

Rubin, Gayle. "The Traffic in Women: Notes on the 'Political Economy' of Sex." In *Toward an Anthropology of Women,* ed. Rayna R. Reiter, 157–210. New York: Monthly Review Press, 1975.

Rush, Florence. *The Best-Kept Secret: Sexual Abuse of Children.* Blue Ridge Summit, Pa.: TAB Books, 1980.

Russell, Diana E. H. *The Secret Trauma: Incest in the Lives of Girls and Women.* New York: Basic Books, 1986.

Said, Edward W. *Culture and Imperialism.* New York: Alfred A. Knopf, 1993.

Salkeld, William. *Reports of Cases Adjudged in the Court of King's Bench.* 2d ed. London, 1722.

Salmon, Thomas. *A Critical Essay concerning Marriage.* 2d ed. London, 1724.

Scarisbrick, J. J. *Henry VIII.* Berkeley: University of California Press, 1968.

Schneider, David M. "The Meaning of Incest." *Journal of the Polynesian Society* 85 (1976): 149–69.

Sedgwick, Eve Kosofsky. *Between Men: English Literature and Male Homosocial Desire.* New York: Columbia University Press, 1985.

Seidel, Michael. *Exile and the Narrative Imagination.* New Haven, Conn.: Yale University Press, 1986.

——. *Satiric Inheritance, Rabelais to Sterne.* Princeton, N.J.: Princeton University Press, 1979.

Shell, Marc. *Children of the Earth: Literature, Politics, and Nationhood.* Oxford: Oxford University Press, 1993.

——. *The End of Kinship: 'Measure for Measure,' Incest, and the Idea of Universal Siblinghood.* Stanford, Calif.: Stanford University Press, 1988.

Shinagel, Michael. *Daniel Defoe and Middle-Class Gentility.* Cambridge, Mass.: Harvard University Press, 1968.

——. "The Maternal Theme in *Moll Flanders:* Craft and Character." *Cornell Library Journal* 7 (1969): 3–23.

Shyllon, F. O. *Black Slaves in Britain.* London: Oxford University Press, 1974.

Silverman, Kaja. *World Spectators.* Stanford, Calif.: Stanford University Press, 2000.

Smith, Barbara Herrnstein. *Contingencies of Value: Alternative Perspectives for Critical Theory.* Cambridge, Mass.: Harvard University Press, 1988.

Smith, Johanna M. " 'My Only Sister Now': Incest in *Mansfield Park.*" *Studies in the Novel* 19.1 (1987): 1–15.

Sollers, Werner. *Neither Black nor White yet Both: Thematic Explorations of Interracial Literature.* Cambridge, Mass.: Harvard University Press, 1997.

Southam, Brian. "The Silence of the Bertrams: Slavery and the Chronology of *Mansfield Park.*" *Times Literary Supplement,* February 7, 1995, 13–14.

Spring, Eileen. "The Heiress-at-Law: English Real Property from a New Point of View." *Law and History Review* 8.2 (fall 1990): 273–96.

———. "Law and the Theory of the Affective Family." *Albion* 16.1 (spring 1984): 1–20.

The Statutes of the Realm (1225–1713). 9 vols. London: G. Eyre & A. Strahan, 1810–22.

Starr, G. A. *Defoe and Casuistry.* Princeton, N.J.: Princeton University Press, 1971.

Staves, Susan. *Players' Scepters: Fictions of Authority in the Restoration.* Lincoln: University of Nebraska Press, 1979.

Steffes, Michael. "Slavery and *Mansfield Park:* The Historical and Biographical Context." *English Language Notes* 34.2 (1996): 23–41.

Stephen, Sir James F. *A History of the Criminal Law of England.* 3 vols. London: Macmillan & Co., 1883.

Sterne, Laurence. *The Life and Opinions of Tristram Shandy.* Ed. Graham Petrie. Harmondsworth: Penguin Books, 1967.

Stewart, Maaja A. *Domestic Realities and Imperial Fictions: Jane Austen's Novels in Eighteenth-Century Contexts.* Athens: University of Georgia Press, 1993.

Stewart, Susan. *Crimes of Writing: Problems in the Containment of Representation.* Durham, N.C.: Duke University Press, 1994.

Stocking, George W. *The Ethnographer's Magic and Other Essays in the History of Anthropology.* Madison: University of Wisconsin Press, 1992.

Stoler, Ann Laura. *Race and the Education of Desire: Foucault's* History of Sexuality *and the Colonial Order of Things.* Durham, N.C.: Duke University Press, 1995.

Stone, Lawrence. *The Family, Sex, and Marriage in England, 1500–1800.* New York: Harper & Row, 1977.

Stranks, C. J. *The Life and Writings of Jeremy Taylor.* London: S.P.C.K., 1952.

Straub, Kristina. *Sexual Suspects: Eighteenth-Century Players and Sexual Ideology.* Princeton, N.J.: Princeton University Press, 1992.

Strauss, Leo. *Natural Right and History.* Chicago: University of Chicago Press, 1953.

Strickland, Agnes. *The Lives of the Queens of England.* 6 vols. Rev. ed. London: George Bell & Sons, 1901.

Surtz, Edward, and Virginia Murphy, eds. *Divorce Tracts of Henry VIII.* Angers, France: Moreana, 1988.

Swender, Catherine. "The Mediating Mother: Desire and Control in *Tom Jones.*" Manuscript.

Tanner, Tony. *Adultery and the Novel: Contract and Transgression.* Baltimore: Johns Hopkins University Press, 1979.

———. *Jane Austen.* Cambridge, Mass.: Harvard University Press, 1986.

Taylor, Jeremy. *Ductor Dubitantium, or The Rule of Conscience.* Part 1. Ed. Alexander Taylor. Vol. 9 of *The Whole Works of the Right Rev. Jeremy Taylor,* ed. Reginald Heber, rev. and corrected by Charles Page Eden. London: Longman, Brown, Green & Longmans, 1855.

Thomas, Keith. "The Puritans and Adultery: The Act of 1650 Reconsidered." In *Puritans and Revolutionaries,* ed. Donald Pennington and Keith Thomas, 257–82. Oxford: Clarendon Press, 1978.

Thompson, E. P. *Whigs and Hunters: The Origin of the Black Act.* New York: Pantheon Books, 1975.

Thorslev, Peter L. "Incest as Romantic Symbol." *Comparative Literature Studies* 2 (1965): 41–58.

Timpanaro, Sebastiano. *On Materialism.* Trans. Lawrence Garner. London: Verso, 1980. Originally published as *Sul materialismo* (Pisa, 1970).

Todd, Janet. *The Secret Life of Aphra Behn.* New Brunswick, N.J.: Rutgers University Press, 1997.

———. *The Sign of Angellica: Women, Writing, and Fiction, 1660–1800.* New York: Columbia University Press, 1989.

Tompkins, J. M. S. *The Popular Novel in England, 1770–1800.* London: Constable & Co., 1932. Reprint, Lincoln: University of Nebraska Press, 1961.

Trumbach, Randolph. *The Rise of the Egalitarian Family: Aristocratic Kinship and Domestic Relations in Eighteenth-Century England.* New York: Academic Press, 1978.

Twitchell, James. *Forbidden Partners: The Incest Taboo in Modern Culture.* New York: Columbia University Press, 1987.

Van Boheemen, Christine. *The Novel as Family Romance: Language, Gender, and Authority from Fielding to Joyce.* Ithaca, N.Y.: Cornell University Press, 1987.

Vaughan, John. *The Reports and Arguments of that Learned Judge, Sir John Vaughan.* London: Edward Vaughan, 1677.

Walpole, Horace. *The Mysterious Mother, a Tragedy.* London: Printed for J. Dodsley, 1781.

Warner, William B. *Licensing Entertainment: The Elevation of Novel Reading in Britain, 1684–1750.* Berkeley: University of California Press, 1998.

Watt, Ian. *The Rise of the Novel: Studies in Defoe, Richardson, and Fielding.* Berkeley: University of California Press, 1957.

Waugh, Scott L. *The Lordship of England: Royal Wardships and Marriages in English Society and Politics, 1217–1327.* Princeton, N.J.: Princeton University Press, 1988.

Wilson, W. Daniel. "Science, Natural Law, and Unwitting Sibling Incest in Eighteenth-Century Literature." *Studies in Eighteenth-Century Culture* 13 (1984): 249–70.

Wolfram, Sybil. *In-Laws and Outlaws: Kinship and Marriage in England.* London: Croom Helm, 1987.

Yeazell, Ruth Bernard. "The Boundaries of Mansfield Park." *Representations* 7 (1984): 133–52.

Index